HOOVER INSTITUTION PUBLICATIONS

THE SPATIAL ECONOMY
OF COMMUNIST CHINA

*Research and publication sponsored by the
Hoover Institution and the Stanford Research Institute
in cooperation with the University of San Francisco*

THE SPATIAL ECONOMY
OF COMMUNIST CHINA

A Study on Industrial Location and Transportation

by
YUAN-LI WU

with
H. C. LING and GRACE HSIAO WU

Published for
**THE HOOVER INSTITUTION
ON WAR, REVOLUTION AND PEACE**
by
FREDERICK A. PRAEGER, PUBLISHERS
New York • Washington
PALL MALL PRESS
London

FREDERICK A. PRAEGER, *Publishers*
111 Fourth Avenue, New York, New York 10003, U.S.A.
PALL MALL PRESS
77–79 Charlotte Street, London W.1, England
Published in the United States of America in 1967
by Frederick A. Praeger, Inc., Publishers
Published in Great Britain in 1967 by Pall Mall Press, Ltd.
All rights reserved
© 1967 by the Board of Trustees of the Leland Stanford Junior University
Library of Congress Catalog Card Number: 67-20739
Printed in the United States of America

PREFACE

The present study focuses attention on two related aspects of economic development: locational policy and the development and use of transport facilities. Recent studies of Communist China in Western countries have tended to neglect the spatial structure of the Chinese economy and its transport industry. This relative neglect was one of the principal reasons the present undertaking was initiated several years ago.

Two further considerations affected the choice of this topic. First, the transport industry and its coordination with locational policy may be regarded as a pivotal strategic variable in determining the economic growth rate in any underdeveloped country. In mainland China, the integration of the vast land area into a viable national economy assumes particular significance. The present study also complements two earlier works on key economic sectors published in the Hoover Institution series, the first on the use of energy resources and the second on the steel industry. Secondly, this study began as an attempt to see what might be done in a regional appraisal while handicapped by severe limitations on available data. In this investigation, as in others, we have been pleasantly surprised by the results of a serious effort.

Nevertheless, this is not a comprehensive study in regional science. Social aspects, such as market integration, urbanization, and agglomeration have been omitted. We have chosen to treat the regional aspect of land utilization only in a most peripheral manner. One excuse is the stability of this aspect of resource use as contrasted with the many changes in industrial location. The chief consideration has been to keep the study manageable and to examine the most important factors first. Another observer of the Chinese scene might have adopted a different emphasis. Our concern was centered on what seemed to be practical considerations. In our discussion of transport, for example, we have concentrated on the railways, which are the primary freight and passenger carriers in China. Those of negligible current importance, such as power transmission nets or the oil and gas pipe lines, have been omitted.

v

Despite the narrow framework of industrial location, delineation of principal market and supply areas, and transportation development, the task has proved to be most time-consuming. Exploratory research began in 1961 under a summer grant of the Joint Committee on Contemporary China. The bulk of data gathering and a partial analysis were completed during the following year, when the author was a Ford Foundation Faculty Research Fellow from the University of San Francisco. Subsequent work continued with partial support from the Committee on the Economy of China of the Social Science Research Council and the continued assistance of the Hoover Institution. Without the indispensable support from these quarters, it would not have been possible to secure the requisite research assistance for processing the vast amount of primary data.

Throughout the years of work on this study, interrupted from time to time by other more urgent demands, the most important sustaining influence in shaping the present volume has been the painstaking and patient effort of the author's long-time associate, Hsien-chang Ling, and that of his able assistant, Mrs. Grace Wei-pan Wu. If this volume proves useful, the credit should be theirs. Sincere thanks are due to Professor Norton Ginsburg of the University of Chicago and Mr. Boyd Ladd of the Surveys and Research Corporation, Washington, D. C., for reviewing the manuscript. Their comments have contributed materially to its improvement. The book has also been made more readable as a result of the careful editing of Ward Smith, assisted by Miss Ruth K. Hersch. Unfortunately, many deficiencies remain. For these the author alone is responsible.

The author wishes to express his special appreciation to Dr. W. Glenn Campbell, Director of the Hoover Institution, and to the Reverend Richard E. Mulcahy, S. J. and Dr. Vincent P. Wright, both of the University of San Francisco, for their frequent encouragement and friendly advice. He is grateful to the SSRC Committee under the chairmanship of Professor Simon Kuznets, and its executive director, Dr. Walter Galenson, for their support and sympathetic appreciation of the importance of timely research on the Chinese economy.

Another small step has been taken in a fascinating and seemingly endless journey. Many other tasks await the researcher. In areas related to the present volume alone, studies of commodity flow and of domestic trade and its role in planning resource allocation are among the topics that beckon. These and other potential studies are essential if we are to deepen our knowledge of modern China.

Yuan-li Wu

Menlo Park, California

March, 1966

CONTENTS

PART I

PART II

TABLES

FIGURES

MAPS

APPENDICES

PART I

1
PRINCIPLES AND PROBLEMS
OF THE SPATIAL ECONOMY

Purpose and Scope of the Inquiry

Every act of production or consumption occurs at a given place, yet economists have tended to ignore the spatial aspects of economic problems--including those of mainland China. Theories on the spatial economy of a country can be advanced on the basis of a single and unified market if the overall economy is small relative to the means and speed of transportation and communication at its disposal. However, such simplifying conditions do not exist for the Chinese economy. To a machine plant in Shanghai or Lo-yang, steel from An-shan in Manchuria is not really the same commodity as steel from Wu-han in Central China. The grain surplus of the Ch'eng-tu plain is of less use to the hungry in the cities on the lower Yangtze than surplus wheat in Canada since the lack of transportation is equivalent to an infinitely high transport cost.

The elementary facts are painfully clear to the economic planners of Communist China, for every major economic decision necessarily entails an important locational decision. Consequently, the critical student of the Chinese economy must be able to grasp the facts of location and their significance in terms of economic development.

One significant question in this inquiry is whether the spatial arrangement of Communist China's industrial activities is properly coordinated with the National developmental program. A corollary question is whether a planned economy like that of Communist China has been able to make better locational arrangements than an unplanned economic system might make in similar circumstances. Since developmental programs in China have been subject to change, sometimes dramatic ones, spatial planning must also be examined from a dynamic point of view, with emphasis on both its flexibility and its time dimension. A second purpose of this inquiry is to determine if spatial and

1

transport decisions are coordinated, and if conflict exists between the two.

Answers to these questions are useful in any evaluation of the soundness of Chinese planning. "Soundness" may be viewed in two ways: (1) Are the plans properly designed for the promotion of economic development as a primary objective? (2) Are the plans properly coordinated in terms of internal consistency? Answers to these questions should also enable us to deduce the magnitude of the contribution of the transport sector to economic development.

Two sets of problems are brought out by the general questions raised above. First, what has transpired in location and transportation in Communist China? For example, what is the spatial distribution of the principal market areas, production sites, and industrial centers; how much is invested in new means of transportation; what are the rate structures and the transport routes; and how efficient are the transport operations? Second, what criteria should be used to judge the appropriateness of such developments? To answer these two questions, consideration must be given to the deliberate policy of the planners and its Zweckmässigkeit as opposed to the haphazard arrangements born of a purely pragmatic and short-term approach. Unfortunately, determining Chinese policy often involves a laborious process of deduction from less than satisfactory data.

Criteria and Constraints in Locational Policy

Three questions should be answered in judging the appropriateness of spatial arrangements:

1. What general proposition can be advanced on the policy of optimal location?

2. What are some of the principal obstacles to the formulation of a policy of optimal spatial arrangements on an operational basis, especially in a planned economy?

3. What specific historical, geographical, ideological, political, or military constraints must be considered, by the Chinese planners and by the dispassionate observer?

In answer to the first question, Isard,[1] on the basis of given transport rates, states:

      ... in a small variation of any production site from its corresponding position in a geographic pattern of production sites which yields maximum surplus, the marginal rate of substitution of one transport input for another must be equal to the reciprocal of the ratio of their transport rates, <u>social</u> surplus plus total revenue less total production costs and less total costs on all other transport inputs being held constant.

This formulation, which identifies the conditions under which it would not be desirable to shift any particular production site in any manner, defines <u>ipso facto</u> the optimal spatial arrangement. Though based on an assumption that each raw material is derived from one specific site only, as Isard pointed out, the statement can be readily broadened to include many sources for all materials and services used. However, what happens if transportation rates are themselves variables, and what is the maximum length of time within which the most beneficial use can be made of surplus?

      Optimal spatial equilibrium may also be visualized in another way. Suppose a planner commanding a colonizing force enters an uninhabited area with a definite number of persons, who represent both the labor force and the consumers, and with a given supply of all movable factors of production. How should this planner choose production and market sites if his goal is to maximize economic welfare as defined by the utility functions of the consumers or of himself, whichever he elects? In this problem of defining general economic equilibrium, Isard's approach can be applied since it makes transport input a variable. At the spatial equilibrium position, one can alternatively say that the marginal rates of return over cost must be equal at all production sites (just as they should be equal in all industries) and that the average rate of return should be maximized. At equilibrium it would not pay to shift any factor of production from one industry to another or from one place to another. In addition, when the workers are also consumers, their dual function and influence on prices must be taken into account. However, even in a simple hypothetical case such as this one, the planner's decisions are subject to definite constraints.

      First, the planner is constrained by the configuration of the area and the uneven distribution of resources, including differences in the fertility of the soil, the climatic conditions, the availability of water, the location of mineral deposits and the discontinuity of the transport surface." These factors in turn

3

define the relationship between transport input and output. The planner can act only on the basis of his knowledge of these factors. Since his knowledge may also be a variable, an optimal spatial arrangement reached at one time might not be optimal if the planner were differently informed. The colonization of a new area presents essentially the same problems as the development of older, underdeveloped countries which have incomplete geographic surveys and only partial information on the availability of resources. Flexibility in any spatial arrangement therefore assumes a special value when the planner has only incomplete knowledge of the facts.

Second, the input-output relationship that defines the usual production functions sets limits on the planner's choice. Specifically, optimal spatial equilibrium is conditioned by (1) the state of technological knowledge, (2) the effect of economies of scale and problems of indivisibility and discontinuity, (3) external economies or diseconomies due to agglomeration, and (4) the time dimension of the production function, which embraces such variables as the "construction" or "gestation period" of investments (except in the "point-input --point-output" of capital theory), the durability of capital goods, and the possibilities of altering the time shape of input and output.

Consequently, spatial variations may have entirely different results if major changes are undertaken instead of small, marginal ones. For instance, a choice may have to be made from among all or some of the following alternatives: (1) expanding the existing plant at location A, (2) establishing a number of small plants at locations B, C, D, ..., (3) establishing a large new plant at B only, and (4) establishing a large new plant at B only but as a part of an integrated program of developing other industries at the same location.

A time dimension means that the concept of return over cost should be transformed into the concept of rate of return over investment, and that the return (net of "current input") over a given period should be discounted to the present or accumulated forward to a specified time in the future. In either case, we need both a rate of discount or accumulation, which will be a variable, and a definite time horizon, which may also be a variable. The discount or accumulation rate becomes a factor in the equilibrium of the economy in the time dimension. The planning horizon may be taken as a parameter, if preselected

4

by the planner. In our hypothetical case, and in all planned societies, the planner must make a deliberate decision as to the period within which economic welfare is to be maximized--assuming that economic welfare is chosen as the criterion. A short horizon would automatically exclude investments with long construction periods or small initial net returns. This condition would definitely affect the spatial optimum in the development of production sites.

The time horizon in a planned society is characteristically an unstable constant. It is affected by a myriad of cultural, political, and ideological factors. In the earlier stages of economic planning in an underdeveloped country, when many urgent problems must be resolved immediately, uniform planning horizons for economic activity are sometimes subordinated to day-to-day operations. Where this is true, the effort to maximize economic welfare, including the correspondent spatial arrangement, is completely vitiated. An unstable time horizon also means that one must consider the effect of every change on the spectrum of choice for future decisions.

Third, the freedom of choice of the planner may be limited merely because men cannot be regarded as automatons or as homogeneous consuming and producing units to be assigned wherever the planner chooses. Allowances must be made for the "herd instinct" and the cultural ties and emotional pulls that induce individuals to live and work together. The planner may not be able to assign individuals to various locations as he pleases. His chances of being able to do so are better in a totalitarian regime, although a loss in labor pro-ductivity may result. However, noneconomic costs are usually disregarded.[2]

Fourth, the breadth of vision of the planner and his freedom of action may be effectively limited by noneconomic factors concerning cultural, ideolog-ical, political, and military matters. For instance, a planner may have a per-sonal preference for a particular geographical pattern of production sites or market areas. For political reasons he may prefer industrial concentration to decentralization because of the greater ease of administrative control. Under different political conditions he might prefer a decentralized spatial pattern because population dispersion weakens the points of concentration from which political and social disturbances could originate. The planner may wish to emphasize the development of areas inhabited by certain racial or other groups.

He may be influenced by considerations of the military vulnerability of particular spatial and transportation arrangements. (Military considerations are in fact important in Communist China from the point of view of domestic political stability and international alliances.)

Although our hypothetical case deals with the colonization of a new country, it would be more realistic to cite examples involving the further economic development, and the corresponding spatial economy, of a settled country. In such countries, the existence of production centers and market areas, which have come about as a result of historical evolution, subjects the planner to additional constraints. The existence of specific production centers limits the manner in which external economies can be brought to play as well as the manner in which the time shape of the production function will behave or can be modified. For instance, a new production area, no matter how well planned, requires a larger initial input in construction, a longer construction period, and a greater overall investment before any benefits of agglomeration are realized. The establishment of a new market area requires migration from other population centers. These migrations tend to be slow unless they are compulsory, but compulsory ones may have an adverse effect on productivity. It is usually much cheaper to expand existing plants than to establish new large plants.

The dichotomy in view points between an emphasis on new production centers and on the improvement of established centers typifies the problems that bring the increasingly significant role of a planning horizon into clearer relief. The longer the planning horizon, the more the planner can afford a policy stressing long-term benefits from the development of new and better production centers and market sites. On the other hand, the longer the planning horizon, the less the possibility of immediate gains in economic welfare and the greater the political pressure for a revision of such plans.

Spatial Characteristics of the Chinese Economy in the Pre-Communist Period

Certain spatial characteristics, which the Communist Chinese regime inherited, have acted as specific constraints on Communist planners.[3] First, the pre-Communist economy was marked by a concentration of modern industry in a few industrial centers, mostly in the coastal areas and in a few inland river ports and cities. Second, railway transportation was confined to a relatively small number of provinces in the eastern part of the country. China proper had only a few important lateral and longitudinal trunk lines although Manchuria had a fairly well developed railway network.

Third, because of the small number of metropolitan industrial and commercial areas, there were few major market areas having a concentrated demand for producer or consumer goods. Even in the large hinterland, with a primarily agricultural population, agricultural production and rural population were concentrated in a relatively small number of provinces of greater soil fertility.

Fourth, the availability of mineral and agricultural resources affected the development of the Chinese economy in the pre-Communist period. For example, coal is found throughout the country, but the limited number of known large iron ore deposits determined the locational development of the iron and steel industry and of machine building in pre-Communist days.[4] Since geological surveys during that period were incomplete and especially rudimentary in western China, including the northwestern and the southwestern parts, Communist planners undoubtedly anticipate that petroleum and nonferrous and rare metals will be found in western China in greater quantities than are now known in the rest of the country.[5]

Similarly, fertile agricultural land has made some eastern, central, southern, and southeastern provinces the prime bases of Chinese agriculture. Because of the greater accessibility of the eastern provinces to the sea and the generally east-west flow of the navigable rivers, the major industries of the pre-Communist period tended for geographical and other reasons to concentrate in the coastal provinces and in major river ports.

Lastly, the historical development of the coastal areas, which resulted in the establishment of the major production and market areas in pre-Communist China for both industry and commerce, was intimately bound to the political development of modern China. For example, the establishment of a separate regime in Manchuria in the 1930's under Japanese sponsorship prompted the Japanese to develop Manchuria as their major industrial base on the Asiatic continent. Despite the denuding of the Manchurian industrial establishments by the Soviet Union after World War II, Communist China has relied on Manchuria

7

first as a base for economic recovery and, second, as a major area for long-term development.

An industrial survey published by the National Economic Commission of Nationalist China in 1948 showed that only 18 cities in 13 provinces (excluding Manchuria) had sufficient manufacturing capacity to be considered even modest industrial centers (Table 1-1). Ten of the 26 provinces and autonomous regions now under the Communist regime (including three provinces in Manchuria) had no important manufacturing centers in 1948. These economically "backward" areas were as follows:

Region	Provinces or Autonomous Regions
North China and Inner Mongolia	Shansi
	Inner Mongolia
East China	Anhwei
	Chekiang
Central-South China	Honan
	Kwangsi
Northwest China	Ningsia
	Tsinghai
	Sinkiang
Southwest China and Tibet	Tibet

The inclusion of Shansi in this list may be questioned because of significant developments in T'ai-yüan in the immediate pre-war and war years. However, the general picture of lagging developments in these provinces and autonomous regions was unmistakable. Of the ten territorial divisions, only Chekiang is a coastal province--one of six in China proper (excluding Manchuria); on the other hand, nine of the 17 inland divisions are found in the list.

The 18 cities and the larger administrative divisions in which they are located may also be ranked according to motive power, employment, and number of factories.

Table 1-2 shows that there was a high degree of concentration in all three variables, but especially in terms of motive power. The lower degree of concentration of employment and number of factories implies that the smaller production centers had factories that were less well-equipped with power equipment and were, therefore, less "modern." The concentrations of the three

Table 1-1

DISTRIBUTION OF MANUFACTURING MOTIVE POWER,
EMPLOYMENT, AND FACTORIES IN
CHINA PROPER AT THE END
OF WORLD WAR II[a]

Cities or City Combinations	Share (%) of Indicated Parameter		
	Motive Power	Employment	Number of Factories
Shanghai	57.7	60.9	60.4
Tientsin	16.8	9.9	9.4
Tsingtao	7.4	4.7	1.4
Peking	6.3	1.5	2.1
Nanking	2.5	1.8	6.9
Wu-han	2.2	3.6	3.6
Chungking	2.2	5.5	5.2
Canton	1.5	4.5	3.7
Kunming	0.7	1.1	0.5
Nan-chang and Chiu-chiang	0.7	1.1	1.3
Sian	0.6	1.1	0.5
Chang-sha and Heng-yang	0.6	1.5	1.7
Foochow	0.4	0.6	1.4
Lan-chou	0.3	0.5	0.3
Kuei-yang	0.2	0.8	0.6
Swatow	--	0.9	0.9
Total	100.0	100.0	100.0

[a]The original data are from the Industrial Survey of Principal Cities in China, Preliminary Report (Nanking: National Economic Commission, 1949), quoted in Yuan-li Wu, An Economic Survey of Communist China (New York: Bookman Associates, 1956), p. 34.

Table 1-2

RANKING OF PRODUCTION AREAS IN MODERN MANUFACTURING IN
CHINA PROPER AT THE END OF WORLD WAR II[a]

	Ranking of City or City Combination According to Indicated Parameter				Ranking of Province According to Indicated Parameter		
Rank	Motive Power	Employment	Number of Factories	Rank	Motive Power	Employment	Number of Factories
1	Shanghai	Shanghai	Shanghai	1	Kiangsu	Kiangsu	Kiangsu
2	Tientsin	Tientsin	Tientsin	2	Hopeh	Hopeh	Hopeh
3	Tsingtao	Chungking	Nanking	3	Shantung	Szechwan	Szechwan
4	Peking	Tsingtao	Chungking	4	Hupeh Szechwan	Kwangtung	Kwangtung
5	Nanking	Canton	Canton	5	Kwangtung	Shantung	Hupeh
6	Wu-han Chungking	Wu-han	Wu-han	6	Yünnan Kiangsi	Hupeh	Hunan
7	Canton	Nanking	Peking	7	Hunan Shensi	Hunan	Fukien Shantung
8	Nan-chang and Chiu-chiang Kunming	Peking	Chang-sha and Heng-yang	8	Fukien	Shensi Yünnan Kiangsi	Kiangsi
9	Sian Chang-sha and Heng-yang	Chang-sha and Heng-yang	Foochow Tsingtao	9	Kansu	Kweichow	Kweichow
10	Foochow	Nan-chang and Chiu-chiang	Nan-chang and Chiu-chiang	10	Kweichow	Fukien	Yünnan Shensi
11	Lan-chou	Kunming Sian	Swatow	11	-	Kansu	Kansu
12	Kuei-yang	Swatow	Kuei-yang				
13	Swatow	Kuei-yang	Kunming Sian				
14	-	Foochow	Lan-chou				
15	-	Lan-chou	-				

	Ranking of Region According to Indicated Parameter		
Rank	Motive Power	Employment	Number of Factories
1	East	East	East
2	North	North	North
3	Central	Southwest	Central
4	Southwest	Central	Southwest
5	South	South	South
6	Northwest	Northwest	Northwest

[a]The original data are from the Industrial Survey of Principal Cities in China, Preliminary Report (Nanking: National Economic Commission, 1949), quoted in Yuan-li Wu, An Economic Survey of Communist China (New York: Bookman Associates, 1956), p. 34.

parameters are as follows:

Number of Cities or City Combinations	Share (%) of Indicated Parameter		
	Motive Power	Employment	Number of Factories
5 Largest	90. 7	85. 5	85. 6
8 Largest	96. 6	92. 4	93. 0

Second, the ranking of the first eight largest cities (Shanghai, Tientsin, Tsingtao, Peking, Nanking, Wu-han, Chungking, and Canton) was the same in terms of motive power and employment. In terms of the number of factories, Tsingtao was replaced by the city combination Chiang-sha and Heng-yang. Except for this minor deviation, the order of importance of the largest established manufacturing centers in China proper was quite unmistakable in the pre-Communist period. These same eight cities were also the cities with the greatest populations in 1948.

Third, the original six most important provinces in modern manufacturing in China proper were Kiangsu, Hopeh, Shantung, Hupeh, Szechwan, and Kwangtung. With one exception they had the largest percentages of motive power, employment, and number of factories. The exception was Shantung province, which was replaced by Hunan in terms of the number of factories as the sixth most important province.

In 1948, East China accounted for 67 to 69 per cent of total modern manufacturing industry in terms of all three criteria. East and North China together accounted for about 80 per cent of the factories and industrial employment in China proper and used 90 per cent of available powered machines. If Manchuria is included, the three industrially most "developed" regions were Manchuria (Northeast), East China, and North China. Central China, a borderline case, followed. Northwest China was the most backward region.

Lastly, five of the six coastal provinces--Hopeh, Shantung, Kiangsu, Chekiang, Fukien, and Kwangtung--accounted for 90 per cent of the motive power and about 80 per cent of the factories and employment in modern manufacturing. in China proper. Chekiang was the only completely laggard coastal province. Approximately 10 per cent of the power and 20 per cent of the number of factories and employment were credited to the 17 inland provinces or autonomous regions. In fact, only eight had one principal center sufficiently important to be surveyed.

11

As late as 1950, when the Communists gained control over the South China coast, there were no operating railways in the following administrative divisions of the country:

Northwest China	Kansu
	Ningsia
	Sinkiang
	Tsinghai
South China	Fukien
Southwest China	Szechwan
	Kweichow
	Yünnan
	Tibet

Nearly half the railway mileage was in Manchuria. In the rest of the country, the density of railways was 5.6 km/1,000 sq km in the coastal provinces as against 3.6 km/1,000 sq km in the interior. In order of diminishing density, after Liaoning, Kirin, and Heilungkiang in Manchuria, the first five provinces were Hopeh, Kiangsu, Honan, Shantung, and Shansi. The first three regions were Northeast China (Manchuria), East China, and Central China (Table 1-3).

Three of the first four provinces with higher railway densities, Hopeh, Shantung, and Kiangsu, were also the first three most developed industrial provinces in China proper in the pre-Communist or early Communist period. Together with Manchuria (especially Liaoning), they constituted the most important geographical areas of the small modern sector of the Chinese economy.

Finally, the individual provinces can be arranged in diminishing order of their importance in food grain production (Table 1-4). By comparing this ranking with a similar ranking of provinces by motive power in manufacturing, we can divide the provinces of China into four groups: (1) relatively developed areas in both industry and agriculture, (2) relatively developed agricultural areas, (3) relatively developed industrial areas, and (4) undeveloped areas. Figure 1-1 shows that five of the seven developed areas in Group 1 were coastal provinces. With the exception of Fukien, the undeveloped areas (Group 4) were in western China. Figure 1-1 graphically illustrates the "irrational" pattern of the Chinese spatial economy frequently mentioned by Communist Chinese planners.

12

Table 1-3

RANKING OF PROVINCES AND REGIONS BY RAILWAY
DENSITY (1949 TO 1950)[a]

Rank	Province	Density of Railways (km/1,000 sq km)	Rank	Region	Density of Railways (km/1,000 sq km)
1	Manchuria	12	1	Northeast (including Jehol)	12
2	Hopeh	8	2	East	6
	Kiangsu	8	3	Central	4
3	Honan	7	4	North	2
4	Shantung	6		South	2
5	Shansi	5	5	Northwest	–
	Anhwei	5		Southwest	–
6	Hunan	4			
	Chekiang	4			
	Kiangsi	4			
7	Shensi	2			
	Kwangtung	2			
	Kwangsi	2			
	Hupeh	2			
8	Inner Mongolia	Negligible			

[a]For railway lengths, see Appendix D, Table D-1.

Table 1-4

PRODUCTION OF GRAIN (CEREALS AND POTATOES) IN
PRE-COMMUNIST CHINA BY ADMINISTRATIVE
DIVISIONS (1931 TO 1937 AVERAGE) [a, b]

Province or Region	Grain Production (1,000 metric tons)
Szechwan	13,676
Manchuria	12,638
Kiangsu	11,219
Shantung	9,175
Kwangtung	8,954
Honan	8,733
Hupeh	6,780
Hopeh	6,728
Hunan	6,008
Chekiang	5,685
Anhwei	4,933
Kiangsi	4,461
Kwangsi	4,367
Fukien	3,063
Shansi	2,953
Yünnan	2,683
Kweichow	2,087
Shensi	1,842
Inner Mongolia	1,719
Kansu	1,184
Tsinghai	381
Ningsia	101
Sinkiang	... [c]
Tibet	...

[a] Source: T. H. Shen, Agricultural Resources of China (Ithaca, N. Y.: Cornell University Press, 1951), Appendix Tables 2 and 5.
[b] The administrative divisions have been adjusted to correspond as closely as possible to those now employed by the Communist regime.
[c] Throughout this text ... denotes no information; - means nil.

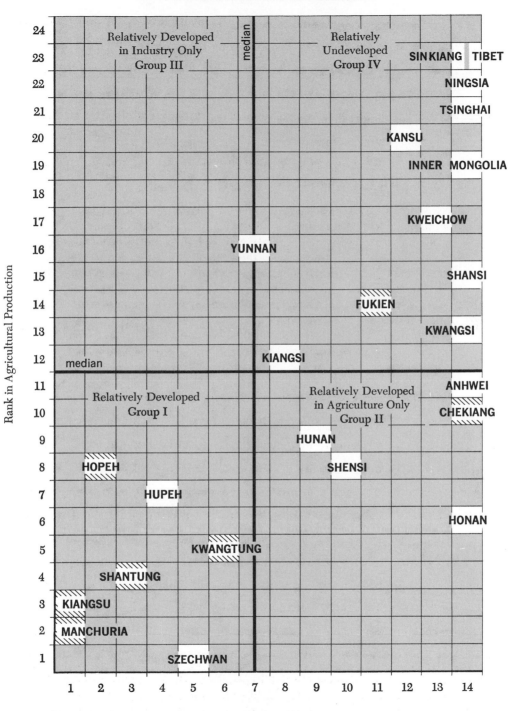

Figure 1.1 Relative Degree of Economic Development by Administrative Divisions in Pre-Communist China

Rank in Agricultural Production

Relatively Developed in Industry Only Group III

median

Relatively Undeveloped Group IV

SIN KIANG   TIBET

NINGSIA

TSINGHAI

KANSU

INNER MONGOLIA

KWEICHOW

YUNNAN

SHANSI

FUKIEN

KWANGSI

median   KIANGSI

ANHWEI

Relatively Developed Group I

Relatively Developed in Agriculture Only Group II

CHEKIANG

HUNAN

HOPEH   SHENSI

HUPEH

HONAN

KWANGTUNG

SHANTUNG

KIANGSU

MANCHURIA

SZECHWAN

Rank in Modern Manufacturing

(coastal provinces)

15

Communist Views on Locational Policy

The Communist locational policy can be deduced from official pronouncements and unofficial writings. In a report to the first session of the First National People's Congress on September 23, 1954, Chou En-lai stated that the First Five-Year Plan would give China new industrial regions and bases, and thereby mark the beginning of a change in the irrational distribution of Chinese industry.[6]

The First Five-Year Plan, published in 1955, contains a statement on the general principles of industrial location:

> We shall locate the productive forces of industry in different
> parts of the country in such a way that they will be close to
> producing areas of raw materials and fuel and also to consumer
> markets. They will also satisfy the requirements for the
> strengthening of national security, lead to the gradual improve-
> ment of the irrational locational pattern, and elevate the econ-
> omic level of the backward areas. In the establishment of in-
> dustrial areas, we shall, first of all, utilize, reconstruct, and
> transform the existing industrial bases so as to avoid over-con-
> centration of enterprises and to bring about a suitable measure
> of decentralization.[7]

Specifically, the First Five-Year Plan called for the further expansion and transformation of Manchuria and the cities of Shanghai, Nanking, Tientsin, Tsingtao, Chinan and Canton. In Manchuria, reconstruction of the industrial sector was to be centered around the An-shan iron and steel complex. Expansion was also scheduled for coal mining at Fu-shun, Fou-shin, Shuang-ya-shan, Chi-hsi, and Ho-kang; and for a metallurgical industry at Pen-ch'i, a machine manufacturing industry at Mukden, a chemical industry at Kirin and an electric power industry in Kirin province. Active construction was to proceed in a number of new industrial areas in North China, Northwest China, and Central China, including T'ai-yüan, Shih-chia-chuang, Lo-yang, Cheng-chou, Chu-chou, Heng-yang, Lan-chow, and Sian. A principal objective, however, was to lay groundwork for the development of two major new iron and steel complexes at Pao-t'ou and Wu-han during the Second Five-Year Plan. Preparatory work was also to be done for the further development of new industrial areas in Southwest China at Chungking, Ch'eng-tu, Tzu-kung, Nei-chiang, and Nan-ch'ung.[8]

Other official and semiofficial comments related to locational policy may also be found. For instance, while commenting on the draft of the First Five-Year Plan during the second session of the First National People's Congress on July 5-6, 1955, Li Fu-ch'un,[9] chairman of the State Planning Commission, said that the problem of industrial location was one of the major issues considered. Li was quoted as saying:

> The original distribution of industrial regions in China was very irrational. On the basis of 1952 statistics, the industrial output of the coastal provinces accounted for over 70 per cent of the total industrial value output of the country. One of the important tasks in developing the Chinese national economy in a planned manner consists, therefore, of altering this irrational state of affairs inherited from old China, of appropriately locating new industries in different parts of the country so that industrial production would be closer to the sources of raw materials and fuels as well as consumer markets,[10] of allowing industrial location to conform to the requirements of national defense and of gradually elevating the economic level of backward areas.[11]

This statement repeated and confirmed earlier statements by Chou and the published version of the First Five-Year Plan, but Li went on to elaborate:[12]

> The Five-Year Plan of capital construction includes a relatively rational spatial arrangement. Industrial bases in Manchuria, Shanghai, and other cities will be appropriately utilized so that they exercise their function in bringing about the rapid expansion of production to meet the demand of the economy and to support the construction of new industrial bases. This effort includes especially certain necessary construction at the industrial base of Manchuria centered around the An-shan iron and steel complex. On the other hand, active efforts will also be made to establish new industrial bases in North China and certain areas in Northwest and Central China, and to begin in part industrial construction in the Southwest. On the basis of this policy, 472 of the 694 above-norm industrial construction projects planned to be started during the first five years will be in the interior provinces and only 222 will be in the coastal areas. Appropriate railway construction arrangements are also being made to meet the requirements of industrial construction and the overall development of the national economy and to provide links between the original and the new industrial bases. At the same time, on the basis of this industrial policy, our present task in urban construction is not to develop the large cities on

the coast, but to develop medium and small cities in the interior and to restrict appropriately the expansion of the large cities (italics added). The present blind or unplanned development of the coastal cities is a phenomenon that has to be corrected.

Since the First Five-Year Plan placed primary emphasis on the development of heavy industry, the statement above was a clear indication that the government planned to concentrate on heavy industry in the medium and small cities in the interior provinces.

The first three years of the First Five-Year Plan were characterized by an overzealousness in developing the new inland industrial centers. This contributed to the relatively slow increase in output during the first half of the Plan. The slow increase can be seen in the changing rates of growth of industrial production and of the GNP. [13]

On June 18, 1956, Li Fu-ch'un emphasized in a report to the third session of the First National People's Congress [14] that it was necessary to place greater reliance on the existing industrial bases on the coast and that industrial development in the coastal and interior areas should be properly coordinated and balanced. According to Li, a principal reason for the slow industrial growth in the coastal industrial centers was the failure to utilize fully the existing industrial facilities. It is quite possible that this statement foreshadowed the institution of Economic Cooperative Regions in mainland China in 1957.

The official position was reviewed by Chou En-lai in September in a speech to the National Congress of the Chinese Communist Party. Chou pointed out that the movement of industrial construction toward the interior and western China had to be accomplished over a long period of time because of the great distance between the eastern and western parts of China. [15]

> During the First Five-Year Plan, our aim is to utilize the original industrial bases in the east in order to build new industrial centers in the middle. The cities of pivotal construction are Wu-han, Pao-t'ou, Cheng-chou, Lo-yang, Sian, and Lan-chow, all of which are situated in the central part of China. Further advance westward must be preceded by the establishment of industrial bases in the center and the completion of necessary preparations in the western regions.... The Second Five-Year Plan will have

18

as its goal the construction of industrial bases in the center and the beginning of construction of industrial bases and some industrial enterprises in the southwest, the northwest, and Sinkiang. As for the general development of industry in western China, this will have to await the completion of future five-year plans. Those who expect the rapid and general establishment of many industrial bases in the far reaches of western China are unrealistic in their outlook.

As a result of an official announcement in July 1957, the country was divided into seven Economic Cooperation Regions.[16] Each region was to be basically self-sufficient and to use in full its particularly favorable conditions. The purposes of the Economic Cooperation Regions were to reduce long-distance transport and cross-country hauls, to accomplish specialization on a regional basis and to promote the development of complementary enterprises within each region. Each region was to have one major iron and steel complex plus a number of secondary steel centers and machine-building production sites. Since each region was to have a number of industries near a major iron and steel complex, the concept of intraregional economic cooperation was tantamount to the delineation of a specific market and supply area for a group of industries organized around the steel industry. The Economic Cooperation Regions also anticipated the further development of central and western China during the second and subsequent Five-Year Plans.

Economic and Ideological Basis of the Apparent Official Policy on Location

It is fairly simple to deduce the general principles embodied in official comments on locational policy. In fact, the principles deduced from official pronouncements have appeared in unofficial writings published in Communist China. For example, a 1957 study by Tseng Wen-ching[17] suggests three principles of industrial location in the socialist Chinese economy: (1) proximity to the sources of raw material supply and consumer markets to make full use of local resources, to lower production costs, and to minimize the requirement of transportation input; (2) regional division of labor although consideration is given to national plans for using fuels, raw materials, and transportation service; and (3) the development of remote and undeveloped areas and the establishment of new industrial bases. These principles point to an optimal spatial arrangement having a proper balance between intraregional self-sufficiency and interregional specialization and exchange. They also underlie the concept of the Economic Cooperation Regions. The emphasis on the even development of the less-developed and neglected areas, including territories inhabited by minority nationalities, is, however, also politically and ideologically oriented.

In December 1959, an article in <u>Geographical Knowledge</u> mentioned national security as another important criterion.[18] The article also pointed out that in developing new industrial bases attention should be given to the proper balance between existing and new industrial centers. The former are better equipped from the point of view of skilled labor, transportation facilities, public utilities, and supply of consumer goods and services to the labor force. Proper exploitation and expansion of existing centers would, therefore, expedite development in general, but development in the new areas would be more costly and time-consuming. Thus, during the first few years of the First Five-Year Plan, the Communist Chinese recognized the practical problems of relocating industry westward and the theoretical difficulties involved in determining the planning horizon.

A further elaboration of this theme is found in another 1959 article in <u>Geographical Knowledge</u>.[19] In this commentary, five classes of industries are ranked according to their role in developing resources of value to national levels and to progressively lower administrative levels. Some industries should supply a national market, and others the regional and lower level markets. Below the national level, distinctions are made between Economic Cooperation Regions since some embrace a number of provinces and others correspond to a single province, a part of a province, or even a single county.

According to one source,[20] the present major Economic Cooperation Regions are as follows:

Region	Provinces
Northeast China (Manchuria)	Liaoning, Kirin, and Heilungkiang
North China	Hopeh, Shansi, and Inner Mongolia
Northwest China	Kansu, Shensi, Sinkiang, Tsinghai and the Ningsia Autonomous Region
East China	Kiangsu, Chekiang, Shantung, and Anhwei
Central-South China Central China	Honan, Hupeh, Hunan, and Kiangsi
South China	Kwangtung, Kwangsi and Fukien
Southwest China	Szechwan, Yünnan, Kweichow, and the Tibetan Autonomous Region

This division, however, is believed to be subject to revision and adjustment,[21] Furthermore, different groupings may prevail for different economic activities.

To recapitulate, the general factors underlying industrial location are regional specialization; intraregional self-sufficiency within the broad framework of interregional trade; proximity to raw materials, fuels, and markets; considerations of national security; and geographical balance between new and established economic bases. A comparison of these general principles with the "objective laws" of socialist production as applied to location shows that they coincide with theoretical propositions developed for the Soviet economy.[22] In fact, the same ideas of parallel regional developments, intraregional self-sufficiency, and interregional specialization and trade were considered by Soviet planners.

In his report to the Central Committee of the Soviet Communist Party's Eleventh Congress, Lenin stated that the Soviet economy was to be divided into a number of regions on the basis of economic conditions, climate, supply of fuels, ways of livelihood, and the nature of local industry.[23] In a resolution of the Russian Regional Planning Commission in 1921,[24] the "economic region" was defined as an integral, individual unit that should be as self-sufficient and self-contained as possible economically. Natural conditions, cultural heritage, and the people's productive capacity must be such as to enable the region to be an effective link in the national economy. If local resources were developed in accordance with the latest techniques and assistance from the outside and in conformity with the national plan, it would then be possible to develop regional economies so that maximum use would be made of resource potentials. Under these conditions, each region would have sectors capable of specialized development, and interregional trade would be kept at the necessary minimum.

However, the desire for a high degree of regional self-sufficiency and a reduction of transport input, despite the underpinnings of erstwhile Soviet ideology, offers only a partial explanation for Chinese regional planning policy in 1957. Another objective probably was to delineate market areas in the hope of maximizing the growth rate of the economy as a whole. In other words, the goal of the Economic Cooperation Region might be self-sufficiency itself or the promotion of the economic growth of the entire economy. The fulfillment of the latter goal would depend on the choice of boundary lines or the delineation of the large market areas for the major steel and machine complexes, as well as the time horizon selected for planning and maximizing the rate of economic growth.

Considerations of Defense

Finally, attention should be called to the political and military considerations of Communist China, both as a member of the Communist group of countries and as an individual regime.

Since some of the Communist nations are highly industrialized, Tseng Wen-ching[25] questioned the need for China--as a member of this united socialist camp--to establish her own heavy industry, and suggested that the Chinese effort be concentrated on the development of agriculture and light industry. Would it be feasible, he asked, for Communist China to confine her trade with the Soviet Union to the exportation of agricultural products in exchange for machinery?

Tseng's answer, reflecting the attitude of the Communist authorities in 1958, was that Communist China would have to build her own integrated industrial economy. He pointed out that the large Chinese population and, consequently, large domestic market demand cannot be satisfied through imports alone. Furthermore, according to the accepted theory, the rapid construction of a socialist economy can be accomplished only through the development of a domestic heavy industry to support light industry and other economic sectors. International specialization would be disadvantageous to Communist China because of the vast distance separating the Chinese mainland from industrial centers in the Soviet Union and Eastern Europe.

From the point of view of world strategy, Tseng also suggests that it would be advantageous for the Communist countries to possess two self-sufficient industrial systems--those of the Soviet Union and Communist China--to which one could then add the industrial power of other European and Asian satellite countries. This combination would offer the socialist camp enough economic potential on the broad Euro-Asian land mass to support any military effort. Dispersion is also desirable because of the reduced threat of military destruction.

These ideas are clearly reflected in a report by Chou En-lai to the Eighth National Congress of the Chinese Communist Party in 1956.[26] As Chou pointed out, because of the great distance between the industrialized areas in the European Communist countries and the Chinese industrial centers on the Pacific coast, the First and Second Five-Year Plans took into account the disposition of the productive capacities of the Communist countries when the location of Chinese industry was selected. The general tendency of the Five-Year Plans of the Soviet Union had been to move industry from the west to the east; therefore, Chinese industry should move from the east to the west toward the Soviet border. Sino-Soviet industrial forces would then be coordinated and linked together, and the industrially underdeveloped land between the major centers of the two countries would be filled. This policy has undoubtedly been modified since the disagreement between Communist China and the Soviet Union came to the fore in the mid-1960's; however, in 1956 this concept was geopolitically sound and was obviously an important consideration in economic planning.

This initial emphasis by Chou En-lai, Li Fu-ch'un, and others on the reorientation of industry from the coastal to the interior provinces also had military significance, primarily because of the experience gained during the

23

Japanese war. The movement west was in part an effort to transfer the bases of industrial production to more sheltered regions. However, beginning in 1957 and reinforced in 1958-59 with the "Great Leap Forward," there was an apparent realization that nuclear weapons have eliminated any real distinction between peripheral and interior industrial bases. Moving industry to the inland provinces would not by itself materially reduce the vulnerability of the industrial complex to attack. Decentralization, on the other hand, would. Industrial decentralization was advocated in the First Five-Year Plan as a corollary justification for the establishment of a large number of medium and small industrial centers. More recent policy statements have broadened the concept to include new industrial centers in coastal areas, as well as inland. Consequently, industrial centers have been developed in Kwangtung, Fukien, Kiangsi, and Chekiang in recent years. The establishment of multiple secondary centers for the iron and steel industry as a part of the steel industry's developmental program seems related to this concept.

Prospects for Locational Policy

The failure of the "Great Leap Forward" and the massive drive to induce the urban population to return to the countryside brought substantial changes in the spatial economy between 1961 and 1965. The main change was a shift of emphasis from the new to the existing industrial centers. This shift indicates a shortening of the planning horizon although another change could occur during the Third Five-Year Plan. At the same time, the disagreement between the Soviet Union and Communist China, which may not be of permanent importance, will undoubtedly influence the westward movement of Chinese industry. If the rift remains unhealed, it may accelerate the development of the western part of the country. An increased westward drive, however, cannot occur before the full resumption of the economic expansion that was curtailed in 1960-62.

Uncertainties continue to surround the spatial aspects of Chinese economic planning. Nonetheless, it is still possible to determine the principal spatial changes that have taken place and to resolve some issues on which only vague statements of policy have been made.[27]

24

2 POPULATION GROWTH AND THE PRINCIPAL URBAN MARKET AND SUPPLY AREAS

Population Growth as A Measure of Change in the Economic Importance of Individual Cities

The spatial pattern of the Chinese economy may be examined in various ways. In this chapter, we will discuss the principal market and supply areas and show how their relative importance and geographic distribution have changed during the Communist period, especially from 1953 to 1958.

Ascertaining the location and relative importance of the principal economic centers, their growth rate differentials, and their status in the industrialization of the country would be easier if it were possible to assemble industrial output, employment, and wholesale and retail trade statistics by cities. Since such data are available for only a few places, crude and indirect methods will have to be used to measure spatial development.

Statistics of population growth in individual cities are of primary importance. In 1953, when the first official census was taken, there were 164 municipalities in Communist China.[1,2] These units included two independent municipalities--Peking and Shanghai--which are administratively on the same level as provinces, and a number of municipalities within provinces, which are administratively on a par with counties. Since all urban places with populations of 100,000 or more are municipalities, all economic centers of any consequence were included in the list of the 164 municipalities. The population statistics of these municipalities, which show their relative rates of growth as well as changes in absolute size, provide useful indications of economic activity.

Since consumption increases with population growth, the latter is an indicator of change in the relative importance of the cities as markets. In addition, if temporary visitors are excluded from population statistics, population growth is also a measure of the importance of a place as an area of productive activity. Inasmuch as people do not remain in an area for long periods without work, any sustained population increase must be accompanied by a corresponding rise of economic activity and employment. This is equally true when population movement is subject to governmental regulation.

The increase in the population of a municipality could understate the importance of the city as a supply area. If large unemployment had prevailed initially, the increase in employment could exceed the increase in population caused by immigrant labor. Similarily, a decrease in population could understate the decrease in employment if unemployment in the city increases. Differences in growth rates for individual industries and in labor intensity per unit of output, which are determined by the production processes used, may also result in population changes that do not correspond to the true magnitude and economic significance of the changes the cities undergo. This is true especially in cities with only a few industries.

These observations underscore the approximate nature of population statistics as an indicator of change in market and supply areas, but they do not destroy the usefulness of the statistics.

Distribution of Municipalities by Size in 1953 and 1958

Despite the limitations of population statistics, a reasonable comparison can be made between midyear populations in 1953 and 1958 in 117 of the 164 municipalities (Table A-1, Appendix A). These 117 municipalities were sampled since population data are not uniformly available for the remaining 47 in both years.

Several factors determined the selection of 1953 and 1958 for comparison. First, by 1953, any sizable unemployment in the cities had disappeared as a result of increasing economic activity during the initial industrial rehabilitation period (1950-52) and the Korean War. Second, by mid-1958, directives issued in 1956 and 1957 requiring recent arrivals in the cities to return to their home villages had had their effect. Temporary visitors who had come to the cities because of rural dislocation during the intensive collectivization program in 1956 were excluded from the 1958 registered population. Changes in midyear populations between 1953 and 1958 may therefore be taken as reasonably accurate reflections of changes in the permanent resident population.

The commune movement wrought havoc in the rural area, and no doubt had a distorting effect on urban population growth figures. But this effect was

26

probably not reflected in the mid-1958 population estimates. Furthermore, in early 1958, when the communes were first organized, heightened activity in the rural areas probably deterred migration to the cities.

The data for 1953 and 1958, adjusted to allow for changes in territorial coverage, span a crucial period--that of the First Five-Year Plan and the first six months of the Second Plan. Population changes during this period may be regarded as a good first measure of the geographical impact of the increase in economic activity in Communist China in terms of individual municipalities. This conclusion seems to be warranted despite the short span of time between 1953 and 1958.

Table 2-1 shows that most of the 117 cities in the sample had populations of less than 300,000. Table 2-1 also shows a sharp discontinuity in frequency distribution between the interval of "200,000 to less than 300,000" and the one immediately above it. A number of cities fall within the intervening intervals between 300,000 and 1,000,000 at more or less decreasing frequency as the class interval in population rises. From 1,000,000 up, the frequency again shows a rise. For convenience we may, therefore, draw two arbitrary dividing lines, one immediately above the class interval of "200,000 to less than 300,000" and the other immediately above the class interval of "900,000 to less than 1,000,000." Cities below the first boundary are described as "small"; those between the two boundary lines as "medium" and those above the 1,000,000 demarcation line as "large." (Map 2-1.)

Frequency distribution for 1958 can also be divided into three major classes on the same basis. The characteristics of the 1953 frequency distribution seem to hold for 1958.

If a close comparison is made, we find a decrease in the number of small cities from 1953 to 1958, accompanied by an increase in the medium and the large groups. The decrease in the small group is not particularly significant; with the same sample size for 1953 and 1958, an increase in the two other groups implies a decrease in the group of small cities. The number in the small group would not necessarily show a decrease if the distribution were made from samples of unequal size. The latter practice was not adopted because of the lack of complete data for all cities in both years and the distortion that might result if different cities are compared with one another in measuring population growth within the city.

27

2.1 Distribution of 117 Cities by Size in 1958

■	Population 1,000,000 and above (Large)
○	Population 300,000 to 1,000,000 (Medium)
▼	Population under 300,000 (Small)

Table 2-1

DISTRIBUTION OF 117 CITIES BY 1953 AND 1958
MIDYEAR POPULATIONS [a,b]

Size of Group	Population (1,000 Persons)	Number of Cities in 1953	Number of Cities in 1958	Change (Number of Cities)	Change (%)
Small	Less than 100	16	2	-14	
	100 to less than 200	47	40	-7	-16.05
	200 to less than 300	18	26	+8	
Medium	300 to less than 400	8	9	+1	
	400 to less than 500	3	5	+2	
	500 to less than 600	4	4	0	
	600 to less than 700	6	4	-2	25.93
	700 to less than 800	2	6	+4	
	800 to less than 900	3	4	+1	
	900 to less than 1,000	1	2	+1	
Large	1,000 to less than 1,500	3	6	+3	
	1,500 to less than 2,000	2	2	0	66.67
	2,000 or more	4	7	+3	
	Total	117	117	–	–

[a]Source: Appendix A, Table A-1.

[b]Medians: 1953 = 126,600
 1958 = 263,500
Upper quartiles: 1953 = 384,400
 1958 = 643,800

Accordingly, attention should be focused on changes in the medium and large groups. The number of cities in the medium group increased by seven between 1953 and 1958. The corresponding increase in the large group was six. In relative terms, the increase in the large group was 67 per cent as compared with 26 per cent for the medium group. The medium group probably corresponds to the medium cities in Li Fu-ch'un's statement in 1955, quoted in Chapter 1. Since these cities, together with the smaller cities, were scheduled for a greater increase in number than the large cities, actual development did not coincide with the policy disclosed in 1955.

A comparison can also be made between 1948 and 1953 using 98 cities for which data are available. Again we find the same characteristics in frequency distribution for 1948. However, during the following five years, there was an increase of 10 in the number of medium cities, as compared with an increase of two in the large group. The relative rates of increase were 59 per cent for the medium cities and 29 per cent for the large cities. This was a notable increase in the number of medium cities as compared with larger cities between 1948 and 1953 (Table 2-2).

Although the percentage figures vary, their overall impact appears to contrast sharply with what might have been expected from an announced policy of discouraging the growth of large metropolitan centers in preference to the extension of medium and small urban units. The medium group expanded under the present regime, but the expansion of large metropolitan areas has been more conspicuous, despite the early policy to discourage it. However, as mentioned in Chapter 1, part of the answer may lie in the change that occurred in 1956 when the planning authorities began to deplore overzealousness in the establishment of new economic areas at the expense of the general rate of economic expansion. Relatively lower rates of increase in medium cities, as compared with those of the large cities from 1953 to 1958, may reflect a shift of policy after 1956. A more detailed picture may be drawn if we examine the provincial and regional patterns of the distribution of the three size groups of cities.

Table 2-2

DISTRIBUTION OF 98 CITIES BY 1948 AND 1953
MIDYEAR POPULATIONS[a, b]

Size of Group	Population (1,000 Persons)	Number of Cities in 1948	Number of Cities in 1953	Change (Number of Cities)	Change (%)
Small	Less than 100	21	2	−19	
	100 to less than 200	34	44	+10	−16.21
	200 to less than 300	19	16	−3	
Medium	300 to less than 400	7	8	+1	
	400 to less than 500	0	3	+3	
	500 to less than 600	5	4	−1	
	600 to less than 700	1	6	+5	58.82
	700 to less than 800	3	2	−1	
	800 to less than 900	0	3	+3	
	900 to less than 1,000	2	1	0	
Large	1,000 to less than 1,500	4	3	−1	
	1,500 to less than 2,000	2	2	0	28.57
	2,000 or more	1	4	+3	
	Total	98	98	--	--

[a]Source: Appendix A, Table A-2

[b]Medians: 1948 = 182,400
1953 = 218,800
Upper quartiles: 1948 = 297,400
1953 − 512,500

Provincial and Regional Distribution of Cities by Size

Table 2-3 presents the change in the frequency distribution of 117 cities from 1953 to 1958 by the three size groups and by provinces. The data show the most-populated provinces or regions in 1955 and 1958 and where the policy of developing medium cities at the expense of large cities has been followed. Table 2-3 also makes it possible to ascertain if the less-developed regions and inland provinces have been given more emphasis in development than the more-developed regions and coastal provinces. (See Maps 2-2 and 2-3.)

As shown in Table 2-4, in 1953 Hopeh and Kiangsu were the two most important provinces in terms of the number of large cities. They were followed by Liaoning, Heilungkiang, Hupeh, Kwangtung, and Szechwan. In 1958, Liaoning was first, followed by Hopeh, Kiangsu, and Szechwan. The greatest number of large cities in any province was two in 1953 and three in 1958. With the exception of the upgrading of Szechwan and Liaoning, the first positions were held by the same provinces in 1953 and 1958. It is to be noted that Hopeh, Kiangsu and Liaoning were also the industrial leaders in pre-Communist China.

The stable composition in this ranking by provinces is paralleled by a similar stability in the ranking of top cities. The first eight large cities in 1953 and 1958 were identical with one exception. In 1953, Chungking ranked above Wu-han, but the order was reversed in 1958. When a comparison is made with 1948, the difference consists principally in the higher places occupied by Nanking and Canton in pre-Communist years, probably because Nanking was the national capital, and Canton was an active seaport. Both conditions changed after 1948. (See Appendix A, Table A-3.)

In 1953, the leading regions were Northeast China (Manchuria), North China, and East China. This ranking again corresponds to the pre-Communist ranking of regions in economic importance.

For medium cities, first place in 1953 was held by Liaoning province followed by Kiangsu and Hopeh. The same general order was maintained in 1958. Northeast China headed the list of regions in 1953, followed by East China and North China. In 1958, East China forged ahead and took the lead over Manchuria and North China. However, this was not a notable change. For

Table 2-3

CHANGES IN THE 1953 AND 1958 FREQUENCY DISTRIBUTIONS
OF 117 CITIES BY SIZE GROUPS IN 24 PROVINCES
AND AUTONOMOUS REGIONS[a]

Region	Province	Number of Cities in Indicated Size Group and Year								
		Large[b]			Medium[c]			Small[d, e]		
		1953	1958	Change	1953	1958	Change	1953	1958	Change
Northeast	Liaoning	1	3	+2	6	4	-2	3	3	0
	Kirin	-	-	-	2	2	0	3	3	0
	Heilungkiang	1	1	0	1	1	0	6	6	0
	Total	2	4	+2	9	7	-2	12	12	0
North	Hopeh	2	2	0	3	4	+1	4	3	-1
	Shansi	-	1	+1	1	-	-1	4	4	0
	Inner Mongolia	-	-	-	-	2	+2	3	1	-2
	Total	2	3	+1	4	6	+2	11	8	-3
East	Kiangsu	2	2	0	4	4	0	7	6	-1
	Shantung	-	1	+1	1	2	+1	3	2	-1
	Anhwei	-	-	-	-	2	+2	5	3	-2
	Chekiang	-	-	-	1	1	0	5	5	0
	Total	2	3	+1	6	9	+3	20	16	-4
Central	Kiangsi	-	-	-	1	1	0	1	1	0
	Honan	-	-	-	1	3	+2	6	4	-2
	Hunan	-	-	-	1	1	0	4	4	0
	Hupeh	1	1	0	-	-	-	1	1	0
	Total	1	1	0	3	5	+2	12	10	-2
South	Kwangsi	-	-	-	-	-	-	4	4	0
	Kwangtung	1	1	0	-	1	+1	6	5	-1
	Fukien	-	-	-	1	2	+1	2	1	-1
	Total	1	1	0	1	3	+2	12	10	-2
Northwest	Shensi	-	1	+1	1	-	-1	1	1	0
	Sinkiang	-	-	-	-	1	+1	3	2	-1
	Kansu	-	-	-	1	1	0	1	1	0
	Tsinghai	-	-	-	-	-	-	1	1	0
	Total	-	1	+1	2	2	0	6	5	-1
Southwest	Szechwan	1	2	+1	1	-	-1	6	6	0
	Kweichow	-	-	-	-	1	+1	1	-	-1
	Yünnan	-	-	-	1	1	0	1	1	0
	Total	1	2	+1	2	2	0	8	7	-1
	GRAND TOTAL	9	15	+6	27	34	+7	81	68	-13

[a] Source: Appendix A, Tables A-1, A-4, and A-5. This table does not include cities in Ningsia and Tibet.

[b] Cities with populations 1,000,000 and above.

[c] Cities with populations 300,000 to less than 1,000,000.

[d] Cities with populations 100,000 to less than 300,000.

[e] See note in Table A-1.

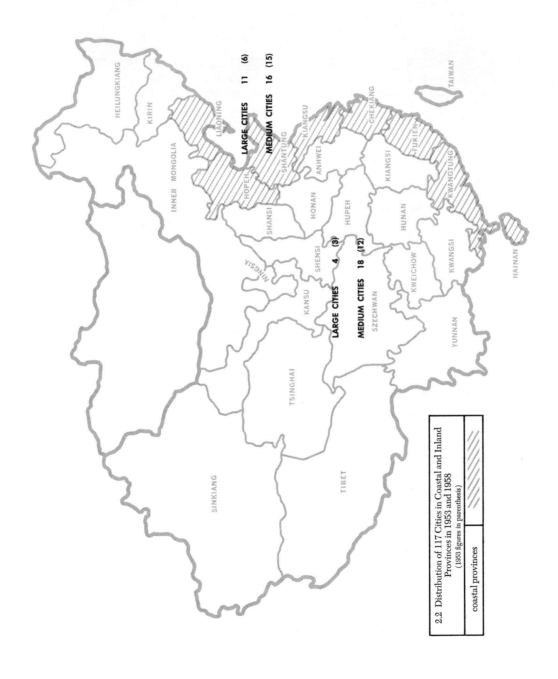

LARGE CITIES 11 (6)
MEDIUM CITIES 16 (15)

LARGE CITIES 4 (3)
MEDIUM CITIES 18 (12)

HEILUNGKIANG
KIRIN
INNER MONGOLIA
LIAONING
HOPEH
SHANTUNG
KIANGSU
ANHWEI
CHEKIANG
KIANGSI
FUKIEN
KWANGTUNG
SHANSI
HONAN
HUPEH
HUNAN
KWANGSI
KWEICHOW
HAINAN
TAIWAN
SHENSI
KANSU
NINGSIA
SZECHWAN
YUNNAN
TSINGHAI
SINKIANG
TIBET

2.2 Distribution of 117 Cities in Coastal and Inland
Provinces in 1953 and 1958
(1953 figures in parenthesis)

coastal provinces

34

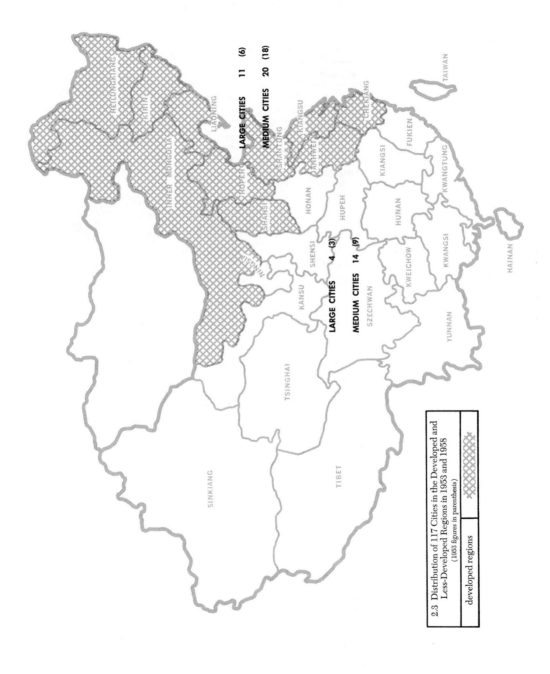

2.3 Distribution of 117 Cities in the Developed and Less-Developed Regions in 1953 and 1958 (1953 figures in parenthesis)

developed regions

LARGE CITIES 11 (6)
MEDIUM CITIES 20 (18)

LARGE CITIES 4 (3)
MEDIUM CITIES 14 (9)

HEILUNGKIANG
KIRIN
LIAONING
INNER MONGOLIA
HOPEH
SHANSI
NINGSIA
SHENSI
KANSU
TSINGHAI
SINKIANG
TIBET
SHANTUNG
HONAN
HUPEH
ANHWEI
KIANGSU
CHEKIANG
KIANGSI
FUKIEN
KWANGTUNG
HUNAN
KWEICHOW
KWANGSI
SZECHWAN
YUNNAN
HAINAN
TAIWAN

35

Table 2-4

RANKING OF PROVINCES AND REGIONS BY THE NUMBER OF CITIES
(FROM A TOTAL OF 117 CITIES) IN THE LARGE AND
MEDIUM GROUPS IN 1953 AND 1958[a]

Group	Rank	1953 Provinces	1953 Regions	1958 Provinces	1958 Regions
Large	1	Hopeh Kiangsu	Northeast North East	Liaoning	Northeast
	2	Liaoning Heilungkiang Hupeh Kwangtung Szechwan	Central South Southwest	Hopeh Kiangsu Szechwan	North East
	3	-	-	Heilungkiang Shansi Shantung Hupeh Kwangtung Shensi	Southwest
	4	-	-	-	Central South Northwest
Medium	1	Liaoning	Northeast	Liaoning Hopeh Kiangsu	East
	2	Kiangsu	East	Honan	Northeast
	3	Hopeh	North	Kirin Inner Mongolia Shantung Anhwei Fukien	North
	4	Kirin	Central	Heilungkiang Chekiang Kiangsi Hunan Kwangtung Sinkiang Kansu Kweichow Yünnan	Central
	5	Shantung Heilungkiang Shansi Chekiang Kiangsi Honan Hunan Fukien Shensi Kansu Szechwan Yünnan	Northwest Southwest	-	South
	6	-	South	-	Northwest Southwest

Table 2-4 (continued)

Group	Rank	1953		1958	
		Provinces	Regions	Provinces	Regions
Large and Medium Combined	1	Liaoning	Northeast	Liaoning	East
	2	Kiangsu	East	Hopeh Kiangsu	Northeast
	3	Hopeh	North	Shantung Honan	North
	4	Heilungkiang Kirin Szechwan	Central	Kirin Heilungkiang Inner Mongolia Anhwei Fukien Szechwan	Central
	5	Shantung Shansi Chekiang Kiangsi Honan Hunan Fukien Shensi Kansu Yünnan	Southwest	Shansi Chekiang Kiangsi Hunan Hupeh Kwangtung Shensi Sinkiang Kansu Kweichow Yünnan	South Southwest
	6	–	–	–	Northwest

[a]Sources: Table 2-3 and Appendix A, Table A-1.

all practical purposes, the relative standing of the three most important regions remained about the same between 1953 and 1958 and also between 1948 and 1953.

As our first finding, we may state, therefore, that as of 1958, or immediately preceding the "Great Leap Forward," the most important market and supply areas as represented by large and medium cities were in Liaoning, Kiangsu, and Hopeh provinces or in the East, Northeast, and North China Economic Cooperation Regions. There was no radical change between 1953 and 1958 and no general change between 1948 and 1958.

Given an increase in the number of medium cities, without any change in the number of large cities or with a smaller decrease in the latter, we may regard the province or region to have increased the number of its urban centers in a manner consistent with the avowed policy to develop medium and smaller cities at the expense of the very large ones. If, on the other hand, we see an increase in the number of cities in the large group with a parallel or smaller increase in that of the medium group, the region or province has increased its degree of urbanization but in a manner contrary to the avowed policy of deemphasizing the larger cities. We may also categorize certain provinces and regions as not having undergone any change in the degree of urbanization or having "contracted."

Table 2-5 indicates a general increase in urbanization from 1953 to 1958 in the sense that the number of large and medium market and supply areas showed a net increase. There was no contraction on a provincial basis, and there was an expansion in all the Economic Cooperation Regions. Furthermore, most provinces appear to have increased urbanization according to official policy. On the other hand, the opposite is true if a regional comparison is made. Table 2-5 shows that a greater proportion of coastal provinces than inland provinces have expanded in this same sense.

Of the increment of six cities in the large group from 1953 to 1958, three were in coastal provinces and three inland (Table 2-3). Two of the added seven cities in the medium group were in the coastal provinces as against an increase of five inland. This represents 30 per cent of the increase for the coastal provinces and 70 per cent for the inland provinces. However, because the coastal provinces are few compared with the other major administrative

38

Table 2-5

PROVINCES AND REGIONS GROUPED BY CATEGORIES OF CHANGE
IN URBANIZATION FROM 1953 TO 1958[a, b]

Group		Change in the Number of Cities in Indicated Group	Provinces	Regions	Nature of Change in Status as Market and Supply Areas
		Medium (M)	Large (L)		
I	I-1	+	0	North: Hopeh, Inner Mongolia; East: Anhwei; Central: Honan; South: Kwangtung, Fukien; Northwest: Sinkiang; Southwest: Kweichow	Central South	Expansion of the number of urban centers according to the policy of developing medium and smaller cities at the expense of very large cities.
	I-2	+ but M ≥ L	-	-	-	
II	II-1	+	+	East: Shantung	East North	Expansion but not according to the policy above
	II-2	0	+	-	Southwest Northwest	
	II-3	- but M ≤ L	+	Northeast: Liaoning; North: Shansi; Northwest: Shensi; Southwest: Szechwan	Northeast	
III	III-1	-	0	-	-	
	III-2	-	-	-	-	
	III-3	0	-	-	-	Contraction
	III-4	+ but M < L	-	-	-	
	III-5	- but M > L	+	-	-	
IV		0	0	Northeast: Heilungkiang, Kirin; East: Kiangsu; Chekiang; Central: Kiangsi, Hunan, Hupeh; Northwest: Kansu, Yünnan		No change
V		No medium or large cities in 1953 and 1958		South: Kwangsi Northwest: Tsinghai	-	No change

[a] Source: Table 2-3 and Appendix A, Tables A-1 and A-6.

[b] Increase: +
Decrease: -
No change: 0

39

Table 2-6

INCREASE IN THE NUMBER OF LARGE AND MEDIUM CITIES
IN THE MORE AND LESS DEVELOPED AREAS
FROM 1953 TO 1958

Type of Area	Region	Increase in Number of Large Cities	Increase in Number of Medium Cities
More Developed	Northeast	+2	-2
	East	+1	+3
	North	+1	+2
	Subtotal	+4	+3
Less Developed	Central	-	+2
	South	-	+2
	Northwest	+1	-
	Southwest	+1	-
	Subtotal	+2	+4
	Total Increase	+6	+7
Proportion of Total Increase Occurring in More Developed Areas		2/3	3/7
Proportion of Total Increase Occurring in Less Developed Areas		1/3	4/7

divisions, they also had a slightly larger than proportionate share of the increment in the number of medium cities.

The same comparison may also be made using regions. As we have seen in Chapter 1, Manchuria, East China, and North China were the three more-developed regions in comparison with Central-South, Northwest, and Southwest China. In the 1953 to 1958 period, these three more-developed regions added four large cities as compared with two in the less-developed regions. Medium cities increased by three in the first group and by four in the second. These findings indicate that development was still very much concentrated in the more developed regions although the coastal provinces alone seemed to have enjoyed a slightly decreased preference. At the same time, we should bear in mind the existence of exceptional enclaves. Some provinces in the less developed regions experienced sizable growth (e. g. , Honan in Central China) while others in the more developed or coastal regions did not (e. g. , Kiangsu and Chekiang in East China, both being coastal provinces and Heilungkiang in the Northeast). (Table 2-3.)

From 1953 to 1958, the less-developed regions became more urbanized but not as greatly as they could have been if the original policy had been fully implemented. Although the number of medium cities increased, the gain was in the order of 50 per cent; the number of large cities showed a 66 per cent gain. (Table 2-6.)

So far, no radical departure from the pre-Communist spatial pattern can be observed from a study of city growth and distribution. However, the inferences which can be drawn from the number of cities and their distribution by size in either provincial or regional groupings are limited. A further examination of the economic significance of individual cities as market and supply areas is necessary for a clearer idea of the spatial pattern.

Classification of Cities by Growth Rates and Absolute Population Increases from 1953 to 1958

A different approach is used to determine the relationship between absolute changes in population and relative rates of change in individual municipalities. Since the sizes of cities differed considerably in 1953, the same

41

absolute change in numbers would not amount to the same relative change. By comparing the absolute changes with the corresponding rates of change, individual cities can be tentatively divided into four groups reflecting the role and relative importance of each city in the changing spatial economy.

Since substantial unemployment was unlikely in 1953, it seems reasonable to assume that the greater the increase in general economic activity within a city the larger the absolute increase in population. A city experiencing a large absolute increase but a small relative change in population was probably one of the large established economic centers that expanded further. These cities have been classed as Group I. Group II includes cities showing both large absolute and relative growths. Since their absolute population increases are comparable to those of Group I and their initial populations are smaller, their economic development would seem to be more intensive and vigorous. One would, therefore, expect to find in Group II most of the newer and rapidly expanding economic centers, including some still of secondary importance in 1958, and most of the formerly large and medium market and supply areas that have undergone economic expansion.

Group III consists of cities that have registered a large relative growth although the absolute increase in population has been small. These cities are predominantly smaller ones that have experienced rapid growth, but that are nevertheless far from being major market or supply areas. Growing mining towns, railway junctions and other cities with specialized industries or economic functions are also in this category. Finally, Group IV consists of cities that have registered only small increases in population as well as low growth rates. Cities in Group IV are lesser economic centers, although a few fairly important industrial towns may offer limited or specialized employment opportunities.

So that large and small absolute increases and rates of growth can be discussed objectively, arbitrary dividing lines have been selected. Since 12 of the 117 cities actually reported declines in populations from 1953 to 1958, they have been eliminated to simplify comparisons. Of the remaining 105 cities, some show extremely large values which would distort the means. Accordingly, medians have been selected as dividing lines for the absolute increases and for the growth rates. The cities on or above the medians are said to have registered

Table 2-7

DISTRIBUTION OF 117 CITIES BY SIZE GROUPS OF
POPULATION CHANGE BETWEEN
1953 AND 1958 MIDYEAR [a, b]

Population Change (1,000 Persons)	Number of Cities
-200 to less than -100	1
-100 to less than 0	11
0 to less than 100	60
100 to less than 200	16
200 to less than 300	11
300 to less than 400	9
400 to less than 500	1
500 to less than 600	2
600 to less than 700	3
700 to less than 800	2
800 or more	1
Total	117

[a] Source: Appendix A, Table A-1.

[b] Median Values: All cities, 77,500 (q_3 = 198,438); Excluding cities with decline of population, 87,500.

Table 2-8

DISTRIBUTION OF 117 CITIES BY RATES OF POPULATION GROWTH BETWEEN 1953 AND 1958 MIDYEAR[a, b]

Change in 1953-58 Population (%) (1953 = 100)	Number of Cities
-60 to less than -40	1
-40 to less than -20	2
-20 to less than 0	9
0 to less than 20	34
20 to less than 40	32
40 to less than 60	10
60 to less than 80	7
80 to less than 100	7
100 to less than 120	2
120 to less than 140	2
140 to less than 160	–
160 to less than 180	–
180 to less than 200	3
200 to less than 220	3
220 to less than 240	2
240 and more	3
Total	117

[a] Source: Appendix A, Table A-1.

[b] Median Values: All cities = 27. 8%.
              Cities without decline of population = 31. 6%.

large increases; those below are said to have shown only small increases (Tables 2-7 and 2-8). A complete list of the 117 cities, grouped by category, is given in Table A-6, Appendix A.

In conformity with what one would expect, the cities in Group I (i.e., the relatively established economic centers) are concentrated in East China, and then in North, Northeast, and Southwest China. The new economic centers and formerly secondary cities being intensively developed (Group II) as well as some of the previously large established centers, are mainly in Northeast China and then in North, Central, East, and Northwest China. The fifteen cities in Group III are fairly evenly divided among all regions, with the exception of Southwest China. (See Table 2-9 and Maps 2-4 and 2-5.)

If the coastal and inland provinces are considered separately, seven cities from Group I are in coastal areas and four are in the inland provinces, which is expected since the major established economic centers of pre-Communist China were in the coastal areas. However, in Groups II and III, more cities are in the inland provinces than in the coastal areas. This breakdown points to a greater role being played by the inland provinces in development, at least in terms of the emergence of new centers and higher growth rates. However, if Northeast, North, and East China are grouped together and contracted to the less-developed regions--Central, South, Northwest, and Southwest China--more cities fall into Groups I, II and III in the more-developed regions than in the less-developed regions. Bearing in mind the existence of exceptional provinces as enclaves, one would infer that there was a tendency to emphasize development in cities removed from the coast, but there was also a relatively heavy emphasis on the development of the more-developed rather than the less-developed areas. This breakdown provides additional evidence that the locational design of the First Five-Year Plan was only partially realized. As previously noted, the Plan itself did not remain consistent and was revised in 1955 or 1956. (See Map 2-6.)

Index of Urbanization

The "index of urbanization" discussed by various authors in connection with the size of the population in cities and the number of cities having populations larger than any given value has an important application in this study.[3]

45

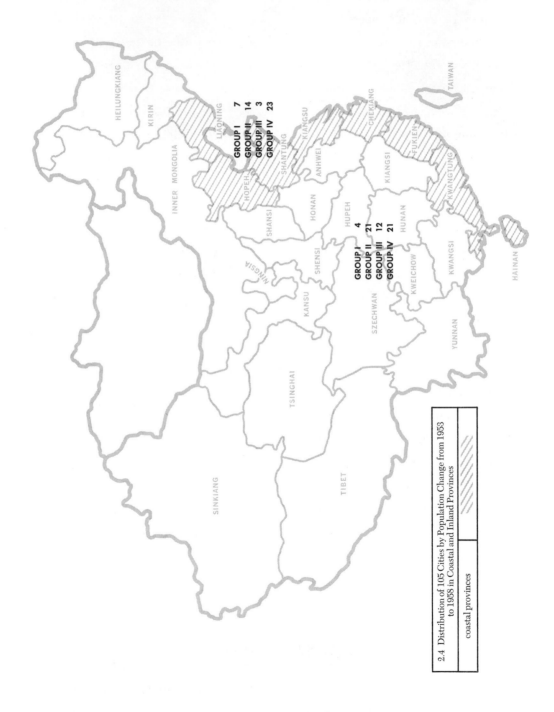

GROUP I	7
GROUP II	14
GROUP III	3
GROUP IV	23

GROUP I	4
GROUP II	21
GROUP III	12
GROUP IV	21

2.4 Distribution of 105 Cities by Population Change from 1953 to 1958 in Coastal and Inland Provinces

coastal provinces

46

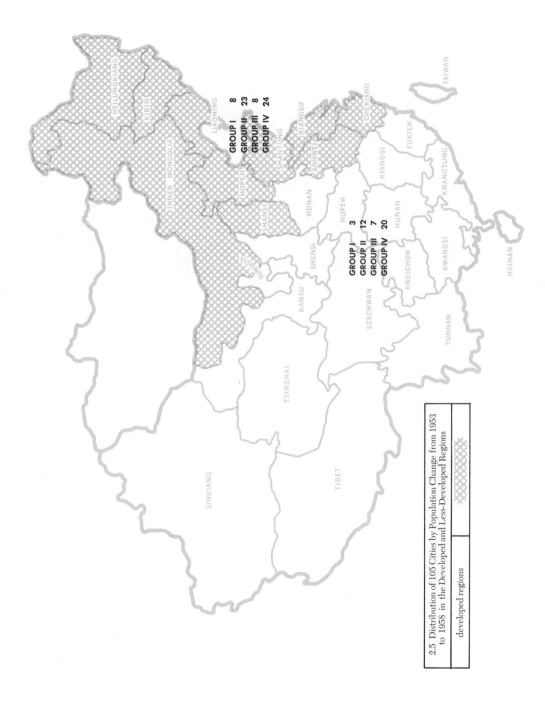

GROUP I   8
GROUP II 23
GROUP III 8
GROUP IV 24

GROUP I   3
GROUP II 12
GROUP III 7
GROUP IV 20

2.5 Distribution of 105 Cities by Population Change from 1953 to 1958 in the Developed and Less-Developed Regions

developed regions

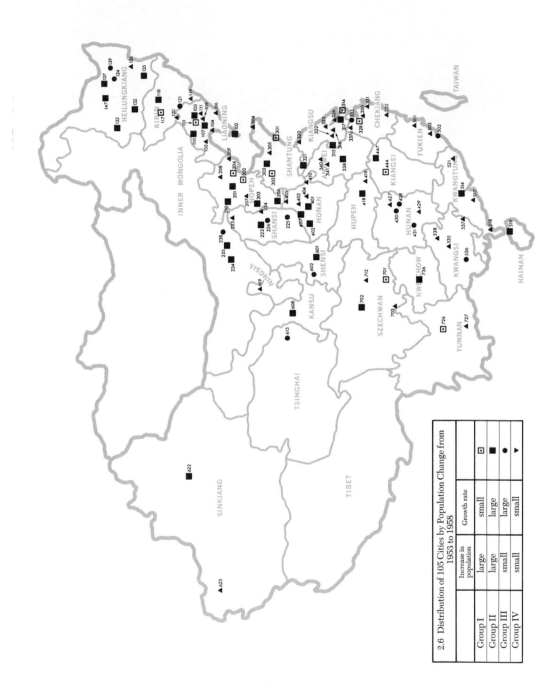

2.6 Distribution of 105 Cities by Population Change from 1953 to 1958

	Increase in population	Growth rate	
Group I	large	small	⊡
Group II	large	large	■
Group III	small	large	●
Group IV	small	small	▲

Table 2-9

REGIONAL AND PROVINCIAL DISTRIBUTION OF 105 CITIES
BY TYPE OF POPULATION CHANGE[a,b]

Region	Province	Number of Cities in Indicated Group			
		Group I	Group II	Group III	Group IV
Northeast	Liaoning	1	4	–	5
	Kirin	1	1	1	2
	Heilungkiang	–	6	2	–
	Total	2	11	3	7
North	Hopeh	2	4	–	3
	Shansi	–	1	2	2
	Inner Mongolia	–	2	1	–
	Total	2	7	3	5
East	Kiangsu	1	3	–	5
	Shantung	2	1	–	2
	Anhwei	–	1	–	2
	Chekiang	1	–	2	3
	Total	4	5	2	12
Central	Kiangsi	1	1	–	–
	Honan	–	3	–	4
	Hunan	–	–	3	2
	Hupeh	–	1	–	1
	Total	1	5	3	7
South	Kwangsi	–	–	1	3
	Kwangtung	–	2	–	3
	Fukien	–	–	1	2
	Total	–	2	2	8
Northwest	Shensi	–	1	1	–
	Sinkiang	–	1	–	1
	Kansu	–	1	–	1
	Tsinghai	–	–	1	–
	Total	–	3	2	2
Southwest	Szechwan	1	1	–	2
	Kweichow	–	1	–	–
	Yünnan	1	–	–	1
	Total	2	2	–	3
	GRAND TOTAL	11	35	15	44
Coastal Provinces		7	14	3	23
Inland Provinces		4	21	12	21
Formerly Developed Regions		8	23	8	24
Underdeveloped Regions		3	12	7	20

---

[a]Source: Appendix A, Table A-6.

[b]Key to Grouping: Median Increase in Population

	III	II	
			Median Rate of
	IV	I	Increase

Median of Growth Rate = 31.6%.   Median of Absolute Increase in Population
= 87,500.

49

As Singer pointed out in his 1936 article:

> In the distribution of population among human agglomerations
> there appears to be a remarkable statistical regularity which,
> besides being interesting in itself and affording a complete
> analogy to Pareto's Law of income distribution, yields an
> exact quantitative measure for the relative roles of the smaller
> and larger types of human agglomerations, so to speak, an
> "Index of Metropolisation. " This regularity can be character-
> ized by the equation log Y = A - αlog X, where X is a certain
> number of inhabitants; Y, the number of towns more than X
> inhabitants; A and α are constants. [4]

If we use the 1953 and 1958 population data for the 117 cities, we can
deduce the linear regression lines of this form. For 1953 we have log Y =
3. 837477 - 0. 924794 log X and for 1958 we have log Y = 4. 143997 - 0. 993881
log X. There was an increase in the value of α or the "Pareto coefficient" between
1953 and 1958, accompanied by a concomitant increase in that of A. However,
the difference between the two values of α is not large. The slight increase of
α in 1958 is compensated for by the increase in A so that for the relevant values
of X the proportions of cities above them in 1958 would still be higher than in
1953. (See Figure 2-1.)

As pointed out by Allen, [5] other things being equal, the highest values
for α should be obtained from statistics based on the legal boundaries or fixed
boundary definitions of town sizes "since the numbers of large towns which
have grown up in recent years by overspilling legal boundaries are many in
most countries. " The population statistics used in computing the values above
for the Pareto coefficients for Communist China are mostly based on the legal
boundaries of towns. But "spilling over" was probably less as a rule in Communist China because of inadequate municipal transportation. The value of α
just under 1 in both 1953 and 1958, may be compared with similar values in
other countries. The corresponding coefficients were 0. 9893 for England and
Wales in 1921 and 0. 9314 for Canada in 1932. [6] It may also be noted that the
relative deviation of the actual data [(Y-Y')/Y, where Y is the actual and Y'
the theoretical] is small for large values of X, but tends to rise as X becomes
smaller. This phenomenon also seems to conform to Allen's observation that
the Pareto function overestimates the number of the smaller towns.

Figure 2.1 Population Size and Rank Relationship of Cities in
Communist China in 1953 and 1958

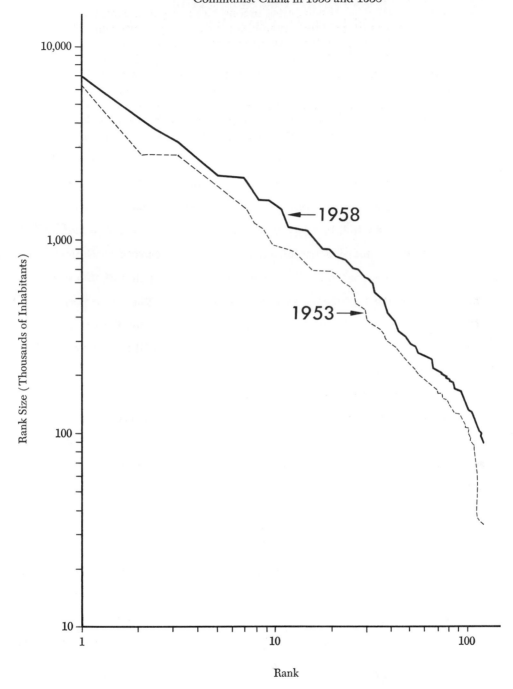

3 SPATIAL PATTERN AND STRUCTURE OF THE INDUSTRIAL ECONOMY

The population data in Chapter 2 present a general view of the development of market and supply areas in the Chinese economy, but they do not provide direct information on the industrial structure of the country. We can deduce the relative importance of the large, small, and medium cities in industrial development, only because city size is likely to vary with industrial importance. Since industrial production is a part of the total supply of goods originating from an area, its significance may be measured in terms of population and population growth. However, factors other than industrial development also affect population growth, and detailed information on industrial location is still meager. As a corrective measure, it is necessary to ferret out all available data on industrial development in cities that can be used to indicate the spatial characteristics of the industrial structure.

Fortunately, by combing journals, newspapers and other sources, it has been possible to construct an industrial profile for 328 cities and smaller locations as of approximately 1960 to 1961. A judicial selection of these data, admittedly a sampling, can be used to derive a general view of the spatial pattern of the industrial economy.

Classification of Industries Used to Describe the Spatial Structure

Fourteen industrial groups are included in the description of the spatial pattern of the industrial economy. With a few exceptions, these classes correspond closely to the 21 industrial groups (excluding defense industries) used in official planning in Communist China.[1] The official classification is as follows:

Heavy Industry	Light Industry
A. Electric power	M. Matches
B. Fuel	N. Paper
C. Iron and steel	O. Textiles
D. Nonferrous metals	P. Clothing
E. Metal processing	Q. Leather
F. Chemicals (including pharmaceuticals)	R. Tallow and cosmetics
	S. Food processing
G. Rubber products	T. Cultural, educational, and art supplies
H. Nonmetallic mining	
I. Building materials	U. Other light industries
J. Glass	
K. Ceramics	
L. Lumber	

The classification used in this compilation is given in the following with the corresponding official classification identity shown in parentheses:

Heavy Industry:

1. Iron and steel (C)

2. Nonferrous metals (D)

3. Electric power (A)

4. Coal mining (B)

5. Petroleum

6. Machinery (E)

    a. Machine tools and parts, including ball-bearings
    b. Transportation machinery and equipment
    c. Mining machinery and equipment
    d. Agricultural machinery and equipment (E)
    e. Textile machinery and equipment
    f. Civil engineering machinery and equipment
    g. Electric and electronic machinery and equipment

7. Chemicals, including paints, dyes, rubber, and glass products (F, G,J)

8. Building materials (I)

9. Lumber (L)

Light Industry:

10. Textiles (O)

11. Food processing (S)

12. Pharmaceutical products (F)

13. Paper (N)

14. Other light industries, including enamel products, ceramics, matches, clothing, leather goods, furs, soap, tallow, cosmetics, printing, and cultural, educational, and art supplies (K, M, P, Q, R, T)

The only industry completely omitted from our list is nonmetallic mining (excluding coal), the importance of which may be safely assumed to be small in Communist China so far.

With the exception of electric power, coal mining, and the iron and steel industry, for which annual capacity data are available, the data we have concern the number of plants in all classes. Both capacity and plant figures must be weighted before they can be combined in a comprehensive index. For this purpose, given the data available, the gross value-added per plant (or per unit capacity) is an appropriate weight. We are fortunate to have some preliminary estimates of gross value-added in 1958, 1959, and 1960.[2]

We first subtract gross value-added in coal mining, power, generation, and iron and steel fabrication, which are estimated separately, from estimates for producer goods in "modern industry." This category covers modern manufacturing, utilities, and modern mining. The remainder in the producer goods sector is then divided by the number of industrial plants in the "other heavy industry" group (i. e., "heavy industry" less the three enumerated industries) in our list. The estimated gross value added per plant is then used as the weight for these " other heavy industries. " In the same manner, we can find the weight for the "light industry" group by dividing the gross value-added in the consumer sector of "modern industry" by the number of industrial plants in the "light industry" group in our sample. The gross value-added estimates for electric power, coal mining, and the iron and steel industries are taken from individual sectoral studies of these industries.[3] The annual capacity figures are then weighted by the corresponding values-added per unit capacity.

Thus, we have at our disposal five large groupings, coal mining, electric power, iron and steel, "other heavy industry" and "light industry," all weighted by their gross values-added per unit capacity or per plant. From these sectoral estimates we can derive the weighted aggregates for "heavy industry," "light industry," and all "modern industry." The details are presented in Table B-1, Appendix B.

The data in Table B-1 can be used to indicate the relative importance of 328 cities and towns in 26 provinces and seven Economic Cooperation Regions on the basis of the weighted values. If we assume that our sample represents the entire industrial sector, the weighted values may also be regarded as gross values-added in modern industry originating from the individual cities, provinces, and regions. In this sense, Table B-1 also gives a general view of the spatial allocation of the gross value-added originating in the modern industry sector.

These estimates constitute only a rough approximation of the spatial pattern of Communist China's modern industry. For one thing, the correspondence between the consumer goods sector and "light industry," on the one hand, and the producer goods sector and "heavy industry" on the other, is far from being complete. Second, some of the capacity and plant data used are probably planned targets rather than realized figures.[4] They would not necessarily correspond to the output statistics even if they were data of realized capacity.

Furthermore, we can not assert that the total number of plants included in the sample constitutes full coverage. Even the estimates of annual capacity for the three enumerated industries are not complete. However, there is no particular reason to believe that the degree of coverage for the industries within the "heavy industry" sector, other than those enumerated, varies significantly from one industry to another. The same may be said of the industries in the "light industry" sector. In addition there is no evidence of significant variations in coverage from one geographical area to another. Other than some possible distortion in the relative degree of coverage between the "heavy" and "light" industry sectors, which will be discussed later, our sample can be legitimately used as an approximate image of the spatial pattern of Chinese industry.

Distribution of Cities by Industrial Capacity

The data in Table B-1 can be used to construct a frequency distribution of the 328 locations by class intervals of total industrial capacity as indicated by weighted values (Table 3-1). One characteristic of the frequency distribution given in Table 3-1 is the marked discontinuity between the first class interval of cities with weighted values of under 50 million 1952 yüan and the next class interval of 50 to under 100 million. A similar discontinuity also exists at the 400 million yüan level. In fact, no cities are in the 400 and 700 million yüan range. Finally, Shanghai stands by itself at a considerable distance above the next two largest cities.

These unmistakable discontinuities serve as convenient dividing lines for grouping by size. The first group of 262 locations are classified as small industrial production sites; the group between 50 million and 400 million yüan annual capacity, as medium-sized industrial centers; and the group beginning at the 700 million yüan level, as large industrial cities.

This tripartite division has been used to construct Table 3-2, which summarizes the distribution of estimated weighted values of annual industrial capacity by city groups. The indicated distribution of industrial capacity, together with the spatial pattern of industrial cities and production sites in Table 3-1, permits several deductions. Although our findings must be treated as preliminary and tentative in view of the incompleteness of available information and the approximate nature of the gross value-added estimates used as weights, they are worth serious consideration. (See Map 3-1.)

Pattern of Industrial Concentration

The Chinese industrial economy shows an extremely high degree of concentration of industrial capacity in the city of Shanghai. The estimated value of annual industrial capacity in Shanghai is more than five times that of the next largest industrial center, Tientsin, and over six times that of the third largest urban complex, Wu-han. Table D-2 shows that the industrial capacity estimates are comparable for Tientsin, Wu-han, and An-shan. These three cities are in turn followed by Chungking, Nanking, and Peking, and, on the next level, by

Table 3-1

FREQUENCY DISTRIBUTION OF 328 CITIES BY INDUSTRIAL CAPACITY
IN 26 PROVINCES AND AUTONOMOUS REGIONS[a]

		Northeast				North				East					Central					South				Northwest						Southwest					
	Annual Capacity of Modern Industry (million yüan)	Liaoning	Kirin	Heilungkiang	Total	Hopeh	Shansi	Inner Mongolia	Total	Shantung	Kiangsu	Chekiang	Anhwei	Total	Honan	Hupeh	Hunan	Kiangsi	Total	Fukien	Kwangtung	Kwangsi	Total	Shensi	Kansu	Tsinghai	Ningsia	Sinkiang	Total	Szechwan	Yünnan	Kweichow	Tibet	Total	ALL CHINA
Small	Under 50	9	12	12	33	15	8	13	36	10	11	9	8	38	15	8	16	11	50	14	20	9	43	6	5	4	3	6	24	20	9	8	1	38	262
Medium	50 to under 100		2	2	4	2	1		3	1	1	2		4	2		2	1	5		2		2							1				1	19
	100 to under 200	2		1	3	4	1		5			1		1	1	1			2		2		2	1				2	3	4	1	1		6	22
	200 to under 300	3	1		4							2	2	4			1		1		1		1	1	1				2						12
	300 to under 400	1			1	1			1				1	1	1				1																4
	400 to under 500																																		
	500 to under 600																																		
	600 to under 700																																		
Large	700 to under 800							1	1												1		1												2
	800 to under 900																																		
	900 to under 1000			1	1					1				1																1				1	3
	1000 to under 1100																																		
	1100 to under 1200	1			1																														1
	1200 to under 1300																																		
	1300 to under 1400															1			1																1
	1400 to under 1500																																		
Very Large	1500 to under 1600							1	1																										1
	.																																		
	.																																		
	.																																		
	Over 4500										1		1																						1
	Total	16	15	15	46	21	12	15	48	13	14	10	13	50	18	10	19	13	60	15	23	11	49	7	7	4	3	8	29	26	10	9	1	46	328

[a] Source: Appendix B, Table B-1.

Table 3-2

DISTRIBUTION OF INDUSTRIAL CAPACITY BY CITY GROUPS
IN 26 PROVINCES AND AUTONOMOUS REGIONS[a]

Region	Province	Number of Large Industrial Centers	Number of Medium Industrial Centers	Number of Small Industrial Centers	Total Number of Industrial Centers
Northeast	Liaoning	1,126	1,241	116	2,483
	Kirin	-	404	76	480
	Heilungkiang	-	265	134	399
	Total	1,126	1,910	326	3,362
North	Hopeh	2,506	596	132	3,234
	Shansi	-	660	49	709
	Inner Mongolia	796	75	137	1,008
	Total	3,302	1,331	318	4,951
East	Shantung	-	831	114	945
	Kiangsu	9,465	56	116	9,637
	Chekiang	-	89	69	158
	Anhwei	-	736	87	823
	Total	9,465	1,712	386	11,563
Central	Honan	-	268	259	527
	Hupeh	1,335	163	60	1,558
	Hunan	-	402	155	557
	Kiangsi	-	394	142	536
	Total	1,335	1,227	616	3,178
South	Fukien	-	242	162	404
	Kwangtung	748	208	187	1,143
	Kwangsi	-	154	84	238
	Total	748	604	433	1,785
Northwest	Shensi	-	276	51	327
	Kansu	-	397	34	431
	Tsinghai	-	-	44	44
	Sinkiang	-	272	11	283
	Total	-	945	175	1,120
Southwest	Szechwan	969	712	159	1,840
	Yünnan	-	170	84	254
	Kweichow	-	169	142	311
	Tibet	-	-	1	1
	Total	969	1,051	386	2,406

[a]Source: Appendix B, Table B-1.

58

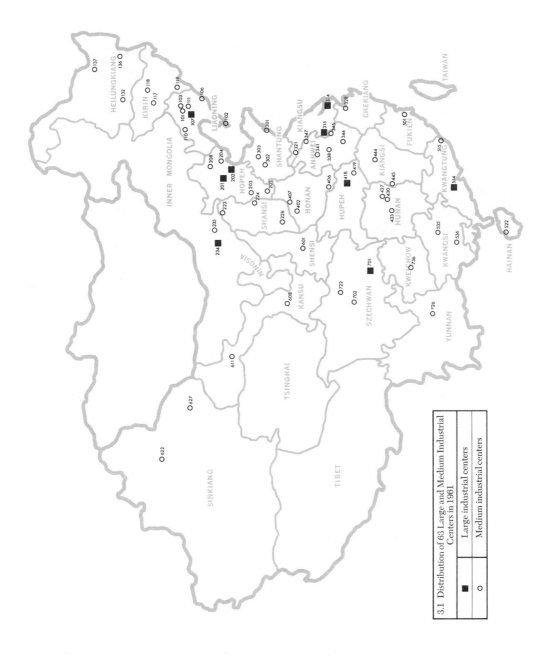

3.1 Distribution of 63 Large and Medium Industrial Centers in 1961	
■	Large industrial centers
○	Medium industrial centers

59

Pao-t'ou and Canton. Other cities are notably smaller and are by no means comparable to Tientsin, Wu-han, or An-shan, not to mention Shanghai. This great disparity between Shanghai and all other industrial centers confirms that the Communist authorities rely on the industrial capacity of Shanghai to a far greater degree than they have admitted. Plant data for Shanghai may have been more completely reported and may have, therefore, exaggerated the relative importance of the city; however, the gap between Shanghai and the next largest industrial center is so vast that no conceivable discounting to compensate for possible error could narrow it significantly.

A second finding (Table 3-3) is that Kiangsu, Hopeh, and Liaoning provinces head the list in terms of annual industrial capacity as they did in the pre-Communist period. Over half the estimated industrial capacity of Communist China is concentrated in these three provinces. If the next two provinces in rank, Szechwan and Hupeh, are included, the five account for two-thirds of the total modern industrial capacity of the country.

However, there is a vast difference between the industrial capacity of Kiangsu and that of Hopeh or Liaoning which again reflects the overwhelming importance of Shanghai. It is also noteworthy that Liaoning is now in third place. The relative importance of this Manchurian province in industrial production appears to be less than would have been expected on the basis of pre-Communist data. If Shanghai, with its commanding industrial position, were disregarded, the most industrialized provinces would be Hopeh and Liaoning.

Relative Geographical Emphasis in Industrial Development

The seven coastal provinces contain six cities with a large industrial capacity in comparison with three in the 19 inland provinces. The coastal provinces also contain proportionately more cities of medium and small industrial capacity than the inland provinces. When the comparison is made between formerly developed regions (Manchuria, North China, and East China) and less-developed regions, the developed ones have proportionately even more medium and small capacity cities than the coastal provinces. These data point to a greater relative emphasis on the establishment of industrial centers in the developed regions vis-a-vis the less-developed ones than in the coastal provinces

Table 3-3

RANKING OF PROVINCES AND ECONOMIC COOPERATION
REGIONS BY INDUSTRIAL CAPACITY[a]

Province	Annual Capacity in Million 1952 Yüan Gross Value Added in 1958-1960 Average	Per Cent in Total Capacity	Region	Annual Capacity in Million 1952 Yüan Gross Value Added in 1958-1960 Average	Per Cent in Total Capacity
Kiangsu	9,637	33.97	East	11,563	40.77
Hopeh	3,234	11.40	North	4,951	17.45
Liaoning	2,483	8.75	Northeast	3,362	11.85
Szechwan	1,840	6.49	Central	3,178	11.20
Hupeh	1,558	5.49	Southwest	2,406	8.48
Kwangtung	1,143	4.03	South	1,785	6.29
Inner Mongolia	1,008	3.55	Northwest	1,120	3.95
Shantung	945	3.33	Total	28,365	100.00
Anhwei	823	2.90			
Shansi	709	2.50			
Hunan	557	1.96			
Kiangsi	536	1.89			
Honan	527	1.86			
Kirin	480	1.69			
Kansu	431	1.52			
Fukien	404	1.42			
Heilungkiang	399	1.41			
Shensi	327	1.15			
Kweichow	311	1.10			
Sinkiang	283	1.00			
Yünnan	254	0.90			
Kwangsi	238	0.84			
Chekiang	158	0.56			
Tsinghai	44	0.16			
Ningsia	35	0.12			
Tibet	1	-			
Total	28,365	100.00			

[a]Source: Appendix B, Table B-1.

61

vis-à-vis the inland provinces. A similar conclusion was drawn in Chapter 2 in relation to the development of principal market and supply areas (Tables 3-4 and 3-5).

If the comparison between coastal and inland provinces and between the developed and the less-developed regions is made in terms of productive capacity (Table 3-5), an even greater degree of industrial concentration is found in the coastal provinces and in the more developed regions. This is true without exception for all size groupings. The cities in the coastal provinces and the more-developed regions obviously have individually larger industrial capacity than those in the inland provinces and the less-developed regions. This marked difference is partially a product of the disproportionate importance of Shanghai as far as the group of large cities is concerned, but no such extreme case exists to distort the comparison for medium and small production sites.

The preceding comparison may be supplemented by ranking individual regions in terms of the number of industrial locations and the total estimated industrial capacity. The details are presented in Tables 3-6, 3-7, and 3-8. They correspond fully with the findings above.

The regional divisions, however, mask notable exceptions in certain provinces. There are some highly developed enclaves in the less-developed regions, as well as some relatively backward provinces in the coastal area. This is again an extension of the pre-Communist pattern, which has not yet been altered.

As a group, the large industrial centers account for about 60 per cent of total industrial capacity, and the medium group accounts for 31 per cent. Small cities and industrial production sites, although numerous, add only a little more than 9 per cent, which is another indication of industrial concentration in Communist China today.

A reasonable explanation of the disparity between large versus medium and small industrial centers or between the single city of Shanghai versus the other large cities is the presence of smaller industrial production sites that are new. Given time, the pattern of industrial location may be greatly altered. However, as of 1961, which is the cut-off date for most of the plant data available, the avowed policy of industrial decentralization of the "Great Leap Forward"

Table 3-4

COMPARISON OF COASTAL PROVINCES WITH INLAND PROVINCES
AND OF DEVELOPED REGIONS WITH LESS DEVELOPED
REGIONS IN TERMS OF THE NUMBER
OF INDUSTRIAL CITIES
AND LOCATIONS[a]

Area	Number of Small Industrial Centers	Number of Medium Industrial Centers	Number of Large Industrial Centers	Total Number of Industrial Centers
Coastal Provinces (7)	88	18	6	112
Inland Provinces (19)	174	39	3	216
Total	262	57	9	328
Formerly Developed Regions (Northeast, North, and East)	107	31	6	144
Less Developed Regions (Central, South, Northwest, and Southwest)	155	26	3	184
Total	262	57	9	328

[a]Source: Table 3-1.

Table 3-5

COMPARISON OF COASTAL PROVINCES WITH INLAND PROVINCES
AND OF DEVELOPED REGIONS WITH LESS DEVELOPED
REGIONS IN TERMS OF INDUSTRIAL CAPACITY [a]

Area	Percentage of Large Cities in Total Capacity	Percentage of Medium Cities in Total Capacity	Percentage of Small Cities in Total Capacity	Percentage Total in Total Capacity
Coastal Provinces	48.8	11.5	3.2	63.5
Inland Provinces	10.9	19.5	6.1	36.5
Total	59.7	31.0	9.3	100.0
Developed Regions (Northeast, North, and East)	49.0	17.5	3.6	70.1
Less Developed Regions (Central, South, Northwest, and Southwest)	10.8	13.5	5.6	29.9
Total	59.8	31.0	9.2	100.0

[a]Source: Appendix B, Table B-1.

Table 3-6

REGIONAL RANKING BY NUMBER OF INDUSTRIAL
CITIES AND LOCATIONS [a]

Region	Rank According to Number of Cities of Indicated Size		
	Medium and Large Cities	Medium Cities Only	Large Cities Only
Northeast (Manchuria)	1	1	3
North	2	3	1
East		2	2
Central	3	3	3
Southwest	4	4	3
South	5	5	3
Northwest	6	5	4

[a]Source: Table 3-1.

Table 3-7

REGIONAL RANKING BY INDUSTRIAL CAPACITY [a]

	Rank According to Number of Cities of Indicated Size			
Region	Large Cities	Medium Cities	Large and Medium Cities	All Cities
East	1	2	1	1
North	2	3	2	2
Central	3	4	4	4
Northeast	4	1	3	3
Southwest	5	5	5	5
South	6	7	6	6
Northwest	–	6	7	7

[a]Source: Table 3-2.

Table 3-8

DISTRIBUTION OF TOTAL INDUSTRIAL CAPACITY
BY CLASSES OF INDUSTRIAL CENTERS[a]

Class of Industrial Center	Percentage in Total Capacity
Large	59.7
Medium	31.0
Small	9.3
Total	100.0

[a]Source: Appendix B, Table B-1.

65

period and, to a lesser extent, of the First Five-Year Plan, has succeeded only in establishing a large number of very small production centers. The preponderant share of productive capacity remains concentrated in a small number of industrial cities. That this distribution implies considerable vulnerability in the military sense is, of course, obvious. Whether it also means that the rate of overall industrial growth has been aided and the transport burden lightened remains to be seen.

Diversification Versus Specialization

One question concerning the spatial aspect of the industrial structure is whether production sites have tended to become specialized. Specialization increases the demand for transport input and exposes residents of a given area to fluctuations in production and demand. Although insufficient demand is not expected to cause unemployment in a planned economy, there is evidence that fluctuations in economic activity have been an integral part of the Chinese developmental experience.[5] Since serious localized unemployment affects the transport sector, the questions arise as to whether the data developed in this chapter provide information on the degree of industrial specialization by production sites and whether any trend toward specialization is a matter of policy.

Industrial specialization can be determined to some extent by the degree to which centers of light and heavy industries have diverged. Table B-1 shows that 241 (73.5 per cent) of the 328 locations reported heavy industry only; four (1.2 per cent) reported light industry only; and the remaining 25.3 per cent reported both heavy and light industries. How should these figures be interpreted?

As mentioned previously, the reorientation of industrial policy in favor of light industry and consumer goods did not take place until the end of 1961, and the results probably could not be seen until 1962. Despite this reorientation, there has been no shift to building consumer goods plants--these goods continue to be produced in existing plants. Inasmuch as new investment up to the 1960 crisis had been concentrated in the heavy industry sector, it is natural to find large numbers of small heavy industry production sites where no modern light manufacturing takes place.

Secondly, because the general policy was to encourage heavy industry until 1961, it is possible that new light industry plants, especially if they are small, have not all been reported in the published sources from which our sample is derived, or, if reported, have been overlooked. The number of locations having heavy industry but no light industry is likely to be smaller than the number reported. Moreover, to compensate, a disproportionately large number of locations with heavy industry may have been reported because of the more comprehensive data that are available on coal mining, the power industry, and ferrous metals production. Many small coal mining and hydro power installations are found at single- or two-industry locations and may account for much of the specialization the figures above seem to show. If the locations with coal mines, power plants, or both, but with no other industries, were eliminated from the list of sites for which only heavy industry has been reported, the number of such locations would be reduced from 241 to 108. If locations with small to negligible annual industrial capacity (less than 50 million yüan) were further eliminated, the number of heavy industry locations without light industry would be reduced to 21, or 6.4 per cent of our 328-site list. If this last screening process were also applied to the locations with light industry alone (i.e., without heavy industry), the number of such locations would in their turn be lowered from four to none, or from 1.2 per cent of the total sample to zero.

Furthermore, if 83 locations (25 per cent of the total) with both heavy and light industry establishments are considered separately, it is significant that a fairly high correlation coefficient (+0.9122) can be established between the productive capacities of the two sectors. One is tempted to conclude that capacities in the two industrial groups tend to expand together and that the absence of one type at any location reflects a relatively early stage of its development. Coal mining, small hydro power, and similar sites are exceptional cases of specialization determined primarily by the fixed location of resources. In the more normal case, the degree of specialization varies inversely with the size of the location and the stage of development and does not appear to be a matter of deliberate policy. Even the exceptions show signs of following the same general rule as their development progresses.

Similar conclusions can be drawn drom an analysis of the number of

Table 3-9

FREQUENCY DISTRIBUTION OF 328 INDUSTRIAL
LOCATIONS BY NUMBER OF INDUSTRIAL
GROUPS AT EACH LOCATION[a]

| Region | Number of Locations Having the Indicated Number of Industrial Groups | | | | | | | | | | | | | | |
	1	2	3	4	5	6	7	8	9	10	11	12	13	14	Total
Northeast	20	3	1	5	4	2	1	3	4	1	1	-	-	1	46
North	27	2	6	2	1	2	2	2	1	1	-	1	1	-	48
East	19	6	8	5	4	1	2	3	1	-	-	-	-	1	50
Central	35	8	2	2	5	2	3	2	-	-	-	1	-	-	60
South	23	9	4	4	2	4	1	1	-	1	-	-	-	-	49
Northwest	13	6	3	3	-	1	-	2	1	-	-	-	-	-	29
Southwest	25	14	1	2	-	-	1	1	1	-	1	-	-	-	46
Total	162	48	25	23	16	12	10	14	8	3	2	2	1	2	328

[a]Source: Appendix B, Table B-3.

industries found at the 328 locations (Table 3-9). Using our selected 14 industry divisions, (pp. 53-54) we find ten cities have 10 to 14 industries; 108 have three to nine; 48 have two; and 162 have one. Four of the latter group are described as having a single industry but in terms which make it appear they may house an industrial composite. These four have been dropped, reducing the number of such "specialized" locations to 158. Of these 134 are sites for coal mines, power plants, or petroleum refineries. The remaining 24 house iron and steel plants. Most of them are bound to fixed resources. A few are thermal power plants, some of which should perhaps be disregarded if their primary function is to supply power for nonindustrial purposes.

At the other extreme, the ten cities boasting 10 to 14 industries are Mukden, Kirin, Harbin, Peking, Tientsin, Tai-yüan, Shanghai, Wu-han, Canton, and Chungking. Of these, six are large industrial centers, and four are medium industrial centers--which shows that diversification is not limited to very large centers only.

Since coal mining and similar activities based on immobile resources have tended to create specialized enclaves of industrial activity, they have added to the vulnerabilities inherent in specialization. These locations are found mostly in the formerly less developed regions.

In general, however, it appears that specialization has not been a deliberate policy where it is not a result of the fixed location of certain resources or where it is not simply a reflection of the early stage of industrial development.

4 KEY ECONOMIC CHARACTERISTICS OF THE CITIES AND OF THE ENTIRE SPATIAL ECONOMY

Ranking of 117 Cities by Industrial and Economic Significance

Chapter 2 analyzed the spatial economy of mainland China and its development under the Communist regime on the basis of available population data, and Chapter 3 focused attention on industrial capacity estimates. The present chapter is a synthesis of the two approaches.

Four variables have been selected to chart the "current" industrial and general economic status of the cities and the nature and rate of their growth under the present regime. Since the available data are primarily from the period prior to the major economic crisis in 1961–62, "current" may seem an unwarrantable term. However, because the pattern presented is primarily relative, comparing each city, and because the ensuing period was characterized more by recovery than economic progress, the "current" status may be looked upon as a reasonably faithful approximation of the 1965–66 situation. This is not to say that significant changes have not taken place but simply that, in terms of the factors which concern us here, there is no marked difference in the overall picture.

The four variables are total population in 1958, total weighted industrial capacity as of 1960–61, population increase from 1953 to 1958, and industrial capacity as represented by new plants constructed since 1949. The first two serve as a guide to the current industrial and general economic status of the cities; the last two shed light on their nature and rate of growth.

The basic reasoning for grouping cities on the basis of these four variables is as follows: First, the larger the total industrial capacity, the larger the population of the city tends to be. A city with a large industrial capacity and a large population must be considered an important industrial and economic center. Second, in general, the larger the capacity of new plants completed or under construction in a city, the larger the increase in population. A city with a large new capacity and a similar increase in population must be an important developing industrial center. Its importance in this respect is measured against the relative size of new plants and population increases compared with other cities. Because of possible shifts of occupations without a population increase or other similar changes, correlation between the number of new plants and increase in population is not so high as that between total number of plants and total population. [1] Third, it follows that the most important cities are rated highest under the first and second criteria. On the other hand, if a city rates high under one criterion, but not so high or low under the second, a different ranking is given, depending on the particular combination of the values of the four variables and, to a lesser extent, the subjective evaluation and interpretation of the analyst. (See Tables 4-1 and 4-2.)

Figure 4-1 shows how cities have been classified on the basis of these four criteria. The classification code consists of two parts, e.g., I-I' and II-V'. Cities with classification codes I-x (except I-III') have been given a rank prefix of "A" to indicate that they are major industrial centers and important economic centers and markets in a broad sense. Cities with codes III-x (including also II-III') have a rank prefix of "C" to denote that they are the least important industrial and economic centers. The remaining cities are in the intermediate range and have the rank prefix "B."

The upper quartiles and medians are used as arbitrary boundary lines to delineate the values of the four variables. The five divisions of regions in each of the two sets of variables used are set forth in Figure 4-1. The classification of some cities is marginal and that of other cities is particularly uncertain. For simplicity, however, these cities are included in regions III and III', respectively. An overall definition for these regions is given in Figure 4-1.

By combining the two regional groupings to which each city can now be assigned, we have established 18 separate classification codes, e.g., I-I' and II-V' from a potential total of 25. These may be reduced further to 16 separate classes; each class is distinguished from the rest by a number which immediately follows the rank prefix. Thus we have such rank index as A1, B2,

71

Table 4-1

FREQUENCY DISTRIBUTION OF 117 CITIES BY
TOTAL INDUSTRIAL CAPACITY[a, b]

Value–Added (million yüan)	Number of Cities
less than 150	87
150 to less than 300	17
300 to less than 450	4
450 to less than 600	0
600 to less than 750	1
750 to less than 900	1
900 to less than 1,050	3
1,050 to less than 1,200	1
1,200 to less than 1,350	1
1,350 to less than 1,500	0
1,500 to less than 1,650	1
Over 1,650	1

[a]Source: Table B-1, Appendix B. The 117 cities are the same as those in Table A-1, Appendix A.

[b]Median = 100.86 million yüan. Q_3 = 156.62 million yüan.

Table 4-2

FREQUENCY DISTRIBUTION OF 117 CITIES BY
CAPACITY OF NEW INDUSTRIAL PLANTS
BUILT OR UNDER CONSTRUCTION
SINCE 1949[a, b]

Value–Added (million yüan)	Number of Cities
less than 100	92
100 to less than 200	14
200 to less than 300	7
300 to less than 400	1
400 to less than 500	1
500 to less than 600	0
600 to less than 700	0
700 to less than 800	2

[a]Source: Table B-1, Appendix B. The 117 cities are the same as those in Table A-1, Appendix A.

[b]Median = 63.59 million yüan. Q_3 = 95.38 million yüan

Figure 4-1

CLASSIFICATION CODES OF CITIES ON THE BASIS OF FOUR CRITERIA
FOR CURRENT INDUSTRIAL AND ECONOMIC SIGNIFICANCE

Region	Size	Present Industrial Status	Region	Rate and Nature of Growth
I	Metropolis (very large)	Major industrial	I'	Very vigorous industrial expansion
II	Large	Principal industrial	II'	Vigorous industrial expansion
III	Mostly medium or small	Mostly least industrial	III'	Fair to vigorous, mostly nonindustrial or new industrial expansion
IV	Very large	Predominantly nonindustrial	IV'	Very vigorous nonindustrial expansion or expansion of existing industry
V	Medium or small	Major industrial (probably new)	V'	Fair growth in size but very strong industrial expansion (probably specialized and/or new development)

First Criterion

Total Population

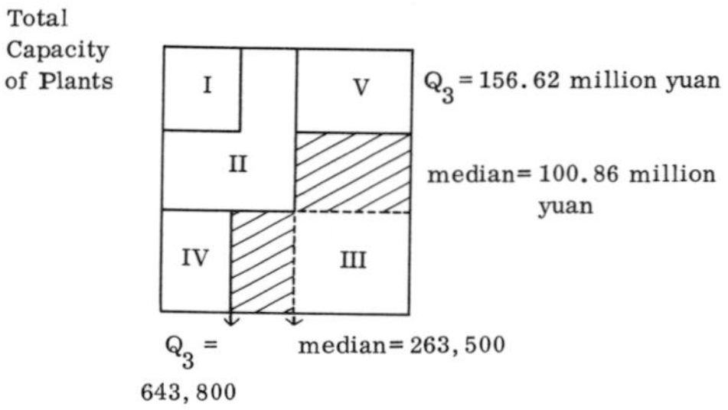

Total
Capacity
of Plants

I	V
II	
IV	III

$Q_3 = 156.62$ million yuan

median= 100.86 million yuan

$Q_3 = 643,800$ median= 263,500

Second Criterion

Increase in Population, 1953-58

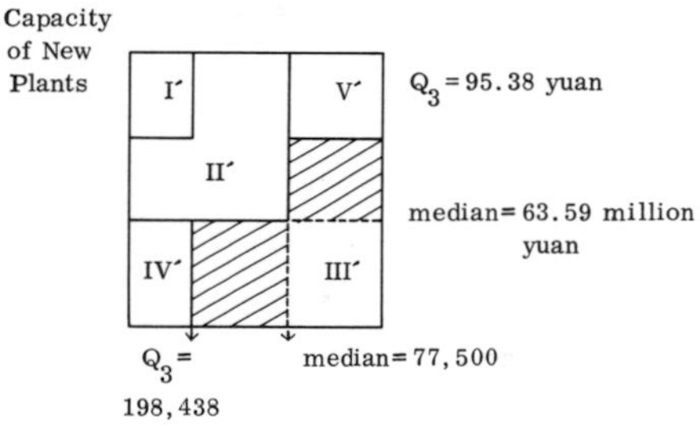

Capacity
of New
Plants

I'	V'
II'	
IV'	III'

$Q_3 = 95.38$ yuan

median= 63.59 million yuan

$Q_3 = 198,438$ median= 77,500

73

and C3. The letter denotes the degree of relative importance or rank, and the number indicates special characteristics of an individual city. These features are more fully described in Table 4-3. Since a number of the classes also include nonindustrial cities--one exclusively--seven nonindustrial rank indexes such as A'1 and B'1 are also created to describe predominantly nonindustrial economic centers. Cities that have high industrial ranking are by no means automatically eliminated from significant nonindustrial roles. The principal nonindustrial activities referred to here consist of transportation, distribution, administration, service, and finance.

Using the full list of cities in Table 4-3, we can consider their regional distribution by class. East China, North China, and Northeast China have by far the largest number of cities in the A group, with the other four regions trailing at a distance. On the other hand, the largest number of cities in the B group is found in Northeast China and Central China, followed by North China and East China. If Ranks A and B are taken together, East China and Northeast China rank equally, closely followed by North China and Central China. Since certain Rank B and C cities are important new industrial centers established or vigorously expanded under the Communist regime during 1953-1960,[2] the largest number of such new centers is found in Central China (particularly in Honan and Hunan), followed by Northeast China and North China. The general picture confirms the findings in Chapter 3, except that the greater importance of Central China, especially in the number of new industrial centers, is brought out in clearer relief. (See Table 4-4.)

The following is a summary of the comparison of coastal provinces with inland provinces and developed regions with previously less-developed regions (Tables 4-5 and 4-6 and Maps 4-1 and 4-2):

(1) a preponderance of the Rank A cities in both coastal provinces
    and the developed regions;

(2) a similar preponderance of the Rank B cities in the developed
    regions, as against a reverse preponderance in the inland
    provinces;

(3) a preponderance of identified important "new" industrial
    centers of Ranks B and C in the developed regions, as against
    a reverse preponderance in the inland provinces.

74

Table 4-4

REGIONAL DISTRIBUTION OF 117 CITIES BY
INDUSTRIAL RANKING[a]

| Region | Number of Cities in Indicated Industrial Rank | | | | | |
	A	B	C	A'	B'	Total
Northeast	3	5 (4)[b]	14 (1)	1	–	23
North	3	4 (3)	10 (2)	–	–	17
East	5	3 (2)	18	2	–[c]	28
Central	1	5 (4)	10 (2)	–	–	16
South	1	–	11	–	2	14
Northwest	1	2 (2)	5	–	–	8
Southwest	1	1 (1)	7	1	1	11
Total	15	20 (16)	75 (5)	4	3	117

[a]Source: Table 4-3.

[b]Numbers in parentheses represent the number of important "new" centers.

[c]Hangchow was included previously in the B group under industrial ranking.

Table 4-5

COMPARISON BETWEEN THE DEVELOPED AND THE LESS
DEVELOPED REGIONS IN THE DISTRIBUTION OF
INDUSTRIAL CENTERS BY RANK[a]

		Formerly Developed Region	Less Developed Region	Total
Rank A Cities	Number	11	4	15
	Per Cent	73.3	26.7	100.0
Rank B Cities	Number	12	8	20
	Per Cent	60.0	40.0	100.0
Total Rank A and B Cities	Number	23	12	35
	Per Cent	65.7	34.3	100.0
Identified Important "New" Industrial Centers (Ranks B and C)	Number	12	9	21
	Per Cent	57.1	42.9	100.0
Minor Rank C[b] Industrial Cities	Number	39	31	70
	Per Cent	55.7	44.3	100.0

[a] Source: Table 4-3.

[b] Ranks C4 and C1.

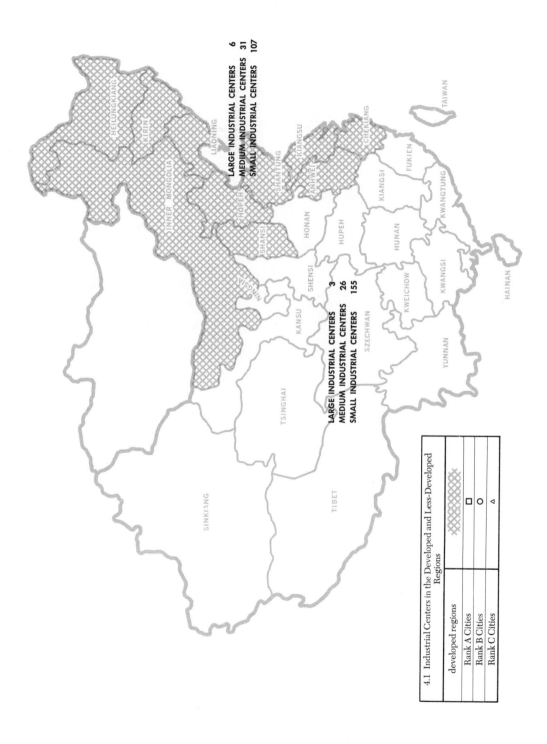

LARGE INDUSTRIAL CENTERS 6
MEDIUM INDUSTRIAL CENTERS 31
SMALL INDUSTRIAL CENTERS 107

LARGE INDUSTRIAL CENTERS 3
MEDIUM INDUSTRIAL CENTERS 26
SMALL INDUSTRIAL CENTERS 155

4.1 Industrial Centers in the Developed and Less-Developed Regions		
developed regions		
Rank A Cities	□	
Rank B Cities	○	
Rank C Cities	△	

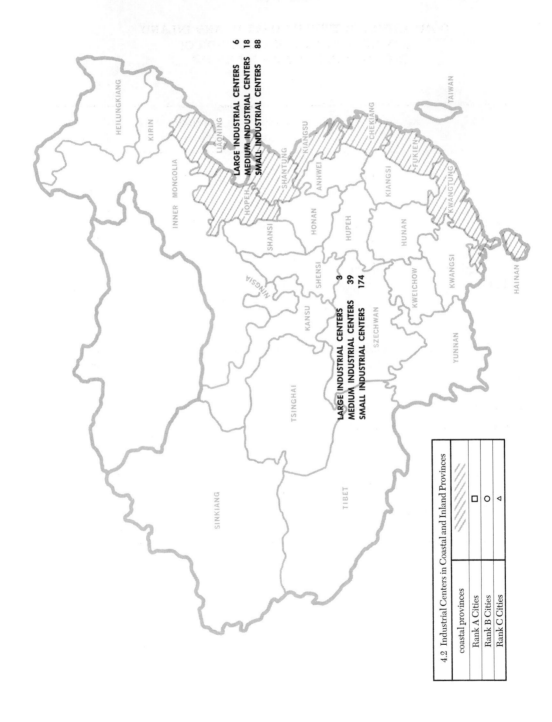

LARGE INDUSTRIAL CENTERS   6
MEDIUM INDUSTRIAL CENTERS   18
SMALL INDUSTRIAL CENTERS   88

LARGE INDUSTRIAL CENTERS   3
MEDIUM INDUSTRIAL CENTERS   39
SMALL INDUSTRIAL CENTERS   174

HEILUNGKIANG

KIRIN

INNER MONGOLIA

LIAONING

HOPEH

SHANTUNG

KIANGSU

ANHWEI

CHEKIANG

FUKIEN

KWANGTUNG

TAIWAN

HAINAN

SHANSI

HONAN

HUPEH

HUNAN

KIANGSI

KWANGSI

KWEICHOW

YUNNAN

SZECHWAN

SHENSI

NINGSIA

KANSU

TSINGHAI

TIBET

SINKIANG

4.2 Industrial Centers in Coastal and Inland Provinces		
coastal provinces		
Rank A Cities	□	
Rank B Cities	○	
Rank C Cities	△	

78

Table 4-6

COMPARISON BETWEEN COASTAL AND INLAND
PROVINCES IN THE DISTRIBUTION OF
INDUSTRIAL CENTERS BY RANK[a]

		Coastal Provinces	Inland Provinces	Total
Rank A Cities	Number	11	4	15
	Per Cent	73.3	26.7	100.0
Rank B Cities	Number	6	14	20
	Per Cent	30.0	70.0	100.0
Total Rank A and B Cities	Number	17	18	35
	Per Cent	48.6	51.4	100.0
Identified Important "New" Industrial Centers (Ranks B and C)	Number	4	17	21
	Per Cent	19.0	81.0	100.0
Minor Rank C[b] Industrial Cities	Number	30	40	70
	Per Cent	42.9	57.1	100.0

[a] Source: Table 4-3.

[b] Ranks C4 and C1.

These relationships point to the relatively greater emphasis given the developed regions as against the coastal provinces, especially with respect to medium, secondary, and new industrial centers. The large established industrial metropolises continue to be concentrated in the coastal provinces. These findings are fully in consonance with the data given in Chapter 3. The presence of exceptional provinces as enclaves in the several regional and larger area groupings may also be noted in Table 4-3.

Further Analysis of the Characteristics
of 110 Cities

We can now compare the ranks assigned in the preceding section with the grouping of cities on the basis of population increases and growth rates developed in Chapter 2. A preliminary step to this cross-classification consists of comparing the ranking procedure with the division of industrial centers into large, medium, and small centers in Chapter 3. This preliminary step is useful inasmuch as the classifications adopted in Chapter 3, which are based on industrial capacity alone, rest on a much larger sample than those used in the population analysis or industrial ranking.

Table 4-7 consists of a matrix of 110 cities (117 less seven predominantly nonindustrial centers) cross-classified by Ranks A, B, and C, and by industrial capacity division of large, medium, and small industrial centers. The distribution of the cities is unmistakably diagonal, with only one outstanding deviation being the spread of medium industrial centers among the three ranks. This result is what one should expect.

Table 4-8 presents a second matrix in which the cities are cross-classified by rank-size categories and four types of population change. Again, the distribution is generally diagonal with a certain amount of horizontal and vertical "spread" in the case of Rank B and Group II cities. The salient features brought out by cross-classification may be summarized as follows:

	Status	Rating	Type	Change under the Communist regime
$A-\frac{I}{M}-1$	Established	Major	Economic and industrial centers	further expanded
$B-_M-I$	Established	Principal	Economic and industrial centers	further expanded

	Status	Rating	Type	Change under the Communist regime
A-$\frac{L}{M}$-II	Formerly established	Large now principal to major	Economic and industrial centers	vigorously expanded
B-$\frac{L}{M/S}$-II	Newer	Principal	Economic and industrial centers (of principally commercial importance formerly)	vigorously expanded
C-$\frac{M}{S}$-II	Newer	Large	Economic and secondary industrial centers	rapidly expanded
C-$\frac{M}{S}$-III	Newer	Medium	Secondary economic and industrial centers	rapidly expanded
B-M-IV	Newer	Small	Secondary economic and industrial centers	little expanded
C-$\frac{M}{S}$-IV	Newer	Small	Secondary economic and industrial centers	little expanded

Admittedly, such descriptive terms as major, principal, and secondary are not precise. However, this characterization of the cities affords a starting point from which further analysis, based on additional information, may proceed.

A comparison of the B-II cities in Table 4-8 with the important new industrial cities of Tables 4-3 and 4-4 shows that ten of the eleven cities in B-II are also in the earlier group of 16 cities.[3] Six other cities in the earlier group are now excluded. On the other hand, one city (Lü-ta) is not included in the earlier grouping although it is now in B-II. These seven cities pose a question, especially in regard to their "newness" and their relative size and importance as industrial centers. Expansion of the criteria used in characterization will probably resolve the issue.

Since the A-II cities are also regarded as among the newer industrial centers, the nine cities in this group may be included with the B-II cities (or the rank B new industrial cities of Tables 4-3 and 4-4) as the new principal to major industrial centers under the present regime. It can be easily shown that

Table 4-7

CROSS-CLASSIFICATION OF 110 CITIES BY INDUSTRIAL RANKING AND INDUSTRIAL CAPACITY[a]

Industrial Ranking	Industrial Capacity		
	Large	Medium	Small
A	Shanghai, Tientsin, Wu-han, An-shan, Chungking, Nanking, Peking, Canton	Fu-shun, T'ai-yüan, Tsingtao, Chinan, Tzu-po, Sian, Mukden	
B	Pao-t'ou	An-tung, Liu-ta, T'ung-hua, Ch'ang-ch'un, Harbin, T'ang-shan, Shih-chia-chuang, Han-tan, Hangchow, Huai-nan, Ho-fei, Lo-yang, Huang-shih, Chang-sha, Nan-ch'ang, Lanchow, Urumchi, Ch'eng-tu	Cheng-chou
C		Pen-ch'i, Fou-hsin, Kirin, Chi-hsi, Ho-kang, Ch'eng-te, Ta-t'ung, Yang-ch'üan, Huhehot, Chiao-tso, Hsiang-t'an, Swatow, Nan-ning, Liu-chou	Chin-chou, Liao-yang, Ying-k'ou, Liao-yüan, Ssu-p'ing, Mu-tan-chiang, Chia-mu-ssu, I-ch'un, Shuang-ya-shan, Kalgan, Pao-ting, Chin-huang-tao, Ch'ang-chih, Yü-t'zu, Chi-ning, Wei-fang, Chefoo, Wu-hsi, Ch'ang-chou, Nan-t'ung, Hsin-hai-lien, T'ai-chou, Chen-chiang, Ch'ang-shu, Yang-chou, Wu-hu, An-ch'ing, Ning-po, Wen-chou, Shao-hsing, Pang-fou, Chia-hsing, Hu-chou, K'ai-feng, Hsin-hsiang, Shang-ch'iu, An-yang, Heng-yang, Chu-chou, Shao-yang, Ching-te-chen, Amoy, Ch'üan-chou, Chan-chiang, Fo-shan, Chiang-men, Ch'ao-chou, Kweilin, Wu-chou, Pao-chi, Yin-ch'uan, Hsi-ning, Kashgar, I-ning, Tzu-kung, Nan-ch'ung, I-pin, Nei-chiang, Wu-t'ung-chiao, Lu-chou, Ko-chiu

[a]Source: Table 4-3 and Appendix B, Table B-2.

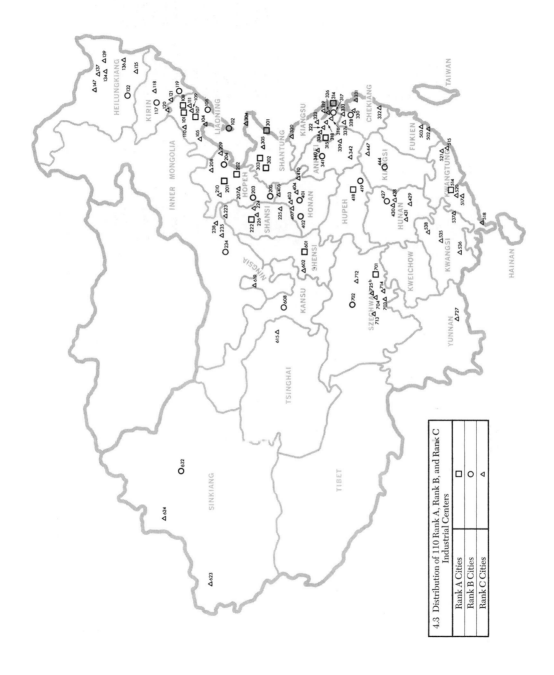

4.3 Distribution of 110 Rank A, Rank B, and Rank C Industrial Centers

Rank A Cities	□
Rank B Cities	O
Rank C Cities	△

Table 4–8

CROSS-CLASSIFICATION OF 110 CITIES BY TYPES OF POPULATION CHANGE FROM 1953 TO 1958 AND COMBINED INDUSTRIAL RANKING AND CAPACITY INDEX[a]

	I	II	III	IV
AL	Shanghai, Tientsin, Chungking	Peking, Canton		
AM	Tsingtao, Chinan, Mukden	Tzu-po, Sian		
	Pao-t'ou			
BM	Ch'ang-ch'un, T'ang-shan, Hangchow, Nan-ch'ang	Lo-yang, Lanchow, Urumchi, Ch'eng-tu		An-tung, T'ung-hua, Huai-nan, Huang-shih, Chang-sha
BS	Cheng-chou			
CM	Fou-hsin, Kirin, Chi-hsi	Ho-kang, Huhehot, Chiao-tso	Hsiang-t'an, Nan-ning	Pen-ch'i, Ch'eng-te, Ta-t'ung, Yang-ch'üan, Swatow, Liu-chou
CS	Mu-tan-chiang, I-ch'un, Kalgan, Ching-te-chen		Liao-yüan, Chia-mu-ssu, Shuang-ya-shan, Ch'ang-chih, Yü-tzu, Chi-ning, Pao-ch'i, Chia-hsing, Hu-chou, Chu-chou, Shao-yang, Amoy, Hsi-ning	Chin-chou, Liao-yang, Ying-k'ou, Ssu-ping, Pao-ting, Chin-huang-tao, Wei-fang, Ning-po, Wen-chou, Shao-hsing, Kai-feng, Chüan-chou, Fo-shan, Ch'ao-chou, Kweilin, Wu-chou, Tzu-kung, I-pin, Wu-t'ung-chia, Ko-chiu, Chefoo, Wu-hsi, Ch'ang-chou, Nan-t'ung, Hsin-hai-lien, T'ai-chou, Ch'ang-shu, Chen-chiang, Hsin-hsiang, Shang-ch'iu, An-yang, Heng-yang, Chan-chiang, Chiang-men, Yin-ch'uan, Kashgar, I-ning, Nan-ch'ung, Nei-chiang, Lu-chou, Yang-chou, Pang-fou, Wu-hu, An-ch'ing

[a]Source: Table 4–7 and Appendix A, Table A–6.

the proportion of cities of this group, which are located in coastal provinces, is somewhat smaller than those located in the developed regions. Of those in inland provinces or the less-developed regions, the largest number is in Central China, followed by Northwest China. This is by far the clearest indication to date of the locational emphasis in the Communist regime's developmental plans.

Role of Soviet Aid

Students of Communist China's economic development usually agree on the important role played by Soviet aid in technical assistance and equipment import. Of 291 projects originally planned or implemented with Soviet assistance from 1950 to the originally projected end of the Third Five-Year Plan in 1967, 132 can be identified.[4] If the eight projects centered in six cities not among the 110 in our sample for industrial ranking are disregarded, 56 projects are located in Rank A cities, 45 in Rank B cities, and 23 in Rank C cities. Soviet-aid projects were reported for 12 cities in each rank, or 80 per cent of all Rank A cities, 60 per cent of Rank B cities, and 16 per cent of Rank C cities. Both the number of Soviet-aid projects and the proportion of cities receiving Soviet aid vary directly with the rank of the cities.

In addition, more Soviet-aid projects exist in cities of all three ranks in the formerly developed regions than in the less-developed regions. The number of cities in each rank reporting Soviet-aid projects is also larger in the developed regions than in the less-developed regions, the difference in number being smallest in the Rank B cities (Tables 4-9, 4-10, and 4-11).

More cities of Ranks B and C reporting Soviet-aid projects are in the inland provinces, and more projects are in these cities, than in the coastal provinces. An inverse relationship holds for the Rank A cities.

Finally, if the "new" industrial centers are taken as a group, (all the cities in the A-II and B-II categories of Table 4-8 plus the six cities designated as new Rank B industrial centers not included in A-II and B-II). They account for 85 projects receiving Soviet aid, or 64 per cent of the 132 projects in our sample. This compares with 16 projects, or 12 per cent of the total, in the A-1 category (Table 4-8).

Table 4-9

DISTRIBUTION OF SOVIET-AIDED INDUSTRIAL PROJECTS IN 110 CITIES BY REGION[a,b]

Classification of Cities [c]	Northeast		North		East		Central		Northwest		Southwest	
	No. of Cities	No. of Projects	No. of Cities	No. of Projects	No. of Cities	No. of Projects	No. of Cities	No. of Projects	No. of Cities	No. of Projects	No. of Cities	No. of Projects
A	3	25	3	11	3	4	1	10	1	5	1	1
B New	2	3	-	-	1	1	1	1	2	6	-	-
B Other	2	14	2	12	-	-	1	4	-	-	1	4
B Total	4	17	2	12	1	1	2	5	2	6	1	4
C New	3	11	-	-	-	-	-	-	-	-	-	-
C Other	5	8	1	1	-	-	2	2	-	-	1	1
C Total	8	19	1	1	-	-	2	2	-	-	1	1
TOTAL	15	61	6	24	4	5	5	17	3	11	3	6
Miscellaneous[d]	2	4	-	-	-	-	1	1	2	2	1	1

[a]Source: Appendix C, Table C-3, and Table 4-3.

[b]No data are available for the number of cities or projects in South China.

[c]B2, B4, B5, B7, and B8 are classified as "new" centers, and B1, B3, and B6 as "other" centers. C1 and C3 are "new" centers, and C2 and C4 are "other" centers.

[d]Cities with Soviet-aid projects but not included in the list of 110 cities and not ranked.

Table 4-10

DISTRIBUTION OF SOVIET-AIDED INDUSTRIAL PROJECTS IN 110 CITIES
BY RANK IN THE DEVELOPED AND THE LESS DEVELOPED REGIONS[a]

Classification of Cities	Developed regions			Less Developed Regions		
	Aid Projects		No. of Cities Without Aid Projects	Aid Projects		No. of Cities Without Aid Projects
	No. of Cities	No. of Projects		No. of Cities	No. of Projects	
A	9	40	2	3	16	1
B New	3	4		3	7	
B Other	4	26	5	2	8	
B Total	7	30		5	15	3
C New	3	11		–	–	
C Other	6	9	33	3	3	
C Total	9	20		3	3	30
TOTAL	25	90	40	11	34	34
Miscellaneous[b]	2	4	–	4	4	–

[a]Source: Appendix C, Table C-3, and Table 4-3.

[b]Cities with Soviet-aid projects but not among the 110 cities in the list.

Table 4-11

DISTRIBUTION OF SOVIET-AIDED INDUSTRIAL PROJECTS IN 110 INDUSTRIAL
CENTERS BY RANK IN COASTAL AND INLAND PROVINCES[a]

Classifi-cation of Cities	Coastal Provinces			Inland Provinces		
	Aid Projects		No. of Cities Without Aid Projects	Aid Projects		No. of Cities Without Aid Projects
	No. of Cities	No. of Projects		No. of Cities	No. of Projects	
A	8	34	3	4	22	0
B New	–	–		6	11	
B Other	2	9	4	4	25	4
B Total	2	9		10	36	
C New	2	6		1	5	
C Other	1	1	28	8	11	35
C Total	3	7		9	16	
TOTAL	13	50	35	23	74	39
Miscel-laneous[b]	1	1	–	5	7	–

[a]Source: Appendix C, Table C-3, and Table 4-3.

[b]Cities with Soviet-aid projects but not among the 110 cities in the list.

The locational pattern of Soviet-aid projects is in complete conformity with a locational policy of industrial development that advocates a shift of emphasis away from the coastal provinces while the center of gravity remains in the formerly developed regions; this correspondence seems complete especially for the newer industrial centers, some of which are in the less-developed regions. Consequently, it is logical to conclude that Soviet aid was an important element in the determination of locational policy. This is not to say that such a locational policy might not have recommended itself otherwise or that Soviet aid was or was not needed to implement any locational policy. What does seem clear is that Soviet aid, especially Soviet planning and design, was a determining factor in the selection of project sites. A related conclusion is that the Chinese planners must have faced serious questions as to the effects of dependence on the Soviet Union.

The Chinese may have asked such questions from the earliest stages of the locational planning process. How, for example, would a locational policy adopted on the assumption of continued Soviet assistance be satisfactorily reoriented if and when this aid was suspended? Or, alternatively, should policy be predicated on the assumption that Soviet aid would ultimately cease, regardless of changes in the relationship between Communist China and the Soviet Union? How much investment waste would be caused by a forced change in policy?

The recognition of such possible future problems was probably reflected in the policy modifications after 1956, which shifted emphasis from an all-out development of the economically backward areas to a compromise. As we have seen, this shift resulted in the retention of essentially the same patterns in the spatial economy that prevailed in the pre-Communist period. The Chinese have not lost sight of the objectives of the First Five-Year Plan, but they have tempered their enthusiasm (although not necessarily for good), especially since the economic debacle that followed in the wake of the "Great Leap Forward" movement of 1958. A detailed analysis of further changes in locational policy planning after the Sino-Soviet rift, which in its open phases dates from 1963, cannot be undertaken on the basis of information currently available.

Summary of the Spatial Pattern of the Economy
At the Beginning of the Third Five-Year Plan

A summary of the relative degree of economic development in individual provinces at the end of the Second Five-Year Plan period may be seen in
Figure 4-2. Because of the absence of radical changes in the pattern of agricultural production, the pre-Communist data on grain output used in Chapter 1
are again used to rank the provinces by relative importance in agricultural output. For industrial production, the weighted industrial capacity data developed
in Chapter 3 are used.

A comparison of Figure 4-2 with Figure 1-1 shows that three provinces
(Honan, Hunan, and Anhwei) succeeded in moving during 1949-61 from the ranks
of the industrially undeveloped (but agriculturally developed) into the industrially
and agriculturally developed sector of the economy. Shansi and Inner Mongolia
both moved from the industrially and agriculturally less-developed sector to
the industrially developed sector. During this period, the distribution of the
provinces became virtually diagonal, which is indicative of industrial advances
in a number of provinces. The beginning of industrialization in such outlying
areas as Sinkiang, Ningsia, Tsinghai, Kansu, and Inner Mongolia was a factor
in this readjustment of the spatial pattern. Tibet alone remained untouched by
the main stream of change. On another level, the relatively most developed
areas in the pre-Communist period continued to retain their ascendancy in the
Communist period. The industrialization of Communist China had not gone
beyond its initial stages before 1961.

A comparison may also be made between Figures 4-2 and 4-3. In the
latter, individual areas are ranked by industrial importance. Distribution on
this basis contrasts sharply with the diagonal distribution in Figure 4-2. A
number of provinces and autonomous administrative regions have become industrially more developed in terms of total industrial capacity rather than in
terms of the number of large industrial centers. In other words, most of the
industrial capacity must have been in smaller industrial centers. This phenomenon probably reflects the early status of industrial development in these areas,
mostly in northwestern and southwestern China, although it may also presage
some effort to decentralize. (See Maps 4-4 through 4-6.)

90

Figure 4.2 Spatial Pattern of Industrial Capacity and Agricultural
Development by Administrative Divisions

(\\\\\\\\ coastal provinces)

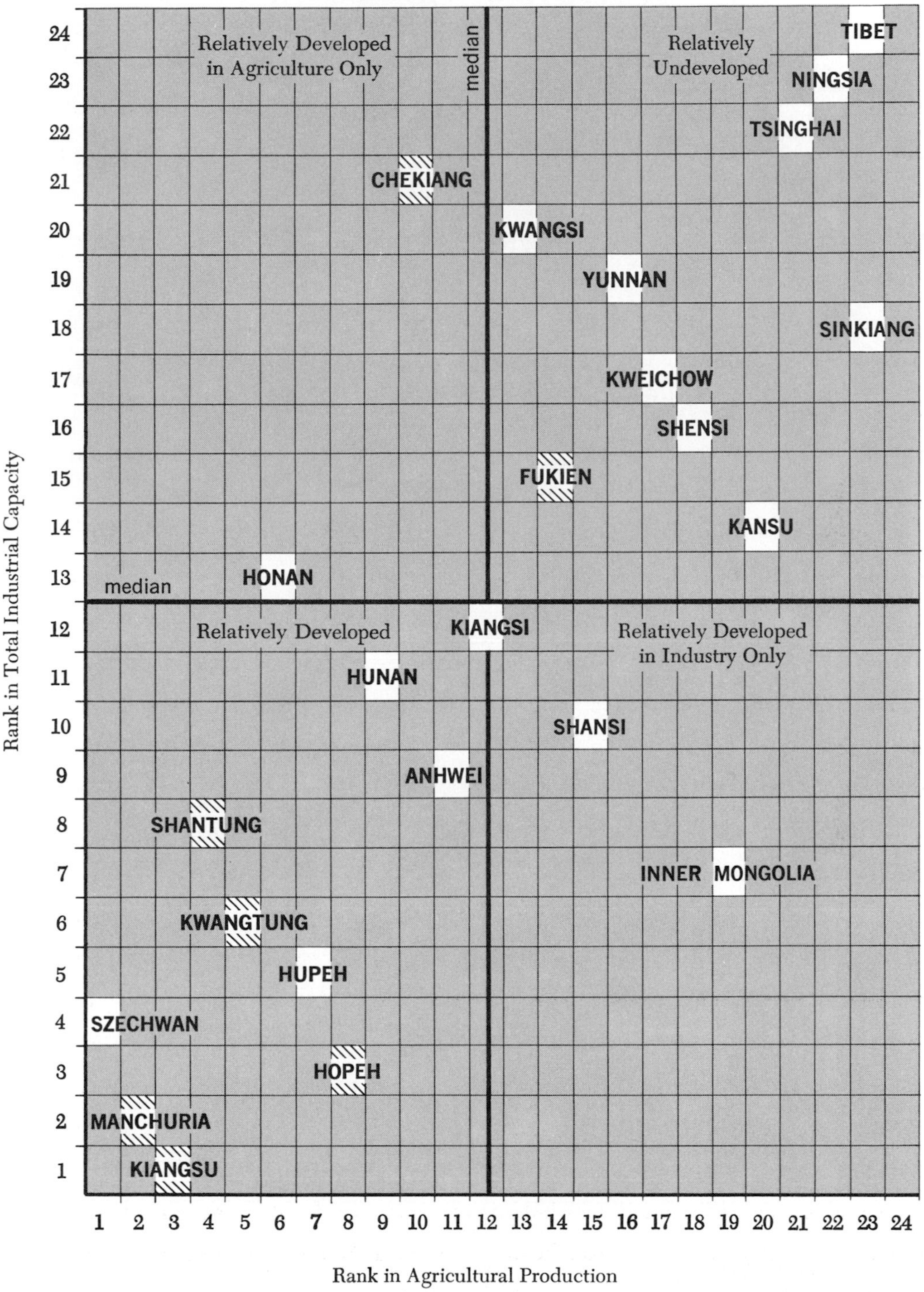

Figure 4.3 Spatial Pattern of Number of Rank A and B Cities and
Agricultural Development by Administrative Divisions

(▨▨▨ coastal provinces)

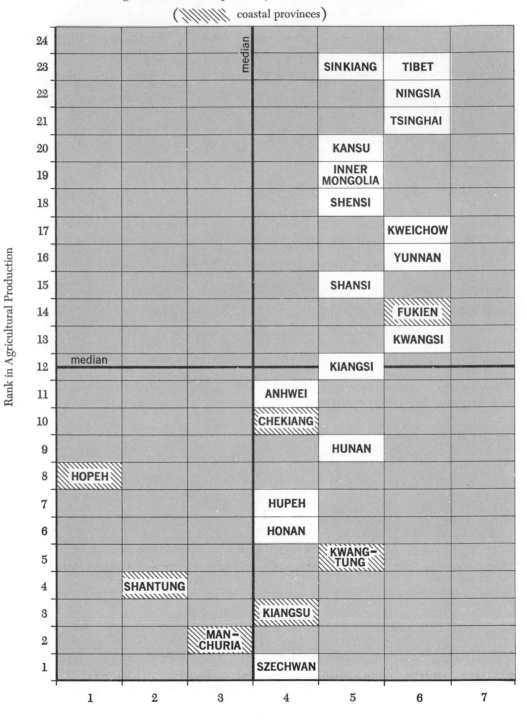

Rank in Agricultural Production

Rank in the Numbers of Rank A and Rank B

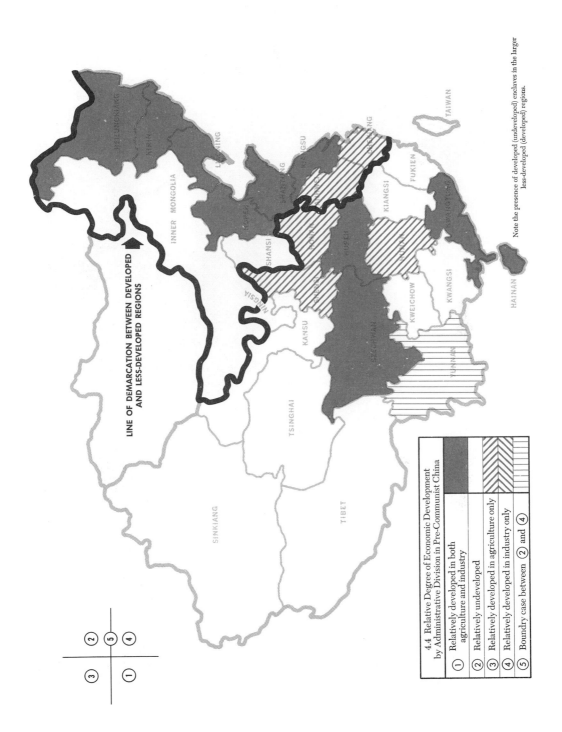

Note the presence of developed (undeveloped) enclaves in the larger less-developed (developed) regions.

LINE OF DEMARCATION BETWEEN DEVELOPED AND LESS-DEVELOPED REGIONS

4.4 Relative Degree of Economic Development by Administrative Division in Pre-Communist China

① Relatively developed in both agriculture and industry

② Relatively undeveloped

③ Relatively developed in agriculture only

④ Relatively developed in industry only

⑤ Boundry case between ② and ④

TAIWAN

HEILUNGKIANG

KIRIN

LIAONING

INNER MONGOLIA

JEHOL

CHAHAR

SUIYUAN

SHANSI

NINGSIA

KANSU

TSINGHAI

SINKIANG

TIBET

SHANTUNG

HONAN

HOPEI

ANHWEI

HUPEH

SZECHWAN

KWEICHOW

YUNNAN

KWANGSI

KIANGSU

CHEKIANG

KIANGSI

FUKIEN

KWANGTUNG

HAINAN

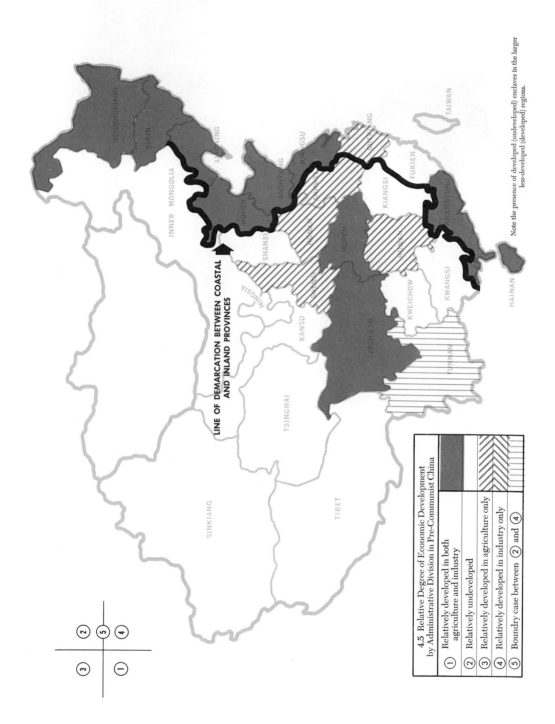

4.5 Relative Degree of Economic Development by Administrative Division in Pre-Communist China

1. Relatively developed in both agriculture and industry
2. Relatively undeveloped
3. Relatively developed in agriculture only
4. Relatively developed in industry only
5. Boundry case between 2 and 4

Note the presence of developed (undeveloped) enclaves in the larger less-developed (developed) regions.

LINE OF DEMARCATION BETWEEN COASTAL AND INLAND PROVINCES

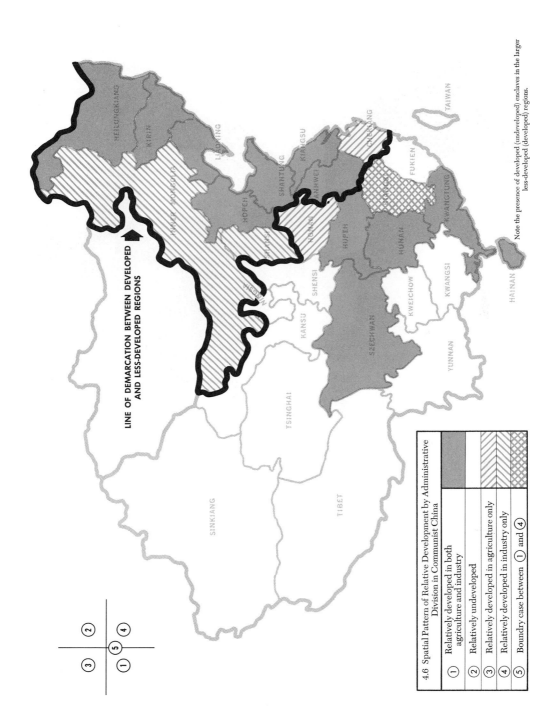

LINE OF DEMARCATION BETWEEN DEVELOPED AND LESS-DEVELOPED REGIONS

4.6 Spatial Pattern of Relative Development by Administrative Division in Communist China

① Relatively developed in both agriculture and industry

② Relatively undeveloped

③ Relatively developed in agriculture only

④ Relatively developed in industry only

⑤ Boundary case between ① and ④

Note the presence of developed (undeveloped) enclaves in the larger less-developed (developed) regions.

95

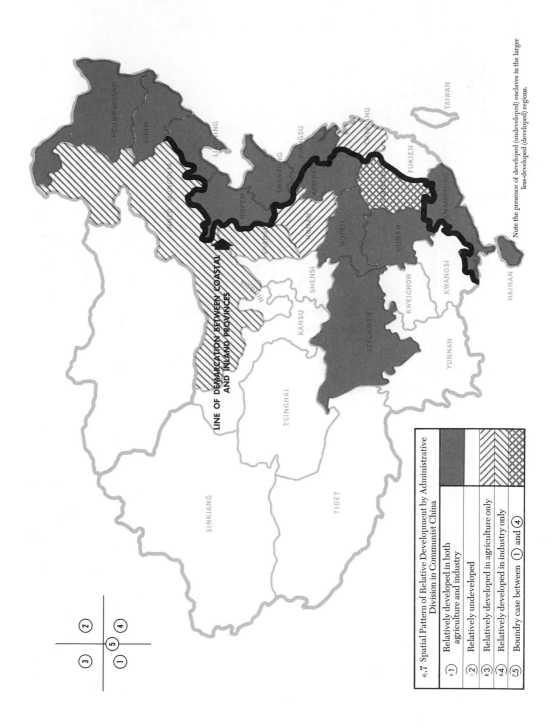

LINE OF DEMARCATION BETWEEN COASTAL AND INLAND PROVINCES

≤.7 Spatial Pattern of Relative Development by Administrative Division in Communist China

①	Relatively developed in both agriculture and industry
②	Relatively undeveloped
③	Relatively developed in agriculture only
④	Relatively developed in industry only
⑤	Boundry case between ① and ④

Note the presence of developed (undeveloped) enclaves in the larger less-developed (developed) regions.

PART II

5 LOCATION AND THE TRANSPORT INPUT

Coordination of Locational Planning and Transport Policy

The adequacy of the transport factor in locational development may be considered in at least two ways. One way is to determine how well transport facilities have met the demands posed by industrial location. A second way is to consider transport as the fixed quantity when determining how effective a locational policy is in obtaining the maximum use of transport facilities. Neither approach can be expected to yield a complete answer. The two must be taken together and attention given primarily to their coordination.

Proper coordination as a criterion of ideal locational policy was discussed in Chapter 1. That chapter pointed out that the objective of a locational policy should be to maximize the rate of economic growth within a given planning horizon. In establishing or expanding economic activity, location should be determined with a view to minimizing the transport input, other things being equal. First consideration should therefore be given to the existing transport plant (including roads, rails, or other media), terminal facilities, installations for transshipment, vehicles, and availability of fuel and other inputs. In choosing between alternative combinations of new transport facilities and new general economic centers or industrial locations, the emphasis should continue to be on minimizing the transport input furnished by a transport plant developed from a certain pattern of investment.

In a comparison between alternative sets of transport-locational policies, the one requiring the least transport input over the entire planning period, other things being equal, would offer the best solution. This theory is sound, but "other things" are not usually equal. Among the "other things," one should note in particular (1) that investments other than those in the transport plant itself will have to be made in conjunction with changes in the transport plant; (2) that still other investments will be made without reference to changes in the transport sector; and (3) that all these investments will affect the productivity of the transport plant. The problem is to achieve a dynamic general equilibrium in which the transport plant and the decision on location are only two of many variables involved.

This cleavage between the theoretical and the practical holds in still another area--no planner, no matter how skilled, can have complete knowledge of all the relevant facts. Consequently, no plan can achieve optimum locational arrangements of the economy and, by implication, optimum coordination between transportation policy and locational decisions.[1] Proper coordination between the two aspects of policy can be thought of only in terms of the avoidance of gross deviations from an indeterminate ideal.

In practice this uncertainty means a marked increase in the attractiveness of criteria based on unalterable physical constraints. If these criteria are followed, the results are not likely to be grossly divergent from the unknown optimum. Such criteria would include, _inter alia_, the following: (1) the establishment of new industrial and transport facilities to exploit major mineral deposits and to contribute to the development of industries that will provide a solid basis for economic growth; (2) the expansion of transport facilities in economically developed areas where inadequate transport seriously restricts economic expansion; and (3) the abstention from investment in transport that will not apparently serve any economic purpose.

Also within this category of "safe" conclusions, as they apply in modern China, would be the extension of transport lines to the inland provinces and less-developed areas. This is not a profitable short-term investment, but it has been recognized as essential for the further development of the vast potential of the Chinese economy. Such a conclusion may be drawn for at least certain trunk lines of transportation even though further network construction may be of secondary concern.

The problem for Chinese planners has been to determine the amount and the timing of investments. The most obvious curb is the ability of the economy to supply the needed capital for the construction of new lines. This ability is not constant, and one of the lurking perils for the planners is commitment to a course of heavy investment.

The discussion above suggests a number of questions. For instance, to what extent have new industrial and general economic centers been established within the framework of the existing transport plant? To the extent that new centers and new transport facilities are correlated, are the new centers obviously justifiable on such grounds as the exploitation of major mineral deposits needed for industrial expansion? To what extent has investment in the transport plant been allocated to the inland provinces and less-developed regions? What has been the division of investment on transportation between additions to existing facilities and the construction of new facilities? To what degree have noneconomic considerations entered into the allocation of investment in transportation? Has there been adequate consideration of the relationship between investment in transport and investment in the other sectors, especially with reference to the possible complementarity between them?

In the short-term utilization of an existing transport plant, minimization of the transport input implies operation at the most efficient level. Operating efficiency must also be considered from the point of view of individual transport sectors, as well as from that of the coordination of the several sectors; and it can be examined from the point of view of the expenditure of input or from that of output. In evaluating the output of the transport sector, one must further bear in mind that, apart from the provision of service to the final consumer, the transport sector supplies an intermediate good the usefulness of which lies in the aid it offers to other sectors of the economy. In the extreme case, it is not inconceivable for a large output of the transport sector to be associated with a general decline of nontransport output as a result of inefficient operations. These and related question focus attention on the day-to-day performance of Communist China's economic administration as distinct from the efficiency of her long-term economic planning.

Centralization in Planning and Its Effect on Transportation and Locational Developments

A number of inherent weaknesses in any planning process create deviations from the optimum. One in particular is the effect of varying degrees of centralization in planning locational and transport patterns.

As pointed out elsewhere,[2] prior to the adoption of the provisional revised procedure for the 1959 annual plan, the balancing of supply and demand or the formulation of "material balance" plans was undertaken on a commodity branch basis by central government ministries. This meant that the available supply of certain key commodities, such as steel, was allocated on a national basis. The users were then more or less free to purchase their quotas from individual suppliers without regard to location. This arrangement would have been harmless if quota holders had consistently tried to minimize the transport input and if the products of individual suppliers had been of equal quality and equal cost ex-factory. In the absence of these conditions, it was not uncommon for a producer to send his supply to a distant buyer while a local buyer had to purchase from a distance. Excessive cross-hauling led to substantial increases in the transport input and a possible malallocation of resources in the transport plant and in the locational planning of new productive facilities.

Following the 1959 revision, the equation of supply and demand was decided on a regional basis. Goods were shipped to an extraregional buyer only if the region of origin was a surplus area. The new policy reduced cross-hauls but had several disadvantages. A high-priority buyer in a deficit region might have to forego certain supplies while a low-priority buyer in a surplus region could obtain his supplies easily. This difficulty could be averted only if allowance was made for differences in priority on a national basis. Second, the transport pattern under the new arrangement was dictated in part by the manner in which the regional boundaries were drawn, an obviously arbitrary matter. The planning agency in a deficit area might, as a consequence, be induced to develop industries that from a national point of view might be better developed elsewhere. The adverse effect on locational and transport planning and investment was evident. It illustrates a wider problem--i.e., maximization of economic growth within a region may not be consonant with maximization of growth for the economy as a whole.

General Indications of Transportation Policy in the First Five-Year Plan

In a theoretical discussion of the problems of coordination between locational planning and transportation policy, a crucial question arises. Are the

100

Communist Chinese authorities aware of these principles and have they followed them? Other than broad generalizations, little has been published in Chinese sources that directly confirms conscious planning of this kind. In large part we must depend on indirect inferences, although several broad official statements may be reviewed.

First, in a report on government operation to the first session of the First National People's Congress on September 23, 1954, Chou En-lai thought if sufficient to say that transportation development should be planned in the light of the major effort to develop heavy industry and that transport policy should attempt to facilitate industrialization and modernization of defense.[3] In a separate speech explaining the First Five-Year Plan,[4] Li Fu-ch'un, chairman of the State Planning Commission, also remarked that appropriate arrangements in railway construction would be made in accordance with industrial development plans and the need for transport connections between the existing plants and the new industrial centers to be built. Thought appears to have been given to the policy of industrial location and the order of priority accorded to the different regions. The coordination of transportation and locational policy, on the other hand, appears to have received relatively little explicit recognition despite evidence it was already a source of difficulty. Lack of forethought must have been a principal factor in failures to coordinate transportation development with the planning and location of industrial centers reported by Chou En-lai in the latter part of 1954.[5]

General indications of underlying considerations in the formulation of Communist China's transportation policy may be gleaned from the published version of the First Five-Year Plan.[6] In this plan, the transport policy contained two parts. One was concerned with improved use of the existing transport plant. It called for (1) a more effective use of highway and waterway transportation to relieve the burden on the railway network and (2) an increase in operating efficiency in the existing railways. Expanded use of waterway and highway transport was to be accomplished partly through the promotion of through shipment by all surface carriers. Highway transportation was to be promoted through new construction, particularly in Southwest China and in other border or coastal areas. Waterway transport was specifically designated as the medium for exporting surplus grain from Szechwan and shipping coal and other materials to the middle and lower reaches of the Yangtze. Mention was also made of plans to expand coastal shipments of coal and timber, partly through the greater use of barges and tugs over short distances. Proposals for the more efficient use of the existing transport plant, especially railways, covered such matters as the average train load, rates of turnover of engines and rolling stock, stopping time in stations, maintenance and repair of railway tracks and equipment, and administrative concerns, such as the introduction of a modern accounting system.

Another part of the plan dealt with new construction, especially of railways. Of the total amount of planned investment in transportation, post, and telecommunications under the First Five-Year Plan, 59 per cent was allocated to the railways. Only 16 per cent was allocated for highways and shipping, one per cent for civil aviation, and nine per cent for local transportation. Of the 5.67 billion yüan of planned investment in the railway transportation sector, 2.37 billion or 41.7 per cent was earmarked for new railway construction 1.85 million, or 32.7 per cent, for improvements on existing lines, and 1.23 million, or 21.5 per cent for additions to equipment. The residual 4.1 per cent was earmarked for investment in the design and construction workshops in general. Of the extentions and improvements, the proposed investment was apparently concentrated in Manchuria and North China, although double-tracking in Central China and constructing the Yangtze River bridge at Wu-han were also scheduled. The bulk of the investment in existing railways was planned for the developed regions; only 19 per cent of planned new rail constructions was in developed regions while 81 per cent was in the less-developed regions.

One pertinent question is whether this particular allocation of funds was in accord with existing locational pattern or conditions of the transport plant at the time. The abbreviated statements make it appear that transport policy had not received careful attention. This impression may reflect our incomplete knowledge of planning objectives at that point in time. We are better able to determine the actual course of events and the further evolution of policy as it was modified in subsequent years.

6

THE TRANSPORT SECTOR AT THE BEGINNING OF THE COMMUNIST PERIOD

Dual Character of the Transport Industry

The transport industry of Communist China presents the typical appearance of a dual economy or, more accurately, of a developing economy in transition. Its modern sector consists of a network of railways and roads, steamships plying inland and coastal waters, air lines, and a few short pipe lines. In addition, a large traditional sector--of junks and sampans, vehicles pulled by animals or laborers, push carts and human carriers--exists alongside the modern carriers.

The relative size of the two sectors varies with the means of measurement and the time chosen. For instance, in terms of national income accounting categories, net value-added in 1952 has been estimated at 1. 92 billion yüan for the modern transport sector, in comparison with 2. 65 billion yüan for the traditional sector.[1] The corresponding relative shares in the total net value-added in the transport sector were 42 per cent and 58 per cent, respectively. Because of the greater capital intensity of the modern sector and its consequently larger depreciation charges, the modern transport sector accounted for 2. 05 billion 1952 yüan in gross value-added or 43. 3 per cent of the total, in contrast to 2. 68 billion yüan or 56. 7 per cent for the traditional sector. If gross receipts are used in the comparison, the modern and traditional sectors would account for 47. 5 per cent and 52. 5 per cent, respectively.[2] The increasing relative importance of the modern sector reflects the greater complexity of modern transport operations and consequently larger purchases from other sectors in order to render transport services.

Compared with estimates for the period before World War II, which antedated the large-scale modernization and construction efforts during the late 1930's and early 1940's in areas under the control of the National

103

Government and the Japanese, the 1952 figures represent considerable advances for the modern sector. According to Ou Pao-san's estimates,[3] the net value-added in the modern transport sector in 1933 was 363 million yüan at current prices (23.2 per cent of the total), and the corresponding amount in the traditional sector was 1.2 billion yüan (76.8 per cent). In terms of gross receipts, the estimates were 618 million 1933 yüan (31.7 per cent) for the modern sector and 1.33 billion yüan (68.3 per cent) for the traditional sector.

If employment data are used, estimates by Liu and Yeh[4] indicate that the modern sector employed 12 per cent of the total number of transportation and communication workers (including those in postal and telecommunication services) in 1952, leaving 88 per cent in the traditional section. However, productivity of labor was much greater in the modern section; even with its smaller share of employment, its output was larger.

For our purpose, the real significance of these statistics lies in the fact, denoted by all three indicators, that as of 1952 a major portion of the contribution of the transport industry to the country's aggregate output continued to originate in the traditional sector--notwithstanding the modernization that had been accomplished by that time. Since 1952 is commonly represented by official Communist Chinese sources, in particular, as the end of economic recovery and the beginning of planned development, this conclusion is tantamount to saying that the industrialization process, which constituted the core of the country's economic development from 1953 to the crisis in 1960, was to be supported, at least initially, by an extremely crude and obsolete transport plant. One would suppose, therefore, that a first step in economic development would necessarily be the modernization of the transport plant. It remains to be seen to what extent this modernization has been accomplished and whether it has been sufficient.

Attention should also be given the large discrepancy in the relative efficiency of the carriers in the two sectors. According to Chin Chia-fung,[5] the cheapest long-distance carrier in the 1930's was the railway (Table 6-1). Junks and steamers were comparable in cost per ton kilometer although the former enjoyed a slight advantage. However, the difference in speed and load capacity made the junk a poor second choice when a choice was possible. Most

Table 6-1

EFFICIENCY OF CARRIERS IN THE MODERN AND
TRADITIONAL SECTORS IN THE 1930's

Carrier	Speed (km/hr)	Unit Load Capacity (kg)	Freight Rate (CN$/ton-km)
Modern Sector:			
Railway	32-45	15,000-40,000	0.013
Steamship	6-25	5,000-3,000,000	0.085
Motor Vehicles	40-60	750-3,000	0.400
Traditional Sector:			
Junk	2-4	1,000-20,000	0.070
Animal-Drawn Cart (1 animal)	1.7-2	300-420	0.117
Hand Cart (1 man)	1.7-2	180	0.125
Human Carrier	1.7-2	50-70	0.320

noteworthy was the apparently uneconomical nature of truck transport, which was far costlier than nonmechanized carts or human carriers. Although these rates have not remained stationary, their relative magnitudes are illuminating. They suggest that the relative efficiency of the carriers during the pre-Communist period dictated that long-distance hauls be made by rail or modern shipping whenever possible. A subordinate role could be played by junks for small and medium loads when speed was not of primary concern. The traditional sector was therefore useful for local transport of all but heavy loads. Truck transport was uneconomical for long and short hauls; it was used in long hauls only when other modern carriers were not available and in short hauls when heavy loads had to be transported.

Some related problems lie in the interaction between locational policy and the relative rates of development of different carriers. If new economic centers and industrial locations are planned in regions where no river transport is available and where, for topographical reasons, rail construction would be slow, highway building must be accelerated. The operating cost of truck traffic, however, is high since the supply of petroleum products is limited. If rail building is not unduly difficult, opening new territories is not subject to the double constraint of high initial investment in transport facilities and high transport input in future production. Added freedom is gained in locational planning. On the other hand, since highways as the only supply routes for new industrial centers are uneconomical under Chinese operational conditions, new centers accessible by road only must be justified by noneconomic or other not immediately apparent economic considerations, especially if the roads are themselves newly built.

Economic development is accompanied by a growth of the transport input in long distance hauls and in local supply and distribution. The limit to which local traffic can be expanded may, however, inhibit general economic development. Since local traffic has been dominated by traditional carriers, their ability to expand and modernize is questionable. The problem involves not only relative line and terminal costs for the different carriers but also capacity limitations.

Size and Structure of the Modern Transport Sector in 1949

Routes in Existence and Operation

Table 6-2 shows the size of the modern transport plant in 1949.

Railways. According to an earlier study,[6] the total length of railways before the Communist regime was 24,940 kilometers of trunk lines and possibly 1,740 kilometers of short branches and spur lines. Of this total of 26,680 kilometers, approximately 3,100 kilometers were dismantled during the war years.

Nearly 22,000 kilometers of railways were in operation in 1949,[7] presumably at the end of the year. The ratio of operating length to total trackage was 21,989/26,680 or 82 per cent.[8] (See Map 6-1.)

Highways. Highway statistics for Communist China are extremely confusing because data are ambiguous for geographic coverage, grades of roads, and matters such as which roads are opened or closed to traffic and which are completed or unfinished. Data are even unclear as to the joint use of highway sections by different routes. A high figure of 599,200 kilometers of highways open to traffic was reported by one Communist source in 1949,[9] but that figure obviously included county and local roads. A July 1950 report placed the total length of national and provincial highways (based on incomplete coverage) at 127,000 kilometers, of which 62,000 kilometers were national highways and 75,000 kilometers, provincial highways.[10]

Highways in Communist China are divided into six grades with the lowest grade further subdivided into two classes.[11] The width of the road surface, average designed speed, and maximum gradients for highways of Grades I through IV correspond roughly to the first three of the four grades used by the Nationalists. Since the first two grades in the Nationalist classification were designated "national highways" and the third "provincial highways," (the fourth was "unclassified road"), we may assume that the 137,000 kilometers of highways referred to in the 1949 statistics correspond to the first four or five grades of the Communist classification. They represent, therefore, all the relatively better surfaced national and provincial highways even though not all are all-weather roads. Mao Shou-chin estimates the latter at one-third of the total, about 77,000 kilometers.[12]

107

Table 6-2

TOTAL LENGTH OF RAILWAYS, INLAND WATERWAYS, AND HIGHWAYS IN 1949[a]

Carrier	Total Length (km)	Length in Operation (km)
Railway Trackage	26,700[b]	22,000
Inland Waterways (identified rivers only)	55,600[c]	24,200
Highways	137,000	75,000
		80,000

[a] Source: See text.

[b] Omitted are 23,600 kilometers of dismantled lines.

[c] For a higher official figure, see Table 7-18.

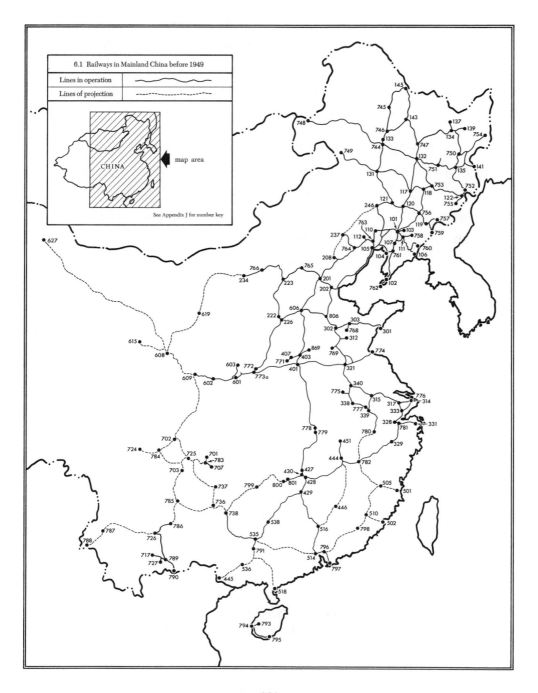

6.1 Railways in Mainland China before 1949

| Lines in operation |
| Lines of projection |

CHINA → map area

See Appendix J for number key

The estimated length of highways open to traffic at the end of 1949 was given as 81,000 kilometers in official 1959 statistics,[13] and as only 75,000 kilometers in a 1953 publication from Hong Kong.[14] It is likely that both sources refer to the same set of roads described above, and that the discrepancy is accounted for principally by minor differences in coverage and measurement and differences in report time.

If these estimates are accurate for total length of highways in existence, the proportion open to traffic was in the range of 55 to 59 per cent.[15] As of the end of 1949, therefore, a far smaller proportion of the roads of Communist China was open to traffic than the railways.

Inland Waterways. According to official statistics in 1956, the total length of inland waterways under the jurisdiction of the Central Government was 21,000 kilometers. In addition, another 34,400 kilometers of waterway routes were navigable.[16] The 1959 statistical report subsequently put the length of inland waterway routes navigable by steamers in 1949 at 24,200 kilometers.[17] Another 49,400 kilometers were navigable by nonmotorized vessels; however, this figure may include double-counting due to overlapping routes. Considerable uncertainty thus surrounds the length of the navigation routes as a whole although the length navigable by steamers seems reasonably definite.

Civil Aviation Routes. Civil aviation routes, serving primarily passengers and mail, included 11,400 kilometers in 1950.[18] No regularly operated routes under Communist control were reported for 1959. However, in the pre-Communist period, 16,900 kilometers of domestic air routes were being flown.[19]

Pipelines. As of 1949, mainland China had no pipelines for the transportation of petroleum and natural gas from producing fields to markets.

Capacity of Transport Equipment

In addition to such impediments as dismantled railway tracks, unrepaired bridges, torn-up roads, and undredged rivers, the modern sector of the transport industry suffered in 1949 from a severe shortage of equipment. The situation had been aggravated by wartime damage and disrepair, loss of rolling stock to Soviet occupation troops in southern Manchuria--which may have been partly regained by the Chinese in northern Manchuria--and losses during the Nationalist retreat. Table 6-3 shows the amount of equipment available in 1949.

The data on railway equipment available at the end of 1949 (Table 6-2) may be further compared with those on equipment reportedly left by the Nationalists. If the latter figures are subtracted from the 1949 data, the remainder would constitute rolling stock already held by the Communists. Since the new regime had no significant rail equipment manufacturing capacity under its control prior to 1949, the bulk of the equipment they held may have been handed over to them by the Soviet Union during the period of the Soviet occupation of Manchuria following World War II. (Some of the equipment held by the Communist Chinese also included some that had not been in the Nationalist records.) One might recall in this connection that some equipment dismantled by Soviet occupation forces in southern Manchuria was reported to have been shipped to Communist-controlled northern Manchuria in railway cars that were left on sidings. A breakdown of these data is given in Table 6-4.

Density and Equipment Capacity per Capita

A clearer conception of the size of the modern transport sector can be obtained if the preceding mileage and capacity statistics are related to the land area and population of Communist China. If we take the approximate land area as 9,561,000 square kilometers[20] and the 1949 year-end population as 542 million,[21] the density and per capita relationships given in Table 6-5 are obtained.

Regional Distribution of Transport Routes

All data confirm the extreme backwardness of the modern transport plant in mainland China in 1949 in relation to the population and size of the country. They do not, however, indicate the uneven geographical distribution of available facilities. A more detailed analysis is therefore needed of the available information on the lengths of railways, highways, and navigable waterways in each province and region.

Table 6-6 shows the total length and distribution of operating railways reportedly in operation in 1949-1950. Approximately 42 per cent of the total trackage was in six coastal provinces, and the remaining 58 per cent was in the inland provinces. Three relatively developed regions accounted for 77 per cent

Table 6-3

MODERN TRANSPORT EQUIPMENT AVAILABLE IN 1949

Equipment	Number Available at the Beginning of 1949	Number Available at the End of 1949
Railway Equipment:[a]		
Engines	1,737	3,355 (1,023)[b]
Freight Cars	29,188	44,401 (4,412)
Passenger Cars	3,145	4,412 (706)
Trucks[c]	...	74,900
Modern Shipping[d]	...	200,000 gross tons

[a]Yuan-li Wu, An Economic Survey of Communist China (New York: Bookman Associates, 1956), p. 364.

[b]Numbers in parentheses indicate the number of damaged engines and cars.

[c]Hung I, Kung-fei Chiao-t'ung Chien-she chih Yen-chiu (A Study on Transportation and Communication in Communist China) (Taipei, 1957), p. 148.

[d]Wu, op. cit.

Table 6-4

SOURCES OF EQUIPMENT AVAILABLE IN 1949[a]

Equipment	Number Held by the Communist Chinese	Number Left by the Nationalist Chinese	Number Available at the End of 1949
Engines	1,010	2,345	3,355
Freight Cars[b]	16,701	27,700	44,401
Passenger Cars[b]	3,116	1,296	4,412

[a]Sources: Table 6-3; and Ting Ch'u-yuan, unpublished manuscript, 1962.

[b]If the equipment left on the mainland were subtracted from the undamaged portion of the 1949 year end estimates, the balance is approximately 12,300 freight cars and 2,410 passenger cars.

112

Table 6-5

DENSITY AND PER CAPITA RELATIONSHIP OF
EQUIPMENT, LENGTH AND CAPACITY

Carrier	Total Length[a] (km/km^2)	Operating Length[b] (km/km^2)	Freight Carrying Capacity[c] (metric tons)	Freight Capacity per Capita[d] (kg)
Railways	0.0028	0.0023	1,332,030	2.5
Highways	0.0143	0.0078-0.0085	187,250	0.3
Waterways	0.0058	0.0025	200,000 gross tons	0.4 gross ton

[a] Taken from Column 1 of Table 6-2 divided by 9,561,000 km^2.

[b] Taken from Column 2 of Table 6-2 divided by 9,561,000 km^2.

[c] Taken from 1949 year-end data in Table 6-3; computed at 30 tons per freight car and 2 1/2 tons per truck.

[d] Freight carrying capacity divided by 542 million.

of total trackage whereas the less developed regions had only 23 per cent. Kansu, Tsinghai, and Sinkiang provinces, together with the autonomous area of Ningsia, all in northwestern China, had no railways in operation at the 1949 year end. In the southwest, Szechwan and Tibet, also an autonomous area, had no trunk line trackage and pre-war lines in Yünnan province had still not been put back in operation. Kweichow had no railway at that time. However, as has been previously noted, a paucity or total absence of railway facilities was not characteristic of the less developed regions of the west alone. Several coastal provinces had negligible trackage and Fukien had none. Railway construction in the pre-Communist period followed the same pattern of distribution as the industrial and economic centers discussed in Chapters 3 and 4.

If navigable inland waterways are similarly compared, using the 55,600 kilometer figure as the national total (Table 6-7), we find the same imbalance but in reverse. The developed regions account for no more than 30 per cent of the total and the underdeveloped regions together account for 70 per cent. Unfortunately, available data do not permit a satisfactory comparison between inland and coastal provinces. One obvious factor which might produce a distortion is that Sinkiang, Tsinghai, Ningsia, and Tibet in the arid northwest and the Himalayan area, have no navigable waterways of particular significance.

The most developed modern carrier, the railway, was concentrated in the developed regions at the beginning of the Communist period, but most of the navigable waterways which were relatively underdeveloped, were found in the underdeveloped regions. The question is therefore raised as to whether the further development of the hitherto underdeveloped regions might not be most rapidly and efficiently advanced by improving and expanding existing navigable water transport routes.

Table 6-8 shows that 42 per cent of the total length of national highways were found in the developed regions in 1949, and 58 per cent were in the underdeveloped regions. This distribution of highways in the two areas resembles that of the inland waterways.

Statistics on lengths of railway, waterway, and highway routes exaggerate the relative development of all modes of transportation in the less developed

Table 6-6

DISTRIBUTION OF OPERATING RAILWAYS
IN 1949-1950[a, b]

Area or Region	Length of Operating Trunk Lines (1,000 km)	Length of Operating Trunk Lines (per cent)
Coastal Provinces	8,404	42
Liaoning	3,820[c]	19
Hopeh	1,791	9
Shantung	950	5
Kiangsu	831	4
Chekiang	443	2
Fukien	--	--
Kwangtung	569	3
All Inland Provinces	11,809	58
Total	20,213	100
Developed Regions	15,680	77
Northeast	9,763	48
North	3,063	15
East	2,854	14
Underdeveloped Regions	4,533	23
Central	3,114	16
South	978	5
Northwest	441	2
Southwest	--	--
Total	20,213	100

---

[a]Source: Appendix D, Table D-1.

[b]These figures are not the same as those in Table E-1 which contains the route lengths of identified lines in operation.

[c]This figure was estimated as follows:

Shen-yang (Mukden) Railway Administration	1,922 km
Ching-chou Railway Administration	1,909 km
Subtotal	3,831 km
Less lines in Kirin	11 km
Total	3,820 km

These data (except for those on Kirin) were taken from Railways in Communist China (Taipei: Communications Research Bureau, Ministry of Communications, 1961), pp. 4-7.

Table 6-7

DISTRIBUTION OF NAVIGABLE INLAND WATERWAY
ROUTES IN 1949-1950[a]

Regions	Length of Waterway Routes (km)	Length of Waterway Routes (per cent)
Developed Regions	16,921	30
Northeast	4,990	9
North	2,933	5
East	8,998	16
Underdeveloped Regions	38,681	70
Central	11,672	21
South	14,838	27
Northwest	2,441	4
Southwest	9,730	18
Total	55,602	100

[a]Source: Appendix D, Tables D-2, D-3, and D-4.

Table 6-8

REGIONAL DISTRIBUTION OF OPERATING NATIONAL
HIGHWAYS IN 1949-1950[a]

Region	Length of Operating Highways (km)	Length of Operating Highways (per cent)
Developed	25,923	42
Northeast	9,142	15
North	9,255	15
East	7,526	12
Underdeveloped	35,902	58
Central and South	10,668	17
Northwest	15,457	25
Southwest	9,777	16
Total	61,825	100

[a]Source: Automobile and Highway (Shanghai), Vol. II, No. 4,
July 21, 1951, p. 41. To conform with the present regional arrangement,
an estimated total of 1,561 km of national highways in Fukien province
was transferred from East China to South China. Fukien also has about
5,460 km of provincial and county highways and short lines. See Fei-ch'ü
Kung-lu She-shih Hsien-k'uang (Highways in Communist China) (Taipei:
Ministry of Communications, 1961), p. 16.

regions since they do not take into account the vast areas traversed by the lone lines in some areas. If a comparison is made of the density of transportation routes in individual areas, great divergences can be seen among the regions (Table 6-9). For example, in 1949-50, the density of railway trunk lines in operation varied from twelve km per 1,000 km^2 in Manchuria to two km per 1,000 km^2 in North China and South China. The density was negligible in Northwest China and nil in Southwest China, but East and Central China showed six and four km per 1,000 km^2, respectively. The density of naviable inland waterways in South China was 26 km per 1,000 km^2 as compared with one, two, and four km per 1,000 km^2 in Northwest, North, and Southwest China, respectively. East and Central China, on the other hand, show density estimates of 18 and 16 km per 1,000 km^2, respectively. Finally, the density of national highways (Table 6-9) in 1949 varied from 15 km per 1,000 km^2 in East China and 11 km per 1,000 km^2 in Manchuria to lows of four, five, and six km per 1,000 km^2, respectively, in Southwest, Northwest, and North China.

In 1949, the developed areas as a whole show densities of railways and national highways of five and nine km per 1,000 km^2, respectively, in contrast to one and five km per 1,000 km^2, respectively, for the rest of the mainland (Table 6-9). Both regions, on the other hand, show the same density of six km per 1,000 km^2 for inland navigable waterways. Much will have to be done if the underdeveloped regions of mainland China are to acquire rail and highway transport plants comparable to those in the developed regions.

If individual regions are arranged in diminishing order of railway, waterway, and highway densities as in Figure 6-1, several obvious deductions may be made. First, Northwest and Southwest China appear on the diagram as very underdeveloped in terms of all three modes of modern surface transportation. However, since little can be done to alter the availability of navigable waterways because of natural conditions, any development of modern transportation in Northwest and Southwest China will depend on railway and highway expansion. Second, at the other extreme, Manchuria and East China are relatively more developed in all three types of transportation, but South and Central China appear to enjoy a favorable status in the density of navigable inland waterways. Thus, all these areas possess the potential for enlarging the major modern means

117

Table 6-9

DENSITY OF TRANSPORTATION ROUTES IN 1949-1950[a, b]

Region or Area	Operating Railways		Navigable Inland Waterways			National Highways	
	Density (km/1,000 km^2)	Rank	Density (km/1,000 km^2)		Rank	Density (km/1,000 km^2)	Rank
Northeast	12	1	6	(2)[c]	4	11	2
North	2	4	2		6	6	4
East	6	2	18	(4)	2	15	1
Central	4	3	16	(2)	3	8	3
South	2	4	26	(22)	1		
Northwest	neg.	–	1		7	5	5
Southwest	–	–	4	(1)	5	4	6
Coastal	8	–	...		...	...	...
Inland	1.4	–	...		...	...	...
Developed	5	–	6		–	9	–
Underdeveloped	1	–	6		–	5	–
Mainland China	2	–	6	(2)	–	6	–

[a]Source: Tables 6-6, 6-7, and 6-8, and Appendix D, Tables D-1 through D-5.

[b]Figures have been rounded off.

[c]Numbers in parentheses indicate the density under the Central Government Administration.

118

Figure 6.1 Density of Transportation Routes by Regions

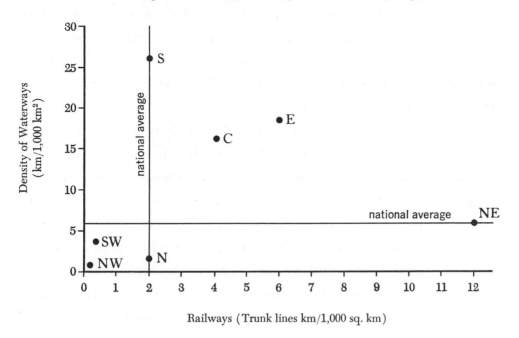

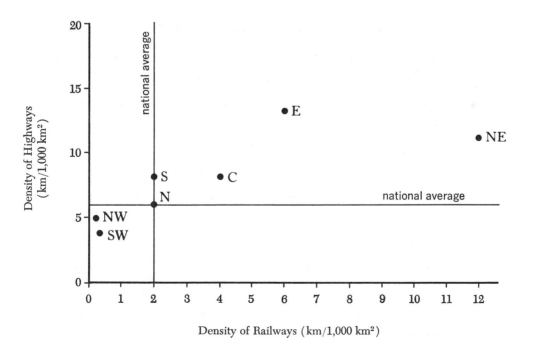

of transportation on the basis of the existing plan. The means of transportation selected for further development will therefore depend on considerations other than the immediate status of the existing transport plant or natural constraints. Finally, North China, with relatively limited possibilities for waterway transport expansion, suffers from no impediments for the further development of other modes of modern transportation.

Figure 6-1 shows that an effort to develop the less developed regions economically will require considerable investment in transport facilities. The heaviest investments called for are in railway and highway construction in Northwest and Southwest China, and even in North China, although at smaller cost. More alternatives are open for developing transport in Central and South China. If the size of investment in the transport sector is a major concern, the economic development of Northwest and Southwest China should be given a lower priority, while Central and South China might be given higher priority. This view, of course, is only a parochial and partial one based on the relative ease of adding transport facilities and are the prospects for an immediate economic return.

Utilization of the Modern Transport Plant

Further understanding of transport conditions in Communist China at the beginning of the present regime may be obtained from an examination of freight traffic. During 1949, the railways accounted for 83 per cent of the 67 million tons of freight carried in the modern transport sector. Modern shipping and highway transport were responsible for no more than eight and nine per cent, respectively, (Table 6-10). In terms of ton-kilometers, 80 per cent of the total was carried by the railways, and modern shipping and highways carried 19 and one per cent respectively. Average hauls in 1949 were 329 kilometers for railway freight, 43 kilometers for highway traffic, and 794 kilometers for modern shipping. These figures show that shipping was used in 1949 mainly for long distance traffic, probably coastal in large part, and highway freight was confined to local hauls. Railways, on the other hand, were responsible for the bulk of medium and long distance hauls.

Table 6-10

VOLUME AND AVERAGE HAUL OF FREIGHT AND PASSENGER TRAFFIC BY MODERN CARRIERS IN 1949

Freight Traffic			
Carrier	Volume (million tons)	Volume-Distance (million ton-km)	Average Haul[a] (tons/km)
Railways[b]	55.89 (83%)	18,400.00 (80%)	329
Shipping[b]	5.43 (8%)	4,310.00 (19%)	794
Highways[b]	5.79 (9%)	250.00 (1%)	43
Civil Aviation[c]	...	0.82	...
Total	67.11 (100%)	22,960.82 (100%)	342

Passenger Traffic[d]			
Carrier	Volume (million passengers)	Volume-Distance (million passenger-km)	Average Trip[e] (passengers/ km)
Railways	102.97 (76%)	13,000.00 (84%)	126
Other Modern Carriers[f]	31.97 (24%)	2,410.00 (16%)	75[g]
Total	134.94 (100%)	15,410 (100%)	...

[a]Although we have taken the tonnage data as "tons carried" rather than "tons originated," the discrepancy between the two is assumed to be relatively small. The average haul is, therefore, the quotient of ton-kilometers divided by tons carried.

[b]Source: Wei-tati Shih-nien (The Great Ten Years) (Peking: People's Publishing House, 1959), Chinese edition, pp. 129-131.

[c]Source: Ibid., p. 135; the figure is for 1950 rather than 1949.

[d]Source: Ibid., pp. 133-135.

[e]Although we have taken the passenger data as "passengers carried" rather than "passengers originated," the discrepancy between the two is assumed to be relatively small. The average trip is, therefore, the quotient of passenger-kilometers divided by passengers carried.

[f]Includes both inland and coastal shipping, highways, and civil aviation.

[g]Shipping only.

If these figures are considered in conjunction with the relative shares of the developed and underdeveloped regions in the distribution of modern surface transport routes, one may deduce that railways were by far the most important carrier of goods in the developed regions. Waterway traffic, disregarding coastal shipping, was perhaps more important in the movement of goods in the less developed regions and in interregional shipments between the less and the more developed regions, e.g., water-borne traffic on the Yangtze River and in the Pearl River Delta. The presence of this water transport potential was also an important factor for the existence of relatively developed provinces as enclaves in the otherwise underdeveloped regions and inland areas.

As already indicated, highway traffic was negligible in comparison with rail traffic because of the high operating cost, the lack of trucks, the slow development of modern roads, and the continued predominance of traditional carriers in local and short hauls.

As for passenger traffic, only the railway passengers can be identified from the 1949 statistics. In 1949, railways accounted for 76 per cent of the passengers carried by modern carriers or 84 per cent of the total passenger-kilometers. These figures show a longer average distance traveled by rail per person than by other modes of transportation. The pattern differs from that of freight traffic, which shows that water-borne shipments averaged more than twice the distance of rail shipments. However, passenger travel by ship on inland waterways and coastal routes was probably not statistically significant. Short-haul highway traffic evidently accounted for most nonrail travel. (Although transport and travel conditions in 1949 were extremely abnormal because of the civil war, they probably had the same effect on all carriers so that the comparison above is still valid.)

A rough comparison of the relative importance of passenger and freight in the railway transport may also be obtained from estimates of distances traveled or hauled (Table 6-11). Estimated passenger train-kilometers in 1949 were 49 million or 64 per cent of the total realized; estimated freight train-kilometers were 28 million or 36 per cent. This large share of passenger traffic is not representative of normal conditions. It reflects the low level of production, incomplete reporting, and confusion that characterized the year the Communists

Table 6-11

RAILWAY PASSENGER AND FREIGHT TRAFFIC IN 1949

Parameter	Quantity
Total Distance of Total Freight Hauled	18,400,000,000 ton-km
Average Freight Train Load	660 tons[a]
Total Distance of Freight Train Hauls	28,000,000 train-km
Total Distance Traveled by All Passengers	13,000,000,000 passenger-km
Average Number of Passengers per Train	265 passengers[b]
Total Distance of Passenger Travel	49,000,000 train-km

[a] Yuan-li Wu, China's Transportation (Menlo Park, Calif.: Stanford Research Institute, 1954), Interim Report 3, Table XI; 1950 figure used for 1949.

[b] Ibid.; figure for 1928-35 average used. Cf., Statistics of Chinese Railways (Nanking: Ministry of Railways, 1928-35).

gained power. Furthermore, the figures quoted probably do not include troop movement.

Composition of Freight Traffic

Prior to World War II, coal dominated the list of commodities carried by the railways. In 1935, for instance, 64 per cent of the total tons carried by railways and 57 per cent of the ton-kilometers were accounted for by mineral products. Since 92 per cent of the mineral products were coal shipments, virtually 60 per cent of the tonnage carried by railways consisted of coal.[22] Manufactured goods accounted for 14 per cent of the tonnage carried and 17 per cent of the ton-kilometers; agricultural products made up 18 per cent of the tonnage and 22 per cent of the ton-kilometers. These figures, which refer to railways in China proper only, are probably also representative of the initial period of Communist control.

According to one Communist report,[23] during the first eight months of 1950, railway coal shipments (35 million tons) were equivalent to 58 per cent of the total tonnage. Since this figure of 35 million tons does not include coal shipments on the Ch'ang-ch'un Railway in Manchuria, it is comparable to the prewar data, which excluded Manchuria. In mainland China as a whole, coal carried by railways in both the prewar and early Communist periods probably constituted an ever larger proportion of total railway freight traffic.

In general, coal moved from Northeast China and North China to East and South China. Both anthracite and bituminous coal produced in Manchuria and North China were shipped to Shanghai and other Yangtze ports for consumption in power plants and households. The railways and the shipping concerns were themselves also very large consumers. Coal produced in K'ai-luan was usually shipped by steamer through the port of Ch'in-huang-tao to Shanghai and other ports on the East China coast. Coal from Fou-hsin, Pei-p'iao, and Fu-shun was usually shipped from the port of Ying-k'ou or Dairen to China proper. In addition to these coastal shipments by water, much coal was shipped by rail in the areas where the mines were located.

124

Size of the Native Transport Sector

Modern transport was only a part of the total transport plant. No adequate data exist for the traditional sector, but its total carrying capacity is estimated to have been as high as 402 million ton-kilometers per day in 1949 (Table 6-12). On the basis of 300 days a year, the annual volume exceeded 90 billion ton-kilometers, or nearly four times that of the modern transport sector.

Three points, however, should be realized:

1. More than half of the carrying capacity was available for very short hauls only.
2. Full mobilization of the theoretical capacity would require a massive organization not then or later available.
3. If full mobilization could have been accomplished, many of the large numbers of workers needed would have had to be recruited from among the peasants; animals and vehicles needed on the farm would also have had to be used.

In practice, therefore, the effectiveness and potential of the traditional sector were, and still are, probably far smaller than the figures suggest.

Table 6-12

ESTIMATES OF THE MAXIMUM TRANSPORTATION CAPACITY OF THE TRADITIONAL SECTOR IN 1949

Carriers	Number of Pieces of Equipment[a] (million)	Number of Animals[b] (million)	Number of Workers[c] (million)	Daily Capacity[d] (tons/unit)	Daily Capacity[e] (million tons)	Daily Capacity[f] (million tons/km)	Total Annual Capacity[g] (million tons/km)
Boats and Junks	0.25	–	0.75	10	2.50	188	42,300
Animal-Drawn Carts:							
Semimodern	0.01	0.03	0.02	2	0.02	1	225
Urban (native)	0.12	0.24	0.24	0.75	0.09	5	1,125
Rural (native)	4.30	0.86	0.86	0.75	3.23	162	36,450
Hand-Drawn Carts	0.26	–	0.26	0.24	0.06	3	675
Wheelbarrows	8.60	–	8.60	0.10	0.86	34	7,650
Rickshas, Pedicabs, and Sedan-Chairs	0.60	–	0.60	0.20	0.12	5	1,125
Coolies and Longshoremen	–	–	0.60	0.04	0.02	1	225
Farmers Working in Transportation	–	–	1.20	0.04	0.05	2	450
Other	–	–	0.77	0.04	0.03	1	225
Total	14.14	1.13	13.90	–	6.98	402	90,450

[a]The 1949 estimates are derived from 1957 figures [Ta-chung Liu and Kung-chia Yeh, The Economy of the Chinese Mainland: National Income and Economic Development, 1933-1959 (Santa Monica, Calif.: The Rand Corporation, April 1963), Vol. II, Table H-10, pp. 766-768], and the lowest value-added index in any year during the First Five-Year Plan or 0.856 (Ibid., p. 291). It is assumed that the 1949 data were approximately equal to the lowest figures thus estimated.

[b]The number of animals used is assumed to be 3 for each semimodern anumal-drawn cart and 2 for other animal-drawn carts. These figures are based on the author's practical experience in this field of transportation.

[c]The number of workers is assumed to be 3 per boat or junk and 2 per animal-drawn cart.

[d]Data from Chin Chia-fung, Chung-kuo Chiao-t'ung chih Fa-chan chi Ch'i Ch'u-hsiang (Transportation Development and Trends in China) (Shanghai: Cheng-chung shu-chü, 1937), pp. 146-147, are used as our basic reference on per unit capacity as well as the average daily journal. A 10-hour day is assumed. The daily haul is assumed to be 75 km for boats and junks; 60 km for semimodern animal-drawn carts; 50 km for urban and rural animal-drawn carts; and 40 km for the other carriers listed in the table.

[e]Maximum capacity per load = 1 x 4.

[f]Daily maximum load x haul (ton-km) = 5 x corresponding average daily haul (km).

[g]Annual capacity is calculated on the basis of 300 operating days per year. One half load is assumed for the return trip.

126

7

NEW CONSTRUCTION IN THE
TRANSPORT SECTOR AND
LOCATIONAL PLANNING

An analysis of the growth of the transport plant requires consideration of major topics, such as the growth of the transport plant; the relationship between the development of transport facilities and economic development; the implicit policy followed in locational planning and in transport development; coordination of plant expansion within the transport subsectors; and the appropriateness of the policy pursued in the light of the a priori discussion in Chapter 5 and the review of the pre-Communist transport structure in Chapter 6. Since our appraisal is necessarily limited by the kind of information available, we shall concentrate our discussion on the railways since more data are available for them than for any other carrier. Fortunately, railways continue to be the most important modern carrier in Communist China and this limitation will not seriously impair the overall picture.

Growth of Railway Trackage and Route Length

Two indexes can be used, inter alia, to measure the growth of the railway transport subsector--(1) railway trackage and (2) route length. The first provides a reasonably accurate reflection of the entire plant inasmuch as most other fixed installations tend to grow simultaneously with trackage. Increases in these installations will be less than increases in trackage, however, when the latter occur in the form of double-tracking or in marshalling yards and sidings. An increase in route length may therefore be compared to an increase in the number of industrial plants, but an increase in trackage without a change in route length may be compared to an increase in the size of individual plants. The first is an "external expansion"; the second, an "internal expansion."

Table 7-1 gives the route lengths in operation in 1949 through 1963, and Table 7-2 gives trackage estimates derived from estimated trackage at the beginning of the Communist period supplemented by data on new rail construc-

Table 7-1

CHANGES IN RAILWAY ROUTE LENGTH IN
OPERATION FROM 1949 TO 1963[a]

Year	Route Length in Operation (km)
1949	21,989
1950	22,512
1951	23,352
1952	24,518
1953	25,072
1954	25,873
1955	27,171
1956	29,237
1957	29,862
1958	31,193
1959	...
1960	32,570
1961	...
1962	...
1963	34,235

[a]Source: Data for 1949 to 1958 are from Wei-ta ti shih-nien (The Great Ten Years) (Peking: People's Publishing House, 1959), p. 127. The 1960 and 1963 estimates are the totals of identified railways known to be in operation. For 1957, the total route length of identified railways is 29,176 km (Table 7-4), which is only 686 km or 2.3 per cent less than the official estimate given above. For 1952, the total route length of identified railways (Table 7-4) is 22,818 or 1,708 km short of the 24,518 km given in the present table (i.e., about five per cent below the official total).

Table 7-2

CHANGES IN RAILWAY TRACKAGE FROM 1949 TO 1963

| Year | Trackage at the Beginning of the Year (km) | Dismantled Main and Branch Trackage (km) | New Construction[a] | | Trackage at the End of the Year (km) |
			Main and Branch Trackage (km)	Spur Trackage (km)	
1949	26,700[b]	3,100[c]	–	–	23,600
1952	23,600	–	1,233	236	25,069
1953	25,069	–	706	494	26,269
1954	26,269	–	1,132	283	27,684
1955	27,684	–	1,406	458	29,548
1956	29,548	–	2,242	866	32,656
1957	32,656	–	1,166	569	34,391
1958	34,391	–	2,376	1,188	37,955
1959	37,955	–	3,136	1,568	42,659
1960	42,659	–	7,344	1,045	51,048
1963	51,048	–	1,566[d]	...	52,614

[a]These data were taken from The Ten Great Years (Peking: Foreign Language Press, 1960), p. 69. The 1959 data were estimated at 132 per cent of the 1958 data (People's Daily, April 9, 1960). For 1960, see Lü Cheng-ch'ao's report to the National People's Congress. The figure of 7,344 km represents the difference between the total amount to be added (8,389 km) and the amount allocated for light rails and spur lines (1,045 km) (People's Daily, April 9, 1960).

[b]Original Nationalist figure. See Ling Hung-hsün, Chung-kuo T'ieh-lu Kai-lun (General Survey of Railways in China) (Taipei, 1950), pp. 27-34, and Yuan-li Wu, An Economic Survey of Communist China (New York: Bookman Associates, 1956), p. 350.

[c]Dismantled during World War II and later (mostly in the civil war). Data were taken from Railways in Communist China (Taipei: Communications Research Bureau, Ministry of Communications, 1961), pp. 25-28.

[d]Estimated from net increase in operating route length from 1960 to 1963.

tions. (See Maps 7-1 and 7-2.) Table 7-3 then presents two series of index numbers based on the operating route lengths and trackage estimates.

Table 7-3 shows that an increase of 123 per cent in trackage occurred in the 14-year period between 1949 and 1963. In contrast, the increase in route length in operation during the same period was only 56 per cent. Average annual growth rates were 5.9 and 3.25 per cent, respectively.

Route length increased at a relatively stable rate varying from two to five per cent in most years--the exception was a nine per cent growth between 1955 and 1956. However, the rate of increase in trackage fluctuated within a wider range, from five to 20 per cent, and exhibited a tendency to accelerate. These divergent tendencies are seen graphically in Figure 7-1 in which the two growth curves intersect each other in 1954-55. Between 1949 and 1955, the growth of the operating route length exceeded that of trackage, reflecting the rapid pace of recovery and rehabilitation over that of new construction. After 1955, the much faster growth of railway trackage reflected increasing double-tracking and construction of spurs and auxiliary tracks. Consequently, the size of the plant, represented by the individual rail route, increased sharply between 1957 and 1960--the well-known period of the "Great Leap Forward." Following the failure of the "Great Leap Forward" and the dramatic cutback in investment, increases in railway trackage were less.

Although lack of complete information for each year precludes a full reconciliation of trackage and route statistics, such a reconciliation may be attempted for 1963:

		Amount (km)
Estimated total railway trackage at the end of 1963 (Table 7-2)		52,614
Accountable railway trackage at the end of 1963:		
Total route length of identified railways in operation at the end of 1963 (Table 7-4)	34,235	
Estimated route length of double tracking completed under the present regime through 1962 (Table E-5, Appendix E)	9,430	
Estimated length of new light spur lines (Table 7-2)	6,707	
Total accountable railway trackage		50,372
Unaccountable railway trackage		2,242

130

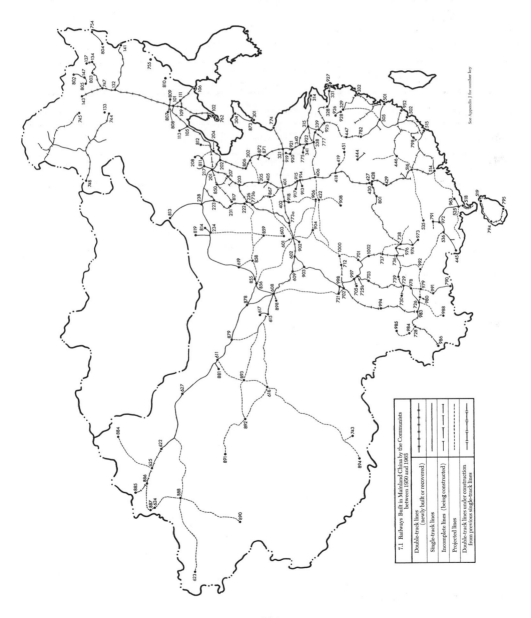

7.1 Railways Built in Mainland China by the Communists between 1950 and 1963

Double-track lines (newly built or recovered)	
Single-track lines	
Incomplete lines (being constructed)	
Projected lines	
Double-track lines under construction from previous single-track lines	

See Appendix J for number key

131

7.2 Railways in Mainland China in 1963			
Railways existing in 1949	narrow-gauge		single-track
Rebuilt or recovered railways[a]	rebuilt *		completed
Double-track lines	projected	under construction	newly built recovered
Newly built railways	projected	under construction	completed
Newly built special lines [b]	projected	under construction	completed
Dismantled railways	··		
Foreign railways	—×—×—×—×—×—		
Principal bridges	under construction (A)—▮—	newly built (B)—▮—	rebuilt (C)—▮—

* not necessarily completed

[a] Rebuilt railways have been in operation continually and were undergoing improvement.

Recovered railways had been abandoned and were being restored to operation.

[b] Special lines are those used exclusively for carrying special loads--i.e., mining lines, refinery lines, etc.

MAP 7.2 IS IN THE BACK POCKET

Table 7-3

INDEXES OF RAILWAY TRACKAGE AND ROUTE
LENGTH FROM 1949 TO 1963[a]

Year end	Indexes for Total Trackage		Indexes for Route Length in Operation	
	1949 = 100	Preceding Year = 100	1949 = 100	Preceding Year = 100
1950	...	...	102	102
1951	...	...	106	104
1952	106	...	112	105
1953	111	105	114	102
1954	117	105	118	103
1955	125	107	124	105
1956	138	111	133	108
1957	146	105	136	102
1958	161	110	142	104
1959	181	112	...	...
1960	216	120	148	...
1961	...	...	...	...
1962	...	...	...	...
1963	223	...	156	...

[a]Source: Tables 7-1 and 7-2.

Figure 7.1 Indexes for Railway Construction
(1949 = 100)

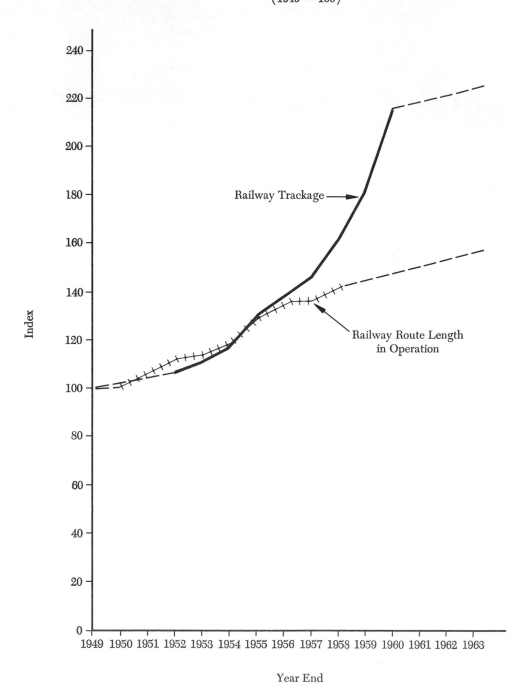

Year End

Table 7-4

ROUTE LENGTH OF <u>IDENTIFIED</u> RAILWAYS
IN OPERATION IN 1949 TO 1963[a]

Region and Province	Operating Route Lengths (km) in Indicated Year				
	1949	1952	1957	1960	1963
Northeast					
Liaoning	2,273	2,906	2,979	3,034	3,096
Kirin	2,046	2,548	2,715	2,749	2,749
Heilungkiang	2,926	3,483	3,925	4,132	4,132
Total	7,245	8,937	9,619	9,915	9,977
North and Inner Mongolia					
Hopeh	1,707	1,905	2,568	2,583	2,583
Shansi	446	1,117	1,210	1,219	1,352
Inner Mongolia	1,178	1,354	2,486	2,764	2,764
Total	3,226	4,376	6,264	6,566	6,699
East					
Shantung	816	881	1,146	1,146	1,146
Kiangsu	1,156	1,167	1,194	1,206	1,248
Chekiang	428	451	619	703	703
Anhwei	168	285	348	348	432
Total	2,568	2,784	3,307	3,403	3,529
Central					
Honan	1,248	1,248	1,346	1,346	1,400
Kiangsi	495	734	806	805	805
Hupeh	159	347	362	460	676
Hunan	502	871	1,064	1,064	1,227
Total	2,404	3,200	3,578	3,675	4,108
South					
Fukien	–	–	621	908	908
Kwangtung	146	529	691	752	752
Kwangsi	608	1,152	1,349	1,349	1,349
Total	754	1,681	2,661	3,009	3,009
Northwest					
Shensi	521	521	521	868	868
Kansu	74	406	1,440	1,968	2,153
Ningsia	–	–	–	470	470
Tsinghai	–	–	–	122	222
Sinkiang	–	–	–	142	707
Total	595	927	1,961	3,570	4,420
Shouthwest					
Szechwan	58	562	655	1,164	1,225
Yünnan	186	186	838	975	975
Kweichow	–	157	293	293	293
Total	244	905	1,786	2,432	2,493
GRAND TOTAL	17,036	22,810	29,176	32,570	34,235

[a] Source: Appendix E, Table E-1.

The unaccounted for trackage can probably be attributed to tracks in switching yards, forest railways and other unidentified lines which do not have regular train schedules.

Regional Pattern of Railway Expansion

Fukien, Kweichow, Ningsia, Tsinghai, Sinkiang, and Tibet had no railways in 1949. The limited rail routes in Kansu and Yünnan were not in operation at the time. The same was probably true of the short line in Szechwan. By the end of 1963, however, Tibet was the only area without one or more operating rail lines. The profile of the Chinese economy has undoubtedly been radically altered by railway building, although the expansion of the railway network did not take place evenly.

A comparison of trunk lines in operation at the beginning of the Communist period and the route length at the end of 1963 (Table 7-5), disregarding any inconsistency in the treatment of double tracking in the initial period, shows that the greatest increase in route length occurred in Northwest China and the smallest in Northeast China. If the regions are ranked, the order would be (1) Northwest Chine, (2) North China and Inner Mongolia, (3) Southwest China, (4) South China, (5) Central China, (6) East China, and (7) Northeast China. Since the increase in the so-called North China region (slightly over 3,600 kilometers) was mainly in Inner Mongolia (2,200 kilometers), and since these lines were closely related to railway extension in Northwest China (just under 4,000 kilometers), we may be justified in thinking of Northwest China as the region with the greatest expansion of railway route length. Secondary priority was given Southwest China (an increment of nearly 2,500 kilometers) and, to a lesser extent, South China (slightly over 2,000 kilometers). Since these three regions were at the bottom of the list in 1949 (Table 7-5), the statistics point to a policy of railway expansion in regions that had been least developed in this transport sector. This conclusion seems to substantiate our view (Chapter 6) of the physical and topographical constraints on the expansion of transport carriers.

The addition of railway routes in some regions between 1949-50 and 1963 (Table 7-5) brought about significant shifts in regional rankings. In terms of rail route length, North China moved from third to second place and Northwest China

Table 7-5

ROUTE LENGTH AND DENSITY OF RAILWAYS IN
OPERATION IN 1949-50 AND 1963

Region and Province	Area[a] (km²)	Route Length (km) of Operating Railways[b]			Density (km/1,000 km²) of Route Length of Operating Railways		
		1949-50	1963	Net Increase	1949-50	1963	Net Increase
Northeast							
Liaoning[c]	151,000	3,820	3,096	724	25	21	4
Kirin	187,000	5,943	2,749	938	9	15	2
Heilungkiang	463,600		4,132			9 }11	
Total	801,600	9,763	9,977	214	12	13	1
North and Inner Mongolia							
Hopeh	219,800	1,791	2,583	792	8	12	4
Shansi	157,100	730	1,352	622	5	9	4
Inner Mongolia	1,177,500	542	2,764	2,222	0.5	2	1.5
Total	1,554,400	3,063	6,699	3,636	2	4	2
East							
Shantung	153,300	950	1,146	196	6	7	1
Kiangsu	108,000	831	1,248	417	8	12	4
Chekiang	101,800	443	703	260	4	7	3
Anhwei[d]	139,900	630	432	198	5	3	2
Total	503,000	2,854	3,529	675	6	7	1
Central							
Honan	167,000	1,205	1,400	195	7	8	1
Kiangsi	164,800	705	805	90	4	5	2
Hunan	210,500	865	1,227	362	4	6	2
Hupeh	187,500	329	676	347	2	4	2
Total	729,800	3,114	4,108	994	4	6	2
South							
Fukien	123,100	–	908	908	–	7	7
Kwangtung	231,400	569	752	183	2	3	1
Kwangsi	220,400	409	1,349	940	2	6	4
Total	574,900	978	3,009	2,031	2	5	3
Northwest							
Shensi	195,800	441	868	427	2	4	2
Kansu and		–	2,153)				
Ningsia	432,900	–	470)	2,623	–	6	6
Tsinghai	721,000	–	222	222	–	0.3	0.3
Sinkiang	1,646,800	–	707	707	–	0.4	0.4
Total	2,996,500	441	4,420	3,979	0.1	1.5	1.3
Southwest							
Szechwan	569,000	--	1,225	1,225	–	2	2
Yünnan	436,200	–	975	975	–	2	2
Kweichow	174,000	–	293	293	–	2	2
Tibet	1,221,600	–	–	–	–	–	–
Total	2,400,800	–	2,493	2,493	–	1	1
GRAND TOTAL	9,561,000	20,213	34,235	14,022	2	4	2

[a]Data are from Appendix D, Table D-1.

[b]The 1949-50 data are from Appendix D, Table D-1; the 1963 data are from Appendix E, Table E-1.

[c]The discrepancy between the 1949-50 and 1963 reported lengths is primarily a result of provincial boundary changes. According to the current boundaries of Liaoning, some of the 3,820 kilometers should probably be placed in Kirin and Hopeh. The total length involved would amount to approximately 700 km.

[d]The difference between 1949-50 and 1963 was due to the dismantled section of the original Ching-kan Railway between Wu-hu and Hsi-hsien.

moved from sixth to third. Central, East, and South China lost ground in their
relative standings.

However, because of the disparity of the sizes of the regions, little change
occurs in the ranking of the regions if the comparison is made in terms of the
density of operating route lengths. The largest change occurred in South China,
followed by (1) Central China, and North China and Inner Mongolia, (2) Northwest
China, and (3) East, Southwest and Northeast China. Consequently, the primary
aim of the Chinese Communists seems to be the expansion of the existing railway
network, especially in Central and East China; however, this aim has not pre-
cluded building new railways in such areas as Northwest China, Inner Mongolia,
and Southwest China.

Availability of Railway Facilities and Degree
of Economic Development

The next question is the economic effect of this expansion. A good starting point is the empirical evidence provided by a comparison of economic development indexes and the availability of railway facilities.

Since railway transportation accounts for the bulk of freight traffic in
modern China, we may presume with some justification that the economically
more developed cities tend to use the railways for larger freight shipments and
therefore have better railway facilities. This thesis can be tested by examining
the relative availability of railway facilities in cities of different economic ranking and industrial importance.

Owing to the absence of detailed information, we have devised our own
indicator to measure the relative availability of railway facilities at individual
localities. As a first approximation only, we have resorted to a crude system of
counting railway radials emanating from various cities. A city with a single-
tracked railway passing through it is treated as having two railway radials. The
number, however, is halved if the rail line is a branch, spur, or special purpose
line. On the other hand, since more complex facilities must be constructed at
railway terminals, an arbitrary weight of four is employed as a multiplier to
give the terminus of a single-tracked line a weighted index of four radials so
that such a city would have a distinctly higher number than a city lying astride
a railway. This relatively better position of cities which are railway termini

Table 7-6

DISTRIBUTION OF 117 CITIES OF ECONOMIC RANK
INDEXES A, B, AND C BY RAILWAY
RADIAL COUNTS[a]

Railway Radial Counts	Number of Cities	Relative Frequency (%)
Rank A Cities[b]		
0 to less than 4	1	4.4
4 to less than 8	8	34.8
8 to less than 12	7	30.4
12 to less than 16	4	17.4
16 to less than 20	1	4.4
20 to less than 24	0	--
24 to less than 28	1	4.3
28 to less than 32	1	4.3
Total	23	100.0
Rank B Cities[c]		
0 to less than 4	5	20.8
4 to less than 8	11	45.8
8 to less than 12	3	12.5
12 to less than 16	2	8.3
16 to less than 20	2	8.3
20 to less than 24	1	4.2
Total	24	100.0[d]
Rank C Cities[c]		
0 to less than 4	34	48.6
4 to less than 8	32	45.7
8 to less than 12	3	4.3
12 to less than 16	1	1.4
Total	70	100.0

[a]Source: Appendix E, Table E-2.

[b]Mean $(\bar{X}_A)$ = 10.87; median (Med_A) = 9.43.

[c]Mean $(\bar{X}_B)$ = 8; median (Med_B) = 6.55.

[d]The total does not equal 100 due to rounding.

[e]Mean $(\bar{X}_C)$ = 4.29; median (Med_C) = 4.

Table 7-7

DISTRIBUTION OF 328 LARGE, MEDIUM, AND SMALL INDUSTRIAL
CENTERS BY RAILWAY RADIAL COUNTS[a]

Railway Radial Counts	Number of Cities	Relative Frequency (%)
Large Industrial Centers[b]		
0 to less than 4	0	--
4 to less than 8	2	22.2
8 to less than 12	1	11.1
12 to less than 16	4	44.4
16 to less than 20	1	11.1
20 to less than 24	0	--
24 to less than 28	0	--
28 to less than 32	1	11.1
Total	9	100.0[c]
Medium Industrial Centers[d]		
0 to less than 4	20	35.1
4 to less than 8	23	40.3
8 to less than 12	8	14.0
12 to less than 16	2	3.5
16 to less than 20	2	3.5
20 to less than 24	1	1.8
24 to less than 28	1	1.8
Total	57	100.0
Small Industrial Centers[e]		
0 to less than 4	214	81.7
4 to less than 8	43	16.4
8 to less than 12	4	1.5
12 to less than 16	1	0.4
Total	262	100.0

[a]Source: Appendix E, Table E-3.

[b]Mean ($\bar{X}_L$) = 14; median (Med_L) = 14.5

[c]The total does not equal 100 due to rounding.

[d]Mean ($\bar{X}_M$) = 6.49; median (Med_M) = 5.48.

[e]Mean ($\bar{X}_S$) = 2.82; median (Med_S) = 2.44.

seems plausible. The number is halved for branches, spurs, and special purpose lines. Finally, the numbers are doubled for all double-track lines.

Using these arbitrary railway radial counts, we have grouped the 117 cities discussed in Chapter 4 as well as the 328 large, medium, and small industrail locations listed in Chapter 3. The results are summarized in Tables 7-6 and 7-7. The corresponding relative frequency charts are illustrated in Figures 7-2 and 7-3.

Rank A cities in the first group have a mean railway radial count of 10.9 as compared with 8 for Rank B cities and nearly 4.3 for Rank C cities. The industrial cities display even wider differences between the successive size groups. The large industrial centers have a radial count of 14, which contrasts with a count of 6.5 for medium and 2.8 for small centers. Similar relationships prevail if medians are used. Although the relatively large gaps between industrial center categories are partly a reflection of the arbitrary system of counting railway radials used, they also indicate a discontinuity in the effect of an expansion of railway facilities on economic growth, especially industrial growth. The attainment of a markedly higher degree of economic or industrial importance by any city may be dependent on a significantly large addition to railway facilities.

Within each rank or industrial group, there is only an insignificant positive correlation between the railway radial count and the industrial capacity. Apart from data deficiencies, this phenomenon may be partly accounted for by the discontinuity factor. Small variations in available railway facilities, as measured by the radial count, are of relatively minor economic consequence. In addition, industrial growth tends to be gradual, but railway radial count always changes by discrete numbers and, consequently, in relatively larger proportions. Second, the lesser status of some smaller and newer industrial and economic centers may reflect little more than that the cut-off point for our industrial capacity data (1961) was too early to permit a closer correlation. The interruption of industrial development by the 1960-62 crisis accentuated this effect. Third, a number of places have high railway radial counts entirely as a result of geographic location. Such cities, including many railway junction towns, do not necessarily become important economic or industrial centers. This point is all the more pertinent if the rail construction is recent. Finally, the railway radial count does not allow for other means of transportation which also play a part.

141

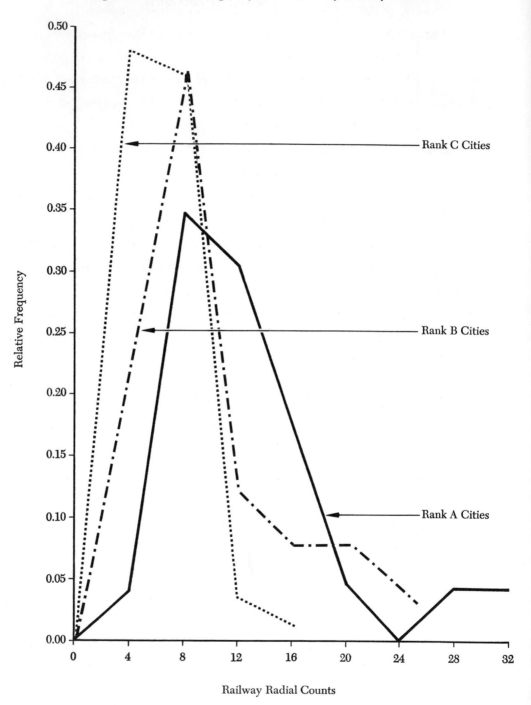

Figure 7.2 Relative Frequency of 117 Cities by Railway Radial Counts

142

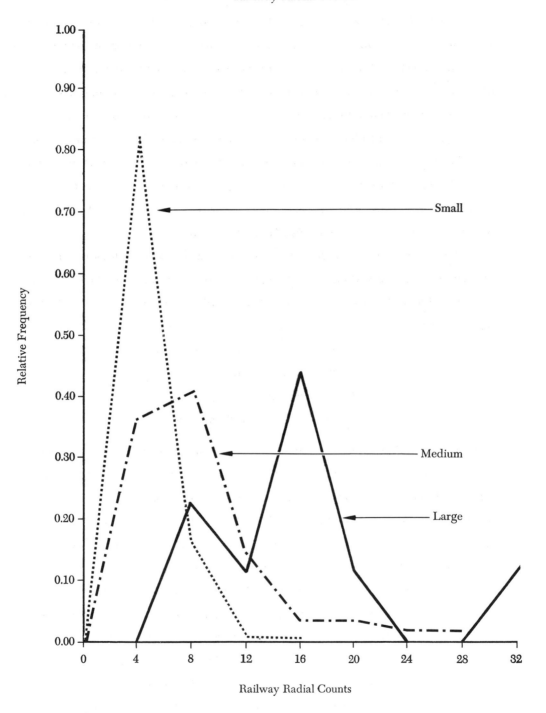

Figure 7.3 Relative Frequency of 328 Industrial Centers by
Railway Radial Counts

143

Relationship between New and Established Economic Centers
and New Railway Construction

Even if every expansion of railway transport facilities at a given place does not result in immediate and noticeable economic expansion or, specifically, industrial growth, continued addition of railway or other transport facilities will ultimately contribute to a rise in the economic or industrial ranking of a locality. Therefore, geographic distribution of new rail construction has an important bearing on locational planning in economic development. A number of questions may, however, be posed. For instance, to what extent are new economic and industrial centers located on railways built prior to the establishment of Communist China? To what degree has new rail construction added to the transport facilities of economic centers established long ago?

As an aid to our analysis, we have used the following letters to classify important economic and industrial centers according to whether they are new or established and whether they lie on railways built during or before the Communist period:

A: new centers on new rail lines

B: new centers on old rail lines

C: old centers on new rail lines

D: old centers on old rail lines

The few economic centers connected by both old and new rail lines are denoted by a "prime." Thus, B' indicates new centers on both old and new rail lines, and C' indicates old centers on both old and new rail lines. For convenience, however, B' cities are combined with the A or B cities depending on whether the new rail lines on which they are situated are trunk or branch lines. The C' cities are added to the D cities if the new rail lines on which they are situated are minor additions in comparison with the existing railways. Otherwise, they are included with the C cities. Whenever these combinations occur, the letter designations, $\overline{A}$, $\overline{B}$, $\overline{C}$, and $\overline{D}$ are employed. Subscripts "u" and "d" indicate if the centers are located in underdeveloped or developed regions.

In general, the B cities are new centers that represent fuller utilization of the existing transport plant. Of the B cities, the B_d category represents cities that have been established because of the existing railway network and the other advantages provided by a more developed economy. The B_u cities do not have these other advantages.

The C category represents cities where additional transport facilities have apparently been provided to facilitate further economic development. The new investment in railway building is, therefore, in a sense marginal. By definition, the cities in the C group are concentrated in the C_d category, and the C_u category is small or nonexistent.

The D cities are established centers that have required relatively little addition to the railway plant, or at least no new railway lines. In these cities, however, one of three things might have prevailed. First, the existing transport plant was more than adequate from the outset and could handle an expanded volume of traffic without expansion. Second, the city in question remained economically static so that no rail expansion was needed. Finally, other transport facilities were developed.

The A cities are the new economic centers developed through new rail construction. Of these, the A_u cities are the vaunted "spearhead" of development in virgin territories. They demand much more investment in "social overhead" capital than other means of industrial development such as various public facilities.

For our purpose new economic centers are defined as those vigorously developed in Communist China prior to the economic crisis in 1960-62, but not necessarily completely new industrial centers. They consist of 26 cities included in categories A-II and B-II in Table 4-8 and B2, B3, B4, B5, and B8 in Table 4-3 (excluding Soochow and Kuei-yang, which are predominantly nonindustrial).[1] The old or established economic centers are the eight cities of Categories A-I and B-I in Table 4-8 not already included as new economic centers. Table 7-8 shows the following numbers of economic centers in these groups:

$$A_d = --$$
$$A_u = 3$$
$$A = 3$$

$B_d = 13$	$B_d' = 3$
$B_u = 6$	$B_u' = 1$
$B = 19$	$B' = 4$

145

$$C_d = \text{--} \qquad\qquad C_d{}' = 1$$
$$C_u = 1 \qquad\qquad C_u{}' = \text{--}$$
$$C = 1 \qquad\qquad C' = 1$$

$$D_d = 6$$
$$D_u = \text{--}$$
$$D = 6$$

The B' and C' categories may be simplified by reassigning the cities in those categories on the basis of the relative importance of the new rail construction:[2]

$B_d{}'$ Peking and T'ai-yüan reassigned to B_d

Pao-t'ou reassigned to A_d

$B_u{}'$ Wu-han reassigned to B_u

$C_d{}'$ Shanghai reassigned to D_d

The adjusted grouping would then read as follows:

$\overline{A}_d = 1$	$\overline{B}_d = 15$	$\overline{C}_d = \text{--}$	$\overline{D}_d = 7$
$\overline{A}_u = 3$	$\overline{B}_u = 7$	$C_u = 1$	$\overline{D}_u = \text{--}$
$\overline{A} = 4$	$\overline{B} = 22$	$C = 1$	$\overline{D} = 7$

The ratio of $\overline{A}$ to $\overline{B} + C$ is 4 to 23 or 17.4 per cent, and that of $\overline{A}_u$ to $\overline{B} + C$ is 3 to 23 or 13.0 per cent. Both ratios reflect a conservative locational policy that tends to limit overhead investment in the development of new centers. It remains to be seen whether this effect was a result of deliberate policy or the result of an initially more ambitious plan that was impeded by the heavy cost of exploiting new areas.

In conformity with our earlier findings, the ratio of $\overline{A}_d + \overline{B}_d + C_d$ to $\overline{A}_u + \overline{B}_u + C_u$ (16 to 11) indicates the much greater emphasis on establishing new economic centers and on adding to the transport plant of old centers in the developed regions rather than the less developed regions. The ratio of $\overline{B}$ to C (22 to 1) points to a policy of developing new centers by taking advantage of transport and other facilities offered by existing railway network in the economically more developed areas rather than of adding new rail facilities to established economic centers.

Table 7-8

PRINCIPAL NEW AND ESTABLISHED ECONOMIC CENTERS
SITUATED ON NEW AND OLD RAILWAY LINES

Category[a]	Centers in Developed Regions			Centers in Underdeveloped Regions				Total
	Northeast	North	East	Central	South	Northwest	Southwest	
A	-	-	-	-	-	Lan-chow Urumchi	Ch'eng-tu	3
B	An-shan Fu-shun Lü-ta Harbin T'ung-hua An-tung Ch'ang-ch'un	Shih-chia-chuang Han-tan	Nanking Tzu-po Ho-fei Huai-nan	Lo-yang Cheng-chou Ch'ang-sha Nan-ch'ang	Canton	Sian	-	19
B'	-	Peking T'ai-yüan Pao-t'ou	-	Wu-han	-	-	-	4
C	-	-	-	-	-	-	Chungking	1
C'	-	-	Shanghai	-	-	-	-	1
D	Mukden	Tientsin T'ang-shan	Tsinan Hangchow Tsingtao	-	-	-	-	6

[a]See Chapter 4, Tables 4-3 and 4-8, and the description in this chapter. (The classification of the cities is based on the criteria discussed in the text first--i.e., before the reassignment described.

Regional Distribution of New Railway Lines

Since only a few new railway lines pass through principal economic centers, the policy underlying new railway building should be analyzed further by examining regional distribution and possible functions of the new lines, as shown in Table 7-9.

The amount of new rail construction was greatest in Northwest China, followed by South China, Southwest China, and North China (including Inner Mongolia). The regional distribution of new construction corresponds closely to that of increments in route length. The differences are attributable to the inclusion of rehabilitated track in the route length statistics. About 19.4 per cent of new construction between 1949 and 1963 was in the developed regions, and 80.6 per cent was in the less developed regions. The average length of the railways in the less developed regions (212.7 kilometers) was also greater than that of new lines in the developed regions (88.8 kilometers).

Primary Functions of New Railways

We have already shown that more new economic centers were established in the developed regions than in the less developed regions ($\bar{A}_d + \bar{B}_d = 16 > \bar{A}_u + \bar{B}_u = 10$), and also that more new economic centers were set up in the less developed regions on existing railway lines than on new railways ($\bar{B}_u > \bar{A}_u$ or $7 > 3$). How can we then interpret the heavy emphasis on the less developed regions in new railway construction?

New railway lines are built for purposes that need not be mutually exclusive. Railways may be built to aid the exploitation of fixed resources; to fulfill a military defense need; to serve as connecting lines that provide missing links, shorter connections or by-passes in the existing system; or to promote regional economic development in general, as distinct from the exploitation of specific fixed resources.

In Tables 7-10 and 7-11 new railways are first divided into two categories: those that do and do not pass through fixed points where important natural resources are known to exist. Known resources considered include coal, water power (where hydrostations are established or planned), petroleum, and iron

148

Table 7-9

REGIONAL DISTRIBUTION OF NEW RAILWAY CONSTRUCTION
FROM 1949 TO 1963 YEAR END[a]

Region	Number of New Lines	Length of New Lines (km)	Percentage of New Lines
Developed Regions			
Northeast	3	115	1.2
North	11	1,194	12.6
East	7	535	5.6
Subtotal	21	1,844	19.4
Underdeveloped Regions			
Central	10	811	8.5
South	8	1,613	17.0
Northwest	11	3,839	40.4
Southwest	7	1,394	14.7
Subtotal	36	7,657	80.6
TOTAL	57	9,501	100.0

[a]These data included all trunk lines and major branches identified, but excluded forest railways, spurs, railways under construction and planned lines. See Appendix E, Table E-4.

ore. Since our knowledge is incomplete especially for nonferrous metals and nonmetallic minerals other than coal, errors of omission cannot be avoided. However, the resources cited include the principal energy and ferrous metal components that modern economics tend to exploit. Only lines not passing through fixed points yielding known resources can be regarded as railways that may have been built solely for other purposes.

Even railways built for the exploitation of specific, fixed resources may also serve other purposes. Therefore, both categories have been divided into four subcategories:

1. Military lines. These railways are obviously designed to serve a potential military front. They include lines to a point on the national border or to a seaport not noted for its commercial traffic.

2. Connecting lines. These railways are designed to complete an existing railway network. They include railways connecting two trunk lines or connecting a trunk line with a seaport or major river port. Lines replacing sections of existing railways are also included in this subcategory.

3. Trunk lines. These railways are neither military nor connecting lines, but they pass through two or more provinces or two or more large industrial, commercial, or culture centers in one or more provinces. They are usually over 100 kilometers long. [3]

4. Other lines. These railways include all other branch and special lines. They are usually less than 100 kilometers long.

If the last category, which is unimportant for our analysis, is disregarded, Tables 7-10, 7-11, and 7-12 support the following conclusions: First, in terms of the length of new rail construction, 51 per cent of the new trackage consists of military or connecting lines. New military trackage (42 per cent) forms by far the largest single subcategory. Even if the number of lines rather than their length is considered, the 12 military and connecting lines still represent 40 per cent of the 30 lines in the first three subcategories.

Second, if trunk lines not passing through fixed points of known resources are considered as purely exploratory lines for spearheading development in a certain area, the ratio of railway length in subcategory 3 is relatively small (about

Table 7-10

NUMBERS OF NEW RAILWAYS[a,b]

Regions	Number of Lines in Indicated Subcategory Passing through Localities with Fixed Resources						Number of Lines in Indicated Subcategory Not Passing through Localities with Fixed Resources						Total Number of Lines in Indicated Subcategory						
	(1)	(2)	(1+2)	(3)	(1+2+3)	(4)	(1)	(2)	(1+2)	(3)	(1+2+3)	(4)	(1)	(2)	(1+2)	(3)	(1+2+3)	(4)	Total
Developed Regions																			
Northeast	-	-	-	-	-	1	-	-	-	-	-	2	-	-	-	-	-	3	3
North	-	3	3	2	5	1	1	-	1	-	1	4	1	2	3	2	6	5	11
East	-	2	2	-	2	2	-	-	-	-	-	3	-	2	2	-	2	5	7
Total	-	5	5	2	7	4	1	-	1	-	1	9	1	4	5	2	8	13	21
Underdeveloped Regions																			
Central	1	-	1	3	4	2	-	-	-	1	1	3	1	1	2	4	5	5	10
South	2	-	2	1	3	2	1	-	1	-	1	2	3	-	3	1	4	4	8
Northwest	1	1	2	3	5	3	-	-	-	2	2	1	1	1	2	5	7	4	11
Southwest	-	-	-	4	4	-	-	-	-	2	2	1	-	-	-	6	6	1	7
Total	4	1	5	11	16	7	1	-	1	5	6	7	5	2	7	16	22	14	36
GRAND TOTAL	4	6	10	13	23	11	2	-	2	5	7	16	6	6	12	18	30	27	57

[a] Source: Appendix E, Table E-4.

[b] Subcategory 1 = military lines. Subcategory 2 = connecting lines. Subcategory 3 = trunk lines. Subcategory 4 = other lines.

151

Table 7-11

LENGTHS OF NEW RAILWAYS[a, b]

Regions	Length (km) of Lines in Indicated Subcategory Passing through Localities with Known Fixed Resources						Length (km) of Lines in Indicated Subcategory Not Passing through Localities with Known Fixed Resources						Total Length (km) of Lines in Indicated Subcategory						
	(1)	(2)	(1+2)	(3)	(1+2+3)	(4)	(1)	(2)	(1+2)	(3)	(1+2+3)	(4)	(1)	(2)	(1+2)	(3)	(1+2+3)	(4)	Total
Developed Regions																			
Northeast	-	-	-	-	-	29	-	-	-	-	-	86	-	-	-	-	-	115	115
North	-	233	233	426	659	61	330	-	330	-	330	144	330	233	563	426	989	205	1,194
East	-	-	-	-	-	79	-	347	347	-	347	109	-	347	347	-	347	188	535
Total	-	233	233	426	659	169	330	347	677	-	677	339	330	580	910	426	1,336	508	1,844
Underdeveloped Regions																			
Central	73	-	73	412	485	46	-	-	-	132	132	148	73	-	73	544	617	194	811
South	976	-	976	168	1,144	72	315	-	315	-	315	82	1,291	-	1,291	168	1,459	154	1,613
Northwest	1,892	185	2,077	1,239	3,316	98	-	-	-	402	402	23	1,892	185	2,077	1,641	3,718	121	3,839
Southwest	-	-	-	864	864	-	-	-	-	469	469	61	-	-	-	1,333	1,333	61	1,394
Total	2,941	185	3,126	2,683	5,809	216	315	-	315	1,003	1,318	314	3,256	185	3,441	3,686	7,127	530	7,657
GRAND TOTAL	2,941	418	3,359	3,109	6,468	385	645	347	992	1,003	1,995	653	3,586	765	4,351	4,112	8,463	1,038	9,501

[a]Source: Appendix E, Table E-4.

[b]Subcategory 1 = military lines. Subcategory 2 = connecting lines. Subcategory 3 = trunk lines. Subcategory 4 = other lines.

11.9 per cent or 1,003/8,463). If, however, all railways not passing through fixed points of known resources are thought of as lines designed to speed up area development in general, the ratio rises to a no longer insignificant ratio (23.6 per cent or 1,995/8,463).

Third, it can be argued that military or connecting lines passing through fixed points of known resources might not have been built or would have been given lower priority had they not had military or connecting functions. If so, these lines might be included with the lines not passing through fixed points of known resources. The ratio of construction for reasons other than the exploitation of known resources would then rise to 63.3 per cent (3,359 + 1,995/8,463).

Finally, the less developed regions account for much higher proportions of these lines than the developed regions.

As we have seen earlier in this chapter, locational policy in the establishment of new economic centers attempted to reduce overhead investment by favoring old railways and the developed regions. The preceding paragraphs have shown that military considerations, as expressed in the construction of military lines, were predominant between 1949 and 1963. Moreover, the policy for railway construction emphasized the less developed regions and gave a significant weight to railways not clearly meant to develop known resources at fixed points. These lines even included a few that were constructed for purely exploratory reasons and that had no other redeeming features including defense potential. Whether such a policy can be justified depends upon the time length of the planning horizon. In a period of capital shortage, one may seriously question its wisdom and the appropriateness of coordination between location planning and transport policy.

Since a larger proportion of the newly constructed lines has been in the less developed regions, it follows that the new lines are, in general, not built to serve existing markets, although they may have been designed to exploit mineral or other resources. It is true, however, that markets expand when workers are brought in. This variety of development has been prominent in Communist China because of the ordering of large population shifts as a matter of state policy. To judge from the frequency and size of such movements, policy at this level may go beyond the ordinary exploitation of resources and look

Table 7-12

DISTRIBUTION OF LENGTHS OF NEW RAILWAYS[a,b]

Regions	Lengths (%) of Lines in Indicated Subcategory Passing through Localities with Known Fixed Resources					Length (%) of Lines in Indicated Subcategory Not Passing through Localities with Known Fixed Resources					Total Lengths (%) of Lines in Indicated Subcategory				
	(1)	(2)	(1+2)	(3)	(1+2+3)	(1)	(2)	(1+2)	(3)	(1+2+3)	(1)	(2)	(1+2)	(3)	(1+2+3)
Developed Regions															
Northeast	-	-	-	-	-	-	-	-	-	-	-	-	-	-	-
North	-	35	35	65	100	100	-	100	-	100	33	24	57	43	100
East	-	-	-	-	-	-	100	100	-	100	-	100	100	-	100
Total	-	35	35	65	100	49	51	100	-	100	25	43	68	32	100
Underdeveloped Regions															
Central	15	-	15	85	100	-	-	-	100	100	12	-	12	88	100
South	85	-	85	15	100	100	-	100	-	100	88	-	88	12	100
Northwest	57	6	63	37	100	-	-	-	100	100	51	5	56	44	100
Southwest	-	-	-	100	100	-	-	-	100	100	-	-	-	100	100
Total	51	3	54	46	100	24	18	24	76	100	46	3	48	52	100
GRAND TOTAL	46	6	52	48	100	32	18	50	50	100	42	9	51	49	100

[a] Source: Table 7-11.

[b] Subcategory 1 = military lines. Subcategory 2 = connecting lines. Subcategory 3 = trunk lines.

154

toward the transportation not only of workers but also of the markets themselves. Industrial plants, therefore, are established near the sources of raw materials and markets, at least in part, are brought to the plants with the population.

Priority in Railway Building and the Nationalist Influence

The planning of railway construction in the Communist period becomes clearer if we look at the sequence in which railways in different categories were built. The two railways constructed from 1950 to 1953--the Ch'eng-tu—Chungking and the Lai-pin—Mu-nan-kuan lines--were both partly built by the Nationalists. During the period through 1957, when the First Five-Year Plan ended, 42 per cent of the new railways represented completion of lines begun under the Nationalist administration. In terms of route length, the proportion is 44 per cent (Table 7-13).

Until 1957, military and connecting lines were proportionately more important in new railway construction than in later years. Military considerations also appeared to be an important factor in railway building prior to the "Great Leap" period. Of the four new military lines (Lai-pin to Mu-nan-kuan, Li-t'ang to Chan-chiang, Ying-t'an to Amoy, and Chi-ning to Erh-lien), the first two are clearly designed to provide logistic support for Chinese activities in Southeast Asia, particularly Vietnam. The early completion of these lines supports the thesis that the Chinese Communist Party decided a decade or more ago to increase its influence in Southeast Asia.

If a comparison is made between railways constructed under the present regime and those planned by the Nationalists for postwar construction, the majority (63 per cent) of the lines built by the Communists but not projected by the Nationalists were nonmilitary and nonconnecting trunk lines (Table 7-14). Furthermore, a larger portion of the lines in each category, with the exception of that of connecting lines, is located in the less developed regions than in the developed regions. This finding, together with points discussed in the preceding section, suggest that the decision to build more railways in less developed areas to promote economic development--possibly without even a prior determination of the fixed resources to be exploited--was largely made under the present regime.

If this conclusion is correct, it follows that the cutback in industrial

Table 7-13

SEQUENCE OF RAILWAY CONSTRUCTION IN COMMUNIST CHINA[a,b]

Category	Railway Length (km) Completed in Indicated Year										
	1950–53	1954	1955	1956	1957	1958	1959	1960	1961–63	Year Unknown	Total
Military	355[c]	–	–	–	694	–	–	–	1,892	–	2,941
(Trunk)	(-)	(-)	(315)	(330)	(-)	(-)	(-)	(-)	(-)	(-)	(645)
Connecting	–	–	104	–	–	9	120	–	185	–	418
(Trunk)	(-)	(-)	(-)	(183)	(-)	(-)	(-)	(-)	(-)	(164)	(347)
Other	504[c]	–	–	280[c]	490[c]	1,260	175	86	314	–	3,109
(Trunk)	(-)	(-)	(-)	(-)	(-)	(669)	(102)	(-)	(100)	(132)	(1,003)
Other	–	–	–	–	14	59	123	–	136	53	385
(Branch)	(-)	(-)	(-)	(-)	(84)	(93)	(-)	(-)	(476)	(-)	(653)
Total	859	–	419	793	1,282	2,090	520	86	3,103	349	9,501

[a]Source: Appendix E, Tables E-4 and E-6.

[b]Numbers in parentheses are for lines not passing through fixed points of known resources; other figures represent lines passing through fixed points of known natural resources.

[c]Lines partly built by the Nationalists.

Table 7-14

NEW RAILWAYS BUILT BY THE COMMUNIST CHINESE
AND NOT PROJECTED BY THE NATIONALISTS[a]

Region	Military Lines		Connecting Lines		Other Lines		Total Lines	
	Number	Length (km)	Number	Length (km)	Number	Length (km)	Number	Length (km)
Developed Regions								
Northeast	-	-	-	-	3	115	3	115
North	-	-	3	233	6	353	9	586
East	-	-	2	347	4	157	6	504
Total	-	-	5	580	13	625	18	1,205
Underdeveloped Regions								
Central	-	-	-	-	9	553	10	553
South	1	315	-	-	4	155	5	470
Northwest	-	-	1	185	5	221	5	406
Southwest	-	-	-	-	3	295	3	295
Total	1	315	1	194	21	1,224	23	1,724
Grand Total	1	315	6	774	34	1,849	41	2,929

[a]Source: Appendix E, Tables E-4 and E-6.

development and the retarded growth of new economic centers from 1961 to 1963 prevented optimal coordination of locational and transport policy, such as was discussed in Chapter 5 as an ideal arrangement. On the other hand, if one looks beyond the present period and assumes renewed and vigorous economic growth in the next decade, it is not inconceivable that a less adverse judgment can be made. Such an assumption would be based on certain bold and perhaps questionable premises at this time. If the economic crisis of 1960-62 can be wholly attributed to noneconomic factors, the poor coordination noted above could be regarded as an unfortunate development beyond the control of Communist China's planners. If, on the other hand, the roots of the economic crisis were inherent in the planning, as we have tried to demonstrate elsewhere,[4] the poor coordination between locational planning and transport policy is yet another planning error, which, because of its inordinate demands on labor and investment for railway building in remote areas at the expense of other more urgent needs, contributed materially to the downswing of the Chinese economy.

Highway Construction

Yet to be analyzed is the relationship of railway construction to the expansion of facilities for the two other principal carriers--the highways and the waterways. The first step is to consider certain characteristics of highway construction in Communist China.

Highway statistics are grossly inadequate, but the total length of all-weather roads open to traffic in 1953 (131,000 kilometers) as well as their distribution by regions are known (Table 7-15). The total road length at the end of 1960 has been estimated at 200,000 kilometers. The increase from 1953 to 1960 may be partly accounted for by new highways, of which 29,500 kilometers can be identified. The identified new roads include most of the trunk lines among the all-weather roads and much of the balance can be attributed to restoration rather than entirely new construction. Accordingly, this remainder (39,500 kilometers) has been distributed among the individual regions in the same proportion as their respective shares in the national total in 1956. The regional estimates for 1956 are found by adding new construction and estimated restorations to the regional figures for 1953. The following findings are based on these reconstructed estimates.

Table 7-15

REGIONAL DISTRIBUTION OF MAJOR ALL-WEATHER OPERATING HIGHWAYS

Region	National Highways in 1949-50[a] (km)	Operating Highways in 1953[b] (km)	New Highways in 1953[c] (km)	Highways Restored during 1953-60[d](km)	Total Density of Highways in 1960[e] (km/1,000 km²)	Total Highways in 1960[e] (km)
Developed Regions						
Northeast	9,142	29,890 (23%)	348	9,076	9	39,314
North	9,255	14,591 (11%)	1,400	4,341	13	20,332
East	7,526	17,723 (13%)	748	5,130	47	23,601
Total	25,923	62,204 (47%)	2,496	18,547	29	83,247
Underdeveloped Regions						
Central and South	10,668	33,234 (26%)	3,236[f]	10,260	36	46,730
Northwest	15,457	18,177 (14%)	9,953	5,524	11	33,654
Southwest	9,777	17,377 (13%)	13,862	5,130	15	36,369
Total	35,902	68,788 (53%)	27,051	20,914	18	116,753
Grand Total	61,825	130,992 (100%)	29,547	39,461	21	200,000

[a]See Table 6-8.

[b]Li Mu-sheng, "Fei-yao Fa-chan-chung ti Hsin-chung-kuo Kung-lu Shih-yeh" (New China's Highways in Rapid Development), Ti-li Chih-shih (Geographical Knowledge) (Peking), Vol. 5, No. 1, January 1954. Adjustments have been made to transfer the total length of highways in Fukien Province, estimated at 4,686 km [Highways in Communist China (Taipei: Ministry of Communications, 1961), pp. 16-21], from East China to Central and South China. Deducted from the estimated total of 7,021 km for Fukien in 1960, are 2,123 km of regular highways and 212 km of "native" highways built since 1953. The remaining 4,686 km are attributed to highways in Fukien in 1953.

[c]See Highways in Communist China, op. cit., pp. 7-77 and Kung-fei Ching-chi (Economy of Communist China) (Taipei: Ministry of Communication, March 1962), pp. 478-484.

[d]The total estimated highway length in 1960 was 200,000 km (Highways in Communist China, op. cit., p. 7). The total amount restored during 1953-60 is estimated by deducting the total length in 1953 and the total length of new construction from the 1960 total. The remainder (39,461 km) is then distributed among the regions in the same ratios as in 1953.

[e]The 1960 regional estimates are obtained by adding the new construction and restoration data to the 1953 figures.

[f]Of this figure, 489 km were constructed in Central China and 2,747 km in South China.

Between 1949 and 1953, the total length of all-weather roads more than doubled. Another 53 per cent increase was registered between 1953 and 1960. The rate of increase exceeded corresponding increases of railway route length in both periods, but fell short of the rate of expansion of railway trackage in 1953-1960. Far more highways were built than railways, although a comparison solely on the basis of route length is not entirely valid as a measure of value. The typical highway, for example, was not engineered for heavy traffic or extended use without constant maintenance.

Far more identified new highways were built in the less developed regions than in the developed regions. Similarly, when regional estimates of restored highways are included, between 1950 and 1960 the increase in the total length of highways was greater in the less developed region. New construction in the 1953-60 period was highest in Southwest China, followed by the Northwest, South China, and North China. These same four regions rank highest in terms of increases in both railway route length and railway trackage although the standings differ in the last three regions. Comparable though unequal emphasis was apparently given to railway as well as highway building in these regions, and this emphasis was considerably greater than that given to the other regions. Far from being only substitutes for each other, roads and railways are often complementary. In addition to the reasons already discussed, roads sometimes have to be built before the construction of railways can begin. Under these circumstances, railway construction in Communist China has begun almost immediately after the completion of the necessary road. Some of these roads specifically built for railway construction are not all-weather roads, and they may eventually be abandoned or deemphasized.

From the data in Table 7-16, a frequency distribution chart can be devised for route lengths (Table 7-17). If roads at least 600 kilometers long are arbitrarily described as "long-distance highways," Table 7-16 shows that five of the 14 routes in this category are found in Northwest China, and two are in Southwest China. These routes will continue to serve as trunk highways until the rail construction is complete, and some may even be maintained afterwards.

The varying requirements for new highways in China proper are partly evident in the data for average road length. The average length was highest in Southwest China (447 kilometers), followed by Northwest China (383 kilometers),

160

Table 7-16

IDENTIFIED NEW HIGHWAYS IN 1960

Regions and Provinces	Terminals		Length (km)	Completion Date
	From	To		
Northeast				
Liaoning	Kai-p'ing	Chuang-ho	150	1955
	T'ung-yüan-pao	Chuang-ho	198	1956
Total			348	
North				Starting
Inner Mongolia	Huhehot	Hai-la-erh	1,400	in 1956
Total			1,400	
East				
Shantung	Wei-fang	Yün-ch'eng	332	1958
Chekiang	Chiang-shan	Feng-lin	77	1954
	Lin-hai	Yung-k'ang	120	1959
	Wen-chou	Fu-ting	144	1956
	Yün-ho	T'ai-shun	75	1959
Subtotal			416	
Total			748	
Central				
Kiangsi	Shang-yao	An-hsien	103	1952
	T'ai-ho	Ching-kang-shan	95	1958
	Kan-chou	Kuei-tung	80	1959
Subtotal			278	
Hunan	T'zu-li	Ta-yung	111	1956
	Tzu-hsing	Kuei-tung	100	1959
Subtotal			211	
Total			489	
South				
Fukien	An-hsien	Foochow	385	1952
	Feng-lin	Chien-ou	203	1954
	Nan-p'ing	Peng-k'ou	266	1955
	Peng-k'ou	Chiao-wei	274	1955
	Foochow	Fu-ting	302	1956
	T'ai-shun	Sh'ou-ning	25	1959
	Pu-ch'eng	Sai-ch'i	280	1959
	Yung-ting	Peng-shih	25	1956
	P'ing-ho	Ch'ao-an	150	1956
Subtotal			1,910	
Kwangtung	Peng-shih	Ta-pu	50	1956
	Ta-pu	Yün-hsiao	180	1956
	P'ing-ho	Jao-p'ing	25	1956
	Ch'ao-an	Jao-p'ing	35	1956
	Hsin-i	Lo-ting	124	1954
	Hai-k'ou	Yü-lin	297	1954
	Na-ta	Pa-so	126	1954
Subtotal			837	
Total			2,747	
Northwest				
Shensi	Nan-cheng	Pa-yü-kuan	40	1955
	Sui-te	Ting-pien	245	1959
Subtotal			285	
Kansu	Hung-liu-yüan	Tun-huang	127	1958
	Tun-huang	Tsinghai Border	100	1954
	Ko-erh-mu	Tsinghai Border	488	1954
	Lan-chou	Lang-mu-ssu	430	1955
	Wu-tu	Szechwan Border	140	1956
Subtotal			1,285	

Table 7-16 (continued)

Regions and Provinces	Terminals From	Terminals To	Length (km)	Completion Date
Northwest (cont'd.)				
Ningsia	Ting-pien	Yin-ch'uan	205	1959
	Shih-tsui-tzu	Chi-lan-t'ai	150	...
Subtotal			355	
Tsinghai	Ko-erh-mu	So-erh-k'u-li	544	1952
	Tao-tang-ho	Yü-shu	723	1953
	Ta-o-po-t'u	Mang-ai	371	1956
	Leng-hu	Cha-leng-k'ou	130	1956
	O-pu-liang	Shao-liang-tzu	150	1956
	Mo-ho	Huang-kua-liang	757	1956
	Tang-chin-shan-k'ou	Mang-ai	363	1956
	Hua-shih-hsia	Chi-mai	340	1955
	Kuo-lo	Chiu-chih	152	1958
	Hsi-ning	T'ung-te	280	1960
	Hsün-hua	T'ung-jen	360	1953
	Hsi-ning	Ko-erh-mu	806	1954
Subtotal			4,976	
Sinkiang	Urumchi	Kashgar	1,513	1958
	Tu-shan-tzu	Ho-shih-t'o-lo-kai	288	1956
	Kashgar	T'u-erh-to-t'e	86	1957
	Yao-ch'iang	Ch'ieh-mo	353	1956
	Yeh-ch'eng	K'ung-ke-shan-k'ou	812	1957
Subtotal			3,052	
Total			9,953	
Southwest				
Szechwan	Pa-yü-kuan	Nan-pu	235	1955
	Kansu Border	Chiang-yu	150	1956
	Ch'eng-tu	A-pa	506	1954
	Lung-jih	Tang-k'e	128	1956
	Hsin-shih	Hsi-ch'ang	336	1956
	Ya-an	Ma-ni-kang-kuo	594	1954
Subtotal			1,949	
Yünnan	Yang-chieh	I-min	243	1953
	Ta-li-yüan	Meng-hai	675	1954
	Meng-hai	Lan-ts'ang	119	1955
	Hai-pa-chuang	Meng-t'ing	574	1956
	Nan-chien	Nan-ta	490	1957
	Hsiang-yün	Pu-erh	328	1959
	Pi-chiang	Mi-chih-na	243	...
	Yang-lin	Hui-tse	280	1956
Subtotal			2,952	
Kweichow	Ssu-nan	T'ung-jen	196	1954
	San-chiang	Ts'e-heng	740	1959
	Lei-shan	Chien-ho	195	1956
	Lei-shan	T'ai-chiang	194	1956
	Hui-shui	Lo-tien	90	1954
	Wei-ning	Shui-ch'eng	49	1956
	Chin-p'ing	Yung-chiang	70	1956
Subtotal			1,534	
Tibet	Ma-ni-kang-kuo	Lhasa	1,661	1954
	Ko-erh-mu	Lhasa	1,217	1954
	K'ung-ke-shan-k'ou	K'o-ta-ke	367	1957
	Lhasa	Ya-tung	607	1955
	Lhasa	Tse-tang	190	1957
	Hei-ho	K'o-ta-ke	1,300	1956
	Jih-ke-tse	Nieh-la-mu	210	1959
	Ko-ta-ke	Pu-lan-tsung	255	1958
	Hei-ho	Ch'ang-tu	720	1956
	Tung-o-lo	Pang-ta	900	...
Subtotal			7,427	
Total			13,862	
GRAND TOTAL			29,547	

[a]Sources: Highways in Communist China (Taipei: 1961), pp. 7-77 and <u>Kung-fei Ching-chi</u> (Economy of Communist China) (Taipei: March 1962), pp. 478-484.

Table 7-17

FREQUENCY DISTRIBUTION OF NEW HIGHWAYS[a,b]

Length (km)	Midpoint (km)	Number	Cumulative Total
1,500 to under 1,800	1,650	2	2
1,200 to under 1,500	1,350	3	5
900 to under 1,200	1,050	1	6
600 to under 900	750	8	14
300 to under 600	450	18	32
under 300	150	54	86

[a] Source: Table 7-16.

[b] Median = 238.9 km. Mean = 355.8 km.

Table 7-18

LENGTH OF NAVIGABLE INLAND WATERWAYS
FROM 1949 TO 1960[a,b]

Year	Official Total Length of Navigable Inland Waterways (km)	Length of Inland Waterways Navigable by Steamers (km)
1949	73,615	24,182
1952	95,025	30,508
1955	99,938	31,685
1956	103,619	38,304
1957	144,101	39,194
1958	150,000	40,000
1959	160,000[c]	40,000[c]
1960	168,000[d]	...

[a] Source: Wei-ta ti Shih-nien (The Great Ten Years) (Peking: : People's Publishing House, 1959), p. 127.

[b] The total length of identifiable rivers is 55,600 km.

[c] People's Daily, February 19, 1960.

[d] People's Daily, March 31, 1960.

163

South China (172 kilometers), East China (150 kilometers), Northeast China (140 kilometers), and Central China (98 kilometers).[5] Roads built in the last four regions can be regarded primarily as feeder roads, as distinct from trunk highways in Southwest and Northwest China.

Waterway Construction

Apart from the development of new harbors and additions to harbor installations, the major investment in waterways has been the dredging of inland waters. The goal in 1958 was 10,000 kilometers dredged, or twice the figure for the entire 1953-57 period. In 1959 and 1960, the goals were 5,000 and 8,000 kilometers, respectively.[6] Because of the general exaggeration of actual performance during the "Great Leap Forward" and the downgrading of goals for 1959 and 1960, in comparison with 1958, we are justified in assuming that the actual length of inland waterways dredged during 1958-60 was lower than the planned figures. Nevertheless, the length of navigable inland waterways was undoubtedly notably increased between 1950 and 1963.

Dredging, together with the installation of navigational aids and facilities, also contributed to a substantial increase in the length of inland waterways navigable by steamer. According to official statistics, the length of such waterways rose from 24,200 kilometers in 1949 to 40,000 kilometers in 1959, or 65 per cent in this decade (Table 7-18). Total length of all navigable inland waterways, including some only nominally navigable, was officially estimated at 168,000 kilometers in 1960, well over twice the total of 73,600 kilometers in 1949. A more valid measure of the increase in the waterway network, however, is the section navigable by steamers. When this criterion is used, the increase of navigable inland waterways from 1949 to 1952 is only 29 per cent--a rate greater than the corresponding one for railway routes (12 per cent from 1949 to 1952), but less than that for highways (112 per cent from 1949-50 to 1953).

According to Kapelinskiy,[7] clearance and dredging of water beds were done on such waterways as the I-ch'ang—Chungking section of the Yangtze, the Min-chiang and the Chiu-lung-chiang in Fukien, and the Shanghai—Pang-fou section of the Grand Canal. Unfortunately, little detailed information is available on the regional distribution of new construction, although work seems to have been concentrated in portions of Southwest China, as well as in East, Central, and

South China. If so, this effort corresponds with the regional distribution of transport routes discussed in Chapter 6.

For a different evaluation of the regional distribution of the construction effort, the locations of new or improved harbor installations were examined by rating the principal seaports on the basis of the number of navigation routes to which they have access (Table 7-19). Of the 20 seaports, several of which are also river ports, ten are in East China, including Shanghai (first in rank), Lung-k'ou, and Chefoo (both fourth), and Tsingtao (fifth). The three second ranking ports are Tientsin, Dairen, and Canton in North, Northeast, and South China respectively. In terms of coastal traffic, East China is therefore undoubtedly the most important and South and North China, as well as Manchuria are of secondary importance.

If this list is supplemented by the addition of seven river ports on which information is available, we find that significant installations were constructed for 12 of the 27 harbors--four each in South and East China and two each in North and Northeast China. Again, more harbors have undergone expansion in South and East China. Furthermore, two of the twelve--Yü-ch'i-k'ou and Harbin--are major river ports.

Finally, a comparison of waterway construction with railway construction (Table E-4) shows that five of the ports listed in Table 7-19 are also terminals for new connecting rail lines. Two of these ports are in South China and two in East China. One in South China, Chan-chiang (formerly known as Kwang-chouwan), is of particular interest since it is the gateway for seaborne traffic to Vietnam.

Economic Ranking of the Principal Ports

Another point of interest emerges if the 27 ports are checked against our data on railway radial counts and grouped according to economic rank and industrial capacity indexes (Tables 7-20 and 7-21).

With the exception of eight ports[8] (five in East China, two in South China, and one in Southwest China), which are not on our lists of economic and industrial centers, the mean railway radial counts of economic centers that are also port cities of Ranks A, B, and C are slightly lower than the corresponding

Table 7-19

SELECTED DATA ON PRINCIPAL PORTS
AND NEW CONSTRUCTIONS[a]

Region	Port	Number of Coastal Navigation Lines	Improvement of Harbor Installations Undertaken in 1949-1961	Connected by New Railway
Northeast	Lü-ta	5	Some	No
	Chia-mu-ssu[b]	–	None	No
	Harbin[b]	–	Some	No
North	Ch'ing-huang-tao	4	Some	No
	Tientsin	5	Major	No
East	Nanking[b]	–	None	No
	Wei-hai	1	None	No
	Lung-k'ou	3	None	No
	Chefoo	3	None	Yes
	Tsingtao	2	Some	No
	Lien-yün	1	Some	No
	Shanghai	13	Some	No
	Ning-po	1	None	Yes
	Ting-hai	1	None	No
	Hai-men	1	None	No
	Wen-chou	1	None	No
	Yü-ch'i-k'ou[b]	–	Major	No
Central	Wu-han[b]	–	None	No
	I-ch'ang[b]	–	None	No
South	Swatow	1	None	No
	Canton	5	Major	No
	Foochow	1	Some	Yes
	Chan-chiang	1	Major	Yes
	Hai-k'ou	1	None	No
	Yü-lin	1	None	No
	Pa-so	–	Major	No
Southwest	Chungking[b]	–	None	Yes

[a]Sources: Shui-yün Yün-chia Hui-pien (Consolidated Tariffs of Water Transportation) (Peking: 1959), No. 5, p. 18; People's Daily (Peking), July 4, 1956; Ta-kung Daily (Peking), December 8, 1956; Ibid., December 14, 1956; Ibid., December 28, 1956; Ibid., January 8, 1957; Ibid., February 17, 1957; Ta-kung (Hong Kong), February 11, 1954; Ibid., June 24, 1954; Ibid., July 4, 1955; Ibid., April 2, 1956; Ibid., July 12, 1957; Ibid., July 19, 1957; Ibid., October 1, 1957; Canton Daily, December 5, 1960; Southern Daily (Canton), December 4, 1956; Heilungkiang Daily (Harbin), November 3, 1961, Anhwei Daily (Ho-fei), February 20, 1957; Ibid., February 21, 1957; Hung I, Kung-fei Chiao-t'ung Chien-she chih Yen-chiu (A Study of Communication Construction in Communist China) (Taipei: 1957), pp. 174-180; Appendix E, Table E-4 of this report.

[b]River port.

Table 7-20

RAILWAY RADIAL COUNTS OF 19 PORTS
GROUPED BY ECONOMIC RANK INDEXES[a]

Rank Index	Region	Port	Railway Radial Counts
A	North	Tientsin	12
	East	Tsingtao	4
		Shanghai	17
		Nanking	12
	Central	Wu-han	12
	South	Canton	9
	Southwest	Chungking	4
	Group Average		10.00
	Average of All Rank A Cities		10.87
B	Northeast	Lü-ta	8
		Harbin	16
	South	Foochow	4
		Hai-k'ou	2
	Group Average		7.50
	Average of All Rank B Cities		8.00
C	Northeast	Chia-mu-ssu	4
	North	Ch'in-huang-tao	4
	East	Chefoo	4
		Lien-yün	8
		Ning-po	4
		Wen-chow	–
	South	Swatow	2
		Chan-chiang	4
	Group Average		3.75
	Average of All Rank C Cities		4.29

[a]Sources: The ports are taken from Table 7-19, and the rank indexes from Appendix E, Table E-2.

Table 7-21

RAILWAY RADIAL COUNTS OF 20 PORTS
GROUPED BY INDUSTRIAL
CAPACITY INDEXES[a]

Industrial Capacity Index	Region	Port	Railway Radial Counts
Large	North	Tientsin	12
	East	Shanghai	17
		Nanking	12
	Central	Wu-han	12
	South	Canton	9
	Southwest	Chungking	4
	Group Average		11.00
	Average of All Large Cities		14.00
Medium	Northeast	Lü-ta	8
		Harbin	16
	East	Tsingtao	4
	South	Foochow	4
		Swatow	2
	Group Average		6.80
	Average of All Medium Cities		6.49
Small	Northeast	Chia-mu-ssu	4
	North	Ch'in-huang-tao	4
	East	Chefoo	4
		Lien-yün	8
		Ning-po	4
		Wen-chou	–
	Central	I-ch'ang	–
	South	Chan-chiang	4
		Hai-k'ou	2
	Group Average		3.33
	Average of All Small Cities		2.82

[a]Sources: The ports are taken from Table 7-19, and the industrial capacity indexes from Appendix E, Table E-2.

means for all the cities of these ranks. With the exception of the large industrial centers, the reverse is true of the cities if they are examined in terms of industrial capacity instead of economic activity in general.

The differences between the averages for the port cities and the corresponding group averages are not large, which seems to indicate that the lack of a strong correlation between railway radial counts and industrial capacity within any group of cities (noted earlier in this chapter) cannot be explained by the possibility that water carriers are more intensively used where railways are not, and vice versa. On the contrary, large ports are also railway centers. The eight ports not on our list of principal economic and industrial centers are examples of pure port cities where railway and industrial development have not yet caught up with the development of waterway facilities.

Regional Profile of the Transport Plant

As a result of new construction and rehabilitation of previously existing routes, both railway and highway densities underwent considerable changes from 1949 to 1960 (Table 7-22). The regional profile of these density estimates is shown in Figure 7-4. When Figures 6-1 and 7-4 are compared, general improvements in all regions can be noted. In particular, however, the relatively greater improvement in highways is especially worth noting. The southwest-northeasterly configuration confirms our earlier suggestion that railway and highway installations complement rather than compete with each other.

Figure 7-4 also shows the gradual transition of less developed regions into more developed regions as may be seen in the shift of the national average densities and that of the regional positions with reference to them. Both Central and South China have railway and highway densities greater than the national average. They appear on the threshold of greater economic development--if and when economic expansion is resumed under the Third Five-Year Plan. [9]

General improvement in the transport plant is evident in Figure 7-5 although the lack of new regional data on waterway routes prevents a fully meaningful interpretation. Natural conditions limit inland waterway development to a greater degree than they do highway and railway construction. For this reason, such regions as Northwest and North China should perhaps be excluded, but a

Table 7-22

DENSITIES OF RAILWAY AND HIGHWAY
ROUTES IN 1960[a]

Region	Indicated Route Densities (km/1,000 km^2)	
	Railway	Highway
Developed Regions		
Northeast	12.4	49.0
East	6.8	46.9
North	4.2	13.1
Average	7.0	29.1
Underdeveloped Regions		
South	5.2 ⎫	
Central	5.0 ⎭	35.8
Northwest	1.2	11.4
Southwest	1.0	15.1
Average	1.9	17.5
National Mean	3.4	20.9

[a]Sources: Railway and highway lengths were taken
from Tables 7-4 and 7-15; area data were taken from
Appendix D, Table D-1.

Figure 7.4 Regional Railway and Highway Densities in 1960

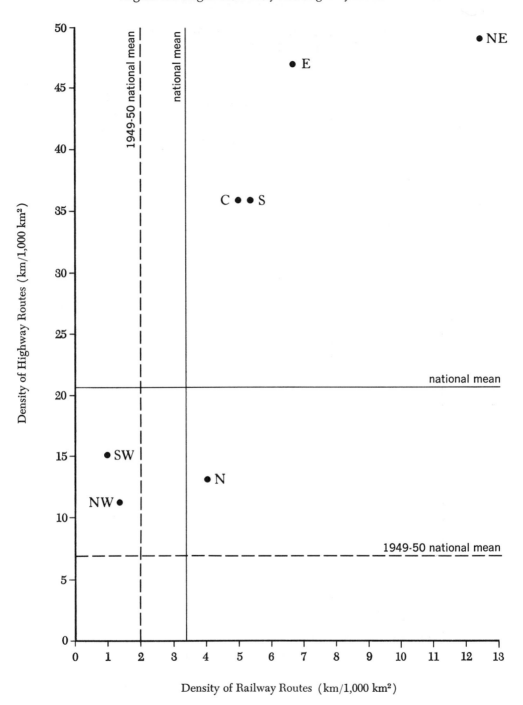

Figure 7.5 Regional Railway and Waterway Densities in 1960

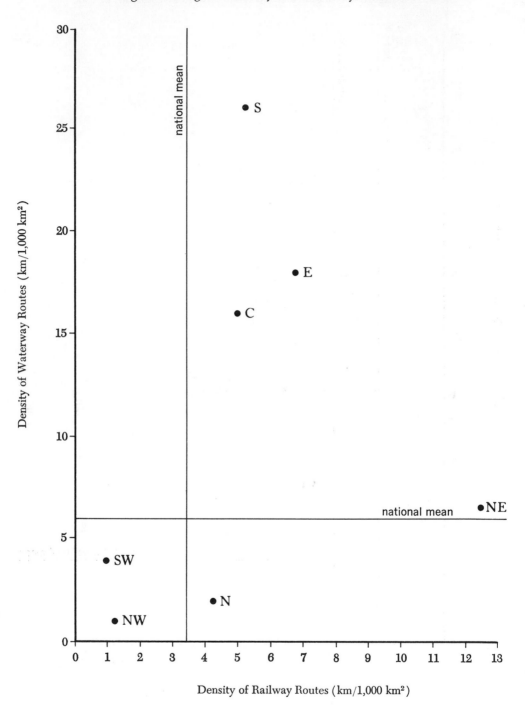

complementary relationship might exist between rail and waterway construction as well. This possibility is not fully established, partly because a growth in waterway traffic is much less a function of increase in route length than is the corresponding increase in railway and highway traffic.

Construction of Native Railways for Local Traffic

In conclusion, a word should be said about construction of railways without the use of standard steel rails and with the use of primitive vehicles. These constructions were common in Central and North China and were a counterpart of the "native" or semimodern steel plants built during the same period--"The Great Leap Forward." Scattered reports, as well as Lü Cheng-ch'ao's statement to the Communist Second National People's Congress in April 1960,[10] indicate that 2,400 kilometers of such lines were in operation in early 1960, and that another 694 kilometers were under construction. However, little progress was reported after April 1960, for the same figure of 2,400 kilometers was quoted in the People's Daily in February 1963.[11] The retrenchment policy pursued from 1961 to 1963 banned the construction of uneconomic industrial and other plants,[12] and consequently probably halted construction of native railways. The problem of expanding facilities for local traffic was apparently relegated once again to the highway sector.

According to one report,[13] 75 per cent of highway and 66 per cent of waterway traffic in 1958 were handled by native carriers or on poorly surfaced roads. Another report puts the total volume of short hauls at about the same time at 60 per cent of total traffic. Later, 70 per cent of the short hauls were said to be handled by native carriers.[14] This continued reliance on the traditional sector in local traffic, apparently a most serious transportation bottleneck, raises the question of whether a different emphasis in the allocation of investment in favor of feeder roads would not have been more appropriate, especially in the light of the shift of locational policy in favor of the more developed regions and the consequently large increase in traffic density in these areas. Such a policy would, of course, have had to be coordinated with an expansion of the production of petroleum products.

8 EFFICIENCY IN THE USE OF TRANSPORT INPUT

In a report to the first session of the Second National People's Congress in April 1959,[1] Lü Cheng-ch'ao, Communist China's Vice-Minister of Railways, stated that railway construction should take into account the location of existing manufacturing and mining plants and that attention should be given to the availability of rail transport when locations are selected for new plants. Specifically, he pointed out the desirability of locating steel mills in areas close to sources of ore and coal and of locating coking and coal concentration facilities at the coal mines. Such pronouncements, however commonplace, are illustrative of at least a vague awareness of the desirability of long-term coordination of transportation and locational policy, and of the need for minimization of transport input in current production.

This chapter discusses the efficiency shown by the economy in using the transport service in production and the operating efficiency of the transport plant itself. Again, attention is centered on the railway system, because of its importance and the relatively larger amounts of information available on it.

Interpretation of the Growth of Passenger and Freight Traffic

The movement of goods and persons takes place for two basic reasons. The first is what may be termed personal "consumption." People travel for pleasure, to visit friends and families, and to relocate for personal reasons. The incidental movement of their personal and household effects may be put in the same category. On the other hand, when persons travel on business, such passenger traffic is really an "intermediate good," a transport service used as input in the production of goods and services, including production in the transport sector itself. When transport service is regarded as an item of consumption, its increase represents an increase in economic welfare. When it is regarded as an intermediate good, it is a part of production cost. Any increase

174

must be related to the output to which it contributes. It is, therefore, incorrect to treat every expansion of traffic as a sign of successful economic development.

Since the beginning of the Communist regime in 1949, mainland China has experienced several large internal migratory movements. One occurred, for instance, when farm workers displaced by the organization of cooperative farms went to the cities to seek work. Following the agricultural crisis and the collapse of the "Great Leap Forward" in the late 1950's and early 1960's, another movement took place when hordes of hungry people moved from one locality to another to look for food. Other large-scale migrations occurred when city dwellers were sent back to the country under successive "hsia-fang movements." The last type of passenger traffic belongs in the same category as the compulsory movement of laborers. Such traffic is clearly an input for the production of other goods and services. Even the mass movement of "surplus" urban population to relieve local social and economic pressure may be regarded as input because the ostensible purpose is to prevent adverse economic effects.

Although no specific information is available on the division of passenger traffic into the consumption-oriented and production-oriented categories, the latter is probably quantitatively significant. Accordingly, the growth of passenger traffic during the Communist period would be expected to exceed the growth of personal consumption since personal consumption has usually lagged behind total output (Tables 8-1 and 8-2 and Figure 8-1). When reduced to a per capita basis (Table 8-3), the difference between the increase in passenger-kilometers per capita and the corresponding increase in per capita consumption, which is of course smaller than the discrepancy between the aggregate values of the two series, shows that the average Chinese travels more under the Communist regime than he did before. Furthermore, the increase exceeds that of consumption in general since his travels are probably more for business than for personal reasons.[2]

All freight traffic can be safely treated as an "intermediate good" since the movement of purely personal goods is probably negligible. A possibly disruptive factor is the movement of military equipment and supplies. Unfortunately, there is no information on the size of this traffic. There is a strong presumption that it is not included, in part or in full, in published traffic statistics.

175

Table 8-1

COMPARISON OF PASSENGER TRAFFIC AND PERSONAL
CONSUMPTION EXPENDITURE FROM 1949 TO 1960

Year	Number of Passengers[a] (million)	Passenger Traffic (million passenger-km) for Indicated Carrier				Personal Consumption[f] (billion 1952 yüan)
		Railways[b]	Waterways[c]	Highways[d]	Total[e]	
1949	102. 97	13,000 (126. 25)[g]	1,395	1,015	15,410	. . .
1950	156. 91	21,240 (135. 36)	1,540	1,120	23,900	. . .
1951	160. 37	23,052 (143. 74)	2,199	1,599	26,850	. . .
1952	163. 52	20,060 (122. 68)	2,658	1,952	24,670	53. 8
1953	228. 61	28,170 (123. 22)	3,482	3,168	34,820	50. 8
1954	232. 86	29,470 (126. 56)	3,690	3,740	36,900	53. 6
1955	208. 01	26,740 (128. 55)	3,519	4,931	35,190	55. 6
1956	252. 11	34,380 (136. 37)	4,638	7,362	46,380	62. 8
1957	312. 62	36,130 (115. 57)	4,550	8,810	49,490	63. 9
1958	345. 69	40,920 (118. 37)	5,040	11,100	57,060	70. 2
1959	480. 52	56,700 (118. 00)	7,798	14,252	78,750	67. 8
1960	530. 00	62,540 (118. 00)	8,686	15,634	86,860	54. 8

[a] The number of passengers figures for 1949 to 1958 are taken from Wei-ta ti Shih-nien (The Great Ten Years) (Peking: 1959), p. 133. The 1959 figure is from Jen-min Shou-t'se, 1960 (People's Handbook, 1960) (Peking: 1960), pp. 448-449; the 1960 figure is a plan estimate.

[b] The railway passenger traffic figures for 1949 to 1958 are taken from The Great Ten Years, op. cit. The figures for 1959 and 1960 are estimates based on the number of passengers and the average distance traveled in 1958 (118 km).

[c] The data include both inland and coastal traffic. The waterway passenger traffic figures for 1949 to 1951 are estimated by distributing the residual of total traffic less railway traffic in the ratio of 11 to 8, which were obtained in 1952. The 1952 and 1957 to 1959 figures are residuals. The 1953 to 1956 and 1960 figures are estimated at 10 per cent of the total passenger traffic, an average of the ratios obtained in 1952 (11 per cent) and in 1957 (9 per cent).

[d] The highway passenger traffic figures for 1949 to 1951 are estimated by distributing the residual of total traffic less railway traffic in the ratio of 11 to 8, which were obtained in 1952. The 1952 and 1957 to 1959 figures are from Highways in Communist China (Taipei: 1961), pp. 153-154. Estimates for 1953 to 1956 and 1960 are derived as residuals.

[e] The total passenger traffic figures for 1949 to 1958 are taken from The Great Ten Years, op. cit. The 1959 and 1960 figures are estimates derived from the corresponding figures for railways, the latter being assumed to be 72 per cent of the total as in 1958.

[f] The personal consumption figures are derived as GNP less gross domestic investment and government consumption from Yuan-li Wu et al., The Economic Potential of Communist China (Menlo Park, Calif.: Stanford Research Institute, 1963), Vol. I, pp. 241 and 340.

[g] The figures in parentheses indicate average distance traveled.

Table 8-2

INDEXES FOR PASSENGER TRAFFIC AND PERSONAL CONSUMPTION
EXPENDITURE FROM 1949 TO 1960[a]

| | Passenger Traffic Index for Indicated Carrier | | | | | | | | Personal Consumption Expenditure Index 1952=100 |
| Year | Railways | | Waterways | | Highways | | Total | | |
	1949=100	1952=100	1949=100	1952=100	1949=100	1952=100	1949=100	1952=100	
1949	100	65	100	52	100	52	100	62	...
1950	163	106	110	58	110	57	155	97	...
1951	177	115	158	83	158	82	174	109	...
1952	154	100	191	100	192	100	160	100	100
1953	217	140	250	131	312	162	226	141	94
1954	227	147	265	139	368	192	239	150	100
1955	206	133	252	132	486	253	228	143	103
1956	264	171	332	174	725	377	301	188	117
1957	278	180	326	171	868	451	321	201	119
1958	315	204	361	190	1,094	569	370	231	130
1959	436	283	559	293	1,404	730	511	319	126
1960	481	312	623	327	1,540	801	564	352	102

[a]Source: Table 8-1.

Figure 8.1 Indexes of Passenger Traffic on Railways, Waterways and
Highways and of Personal Consumption Expenditures from 1952 to 1960

(1952 = 100)

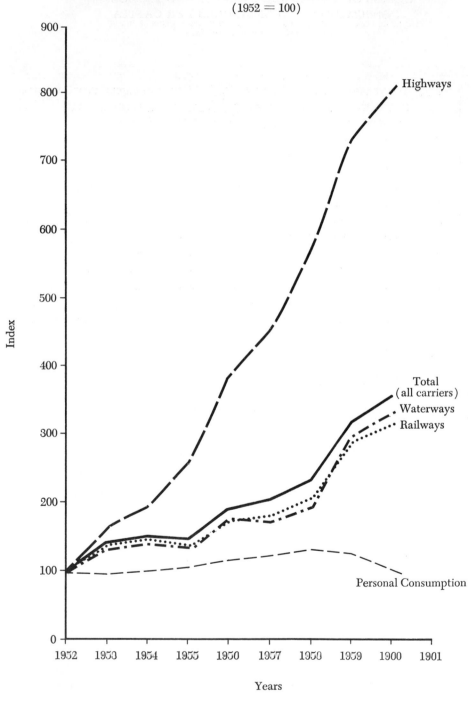

Table 8-3

INDEXES OF PASSENGER TRAFFIC AND PERSONAL
CONSUMPTION EXPENDITURES PER CAPITA
FROM 1952 TO 1960[a]

Year	Passenger Traffic Index	Personal Consumption Index 1952=100	Passenger Traffic Index Minus Personal Consumption Index	
1953	138	92	46	(47)[b]
1954	143	95	48	(50)
1955	133	97	36	(40)
1956	172	107	65	(71)
1957	179	106	73	(82)
1958	201	113	88	(101)
1959	272	107	165	(193)
1960	294	85	209	(250)

[a]Sources: Aggregate data are taken from Table 8-1. Population estimates used are midyear figures from Yuan-li Wu et al., The Economic Potential of Communist China (Menlo Park, Calif. : Stanford Research Institute, 1963), Vol. I, pp. 16 and 18.

[b]Figures in parentheses are the corresponding differences from Table 8-2.

Since we cannot isolate it, its rank as an intermediate good remains questionable.

Tables 8-4 and 8-5, as well as Figures 8-2 and 8-3, show that the growth rate of freight traffic was extremely high in the first two to three years of economic rehabilitation and again in the period from 1957 through 1960. Specifically, the annual increases in traffic were 46 per cent from 1949 to 1952 and 36.7 per cent from 1957 to 1960, as against 19.3 per cent from 1952 to 1957. If the entire period is taken into account, rail and waterway traffic progressed at comparable speeds with shipping showing a slight edge.[3] By far the fastest growing subsector, however, was highway traffic, which began to forge ahead after 1952. Taken at face value, these statistics indicate an extremely rapid growth of the transport sector consistent with an accelerated industrialization program.

Factors Underlying an Increase in the Transport Input Coefficient

Since freight traffic is essentially a measure of transport input used in production, the growth of freight traffic in Communist China is noticeably out of proportion to overall production growth. Table 8-6 gives total freight traffic by rail and inland and coastal shipping for 1952 to 1963. When these totals are divided by the corresponding gross domestic product, the quotient, which represents freight transport input per yüan of domestic product, shows an uninterruptedly rising trend from 1952 to 1961. The trend was then broken during the recovery in 1962 and 1963. The coefficient of freight transport input (per unit of output) rose from 0.95 ton-km in 1952 on the eve of the First Five-Year Plan to 1.73 ton-km in 1957, when the Plan ended. This figure more than doubled during the "Great Leap Forward," reaching 3.66 ton-km in 1960. As the domestic product sank in 1961, the coefficient rose again to a peak of 4.56 ton-km.

Several plausible reasons explain why an increase in the transport input coefficient might be expected. First, as local self-sufficiency gives way to greater geographical division of labor, an increased exchange of goods leads to greater demands on the transport sector. Increasing "metropolization" accentuates this tendency. The higher transport input per unit of output is presumably justified by savings in other costs (inputs) owing to newly gained access

Table 8-4

VOLUME OF FREIGHT CARRIED BY RAILWAYS, WATERWAYS,
AND HIGHWAYS FROM 1949 TO 1963

Year	Volume of Freight (million metric tons) on Indicated Carrier							
	Railways[a,b,d]		Waterways[a,c,d] (Inland and Coastal)		Highways[a,c,d]		Total[a,d]	
1949	55.89	(100)[e]	5.43	(100)	5.79	(100)	67.13	(100)
1950	99.83	(179)	6.65	(122)	9.21	(159)	115.69	(172)
1951	110.83	(198)	10.11	(186)	14.21	(245)	135.06	(201)
1952	132.17	(236)	14.32	(264)	22.10	(382)	168.59	(251)
1953	161.31	(289)	20.01	(369)	30.94	(534)	212.27	(316)
1954	192.88	(345)	28.75	(529)	43.03	(743)	264.67	(394)
1955	193.76	(347)	35.70	(657)	48.96	(846)	278.43	(415)
1956	246.05	(440)	46.96	(865)	79.13	(1367)	372.15	(554)
1957	274.20	(491)	53.77	(990)	83.73	(1446)	411.71	(613)
1958	381.09	(682)	76.36	(1406)	176.30	(3045)	633.76	(944)
1959	542.00	(970)	121.09	(2230)	343.95	(5940)	1,007.04	(1500)
1960	666.60	(1193)	150.91	(2779)	421.14	(7274)	1,238.65	(1845)
1961	540.00	(966)	142.00	(2615)	418.00	(7219)	1,100.00	(1639)
1962	577.50	(1033)	150.15	(2765)	427.35	(7381)	1,155.00	(1721)
1963	611.13	(1093)	158.89	(2926)	452.24	(7811)	1,222.26	(1821)

[a]The railway, waterway, highway, and total freight figures for 1949 to 1958 are taken from Wei-ta ti Shih-nien (The Great Ten Years) (Peking: 1959), p. 129. The 1959 figures are derived from a report by Li-Fu-ch'un on the 1960 economic plan.

[b]The railway freight figures for 1960 and 1961 are taken, respectively, from Liberation Army Daily, March 21, 1961, and Liberation Army Daily, April 28, 1963. The 1962 figure is estimated at 50 per cent of the total freight, according to Railway Traffic (Peking), No. 3, 1963.

[c]The 1960 waterway and highway freight figures are derived from a report by Li Fu-ch'un on the 1960 economic plan. The 1961 and 1962 figures are derived by apportioning railway, waterway, and highway freight in the same ratio as that of their shares in 1959.

[d]Derivation of the 1963 freight estimate is more complicated. First, according to returns from the Chi-nan, Ch'ang-sha, Shanghai, T'ai-yüan, Lan-chou and Liaoning Railway Administrations, consumer goods and agricultural products carried in local traffic to and from the villages amounted to 8.54 million tons. This volume was estimated at 15 per cent of total freight shipped locally in this manner; the total freight would then be 56.93 million tons. To the last figure we must add twice the amount to account for direct shipments between major urban centers, making the grand total for the six railway administrations 170.80 million tons. Second, the total route length under the six railway administrations was 32.14 per cent of the national total. Assuming equal traffic density for the remaining two-thirds of the railway system, total railway freight for the country as a whole would be 531.42 million tons. An addition equivalent to 15 per cent of the last figure to allow for traffic on the native railways brings the total to 611.13 million tons. Total freight by all carriers and by shipping and highway are then estimated by assuming the same percentage distribution as in 1962. See Tsingtao Daily, March 9, 1963; New Hunan Daily, March 11, 1963; Liberation Daily (Shanghai), March 16, 1963; Shansi Daily, December 12, 1962; Kansu Daily, January 7, 1963; Liaoning Daily, February 20, 1963; Honan Daily, October 12, 1959; Railway Traffic (Peking), No. 23, 1961; Hopeh Daily, March 17, 1963.

[e]Numbers in parentheses are the corresponding indexes.

Table 8-5

VOLUME OF FREIGHT TRAFFIC CARRIED BY RAILWAYS, WATERWAYS,
AND HIGHWAYS FROM 1949 TO 1963[a]

Year	Volume of Freight Traffic (billion ton-km) on Indicated Carrier			
	Railways	Waterways (Inland and Coastal)	Highways	Total
1949	18.40 (100)[b]	4.31 (100)	0.25 (100)	22.98 (100)
1950	39.41 (214)	2.90 (67)	0.38 (152)	42.69 (186)
1951	51.56 (280)	7.21 (167)	0.57 (228)	59.34 (258)
1952	60.16 (327)	10.61 (246)	0.77 (308)	71.54 (311)
1953	78.14 (425)	13.57 (315)	1.30 (520)	93.01 (405)
1954	93.24 (507)	18.64 (432)	1.94 (776)	113.83 (495)
1955	98.15 (533)	24.44 (567)	2.52 (1008)	125.12 (544)
1956	120.35 (654)	28.21 (655)	3.49 (1396)	152.06 (662)
1957	134.59 (731)	34.39 (798)	3.94 (1576)	172.93 (753)
1958	185.52 (1008)	43.91 (1019)	6.96 (2784)	236.40 (1029)
1959	265.58 (1443)	77.26 (1793)	15.48 (6192)	358.32 (1559)
1960	326.63 (1775)	96.28 (2234)	18.95 (7580)	441.86 (1923)
1961	264.60 (1438)	90.60 (2102)	18.81 (7524)	374.01 (1628)
1962	282.97 (1538)	95.80 (2223)	19.23 (7692)	398.00 (1732)
1963	299.45 (1627)	101.37 (2352)	20.35 (8140)	421.17 (1833)

[a]The 1949 to 1958 data are from Wei-ta ti Shih-nien (The Great Ten Years)(Peking: 1959), pp. 129-131. The 1959 to 1963 figures are estimated by multiplying the tonnage estimates in Table 8-4 by their respective average hauls for 1953 to 1958. The average haul estimates are as follows:

Year	Average Haul (km) of Freight Traffic on Indicated Carrier		
	Railways	Waterways	Highways
1953	484	678	42
1954	483	648	45
1955	507	685	51
1956	489	601	44
1957	491	640	47
1958	487	575	40
Average	490	638	45

The average haul is derived from the freight traffic data divided by the corresponding freight tonnage. This was done on the assumption that the discrepancy between tons originated and tons carried remained fairly stable in 1959 to 1963 and that tonnage statistics published are consistently of the same category.

[b]Numbers in parentheses are the corresponding indexes.

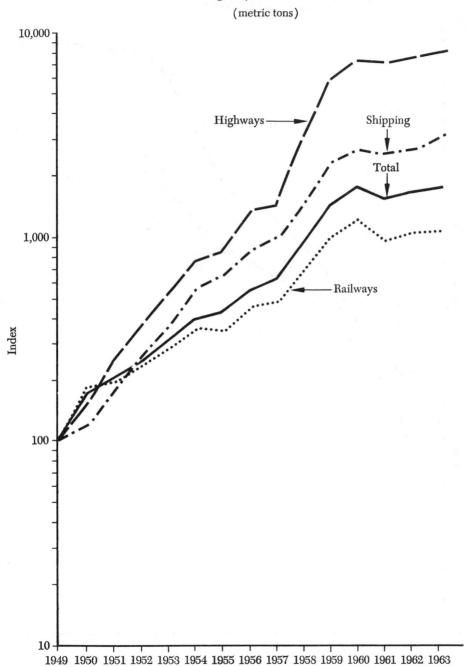

Figure 8.2 Indexes of Volume of Freight Carried by Railways, Waterways and Highways from 1949 to 1963

(metric tons)

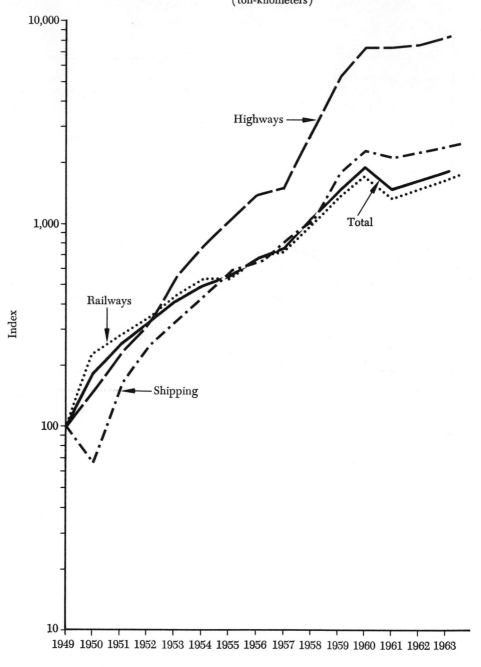

Figure 8.3 Indexes of Volume of Freight Traffic Carried by Railways, Waterways and Highways from 1949 to 1963

(ton-kilometers)

Table 8-6

COEFFICIENTS OF TRANSPORT INPUT
PER YÜAN OF GROSS DOMESTIC
PRODUCT FOR 1952 TO 1963

Year	Total Freight Traffic[a] (billion ton-km)	Gross Domestic Product (billion yüan)	Coefficient of Transport Input (ton-km/yüan)
1952	71.54	75.6	0.95
1953	93.01	78.9	1.18
1954	113.83	82.2	1.38
1955	125.12	86.1	1.45
1956	152.06	96.6	1.57
1957	172.93	100.0	1.73
1958	236.40	110.7	2.14
1959	358.32	119.1	3.01
1960	441.86	120.7	3.66
1961	374.01	82.1	4.56
1962	398.00	109.0	3.65
1963	421.17	113.9	3.70

[a]Source: Table 8-5.

[b]Source: Yuan-li Wu et al., The Economic Potential of Communist China (Menlo Park, Calif.: Stanford Research Institute, 1964), Vol. III, p.120, Table 27, and Appendix C, Table C-1.

to cheaper or more productive raw materials at greater distances.

Second, in a country with a large undeveloped hinterland, development in the more remote areas means that more goods have to be moved over longer distances. The transport input coefficient would thus increase until output in the hitherto remote and backward hinterland catches up. To the extent that development of remote areas is not emphasized, an increase in the transport input coefficient must be explained by greater geographical division of labor or other factors.

Third, an increase in transport input per unit of output may arise because of a larger proportion of goods produced in the "transport-intensive" sectors.

Finally, a "residual factor" is present which may be simply described as inefficiency and poor planning.

The precise effect of this factor in Communist China is not susceptible to complete statistical analysis except as we will show later in this chapter, but it has evidently been considerable. In fact, numerous items of evidence occur in official records, some in the form of condemnations of transport officials and others in announced rectifications of procedures. A curious example which received wide publicity in the mid-1950's was the accolade given a "labor hero," a locomotive engineer, who made the remarkable discovery that he could reduce lubricating costs by mixing his oil with water.

The human factor aside, Communist China has been handicapped by inadequate supplies of rolling stock, poorly designed and constructed roadbeds, and overaged equipment. Most existing lines in 1949 dated back several decades and no substantial improvements or additions had been made for many years. Wartime damage, too, was heavy. Given these conditions, a high level of operating efficiency would be surprising.

Comparison of the Transport Input Coefficients of the Soviet Union, United States and Japan

The first two factors in the preceding discussion seem to apply at first glance quite definitely for Communist China. Careful analysis, however, shows that this is not necessarily true. A comparison with the experience of other countries is therefore pertinent.

The GNP of the Soviet Union at 1937 factor cost rose from 215. 6 billion rubles in 1937 to 322. 4 billion rubles in 1950.[4] During the same period, freight traffic by rail, highway, inland and coastal waterway, and pipe line rose from 417. 74 billion ton-km to 700. 30 billion ton-km.[5] These figures yield 1. 94 and 2. 17 ton-km per ruble of GNP in 1937 and 1950, respectively--an increase of 12 per cent. During the same period, the average railway freight haul increased by five per cent from 686 kilometers to 722 kilometers,[6] while the average waterway traffic haul increased from 494 kilometers to 502 kilometers. Highway traffic hauls decreased very slightly, from 10. 9 kilometers to 10. 8 kilometers. There was, therefore, no significant change in the transport input coefficient (per unit output) in terms of traffic, and the change in terms of tonnage alone was even less noticeable. This growth is in sharp contrast to the increase of nearly 285 per cent in transport input in Communist China in 1952-60 or the 112 per cent increase during the "Great Leap" period alone.

In the United States, the transport input coefficient in freight ton-miles (including rail, highway, inland waterway, and pipeline traffic) per dollar of GNP fluctuated between a low of 4. 79 in 1939 to a high of 6. 46 in 1947. The change from 1939 to 1953, a period which spanned both World War II and the Korean war, was from 4. 79 ton-miles to 5. 76 ton-miles, a 20 per cent increase.[7] The average haul by rail in a comparable period rose from 351. 13 miles (1940) to 416. 32 miles (1950), and that of inland waterway freight traffic increased from 237. 8 miles to 392 miles. There was little increase in the transport input coefficient measured in freight tonnage.

During the post-World War II economic expansion, the transport input coefficient in Japan declined slightly from 13. 37 ton-km per 1,000 yen of GNP (at 1956 prices) in 1950 to 12. 35 ton-km per 1,000 yen in 1959.[8] It may be presumed that there was little change in the average haul so that a similar decline probably occurred in unit transport input in terms of freight tonnage.

These comparisons make it plausible to postulate that periods of rapid economic development need not be associated with large increases in transport input per unit of output either in terms of freight traffic or in terms of freight tonnage. Communist China's experience seems to present, therefore, certain unique features.

As noted in Table 8-6, the average haul by rail remained stable between 1952 and 1957 when there was an 82 per cent increase in ton-kilometers per yüan of GNP. This increase in freight tonnage input was significant, but, until the end of the First Five-Year Plan, there was relatively little traffic to and from areas at a great distance from established economic centers. In this period, Chinese locational policy stressed the establishment of new economic centers in the more developed rather than in the less developed areas even though the tendency was to locate them away from the coastal provinces. The exploitation of the existing railway network in developing new economic centers served to increase traffic over comparable distances. The development of the more remote areas from 1953 to 1957 was insufficient to affect the average haul, but this situation changed materially during and after the "Great Leap Forward" period. Development of the more remote areas was given greater emphasis and an increase in the average haul may have occurred. If so, estimated freight traffic in Table 8-5 is understated. The same comment would apply to the already high transport input coefficient in ton-kilometers noted above.

Transport Input Coefficient and Industrial Development

Two factors remain to be considered as plausible explanations for the increase in transport input in ton-kilometers, other than simple inefficiency or the underestimate of the gross domestic product. The last possibility could not, however, explain away the large increase in the coefficient of transport input. These factors are a greater geographical division of labor, as a result of accelerated industrialization and the increasing integration of formerly separated, if not isolated, regional markets, and the expansion of "transport-intensive" sectors of the economy.

The increase in the geographical division of labor is greater at the beginning of the integration of a national economy than at later stages when an integrated economy is already in existence. In particular, the process of building new industries tends to increase the demand for inputs not produced on the spot. Compared with nonindustrial production, industrial production requires a greater transport input coefficient, because of greater use of raw materials produced by others. Accelerated industrial development, coupled with the integration of a fragmented economy, may, therefore, increase the transport

188

input coefficient more than it would after the economy has already reached a stage of advanced industrialization. This hypothesis is supported by the experience of the Soviet Union if the comparison is made between 1928 and 1937 instead of between 1937 and 1950. The transport input coefficient per ruble of GNP at factor cost increased from 0.82 ton-km in 1928 to 1.94 ton-km in 1937. This 137 per cent increase in nine years compares with a 125 per cent increase between 1952 and 1958 in Communist China. It can be argued that Chinese industrialization during the First Five-Year Plan was closer to the early Soviet model than to the more mature and developed economies of the United States or Japan.

According to Yin,[9] data can be aggregated for the total railway freight tonnage of coal and coke, petroleum products, ferrous metals, metal ores, timber, and cement during 1950 and 1955 to 1958 inclusive. These items constitute the bulk of industrial products and raw materials that require railway freight transport input. The aggregate tonnage statistics, multiplied by the average hauls for railway freight traffic, provide annual estimates in ton-kilometers. If the ton-kilometer estimates are then divided by corresponding estimates of gross value output, the quotient represents transport input in ton-kilometers per yüan of value output of modern industry (Table 8-7). Since the value output figures are considerably larger than corresponding estimates of values-added, it follows that the corresponding transport input per yüan of gross value-added would be larger.

Some significant characteristics are as follows: (1) the higher transport input coefficient of the modern industry sector (Table 8-7) compared with the mean input coefficient per yüan of domestic product noted in Table 8-6; (2) the relative stability of this input coefficient when a comparison is made between 1955 and 1957; and (3) the more rapid advance of the same coefficient between 1950 and 1955 and again in 1957 to 1958 with the onset of the "Great Leap Forward."

The following are still much in evidence: (1) the rise of the average input coefficient per yüan of domestic product as a result of the expansion of the industrial sector, which is more "transport-intensive" throughout the period under study and (2) the additional boost given to the input coefficient in the first phase of economic recovery and integration (1950 to 1955 in Table 8-7) and later, during the "Great Leap."

Table 8-7

ESTIMATE OF RAILWAY TRANSPORT INPUT OF MODERN INDUSTRIAL SECTOR
BASED ON FREIGHT TRAFFIC OF KEY INDUSTRIAL MATERIALS[a]

Year	Volume of Coal and Coke, Petroleum Products, Metal Ores, Ferrous Metals, Timber and Cement (million metric tons)	Average Haul (km)	Freight Traffic (billion ton-km)	Modern Industrial Output (billion 1952 yüan)	Modern Industrial Gross Value-Added (billion 1952 yüan)	Transport Input Coefficient (ton-km/yüan) for Output	Transport Input Coefficient (ton-km/yüan) for Gross Value-Added
1950	32.55	490	15.95	13.5	...	1.18	...
1955	108.21	507	54.86	35.6	15.1	1.54	3.63
1956	128.33	489	62.75	45.0	19.8	1.39	3.17
1957	155.13	491	76.17	49.7	21.9	1.53	3.48
1958	225.72	487	109.93	61.0	27.1	1.80	4.06

[a]For metric tons of freight, see A. I. Yin, "Railroad Transport in the Chinese People's Republic," J. P. R. S., No. 3484, July 6, 1960, p. 72. The average haul estimates for 1955 to 1958 are taken from Table 8-5. For 1950, the 1953 to 1958 average of 490 km is used. The industrial output data and the GNP estimates for 1955 to 1958 are taken from Yuan-li Wu et al., The Economic Potential of Communist China (Menlo Park, Calif.: Stanford Research Institute, 1963), Vol. I. The 1950 modern industry output estimate is derived in the same manner on the basis of equations in the same volume on pages 213 and 217. The electric power output of finished steel used in the equations are 2,737 million kw-hr and 463,000 metric tons, respectively. Allowance is made for the value output of the power plants themselves.

In the light of events during these periods, we can assume that some of the sharper increases must be attributed to inefficiency and planning errors.

Inefficient Planning and Execution of Plans

Inefficient planning or execution of plans has been the subject of considerable discussion since 1958. This discussion involves the distinction between (1) excessive use of transport input associated with a rise of freight traffic and (2) excessive use of the transport plant not necessarily reflected in an increase in freight traffic but, nevertheless, giving rise to higher than necessary transport costs.

Several causes can be singled out for the first category. First, transport input may be unnecessarily increased because of the need to ship more goods as a result of high spoilage or other transit losses. Second, transport input may be unnecessarily increased because of the planners having disregarded transport costs. Third, the demand for transport may be unnecessarily exaggerated because of the method used in distribution and transportation planning. In fact, the obstacles to the minimization of transport input lie in the planning system itself. Finally, transport input may become greater than necessary because of poor locational planning.

Railway equipment shortages in 1952 and during the first phase of the First Five-Year Plan tempted the Communist Chinese to overload railway cars and to put as many cars as possible in each train. This effort to increase both the train and the carload increased the deterioration of rolling stock and also added to the waste of goods in transit. However, little has been heard of this practice since 1956. As the First Five-Year Plan approached completion, thinking on means to increase transport capability shifted to additional double-tracking, station facilities, signals en route, equipment in marshalling yards, and rolling stock. The ineffectiveness of a policy calling for overloaded trains was apparently realized.[10] However, as late as 1963, there continued to be constant complaints about the large volume of goods damaged in transit. Many examples are concerned especially with the distribution of such goods as chemical fertilizers to farm communities.[11] Waste in transit also occurs in warehouses and at transshipment or concentration points where goods are inadequately stored while awaiting shipment.

191

Another complaint about inefficient use of transportation during the recent economic crisis was the practice on the part of many enterprises of shipping products to prospective markets without prior knowledge of the size or nature of the demand. This was said to be especially common in the marketing of industrial products in rural communities. Following the call to concentrate industrial effort on agricultural needs, some industries followed the directive literally but without considering the demand for their particular products.[12,13] The failure to match supply to demand is not a unique problem that occurs only when producers are pressed to ship goods. It is a far more general problem involving the allocation of resources in response to changes in market demand. If the planning system is incapable of resolving this issue adequately, waste of transport, as well as general waste of resources in inevitable.[14]

Examples of wastefulness in shipments from production centers to markets abound in Chinese economic literature. According to one article, large quantities of coal had been shipped from the Chiao-tso coal mine in Honan to Manchuria where local supplies were readily available.[15] Other large shipments were regularly made from the Huai-nan coal mine in Anhwei Province (East China) to Wu-han, although East China has consistently been a coal deficit area. Logically, coal should have been imported from the P'ing-ting-shan mine which is far closer to the Wu-han market. Again, coal was shipped eastward from Kuan-yin-t'ang in Honan while the same kind of coal was being shipped westward from the Feng-feng and Chiao-tso mines--a typical instance of cross-hauling. Another example is the shipment of coal for household consumption from Yang-ch'üan in Shansi to Peking where local coal from Men-t'ou-kou was available, even though there may have been some quality difference. Even coal from Manchuria was shipped to the Shantung peninsula, which is well supplied by local sources.

Why such disregard of the need to minimize transport input? Until 1959, when an attempt was made to decentralize planning and to balance commodity supply and demand within individual regions, balancing supply and demand was the concern of the central government ministries responsible for the various industrial branches. These ministries performed their functions on an industry and national basis, and failed to relate buyers to their nearest suppliers. The

192

result was excessive long-distance hauling and cross-hauls. Where there were only a few large suppliers, the likelihood of such aberations rose. As late as 1957, some 30 per cent of the iron ore used at the An-shan steel complex had to be shipped in from China proper, which added 20 yüan per ton of ore to the cost.[16]

However, even after the 1959 planning "reform," the adoption of administrative supply areas (such as provinces) and the rigidity of the boundaries often caused the shipment of goods from distant suppliers within the area rather than from nearby suppliers outside the designated area.[17] One effort to reduce waste of transport input in 1963 was the relaxation of rigid boundary rules.

A far more important cause of waste of transport resources was the practice of shipping goods by circuitous routes through a series of points of concentration in the distribution network instead of directly from supplier to consumer. According to the Ta-kung Daily,[18] before agricultural products could reach the consumer, they had to pass through a local collection point, a point of concentration in the town, a county center, an urban specialized trading company, a processing factory, if needed, and finally a retail store. If a portion of these goods was to be redistributed to another rural area, a reverse movement through an almost equal number of distribution points was required. When the collection of agricultural products, including grains, cotton, and other items, was stepped up in the "Great Leap Forward," the volume of traffic back and forth reached monumental proportions and was a major factor causing delay and bureaucratic confusion.[19] Furthermore, a large proportion of the transport needed for local distribution was provided by human labor, and the inability of the labor force to meet demands became a serious bottleneck which contributed to the downturn of the economy in 1960.[20]

The same factors hampered the flow of industrial goods from urban areas to rural consumers. As the Ta-kung Daily reported,[21] goods had to go through a chain of central wholesale warehouses, provincial wholesale centers, and county wholesale stations before reaching retail outlets in the villages. A reform, which began in the latter part of 1962 and continued through 1963, focused on the reduction of these circuitous routes through the institution of direct shipment from the factory to the railway station, or from the warehouse directly to the consumer. How far these efforts have been successful remains to be seen.

Another factor causing high transportation input is less apparent--the practice of using "transfer prices" to regulate the supply of goods from one government enterprise to another. According to Fan Jo-i,[22] transfer prices are established on a regional basis by combining production cost, enterprise profit, and an average transportation cost. The gross price paid by a purchaser is not necessarily related to actual transport cost. In fact, sometimes the actual freight paid exceeds the transportation cost incurred, or vice versa (freight absorption). The advantage of purchasing from a nearby supplier rather than from one farther away is eliminated in a manner reminiscent of basing point and zone pricing systems in other countries.

Transport cost is often higher than necessary because of poor planning for industrial plant location. For example, a number of Chinese coal mines do not have coal concentration plants, and the coal has to be shipped to other mines for concentration. This expensive hauling of waste materials was so commonplace that during the "Great Leap Forward," the coal concentration process was bypassed, which led to an even greater waste of transportation and a further decline in production efficiency.

Not all locational problems could be avoided, however. As long as industrial plant construction is limited by lack of capital or of indispensable imported equipment, site selection will require a number of compromises. No substantial improvement can be expected until further economic development can take place. On the other hand, a recent study of the steel industry of Communist China indicates that locational planning errors resulting in regional intraindustry imbalance have been excessive and greater than necessary.[23]

Other failures to minimize transportation input have resulted from hurried industrial development and underestimation of the need for transport facilities. A lack of coordination has been evident, according to an article in Planned Economy,[24] in the development of the oil resources of the Tsaidam basin and at Karamai. Because road construction was not given enough attention initially, delays in the development of the oil fields were a serious concern.

Equipment Utilization and Transport Cost

Excessive transportation cost associated with unnecessary freight movement is one aspect of a larger complex. In addition, higher transport input, even in unavoidable freight movements, is caused by the poor utilization of railway equipment. The consequences of haphazard use of this equipment include empty runs, delays in switching and transfer of rolling stock and engines, delays in loading and unloading at terminals, multiplication of loadings and unloadings because of poor transshipment arrangements, crowding at marshalling yards, and other factors that increase the time needed for moving freight from one point to another.

Transport authorities in Communist China have attempted to increase the average daily operation of engines and freight cars and to reduce the turn-around time of the freight cars. Through their efforts, the average daily run of railway locomotives increased from 308. 7 kilometers in 1949 to 336. 7 in 1950 and 396. 8 in 1952.[25] Similarly, the freight car average increased from 154. 9 kilometers in 1949 to 233. 1 in 1951 and 255. 6 in 1958.[26] The average turn-around time for freight cars was reduced from 4. 39 days in 1949 to 2. 9 days in 1952 and 2. 47 days in 1959.[27] However, mainly because of technical limitations, increases were more difficult to achieve for train and car loads and for train speeds, which remained between 360 and 370 km per day during most of the period of the Five-Year Plan after having reached a peak in 1952. Further increases in efficiency and in reduced transport cost can only be achieved by reducing transport input through improved planning outside the transport sector. In short, the Chinese Communists have found from experience that it is not enough to be able to ship goods from point A to point B with the most efficient use of equipment and expenditure of time if it would have been better to make the shipment from A to C. Their goal should be to maximize profits rather than to minimize losses.

Linear Programming and Other Measures to Minimize Transport Input

To correct the wasteful expenditure of transport input, Communist China's planners instituted a set of regulations for the "rational transport" of

195

a number of key commodities, including coal and coke, petroleum, timber, salt, iron ore, and cement--six principal commodities using bulk railway transport. These regulations were promulgated in the early part of 1959.[28] Little is known about their details except that by 1963 linear programming had apparently been used to solve "transportation problems. " It was first used in the solution of the direction of coal shipments in Manchuria and later in the solution of similar problems on a national scale.[29] Linear programming is used to prepare direction or flow charts for transportation of key commodities; exceptions to these flow charts must be authorized in advance.

Still other measures for the reduction of transport input have included additional local freight stations, greater use of joint transport (railways and highway or railways and waterways), decreased loading and unloading time, and other techniques to increase traffic volume including the development of "native" carrier routes by road and small river traffic.[30] But the difficulties confronting local distribution remain.

Freight Rates and Minimization of
Transport Input

It is not clear whether the "objective function, " employed in linear programming solutions in Communist China, consists of the minimization of transportation cost or of ton-kilometers. There has been discussion of minimizing ton-kilometers, which would not necessarily correspond to a minimization of transport cost. Effective use of linear programming should refer to total transport cost and must, of course, rely upon certain data on unit transportation and other incidental costs. For instance, freight rates charged on different categories of commodities over varying distances must reflect the transport input used. Furthermore, deficits and surpluses of goods available for transportation must themselves reflect the result of rational allocation of resources.

The railway freight rate tables (Appendix F)[31] show that up to a certtain point the rates are progressively lower per freight unit as the distance increases. After this point has been passed, the rate ceases to decrease or begins to rise. The distance in kilometers over which the tariff declines depends on the commodity--an apparently conscious arrangement planned to discourage shipments over extremely long distances but, except for this reservation, to reflect the lower unit costs for shipments over longer distances. The same rule applies to waterway traffic.

One would assume that minimization of transportation input could be accomplished if producers outside the transport sector were free to select their suppliers on the basis of a system of freight rates reflecting true transportation cost, or if transportation routes were selected for them on the basis of freight cost minimization. One difficulty lies in the fact that transport input has both a space and a time dimension. Although movement over a long distance results in a low unit transport cost in the current operation of the transport sector, it also ties up transportation equipment over a longer period. The delay may also have an adverse effect on production. This cost factor can be assessed if appropriate interest charges are made on equipment tied up in transit and are made a part of the transportation cost the shipper is to pay. The obstacle lies in the aversion of the Communist planning system to interest charges. The same ideological difficulty has prevented Communist Chinese planners from adjusting commodity prices to changing conditions of supply and demand or from calculating the rate of return over investment rather than over cost.[32] Without flexible pricing, it is next to impossible to eliminate wasteful shipment, although such waste can be reduced by methods such as linear programming.

9 SUMMARY AND CONCLUSIONS

The Questions (Chapters 1 and 5)

What is the effect of the spatial arrangement of Chinese economic activities on the development program of the country as a whole? In particular, has the spatial aspect of Chinese economic planning served to promote or impede general development? What is the degree of coordination between transportation and locational policies? Has Communist China as a planned economy been able to make better locational arrangements than a market economy might have? Has the spatial arrangement been sufficiently flexible over time and has a degree of flexibility been secured at reasonable cost?

An evaluation of Communist Chinese locational policy must be preceded by a proper definition of the optimum. This definition requires the choice of a definite time dimension as the planning horizon. Because of imperfect knowledge about resources and their geographical distribution, flexibility in planning has special virtue. But flexibility, as hinted above, may also entail a cost.

How stable is the planning horizon? If and when it is changed, will the change adversely affect the future? Will it vitiate the accomplishment of the past?

Some Historical Background (Chapters 1 and 6)

Before the establishment of the Communist regime, the Chinese economy was characterized by the following spatial features:

1. Modern industry was heavily concentrated in a few centers. Outside Manchuria, not more than 18 cities in 13 provinces could be regarded as principal industrial centers.

2. Again excluding Manchuria, East China and North China ranked first in terms of motive power, employment, and number of factories in modern manufacturing. Together with Manchuria (or Northeast China), the three regions

198

constituted the relatively more developed regions in contrast to the remaining underdeveloped regions of the country.

3. Five of seven coastal provinces--Hopeh, Shantung, Kiangsu, Fukien, and Kwangtung (omitting Chekiang and Liaoning)--accounted for 80 per cent of the number of factories and amount of employment and 90 per cent of the motive power in modern manufacturing. There were, however, exceptional enclaves in the division of the country into the developed coastal areas and the less developed inland provinces. Similar exceptions existed in the decision between the developed and the less developed regions under (2) above.

4. Eight of the 26 provinces and autonomous regions, based on the administrative divisions of the Communist period, had no railways in operation in 1949-50. There was also great variance in railway density. Of railway trackage in operation 42 per cent was in the seven coastal provinces (the seven mentioned above) as against 58 per cent in 19 inland provinces and autonomous regions. Seventy-seven per cent of the same total trackage was located in the economically more developed regions [Manchuria or Northeast China, North China, (including Inner Mongolia), and East China] as compared with 23 per cent in the less developed regions (Central, Northwest, Southwest, and South China). The density averages were 5 km per 1,000 km^2 in the more developed regions as against 1 km per 1,000 km^2 in the underdeveloped regions.

5. Five of the seven relatively more developed provinces in both industry and agriculture were coastal. Hupeh and Szechwan were the inland exceptions. The underdeveloped provinces, except Fukien, were generally in western China.

In 1952, with the economy about to begin a more rapid development, more than half of the gross receipts of the transport sector was still derived from obsolescent and inefficient traditional carriers. This figure may be compared with an estimate of 68 per cent in 1933 before the war with Japan. The major portion of long distance freight traffic was carried on 26,700 kilometers of railways, of which 82 per cent had been in operation at the end of 1949. Less than 60 per cent of the highway routes, which were five times longer than those of the railways, were in operation at the time. Inland waterways, which were twice as long as the railway network, carried only a small portion of the traffic. The developed regions had only 30 per cent of navigable inland waterways and

42 per cent of the better surfaced highways. This geographical distribution in favor of the less developed regions was the reverse of the railway pattern.

Ostensible Policy (Chapters 1, 5, and 6)

The stated goals of Communist China's locational policy are as follows: (1) to correct the "irrational" pattern of the pre-Communist spatial economy; (2) to establish new economic and industrial centers closer to raw materials and consumer markets; (3) to strike a proper balance between intraregional self-sufficiency and interregional specialization; (4) to enhance national security, evaluation of which has, however, changed with increasing appreciation of the rising vulnerability of inland provinces to modern long-range weapons systems; (5) to allow for requirements in international geopolitics; and (6) to develop medium and small cities in the interior rather than large cities on the coast. As evidence of the last, the number of "above-norm" construction projects in the interior provinces during the First Five-Year Plan were twice as many as in the coastal areas. This emphasis, however, was modified in 1956.

The announced transport policy was to expand the use of inland waterways and highways to reduce traffic congestion on railways and to increase railway operating efficiency. To support this policy, 59 per cent of the planned total investment in transportation and communications under the First Five-Year Plan was assigned to railways, 16 per cent to highways and waterways, 9 per cent to local transportation, and 1 per cent to air transport. It was further planned to allocate 41.7 per cent of the railway investment to new railway construction, 32.7 per cent to improvements of the existing network, and 21.5 per cent to equipment additions. The remaining 4.1 per cent was allocated to investment in design and construction workshops.

Several guidelines are used to coordinate transportation and locational policies in China. First, new industrial centers should be established close to fixed natural resources and the transport plant expanded to serve these new centers. Second, the transport plant in the economically more developed regions should be expanded but chiefly where it appears inadequate to permit further economic development. Third, if defense and political considerations can be ignored, the transport plant should not be expanded for noneconomic

reasons. Finally, extension of the transport plant to the economically less developed regions should be undertaken to spearhead development. The amount
of expansion would depend on the planning horizon of the planners.

Changes in the Pattern of the Spatial Economy

Population Growth in Cities (Chapter 2)

An analysis of population growth of 117 municipalities from 1953 to 1958
showed 67 per cent (or 6) more large cities (population over one million) and
26 per cent (or 7) more medium cities (population between 300,000 and
1,000,000). In comparison with the 1948 to 1953 period, when the rate of increase was greater for medium cities, the rate of "metropolization" was
stepped up in the following five years.

As of 1958, the most important market and supply areas, as represented
by large and medium cities were in the provinces of Liaoning, Hopeh, and
Kiangsu (East, Northeast, and North China). Development effort between 1953
and 1958 was concentrated in the more developed regions, but with a lower priority given the coastal provinces. This finding is substantiated when cities are
grouped according to absolute increments in population and population growth
rates. The developed regions had eight large economic centers, which were
further expanded during this period, in contrast to three such centers in the
less developed regions. Twenty three cities experienced intensive population
growth in the developed regions as against twelve in the less developed regions.
The ambivalence between population growth in the coastal provinces as compared with the inland provinces seems to reflect a midcourse change in policy.

Industrial Capacity in Cities (Chapter 3)

In terms of industrial capacity, based mainly on plant data weighted by
the gross value-added, the most important center in Communist China is Shanghai, followed at a considerable distance by Tientsin, Wu-han, and An-shan. The
dependence on the established industrial metropolis, Shanghai, is greater than
has been officially admitted or generally realized.

The degree of industrial concentration is further illustrated by the fact
that one half the country's modern industrial capacity is in three provinces--

Kiangsu, Hopeh, and Liaoning. The same was true in the pre-Communist period. Two-thirds of total capacity is in the five most industrialized provinces--the preceding three, plus Hupeh and Szechwan. Furthermore, the seven coastal provinces have twice as many large industrial centers as the inland provinces. The same ratio is obtained between developed and underdeveloped regions. There are, however, fewer medium industrial centers in the coastal provinces than in the inland provinces, although the number per province is larger in the coastal group. The economically developed regions again have more medium industrial centers than the less developed regions. An even greater degree of concentration is found in coastal (versus inland) provinces and in developed (versus less developed) regions if the comparison is made in terms of industrial capacity rather than in the number of large or medium industrial centers.

The degree of concentration may also be seen in the fact that in the country as a whole, nine large industrial centers account for about 60 per cent of total industrial capacity, and the 57 medium industrial centers represent only 31 per cent. The degree of industrial specialization varies inversely with the size of the location and the stage of its development. Diversity, on the other hand, is not limited to the large centers only.

Economic Ranking of Cities (Chapter 4)

An analysis of the economic ranking of 117 cities showed that 73 per cent of Rank A cities are in the coastal provinces and in the developed regions. The economically developed regions account for 60 per cent of Rank B cities, but 70 per cent are in inland provinces. Most (57 per cent) identified new industrial centers of Ranks B and C are in the developed regions, and even more (81 per cent) are in inland provinces. The relatively heavier emphasis given to the developed regions as against the coastal provinces in medium cities and secondary or new industrial centers is unmistakable, but the large established industrial metropolises are still concentrated in the coastal provinces. Note should be taken, however, of exceptional enclaves in the larger areas conveniently designated as "developed" and "less" or "under-developed," respectively.

Of 124 identified industrial projects receiving Soviet aid prior to mid-1960, 56 were in Rank A cities, 45 in Rank B cities, and 23 in Rank C cities.

Eighty per cent of Rank A cities, 60 per cent of Rank B cities, and 16 per cent of Rank C cities had Soviet aid projects. More cities receiving aid and more Soviet aid projects were in the developed regions than in the less developed regions. The same pattern prevailed for the Rank B and Rank C cities in the inland provinces, but the reverse was true for the Rank A cities. The role played by Soviet aid planners in the choice of project sites may have a substantial effect on Chinese industrial locations.

During the period under study, Honan, Hunan, and Anhwei, all inland provinces, moved from the ranks of the industrially underdeveloped and agriculturally developed into a sector in which both industry and agriculture are relatively more developed. Shansi and Inner Mongolia moved to the industrially developed sector. These shifts constitute notable changes from the pre-Communist spatial pattern of provinces.

Expansion in the Transport Sector (Chapter 7)

From 1949 to 1963, railway trackage increased 123 per cent, and railway route length increased 56 per cent. The annual rate of increase averaged 5.9 per cent for trackage and 3.25 per cent for route length. The highest rate of trackage increase was seven per cent in 1954-55. The highest annual rate of increase attained in railway route length was eight per cent in 1955-56. From 1953 to 1960, the increase in the length of highways was 56 per cent, and most of this increase was in the less developed regions.

Railway construction has been concentrated in the northwestern region (including both Northwest China proper and parts of Inner Mongolia bordering on the Northwest) and in South and Southwest China. The less developed regions accounted for 80 per cent of total new railway construction under the Communists through 1963. The largest increment in rail density, however, was in South China.

Expansion of the existing transport plant through double-tracking and the like grew after 1955, corresponding roughly to the shift of emphasis in locational planning to the developed regions. Considered as a response to the increase in volume of railway traffic in these areas, it was, however, insufficient.

Railway Construction and Economic Development (Chapter 7)

The average count of railway radials of the Rank A cities was 10.9, which compares with a count of eight for Rank B cities and 4.3 for Rank C cities. Railway radial counts averaged 14 for large industrial centers, 6.5 for medium centers, and 2.8 for small centers. It appears, however, that small variations in railway radial counts, representing railway development within any given group of cities of a particular size or economic ranking, have no marked economic effect.

An examination of the new economic centers established under the Communist regime shows that the ratio of the number of new centers on new lines to the total number of new centers located on old lines plus old centers on new lines was 17.4 per cent. This ratio reflects in part a greater emphasis on establishing new centers and adding to the transport plant of old centers in the developed regions than in the less developed regions.

In terms of route length, 51 per cent of new railway lines built are military or connecting lines. These two categories include twelve of the 30 lines built up to 1963. A significant proportion (at least 11.9 per cent) of the new lines were evidently built to speed economic development, since they do not serve existing markets. On the other hand, many lines were built through areas with known natural resources. The emergence of new market areas will presumably follow the development of these resources.

This approach is, from all indications, a product of Communist planning rather than an inheritance from the Nationalist period. The absence of a historical relationship in this sense is perhaps more pronounced in transportation development than in other sectors of the economy.

The development of highways and railways has apparently been complementary. Where more new railways have been built, more new highways have also been constructed. Only in the more developed areas has the construction of short feeder roads been significant.

Use of Transportation Input (Chapter 8)

During this period, passenger traffic grew faster than personal consumption. The growth of railway freight traffic averaged 46 per cent a year from

1949 to 1952, 19.3 per cent from 1952 to 1957, and 36.7 per cent from 1957 to 1960. Growth in waterway and highway freight traffic was even faster. However, in terms of ton-kilometers, railway traffic in 1963 was nearly fifteen times greater than highway traffic and about three times greater than inland and coastal waterway traffic.

Railway freight input in total production measured by ton-kilometers per yüan of gross domestic product increased from 0.95 ton-kilometer in 1952 to 3.66 in 1960 and 4.56 in 1961. This rate of increase was contrary to the experience in Japan and the United States and greater than a similar increase in the Soviet Union from 1928 to 1937. The following explanations of the increase are offered: (1) increasing geographical division of labor followed by more integration and "metropolization"; (2) a change in the composition of the total output with an increase in the proportion of "transport-input-intensive" goods; (3) the attempted development of remote areas; and (4) inefficient management and planning. The first three are characteristic of an initial stage of industrial growth, but the third was apparently not quantitatively important for Communist China, because the average haul remained nearly stable during most of the period.

Inefficiency in management and planning was an important factor. It may be broken down into several categories: (1) waste in transit; (2) shipment of goods without prior determination of market demand; (3) the early parctice of balancing supply and demand of key commodities by industrial branches and, since 1959, rigidly bounded supply areas with supply and demand balanced on a zonal basis; (4) the long series of intermediary agencies handling the distribution of goods; (5) inclusion of average transportation cost in a uniform "transfer price," thus eliminating differential transport costs from consideration; and (6) poor locational planning as shown by intraindustry imbalances at certain locations of major industries.

Improvement in equipment utilization has not offset planning errors. Linear programming and other operational research methods are used to minimize transportation input, but two basic problems remain: (1) freight rates, usually set on a declining scale as the length of the haul is increased do not allow for interest charges on tied-up transport equipment and (2) commodity prices are not responsive to changing conditions of supply and demand. These two problems are, however, fundamental to the planning system as a whole and not to the transport sector alone.

Adequacy of Investment

The First Five-Year Plan allocated 5.67 billion yüan to investment in railway transport. Of this amount. 2.37 billion yüan was earmarked for the construction of new railways. Actual investment was probably higher. With estimated cost construction at 400,000 yüan per km, the total in 1953 and 1954 amounted to 3.73 billion yuan, well in excess of the planned investment. The apparent shift in locational planning in 1956 to greater emphasis on the development of existing economic centers and the economically more developed regions as against new centers and the less developed regions, makes it appear that insufficient funds were allocated for the improvement of the existing transport network. Because of the greater unit transport input required, traffic congestion became a major obstruction to economic development during the period of the "Great Leap Forward." Even in the economic crisis of 1960 to 1962, when rail traffic declined, the same difficulties in local short-distance traffic had not been resolved, despite the increased attention paid the subject by Communist authorities.

Change in the Planning Horizon

If the original proposals in the First Five-Year Plan had been carefully followed, the gradual development of the less developed areas and the inland provinces would have been reasonably well coordinated with transportation policy. However, after a large proportion of new railway construction had been completed in the less developed regions, locational policy--but not transportation development--shifted to planning favoring the more developed regions. Consequently, one may question the economic viability of the many small new economic and industrial centers, which have only just begun to emerge. When long-term planning gives way to near-term improvisation, many advantages arc lost. Improvisation may bc incvitablc if unoxpootod diffioultioo havo to bo met. However, if such difficulties arise as a direct consequence of economic policy, one may question whether the original goals were realistic.

Communist Chinese planners were fairly skillful in formulating locational and transportation plans in the first two Five-Year Plans. The results were, however, marred by the "great depression" of 1960 to 1962. Even if Chinese locational planning has been moderately competent, the planners have failed to anticipate the instability of the economic system. The relative efficiency of Chinese locational planning cannot be compared with that of a market economy without a comparison of their respective vulnerability to economic fluctuation. The Chinese Communist model has shown serious deficiencies in this aspect of planning. Both the theory of location and that of economic fluctuations need to be examined more closely within the context of planned economies.

POPULATION DATA

Table A-1

POPULATIONS OF THE 117 MUNICIPALITIES HAVING
POPULATIONS OVER 100,000 IN 1953 OR 1958 MIDYEAR[a, b]

Province	City	Population (1,000 Persons)			Population Change (%) (1958=100)
		in 1953	in 1958	Increase	
Northeast China					
Liaoning	Mukden	2,300	2,423	123	5
	Lü-ta	892	1,590	698	78
	Fu-shun	679	1,019	340	80
	An-shan	549	833	284	52
	Pen-ch'i	449	449	0	0
	Chin-chou	352	400	48	14
	An-tung	360	370	10	3
	Fou-hsin	189	290	101	53
	Liao-yang	147	169	22	15
	Ying-k'ou	131	161	30	23
Kirin	Ch'ang-ch'un	855	988	133	16
	Kirin	435	583	148	34
	Liao-yüan	120	177	57	48
	T'ung-hua	129	158	29	22
	Ssu-p'ing	126	130	4	3
Heilungkiang	Harbin	1,163	1,595	432	37
	Ch'i-ch'i-ha-erh	345	704	359	104
	Chi-hsi	35	253	218	623
	Mu-tan-chiang	151	251	100	66
	Chia-mu-ssu	146	232	86	59
	Ho-kang	90	200	110	122
	I-ch'un	35	200	165	471
	Shuang-ya-shan	35	110	75	214

Table A-1 (continued)

Province	City	Population (1,000 Persons)			Population Change (%) (1958=100)
		in 1953	in 1958	Increase	
North China					
Hopeh	Peking	2,768	4,148	1,380	50
	Tientsin	2,694	3,278	584	22
	T'ang-shan	693	812	119	17
	Shih-chia-chuang	373	623	250	67
	Kalgan	343	480	137	40
	Han-tan	125	380	255	204
	Pao-ting	197	250	53	27
	Ch'in-huang-tao	187	210	23	12
	Ch'eng-te	93	120	27	29
Shansi	T'ai-yüan	721	1,053	332	46
	Ta-t'ung	228	243	15	7
	Yang-ch'üan	177	200	23	13
	Ch'ang-chih	98	180	82	84
	Yü-t'zu	60	100	40	67
Inner Mongolia	Pao-t'ou	149	490	341	229
	Huhehot	148	320	172	116
	Chi-ning	30	100	70	203
East China					
Kiangsu	Shanghai	6,204	6,977	773	12
	Nanking	1,092	1,455	363	33
	Hsü-chou	373	710	337	90
	Soochow	474	651	177	37
	Wu-hsi	582	616	34	6
	Ch'ang-chou	296	300	4	1
	Nan-t'ung	260	240	-20	-8
	Hsin-hai-lien	208	210	2	1
	T'ai-chou	160	200	40	25
	Chen-chiang	201	190	-11	-5
	Yang-chou	180	160	-20	-11
	Ch'ang-shu	101	101	0	0
Shantung	Tsingtao	917	1,144	227	25
	Tsinan	680	882	202	30
	Tzu-po	259	875	616	238
	Wei-fang	149	190	41	28
	Chefoo	116	140	24	21
Anhwei	Ho-fei	184	360	176	96
	Pang-fou	253	330	77	30
	Huai-nan	287	280	-7	-3
	Wu-hu	242	240	-2	-1
	An-ch'ing	105	129	24	23

Table A-1 (continued)

Province	City	Population (1,000 Persons) in 1953	in 1958	Increase	Population Change (%) (1958=100)
Chekiang	Hangchow	697	794	97	14
	Ning-po	238	280	42	18
	Wen-chou	202	210	8	4
	Shao-hsing	131	160	29	22
	Chia-hsing	78	132	54	69
	Hu-chou	63	120	57	90
Central China					
Kiangsi	Nan-ch'ang	398	520	122	31
	Ching-te-chen	92	266	174	189
Honan	Cheng-chou	595	785	190	32
	Lo-yang	171	500	329	192
	K'ai-feng	299	318	19	6
	Chiao-tso	35	250	215	614
	Hsin-hsiang	170	203	33	19
	Shang-ch'iu	134	165	31	23
	An-yang	125	153	28	22
Hunan	Ch'ang-sha	651	709	58	9
	Hsiang-t'an	184	247	63	34
	Heng-yang	235	240	5	2
	Chu-chou	127	190	63	50
	Shao-yang	118	170	52	44
Hupeh	Wu-han	1,427	2,226	799	56
	Huang-shih	110	135	25	23
South China					
Kwangsi	Nan-ning	195	260	65	33
	Liu-chou	159	190	31	20
	Kweilin	145	170	25	17
	Wu-chou	111	120	9	8
Kwangtung	Canton	1,599	2,200 [c]	601	38
	Hai-k'ou	135	402	267	198
	Swatow	280	250	-30	-11
	Chan-chiang	166	170	4	2
	Fo-shan	122	120	-2	-2
	Chiang-men	85	110	25	29
	Ch'ao-chou	101	101	0	0
Fukien	Foochow	553	623	70	13
	Amoy	224	308	84	38
	Ch'üan-chou	108	110	2	2
Northwest China					
Shensi	Sian	787	1,368	581	74
	Pao-chi	130	180	50	38

Table A-1 (continued)

| Province | City | Population (1,000 Persons) | | | Population Change (%) (1958=100) |
		in 1953	in 1958	Increase	
Sinkiang	Urumchi	141	320	179	127
	Kashgar	91	100	9	10
	I-ning	108	85	-23	-21
Kansu	Lan-chou	397	732	335	84
	Yin-ch'uan[d]	84	91	7	8
Tsinghai	Hsi-ning	94	150	56	60
Southwest China					
Szechwan	Chungking	1,847	2,165	318	17
	Ch'eng-tu	857	1,135	278	32
	Tzu-kung	291	280	-11	-4
	Nan-ch'ung	165	206	41	25
	I-pin	178	190	12	7
	Nei-chiang	190	180	-10	-5
	Wu-t'ung-chiao	199	140	-59	-26
	Lu-chou	289	130	-159	-55
Kweichow	Kuei-yang	271	530	259	96
Yunnan	K'un-ming	699	900	201	29
	Ko-chiu	160	180	20	13

[a]This table includes the cities for which population data are available for both 1953 and 1958. The cities in each province are arranged in order of population size in 1958.

[b]Morris B. Ullman, Cities of Mainland China: 1953 and 1958 (Washington, D. C.: Bureau of the Census, Foreign Manpower Research Office, U. S. Department of Commerce, 1961), Series P-95, No. 59, p. 2.

[c]Source: Geographical Knowledge, No. 2, 1959, p. 73.

[d]Although this city had a population under 100,000 in both 1953 and 1958, it is included because of its importance as a trade center in the area.

Table A-2

POPULATIONS OF THE 98 MUNICIPALITIES HAVING POPULATIONS
OVER 100,000 IN 1948 OR 1953 MIDYEAR[a]

Province	City	Population (1,000 Persons)			Population Change (%) (1948=100)
		in 1948	in 1953	Increase	
Northeast China					
Liaoning	Mukden	1,121	2,300	1,179	105
	Lü-ta	569	892	323	57
	Fu-shun	513	679	166	32
	An-shan	166	549	383	231
	Pen-ch'i	321	449	128	40
	Chin-chou	148	352	204	138
	An-tung	271	360	89	33
	Fou-hsin	180	189	9	5
	Liao-yang	110	147	37	34
	Ying-k'ou	159	131	-28	-18
Kirin	Ch'ang-ch'un	630	855	225	36
	Kirin	247	435	188	76
	Liao-yüan	185	120	-65	-35
	T'ung-hua	80	129	49	61
	Ssu-p'ing	76	126	50	66
Heilungkiang	Harbin	760	1,163	403	53
	Ch'i-ch'i-ha-erh	175	345	170	97
	Mu-tan-chiang	200	151	-49	-25
	Chia-mu-ssu	168	146	-22	-13
North China					
Hopeh	Peking	1,603	2,768	1,165	73
	Tientsin	1,686	2,694	1,008	60
	T'ang-shan	137	693	556	401
	Shih-chia-chuang	198	373	175	88
	Kalgan	151	343	192	127
	Han-tan	30	125	95	32
	Pao-ting	130	197	67	52
	Ch'in-huang-tao	100	187	87	87
Shansi	T'ai-yüan	200	721	521	261
	Ta-t'ung	80	228	148	185
Inner Mongolia	Pao-t'ou	82	149	67	82
	Huhehot	104	148	44	42
East China					
Kiangsu	Shanghai	4,423	6,204	1,781	40
	Nanking	1,230	1,092	-138	-11
	Hsü-chou	340	373	33	10
	Soochow	381	474	93	24

213

Province	City	Population (1,000 Persons)			Population Change (%) (1958=100)
		in 1948	in 1953	Increase	
	Wu-hsi	273	582	309	113
	Ch'ang-chou	239	296	57	24
	Nan-t'ung	226	260	34	15
	Hsin-hai-lien	125	208	83	66
	T'ai-chou	131	160	29	22
	Chen-chiang	179	201	22	12
	Yang-chou	127	180	53	42
	Ch'ang-shu	64	101	37	58
Shantung	Tsingtao	788	917	129	16
	Tsinan	575	680	5	1
	Wei-fang	134	149	15	11
	Chefoo	227	116	-111	-49
	Wei-hai	175	35	-140	-80
Anhwei	Ho-fei	153	184	31	20
	Pang-fou	201	253	52	26
	Wu-hu	204	242	38	19
	An-ch'ing	109	105	-4	-4
Chekiang	Hangchow	570	697	127	22
	Ning-po	210	238	28	13
	Wen-chou	157	202	45	29
	Shao-hsing	92	131	39	42
Central China					
Kiangsi	Nan-ch'ang	267	398	131	49
	Chiu-chiang	121	65	56	46
Honan	Cheng-chou	150	595	445	297
	Lo-yang	60	171	11'	185
	K'ai-feng	300	299	1	0
	Shang-ch'iu	70	134	64	91
	An-yang	115	125	10	9
	Chou-k'ou	104	121	17	16
Hunan	Ch'ang-sha	396	651	255	64
	Hsiang-t'an	133	184	51	38
	Heng-yang	184	235	51	28
	Chu-chou	7	127	120	1,714
	Shao-yang	106	118	12	11
Hupeh	Wu-han	910	1,427	517	57
	Huang-shih	28	110	82	293
South China					
Kwangsi	Nan-ning	200	195	-5	-3
	Liu-chou	194	159	-35	-18
	Kweilin	131	145	14	10
	Wu-chou	207	111	-96	46

Table A-2 (continued)

Province	City	Population (1,000 Persons)			Population Change (%) (1948=100)
		in 1948	in 1953	Increase	
Kwangtung	Canton	1,414	1,599	-185	13
	Hai-k'ou	60	135	75	125
	Swatow	215	280	65	30
	Chan-chiang	271	166	-105	-39
	Fo-shan	96	122	26	27
	Ch'ao-chou	60	101	41	68
Fukien	Foochow	331	553	222	67
	Amoy	158	224	66	42
	Ch'üan-chou	121	108	-13	-11
Northwest China					
Shensi	Sian	503	787	284	56
	Pao-chi	56	130	86	154
Sinkiang	Urumchi	88	141	53	60
Kansu	Lan-chou	204	397	193	95
Southwest China					
Szechwan	Chungking	1,040	1,847	807	78
	Ch'eng-tu	727	857	130	18
	Tzu-kung	223	291	68	30
	Nan-ch'ung	60	165	105	175
	I-pin	80	178	98	123
	Nei-chiang	32	190	158	49
	Lu-chou	50	289	239	478
Kweichow	Kuei-yang	240	271	31	13
Yunnan	K'un-ming	300	699	399	133
	Ko-chiu	16	160	144	900

[a]Sources: Appendix A, Table A-1; and Morris B. Ullman, Cities of Mainland China: 1953 and 1958 (Washington, D. C. : Bureau of the Census, Foreign Manpower Research Office, U. S. Department of Commerce, 1961), Series P-95, p. 2.

CITIES RANKED BY 1948, 1953, AND 1958 POPULATIONS[a]

Rank No.	Rank of Cities in 1948	Rank of Cities in 1953	Rank of Cities in 1958
1	Shanghai	Shanghai	Shanghai
2	Tientsin	Peking	Peking
3	Peking	Tientsin	Tientsin
4	Canton	Mukden	Mukden
5	Nanking	Chungking	Wu-han
6	Mukden	Canton	Canton
7	Chungking	Wu-han	Chungking
8	Wu-han	Harbin	Harbin
9	Tsingtao	Nanking	Lü-ta
10	Harbin	Tsingtao	Nanking
11	Ch'eng-tu	Lü-ta	Sian
12	Ch'ang-ch'un	Ch'eng-tu	Tsingtao
13	Tsinan	Ch'ang-ch'un	Ch'eng-tu
14	Hangchow	Sian	T'ai-yüan
15	Lü-ta	T'ai-yüan	Fu-shun
16	Fu-shun	K'un-ming	Ch'ang-ch'un
17	Sian	Hangchow	K'un-ming
18	Ch'ang-shu	T'ang-shan	Tsinan
19	Soochow	Tsinan	Tzu-po
20	Hsü-chou	Fu-shun	An-shan
21	Foochow	Ch'ang-shu	T'ang-shan
22	Pen-ch'i	Cheng-chou	Hangchow
23	K'ai-feng	Wu-hsi	Cheng-chou
24	K'un-ming	Foochow	Lan-chou
25	Wu-hsi	An-shan	Hsü-chou
26	Chan-chiang	Soochow	Ch'ang-shu
27	An-tung	Pen-ch'i	Ch'i-ch'i-ha-erh
28	Nan-ch'ang	Kirin	Soochow
29	Kirin	Nan-ch'ang	Foochow
30	Kuei-yang	Lan-chou	Shih-chia-chuang
31	Ch'ang-chou	Hsü-chou	Wu-hsi
32	Chefoo	Shih-chia-chuang	Kirin
33	Nan-t'ung	An-tung	Kuei-yang
34	Tzu-kung	Chin-chou	Nan-ch'ung
35	Swatow	Ch'i-ch'i-ha-erh	Lo-yang
36	Ning-po	Kalgan	Pao-t'ou
37	Wu-chou	K'ai-feng	Kalgan
38	Wu-hu	Ch'ang-chou	Pen-ch'i
39	Lan-chou	Tzu-kung	Hai-k'ou
40	Pang-fou	Lu-chou	Chin-chou
41	Mu-tan-chiang	Huai-nan	Han-tan
42	Nan-ning	Swatow	An-tung

Table A-3 (continued)

Rank No.	Rank of Cities in 1948	Rank of Cities in 1953	Rank of Cities in 1958
43	T'ai-yüan	Kuei-yang	Ho-fei
44	Shih-chia-chuang	Nan-t'ung	Pang-fou
45	Liu-chou	Tzu-po	Urumchi
46	Liao-yüan	Pang-fou	Huhehot
47	Heng-yang	Wu-hu	K'ai-feng
48	Fou-hsin	Ning-po	Amoy
49	Chen-chiang	Heng-yang	Ch'ang-chou
50	Wei-hai	Ta-t'ung	Fou-hsin
51	Ch'i-ch'i-ha-erh	Amoy	Tzu-kung
52	Chia-mu-ssu	Hsin-hai-lien	Ning-po
53	An-shan	Wen-chou	Huai-nan
54	Ying-k'ou	Chen-chiang	Ching-te-chen
55	Amoy	Wu-t'ung-ch'iao	Nan-ning
56	Wen-chou	Pao-ting	Chi-hsi
57	Ho-fei	Nan-ning	Mu-tan-chiang
58	Kalgan	Nei-chiang	Swatow
59	Cheng-chou	Fou-hsin	Chiao-tso
60	Chin-chou	Ch'in-huang-tao	Pao-ting
61	T'ang-shan	Ho-fei	Hsiang-t'an
62	Wei-fang	Hsiang-t'an	Ta-t'ung
63	Hsiang-t'an	Yang-chou	Heng-yang
64	T'ai-chou	I-pin	Wu-hu
65	Kweilin	Yang-ch'üan	Nan-t'ung
66	Pao-ting	Lo-yang	Chia-mu-ssu
67	Yang-chou	Hsin-hsiang	Hsin-hai-lien
68	Hsin-hai-lien	Chan-chiang	Ch'in-huang-tao
69	Ch'üan-chou	Nan-ch'ung	Wen-chou
70	Chin-chiang	Ko-chiu	Nan-ch'ung
71	An-yang	T'ai-chou	Hsin-hsiang
72	Liao-yang	Liu-chou	Yang-ch'üan
73	An-ch'ing	Mu-tan-chiang	T'ai-chou
74	Shao-yang	Pao-t'ou	I-ch'un
75	Chou-k'ou	Wei-fang	Ho-kang
76	Huhehot	Huhehot	Chen-chiang
77	Ch'in-huang-tao	Liao-yang	Wei-fang
78	Fo-shan	Chia-mu-ssu	Chu-chou
79	Shao-hsing	Kweilin	Liu-chou
80	Urumchi	Urumchi	I-pin
81	Pao-t'ou	Hai-k'ou	Ko-chiu
82	I-pin	Shang-ch'iu	Nei-chiang
83	T'ung-hua	Shao-yang	Pao-chi
84	Ta-t'ung	Ying-k'ou	Ch'ang-chih
85	Ssu-p'ing	Pao-chi	Liao-yüan
86	Shang-ch'iu	T'ung-hua	Chan-chiang
87	Ch'ang-sha	Chu-chou	Kweilin

217

Table A-3 (continued)

Rank No.	Rank of Cities in 1948	Rank of Cities in 1953	Rank of Cities in 1958
88	Lo-yang	Ssu-p'ing	Shao-yang
89	Hai-k'ou	Han-tan	Liao-yang
90	Ch'ao-chou	An-yang	Shang-ch'iu
91	Nan-ch'ung	Fo-shan	Ying-k'ou
92	Pao-chi	Liao-yüan	Shao-hsing
93	Lu-chou	Shao-yang	Yang-chou
94	Nei-chiang	Chefoo	T'ung-hua
95	Han-tan	Wu-chou	An-yang
96	Huang-shih	Huang-shih	Hsi-ning
97	Ko-chiu	I-ning	Wu-t'ung-ch'iao
98	Chu-chou	Ch'üan-chou	Chefoo
99	--	An-ch'ing	Huang-shih
100	--	Ch'ang-shu	Chia-hsing
101	--	Ch'ao-chou	Lu-chou
102	--	Ch'ang-chih	Ssu-p'ing
103	--	Hsi-ning	An-ch'ing
104	--	Ch'eng-te	Hu-chou
105	--	Ching-te-chen	Fo-shan
106	--	Kashgar	Wu-chou
107	--	Ho-kang	Ch'eng-te
108	--	Chiang-men	Shuang-ya-shan
109	--	Yin-ch'uan	Ch'üan-chou
110	--	Chia-hsing	Chiang-men
111	--	Hu-chou	Ch'ao-chou
112	--	Yü-tzu	Ch'ang-shu
113	--	Chiao-tso	Chi-ning
114	--	Chi-hsi	Yü-tzu
115	--	I-ch'un	Kashgar
116	--	Shuang-ya-shan	Yin-ch'uan
117	--	Chi-ning	I-ning

[a]Sources: Appendix A, Tables A-1 and A-2.

Table A-4

DISTRIBUTION BY SIZE OF 101 CITIES HAVING POPULATIONS OVER 100,000 IN 1953[a]

Province	Cities Having Indicated Populations									
	1 Million or above	900,000 to under 1 Million	800,000 to under 900,000	700,000 to under 800,000	600,000 to under 700,000	500,000 to under 600,000	400,000 to under 500,000	300,000 to under 400,000	200,000 to under 300,000	100,000 to under 200,000
Northeast China (19 Cities)										
Liaoning	Mukden		Lü-ta		Fu-shun	An-shan	Pen-ch'i	Chin-chou An-tung		Fou-hsin Liao-yang Ying-k'ou
Kirin			Ch'ang-ch'un				Kirin			Liao-yüan T'ung-hua Ssu-p'ing
Heilungkiang	Harbin							Ch'i-ch'i-ha-erh		Mu-tan-chiang Chia-mu-ssu
North China (13 Cities)										
Hopeh	Peking Tientsin				T'ang-shan			Shih-chia-chuang Kalgan		Han-tan Pao-ting Ch'in-huang-tao
Shansi				T'ai-yüan					Ta-t'ung	Yang-ch'üan
Inner Mongolia										Huhehot Pao-t'ou
East China (26 Cities)										
Kiangsu	Shanghai Nanking					Wu-hsi	Soochow	Hsü-chou	Ch'ang-chou Nan-t'ung Hsin-hai-lien Chen-chiang	T'ai-chou Yang-chou Ch'ang-shu
Shantung		Tsingtao			Tsinan				Tzu-po	Wei-fang Chefoo
Anhwei									Huai-nan Pang-fou Wu-hu	Ho-fei An-ch'ing
Chekiang					Hangchow				Ning-po Wen-chou	Shao-hsing
Central China (14 Cities)										
Kiangsi								Nan-ch'ang		
Honan						Cheng-chou			K'ai-feng	Lo-yang Hsin-hsiang Shang-ch'iu An-yang

Table A-4 (continued)

	Cities Having Indicated Populations									
Province	1 Million or above	900,000 to under 1 Million	800,000 to under 900,000	700,000 to under 800,000	600,000 to under 700,000	500,000 to under 600,000	400,000 to under 500,000	300,000 to under 400,000	200,000 to under 300,000	100,000 to under 200,000
Hunan					Ch'ang-sha				Heng-yang	Hsiang-t'an Chu-chou Shao-yang
Hupeh	Wu-han									Huang-shih
South China (13 Cities)										
Kwangsi										Nan-ning Liu-chou Kweilin Wu-chou
Kwangtung	Canton								Swatow	Hai-k'ou Chan-chiang Fo-shan Ch'ao-chou
Fukien						Foochow			Amoy	Ch'üan-chou
Northwest China (5 Cities)										
Shensi				Sian						Pao-chi
Sinkiang										Urumchi I-ning
Kansu								Lan-chou		
Southwest China (11 Cities)										
Szechwan	Chungking		Ch'eng-tu						Tzu-kung Lu-chou	Nan-ch'ung I-pin Nei-chiang Wu-t'ung-chiao
Kweichow									Kuei-yang	
Yunnan					K'un-ming					Ko-chiu
Total	9	1	3	2	6	4	3	8	18	47

[a]Source: Appendix A, Table A-1.

220

Table A-5

DISTRIBUTION BY SIZE OF 117 CITIES HAVING POPULATIONS OVER 100,000 IN 1958[a]

Province	Cities Having Indicated Population									
	1 Million or above	900,000 to under 1 Million	800,000 to under 900,000	700,000 to under 800,000	600,000 to under 700,000	500,000 to under 600,000	400,000 to under 500,000	300,000 to under 400,000	200,000 to under 300,000	100,000 to under 200,000
Northeast China (23 Cities)										
Liaoning	Mukden Li-ta Fu-shun		An-shan				Pen-ch'i Chin-chou	An-tung	Fou-hsin	Liao-yang Ying-k'ou
Kirin		Ch'ang-ch'un				Kirin				Liao-yüan T'ung-hua Ssu-p'ing
Heilungkiang	Harbin			Ch'i-ch'i-ha-erh					Chi-hsi Mu-tan-chiang Chia-mu-ssu Ho-kang I-ch'un	Shuang-ya-shan
North China (17 Cities)										
Hopeh	Peking Tientsin		T'ang-shan		Shih-chia-chuang		Kalgan	Han-tan	Pao-ting Ch'in-huang-tao	Ch'eng-te
Shansi	T'ai-yüan									
Inner Mongolia							Pao-t'ou	Huhehot		Chi-ning
East China (28 Cities)										
Kiangsu	Shanghai Nanking			Hsü-chou	Soochow Wu-hsi			Ch'ang-chou	Nan-t'ung Hsin-hai-lien T'ai-chou	Chen-chiang Yang-chou Ch'ang-shu
Shantung	Tsingtao		Tsinan Tzu-po							Wei-fang Chefoo
Anhwei								Ho-fei Pang-fou	Huai-nan Wu-hu	An-ch'ing
Chekiang				Hangchow					Ning-po Wen-chou	Shao-hsing Chia-hsing Hu-chou

Table A-5 (continued)

Province	Cities Having Indicated Population									
	1 Million or above	900,000 to under 1 Million	800,000 to under 900,000	700,000 to under 800,000	600,000 to under 700,000	500,000 to under 600,000	400,000 to under 500,000	300,000 to under 400,000	200,000 to under 300,000	100,000 to under 200,000
Central China (16 Cities)										
Kiangsi						Nan-ch'ang			Ching-te-chen	
Honan				Cheng-chou		Lo-yang		K'ai-feng	Chiao-tso Hsin-hsiang	Shang-ch'iu An-yang
Hunan				Ch'ang-sha					Hsiang-t'an Heng-yang	Chu-chou Shao-yang
Hupeh	Wu-han									Huang-shih
South China (14 Cities)										
Kwangsi									Nan-ning	Liu-chou Kweilin Wu-chou
Kwangtung	Canton						Hai-k'ou		Swatow	Chan-chiang Fo-shan Chiang-men Ch'ao-chou
Fukien					Foochow			Amoy		Ch'üan-chou
Northwest China (7 Cities)										
Shensi	Sian									Pao-chi
Sinkiang								Urumchi		Kashgar
Kansu				Lan-chou					Yu-men	
Tsinghai										Hsi-ning
Southwest China (12 Cities)										
Szechwan	Chungking Ch'eng-tu								Tzu-kung Nan-ch'ung	I-pin Nei-chiang Wu-t'ung-chiao Lu-chou
Kweichow						Kuei-yang			Tsun-i	
Yunnan		K'un-ming								Ko-chiu
Total	15	2	4	6	4	4	5	9	28	40

aSource: Appendix A, Table A-1.

Table A-6

DISTRIBUTION OF CITIES BY ABSOLUTE AND RELATIVE POPULATION
CHANGES BETWEEN 1953 AND 1958[a, b]

| | Cities in Indicated Group | | | |
Province	Group I	Group II	Group III	Group IV
Northeast China				
Liaoning	Mukden	Lü-ta Fu-shun An-shan Fou-hsin		Pen-ch'i Chin-chou An-tung Liao-yang Ying-k'ou
Kirin	Ch'ang-ch'un	Kirin	Liao-yüan	T'ung-hua Ssu-p'ing
Heilungkiang		Harbin Ch'i-ch'i-ha-erh Chi-hsi Mu-tan-chiang Ho-kang I-ch'un	Chia-mu-ssu Shuang-ya-shan	
North China				
Hopeh	Tientsin T'ang-shan	Peking Shih-chua-chuang Kalgan Han-tan		Ch'in-huang-tao Ch'eng-te Pao-ting
Shansi		T'ai-yüan	Yü-t'zu Ch'ang-chih	Ta-t'ung Yang-ch'üan
Inner Mongolia		Pao-t'ou Huhehot	Chi-ning	
East China				
Kiangsu	Shanghai	Nanking Hsü-chou Soochow		Ch'ang-chou Nan-t'ung[c] Hsin-hai-lien T'ai-chou[c] Yang-chou[c] Ch'ang-shu Wu-hsi[c] Chen-chiang
Shantung	Tsingtao Tsinan	Tzu-po		Wei-fang Chefoo
Chekiang	Hangchow		Chia-hsing Hu-chou	Ning-po Wen-chou Shao-hsing
Anhwei		Ho-fei		Pang-fou Huai-nan[c] Wu-hu[c] An-ch'ing

223

Table A-6 (continued)

| | | Cities in Indicated Group | | |
Province	Group I	Group II	Group III	Group IV
Central China				
Kiangsi	Nan-ch'ang	Ching-te-chen		
Honan		Cheng-chou		K'ai-feng
		Lo-yang		Hsin-hsiang
		Chiao-tso		An-yang
				Shang-ch'iu
Hupeh		Wu-han		Huang-shih
Hunan			Shao-yang	Heng-yang
			Hsiang-t'an	Ch'ang-sha
			Chu-chou	
South China				
Kwangtung		Canton		Swatow[c]
		Hai-k'ou		Chan-chiang
				Fo-shan[c]
				Chiang-men
				Ch'ao-chou
Kwangsi			Nan-ning	Liu-chou
				Kweilin
				Wu-chou
Fukien			Amoy	Foochow
				Ch'ao-chou
Northwest China				
Shensi		Sian	Pao-chi	
Kansu		Lan-chou		Yin-ch'uan
Sinkiang		Urumchi		Kashgar
				I-ning[c]
Tsinghai			Hsi-ning	
Southwest China				
Szechwan	Chungking	Ch'eng-tu		Tzu-kung[c]
				Nan-ch'ung
				I-pin
				Nei-chiang[c]
				Wu-t'ung-chiao
				Lu-chou[c]
Yúnnan	K'uń-ming			Ko-chiu
Kweichow		Kuei-yang		

[a] Sources: Tables 2-7, 2-8, 2-9, and A-1.

[b] Key to groups: Median Increase in Population (87,500)

III	II
IV	I

Median Rate of Increase (31.6%)

[c] Population decreased in these cities.

224

B INDUSTRIAL CAPACITY DATA

Table B-1

DISTRIBUTION AND VALUE OF INDUSTRIAL PLANTS IN 328 CITIES[a, b]

Province	City	Heavy Industry		Light Industry		Total	
		Number of Plant Units	Allocated Amount of Gross Value-Added (million yüan)	Number of Plant Units	Allocated Amount of Gross Value-Added (million yüan)	Number of Plant Units	Allocated Amount of Gross Value-Added (million yüan)
Northeast China							
Liaoning	Mukden	926	206	17	15	943	221
	Lü-ta	261	84	49	41	310	125
	Fu-shun	741	240	-	-	741	240
	Ying-k'ou	10	13	28	23	38	36
	Chin-chou	7	9	5	5	12	14
	An-tung	455	330	25	21	480	351
	An-shan	1,540	1,126	-	-	1,540	1,126
	Chin-hsi	42	10	-	-	42	10
	Liao-yang	19	11	4	4	23	15
	Fou-hsin	516	102	-	-	516	102
	Pen-ch'i	355	202	-	-	355	202
	Pei-p'iao	27	6	-	-	27	6
	Nan-p'iao	38	14	-	-	38	14
	T'ien-shih-fu	30	2	-	-	30	2
	T'ien-chang-tzu	1	neg.	-	-	1	-
	Huan-jen	294	19	-	-	294	19
Kirin	Ch'ang-ch'un	184	75	8	7	192	82
	Kirin	991	88	8	7	999	95
	T'ung-hua	404	225	2	2	406	227

225

Province	City	Heavy Industry		Light Industry		Total	
		Number of Plant Units	Allocated Amount of Gross Value-Added (Million yüan)	Number of Plant Units	Allocated Amount of Gross Value-Added (Million yüan)	Number of Plant Units	Allocated Amount of Gross Value-Added (Million yüan)
	Ssu-p'ing	5	7	1	1	6	8
	Liao-yüan	89	20	–	–	89	20
	Yen-chi	1	1	–	–	1	1
	Chiao-ho	121	43	–	–	121	43
	Chien-kuo-chi	1	neg.	–	–	1	–
	Tu-hsi	3	neg.	–	–	3	–
	Lung-ch'ing	60	4	–	–	60	4
	Chien-ch'en	3	neg.	–	–	3	–
	Hun-ch'un	6	neg.	–	–	6	–
	Chi-ning	2	neg.	–	–	2	–
	Tao-nan	2	neg.	–	–	2	–
	Tao-an	1	neg.	–	–	1	–
Heilungkiang	Harbin	322	107	55	46	377	153
	Ch'i-ch'i-ha-erh	72	18	3	3	75	21
	Chia-mu-ssu	229	43	4	3	233	46
	Mu-tan-chiang	23	15	3	3	26	18
	Chi-hsi	192	61	–	–	192	61
	Ho-kang	139	51	–	–	139	51
	Fu-la-erh-chi	151	45	–	–	151	45
	Shuang-ya-shan	2	2	–	–	2	4
	I-lan	1	neg.	–	–	1	–
	Sui-fen-ho	2	neg.	–	–	2	–
	Ti-tao	6	neg.	–	–	6	–
	Pei-an	4	neg.	–	–	4	–
	Sun-wu	7	neg.	–	–	7	–
	Hei-ho	1	neg.	–	–	1	–
	Ching-po-hu	36	2	–	–	36	2
North China							
Hopeh	Peking	1,607	792	151	131	1,758	923
	Tientsin	1,148	1,061	621	522	1,769	1,583
	Shih-chia-chuang	323	135	9	8	332	143
	T'ang-shan	462	180	3	3	465	183
	Han-tan	168	134	1	1	169	135
	Hsüan-hua	94	37	–	–	94	37
	Pao-ting	56	11	–	–	56	11
	Ch'eng-te	425	135	–	–	425	135
	Ch'in-huang-tao	6	2	–	–	6	2
	Kalgan	2	2	2	2	4	4
	Cho-hsien	19	14	–	–	19	14
	Cheng-ting	10	8	–	–	10	8
	Hsing-t'ai	2	2	–	–	2	2

Province	City	Heavy Industry		Light Industry		Total	
		Number of Plant Units	Allocated Amount of Gross Value-Added (million yüan)	Number of Plant Units	Allocated Amount of Gross Value-Added (million yüan)	Number of Plant Units	Allocated Amount of Gross Value-Added (million yüan)
	T'zu-hsien	99	38	–	–	99	38
	Kuan-t'ing	30	2	–	–	30	2
	Shuang-t'ou-shan	6	neg.	–	–	6	–
	Mi-yün	90	6	–	–	90	6
	Shih-hsia-li	30	2	–	–	30	2
	Hsiang-kuang-t'ung	10	1	–	–	10	1
	Yu-chou	40	3	–	–	40	3
	Chiao-chia-wan	30	2	–	–	30	2
Shansi	T'ai-yüan	706	376	10	8	716	384
	Ta-t'ung	202	80	1	1	203	81
	Yang-ch'üan	132	66	–	–	132	66
	Ch'ang-chih	32	26	–	–	32	26
	Yü-t'zu	2	3	–	–	2	3
	P'ing-wang	12	1	–	–	12	1
	Lin-fen	170	129	–	–	170	129
	Yü-hsien	5	4	–	–	5	4
	Ling-shih-hsien	2	1	–	–	2	1
	Ning-wu	5	2	–	–	5	2
	Shou-yang	4	2	–	–	4	2
	Fen-hsi	25	10	–	–	25	10
Inner Mongolia	Pao-t'ou	1,252	793	3	3	1,255	796
	Huhehot	73	71	5	4	78	75
	Hai-la-erh	34	26	2	2	36	28
	Ch'ih-feng	41	18	1	1	42	19
	Chi-ning	1	1	1	1	2	2
	Wu-lan-hao-t'e	21	16	–	–	21	16
	Lao-ha-ho	50	19	–	–	50	19
	Ta-hsing-an-ling	6	2	–	–	6	2
	P'ing-chuang	100	38	–	–	100	38
	Yü-erh-ai	1	neg.	–	–	1	–
	Cha-lai-no-erh	12	1	–	–	12	1
	Ssu-shih-sha-ho	100	6	–	–	100	6
	T'ung-liao	2	neg.	–	–	2	–
	Wu-ho-hao-t'e	1	1	–	–	1	1
	Wu-lan-cha-pu-meng	6	5	–	–	6	5
East China							
Shantung	Tsingtao	219	177	138	116	357	293
	Tsinan	468	227	4	3	472	230
	Tzu-po	446	308	–	–	446	308
	Chefoo	6	6	2	2	8	8
	Wei-fang	11	10	2	2	13	12

Table B-1 (continued)

Province	City	Heavy Industry		Light Industry		Total	
		Number of Plant Units	Allocated Amount of Gross Value-Added (million yüan)	Number of Plant Units	Allocated Amount of Gross Value-Added (million yüan)	Number of Plant Units	Allocated Amount of Gross Value-Added (million yüan)
	I-hsien	18	7	-	-	18	7
	Hung-shan	27	10	-	-	27	10
	Tsao-chuang	65	25	-	-	65	25
	Tzu-ch'uan	50	19	-	-	50	19
	Liang-chuang	60	23	-	-	60	23
	Han-chuang	52	3	-	-	52	3
	Hsin-t'ai-hsien	24	2	-	-	24	2
	Nan-ting	74	5	-	-	74	5
Kiangsu	Shanghai	3,809	3,801	5,612	4,714	9,421	8,515
	Nanking	455	376	684	574	1,139	950
	Wu-hsi	18	23	7	6	25	29
	Soochow	54	42	3	3	57	45
	Ch'ang-chou	8	5	1	1	9	6
	Nan-t'ung	14	6	1	1	15	7
	Hsin-hai-lien	38	5	-	-	38	5
	Hsü-chou	133	56	-	-	133	56
	Chen-chiang	7	5	-	-	7	5
	T'ai-chou	1	1	-	-	1	1
	Yang-chou	7	3	-	-	7	3
	Ch'i-shu-yen	20	2	-	-	20	2
	Ch'ang-shu	1	neg.	-	-	1	-
	Wang-t'ing	200	13	-	-	200	13
Chekiang	Hangchow	113	80	11	9	124	89
	Chin-hua	1	1	-	-	1	1
	Shao-hsing	6	4	-	-	6	4
	Ning-po	11	2	-	-	11	2
	Wen-chou	5	neg.	2	2	7	2
	Chia-hsing	-	-	1	1	1	1
	Hsin-an-chiang	382	24	-	-	382	24
	Chi-li-lung	300	20	-	-	300	20
	Hu-nan-chen	195	13	-	-	195	13
	Huang-t'an-k'ou	30	2	-	-	30	2
Anhwei	Ho-fei	195	124	2	2	197	126
	Wu-hu	10	8	2	2	12	10
	Pang-fou	17	16	1	1	18	17
	Huai-nan	596	226	-	-	596	226
	An-ch'ing	39	31	1	1	40	32
	Tang-t'u	2	3	-	-	2	3
	T'ung-ling	104	81	-	-	104	81
	Ma-an-shan	339	241	-	-	339	241
	Feng-t'ai	22	17	-	-	22	17
	Su-hsien	170	62	-	-	170	62

Table B-1 (continued)

Province	City	Heavy Industry		Light Industry		Total	
		Number of Plant Units	Allocated Amount of Gross Value-Added (million yüan)	Number of Plant Units	Allocated Amount of Gross Value-Added (million yüan)	Number of Plant Units	Allocated Amount of Gross Value-Added (million yüan)
	Chin-sai-hsien	80	5	–	–	80	5
	Hsiang-kung-miao	11	1	–	–	11	1
	Mao-chien-shan	30	2	–	–	30	2
Central China							
Honan	Cheng-chou	66	25	10	8	76	33
	Lo-yang	181	109	60	50	241	159
	Hsin-hsiang	12	12	3	3	15	15
	Kai-feng	10	10	–	–	10	10
	An-yang	47	37	–	–	47	37
	Hsin-yang	101	50	1	1	102	51
	Chiao-tso	147	58	–	–	147	58
	Nan-yang	49	37	–	–	49	37
	Hao-pi	8	3	–	–	8	3
	Shang-ch'iu	–	–	1	1	1	1
	Hsü-ch'ang	55	21	–	–	55	21
	San-men-hsia	376	24	–	–	376	24
	Pa-pan-hsia	288	19	–	–	288	19
	Hsin-cheng	125	8	–	–	125	8
	Chai-chia-hsia	125	8	–	–	125	8
	Shui-yen	15	11	–	–	15	11
	Sha-p'o-t'ou	90	6	–	–	90	6
	Hsiao-lang-ti	400	26	–	–	400	26
Hupeh	Wu-han	1,418	1,200	161	135	1,579	1,335
	Huang-shih	372	163	–	–	372	163
	I-ch'ang	2	3	–	–	2	3
	O-ch'eng	33	25	–	–	33	25
	Hsiang-fan	1	1	–	–	1	1
	Chi-chi	18	1	–	–	18	1
	Pai-lien-ho	64	4	–	–	64	4
	Tan-chiang-k'ou	288	18	–	–	288	18
	Ch'ang-t'an	96	6	–	–	96	6
	Ma-ch'eng	3	2	–	–	3	2
Hunan	Ch'ang-sha	113	138	123	104	236	242
	Chu-chou	65	23	2	2	67	25
	Heng-yang	39	12	1	1	40	13
	Hsiang-t'an	126	98	1	1	127	99
	Shao-yang	1	1	1	1	2	2
	Ch'ang-te	1	1	1	1	2	2
	Cha-ling	3	2	–	–	3	2
	Tzu-hsing	33	3	–	–	33	3
	Yao-yang	8	1	–	–	8	1

229

Table B-1 (continued)

Province	City	Heavy Industry		Light Industry		Total	
		Number of Plant Units	Allocated Amount of Gross Value-Added (million yüan)	Number of Plant Units	Allocated Amount of Gross Value-Added (million yüan)	Number of Plant Units	Allocated Amount of Gross Value-Added (million yüan)
	Chi-ch'i	299	19	-	-	299	19
	Tung-chiang	283	18	-	-	283	18
	Chao-shih	96	6	-	-	96	6
	Shih-mo-ch'i	175	11	-	-	175	11
	Ling-ching-t'an	250	16	-	-	250	16
	An-hua	305	20	-	-	305	20
	An-chiang	150	10	-	-	150	10
	Ch'ang-ning	2	2	-	-	2	2
	P'ing-an	6	5	-	-	6	5
	Lien-yüan	80	61	-	-	80	61
Kiangsi	Nan-ch'ang	264	213	118	99	382	312
	P'ing-hsiang	127	81	1	1	128	82
	Kan-chou	5	5	2	2	7	7
	Ching-te-chen	1	1	3	3	4	4
	Hsin-yü	50	38	-	-	50	38
	Chi-an	4	3	-	-	4	3
	Feng-ch'eng	86	33	-	-	86	33
	Chin-chiang	7	neg.	1	1	8	1
	Chiang-k'ou	36	2	-	-	36	2
	Shang-yu	60	4	-	-	60	4
	Wan-an	300	20	-	-	300	20
	Shang-yao	-	-	1	1	1	1
	Ching-kang-shan	38	29	-	-	38	29
South China							
Fukien	Foochow	183	156	103	86	286	242
	Amoy	25	25	6	5	31	30
	Ch'üan-chou	6	8	2	2	8	10
	Chang-chou	4	5	5	4	9	9
	Nan-p'ing	8	9	1	1	9	10
	San-ming	49	37	-	-	49	37
	Kuo-k'eng	9	7	-	-	9	7
	Yung-ch'un	3	2	-	-	3	2
	Chang-p'ing	13	7	-	-	13	7
	Lung-yen	1	1	-	-	1	1
	Chien-ch'i	277	18	-	-	277	18
	Ku-tien	224	14	-	-	224	14
	Fu an	?	?	-	-	3	2
	Lung-ch'i	3	2	-	-	3	2
	Shang-hang	200	13	-	-	200	13

Table B-1 (continued)

Province	City	Heavy Industry		Light Industry		Total	
		Number of Plant Units	Allocated Amount of Gross Value-Added (million yüan)	Number of Plant Units	Allocated Amount of Gross Value-Added (million yüan)	Number of Plant Units	Allocated Amount of Gross Value-Added (million yüan)
Kwangtung	Canton	641	601	174	147	815	748
	Swatow	16	21	104	87	120	108
	Shao-kuan	8	10	–	–	8	10
	Chiang-men	13	15	3	3	16	18
	Chan-chiang	9	11	1	1	10	12
	Hai-k'ou	40	7	3	3	43	10
	Fo-shan	2	2	13	11	15	13
	Ch'ao-chou	1	1	–	–	1	1
	Shih-lu	153	100	–	–	153	100
	Yang-ch'un	40	22	–	–	40	22
	Lo-chiang	10	8	–	–	10	8
	Lien-chiang	3	2	–	–	3	2
	Ch'ang-ch'ang	1	neg.	–	–	1	–
	Ch'ü-chiang	2	1	–	–	2	1
	Jen-hua	10	4	–	–	10	4
	Nan-lin	10	4	–	–	10	4
	Wu-shih	200	13	–	–	200	13
	Fang-ch'eng	18	1	–	–	18	1
	Feng-huang-shan	22	1	–	–	22	1
	Hsin-feng	300	19	–	–	300	19
	Ju-yüan	50	3	–	–	50	3
	Hsing-ning	20	15	–	–	20	15
	Ho-nan	39	30	–	–	39	30
Kwangsi	Liu-chou	265	68	–	–	265	68
	Nan-ning	297	83	3	3	300	86
	Wu-chou	5	5	–	–	5	5
	Kuei-lin	10	7	–	–	10	7
	Lu-chai	14	11	–	–	14	11
	Pa-pu	3	neg.	–	–	3	–
	Chung-shan	3	1	–	–	3	1
	Chao-p'ing	272	17	–	–	272	17
	Heng-hsien	216	14	–	–	216	14
	Hsi-chung	5	14	–	–	5	14
	P'ing-kuei	240	15	–	–	240	15
Ningsia	Yin-ch'uan	3	4	1	1	4	5
	Shih-tsui-shan	20	13	–	–	20	13
	Chin-chi	260	17	–	–	260	17
Sinkiang	Urumchi	469	163	3	3	472	166
	Kashgar	8	3	1	1	9	4
	I-ning	1	1	2	2	3	3
	Tu-shan-tzu	2	2	–	–	2	2
	Karamai	1	1	–	–	1	1

231

Table B-1 (continued)

Province	City	Heavy Industry		Light Industry		Total	
		Number of Plant Units	Allocated Amount of Gross Value-Added (million yüan)	Number of Plant Units	Allocated Amount of Gross Value-Added (million yüan)	Number of Plant Units	Allocated Amount of Gross Value-Added (million yüan)
	Ha-mi	140	106	-	-	140	106
	Ko-ko-to-hai	12	1	-	-	12	1
	Wu-la-po	2	neg.	-	-	2	-
Southwest China							
Szechwan	Chungking	811	650	379	319	1,190	969
	Ch'eng-tu	398	134	5	4	403	138
	I-pin	24	5	2	2	26	7
	Tzu-kung	6	2	-	-	6	2
	Wei-yüan	15	11	-	-	15	11
	Ta-hsien	40	30	-	-	40	30
	Ch'i-chiang	10	8	-	-	10	8
	Wan-hsien	3	2	-	-	3	2
	Lo-shan	2	2	-	-	2	2
	Ho-ch'uan	1	1	-	-	1	1
	Kuang-yüan	11	5	-	-	11	5
	Nan-ch'ung	8	3	-	-	8	3
	Wu-t'ung-chiao	3	neg.	-	-	3	-
	Lu-hsien	42	30	-	-	42	30
	Chien-wei	2	neg.	-	-	2	-
	Pien-chüang-tzu	2,000	128	-	-	2,000	128
	Shih-p'eng	3,000	192	-	-	3,000	192
	Shih-chiu-t'an	200	13	-	-	200	13
	Tzu-p'ing-pu	283	18	-	-	283	18
	So-chia	70	5	-	-	70	5
	K'uan-hsien	70	5	-	-	70	5
	Chiang-yu	155	62	-	-	155	62
	Ch'ang-shou	99	6	-	-	99	6
	K'ang-t'ing	1	neg.	-	-	1	-
	Chu-yang-ch'i	3,000	192	-	-	3,000	192
	San-chiang	15	11	-	-	15	11
Northwest China							
Shensi	Sian	302	224	62	52	364	276
	Pao-chi	63	15	-	-	63	15
	T'ung-ch'uan	6	2	-	-	6	2
	Hu-hsien	250	16	-	-	250	16
	Nan-cheng	2	neg.	-	-	2	-
	Shih-ch'üan	200	13	-	-	200	13
	Hsien-yang	-	-	6	5	6	5

Table B-1 (continued)

Province	City	Heavy Industry		Light Industry		Total	
		Number of Plant Units	Allocated Amount of Gross Value-Added (million yüan)	Number of Plant Units	Allocated Amount of Gross Value-Added (million yüan)	Number of Plant Units	Allocated Amount of Gross Value-Added (million yüan)
Kansu	Lan-chou	630	103	26	22	656	125
	T'ien-shui	5	6	-	-	5	6
	Yü-men	14	6	-	-	14	6
	Chiu-ch'üan	358	272	-	-	358	272
	Yung-teng	4	3	-	-	4	3
	Shan-tan	3	1	-	-	3	1
	Yen-kuo-hsia	288	18	-	-	288	18
Tsinghai	Hsi-ning	40	17	3	3	43	20
	Tsaidam	7	9	-	-	7	9
	Ta-t'ung	36	14	-	-	36	14
	Ko-erh-mu	12	1	-	-	12	1
Southwest China							
Yünnan	Kun-ming	178	145	29	25	207	170
	Ko-chiu	2	2	-	-	2	2
	Hsia-kuan	252	19	-	-	252	19
	Hsüan-wei	204	16	-	-	204	16
	Hui-tse	402	26	-	-	402	26
	Liu-lang-tung	26	2	-	-	26	2
	Shih-lung-pa	6	neg.	-	-	6	-
	Liu-shui-ho	60	4	-	-	60	4
	Hsiao-chiang-k'ou	180	12	-	-	180	12
	Yang-tsung-hai	40	3	-	-	40	3
Kweichow	Kuei-yang	271	130	47	39	318	169
	Tsun-i	25	20	-	-	25	20
	Tu-yün	114	13	-	-	114	13
	Shui-ch'eng	102	39	-	-	102	39
	Hsia-ssu	40	3	-	-	40	3
	Ching-chen	250	16	-	-	250	16
	Ta-yen-men	2	neg.	-	-	2	-
	Pi-ch'ieh	40	30	-	-	40	30
	An-shun	28	21	-	-	28	21
Tibet	Lhasa	16	1	-	-	16	1

[a]Sources: News services and radio broadcasts: Radio Peking; New China News Agency; and Asia News Service (Tokyo). Newspapers: People's Daily (Peking); Daily Worker; Ta-kung Daily (Peking); Ta-kung Daily (Hong Kong); Wen-hui Daily (Hong Kong); China Youth Daily (Peking); Enlightenment Daily (Peking); and China News (Canton).
Periodicals: New China Semimonthly (Peking); China Pictorial (Peking); Popular Science (Peking); Economic Bulletin (Hong Kong); Planned Economy (Peking); Coal Industry (Peking); Water Conservation and Electric Power (Peking); Statistical Research (Peking); Statistical Work (Peking); Peking Review; Hydroelectric Power (Peking); People's Electric Power Industry (Peking); Geographical Knowledge (Peking); Research on Communist China (Taipei); Far Eastern Economic Review (Hong Kong); Metallurgical Report (Peking); China Youth (Peking); and Red Flag (Peking).
Books: Wo-k'uo Kang-t'ieh Tien-li Mei-t'an Chi-hsieh Fang-chih Kung-yeh ti Chin-hsi (Major Aspects of the Chinese Economy through 1956) (Peking: 1958); Chao I-wen, Hsin Chung-kuo ti Kung-yeh (New China's Industry) (Peking: 1957); Jen-min Shou-t'se (People's Handbook) (Peking: 1950-1962); and Wei-ta ti Shih-nien (The Great Ten Years) (Peking: 1960).

Table B-1 (continued)

[b]neg. = negligible.

[c]For the iron and steel industry, the gross value-added weight per plant or per unit capacity is derived as follows: The average of the gross value-added between 1958 and 1960 is 9,300 million yüan, and the total number of modern iron and steel plants is 11,722. Therefore, 9,300/11,722 = 0.79 million yüan per plant. See Yuan-li Wu, The Steel Industry in Communist China (Stanford, Calif.: Hoover Institution, 1965), Table IV-16 and accompanying text.

For the electric power industry, the average of gross value-added between 1958 and 1960 is 1,948.6 million yüan, and the total number of electric power plants, in units of 1,000 km each, is 30,232. Therefore, 1,948.6/30,232 = 0.065 million yüan/per plant. See Yuan-li Wu, Economic Development and the Use of Energy Resources in Communist China (New York: Praeger, 1963), p. 135. Since some industrial enterprises have their own power plants, which, if small, may not be listed separately, the allocation of value-added in power generation underestimates the importance of locations where intraenterprise power plants exist. The distortion is believed, however, to be relatively small and has been ignored.

For the coal industry, the average gross value-added between 1958 and 1960 is 1,208.4 million yüan, and the total number of modern coal mines, in equivalent units of 100,000 tons per year, is 3,188. Therefore, 1,208.4/3,188 = 0.38 million yüan per plant. See Yuan-li Wu, Economic Development and the Use of Energy Resources in Communist China, op. cit., p. 144.

For the other heavy industries, the weight used is derived by subtracting the total average gross value-added of iron and steel, electric power, and coal industries between 1958 and 1960 from the total average gross value-added of the producer goods sector in the same period. The difference is the total average gross value-added for other heavy industry. Thus, the total average gross value-added in the producer goods sections between 1958 and 1960 is 20.7 billion 1952 yüan. The total average gross value-added for iron and steel, electric power, and coal mining is 12.46 billion yüan. Therefore, 20.7 - 12.5 = 8.2 billion yüan. The total number of the other heavy industrial plants is 6,142. Therefore, 8,200/6,142 = 1.34 million per plant. See Yuan-li Wu, The Economic Potential of Communist China (New York: Praeger, 1963).

For light industry the average of the gross value-added in consumer goods industries between 1958 and 1960 is 7.5 billion 1952 yüan. Thus, 7.5 billion yüan per 8.977 plants = 0.84 million yüan per plant.

Table B-2

RANKING OF INDUSTRIAL CITIES AND PRODUCTION SITES
BY ANNUAL CAPACITY IN VALUE-ADDED[a]

City	Annual Capacity in Value-Added (million yüan)	Percentage of Total Added	City	Annual Capacity in Value-Added (million yüan)	Percentage of Total Added
Shanghai	8,515	30.02	Lan-chou	125	0.44
Tientsin	1,583	5.58	Lü-ta	125	0.44
Wu-han	1,335	4.71	Swatow	108	0.38
An-shan	1,126	3.97	Ha-mi	106	0.37
Chungking	969	3.42	Fou-hsin	102	0.36
Nanking	950	3.35	Shih-lu	100	0.35
Peking	923	3.25	Hsiang-t'an	99	0.35
Pao-t'ou	796	2.81	Kirin	95	0.33
Canton	748	2.64	Hangchow	89	0.31
T'ai-yüan	384	1.35	Nan-ning	86	0.30
An-tung	351	1.24	P'ing-hsiang	82	0.29
Nan-ch'ang	312	1.10	Ch'ang-ch'un	82	0.29
Tzu-po	308	1.09	Ta-t'ung	81	0.29
Tsingtao	293	1.03	T'ung-ling	81	0.29
Sian	276	0.97	Huhehot	75	0.26
Chiu-ch'üan	272	0.96	Liu-chou	68	0.24
Ch'ang-sha	242	0.85	Yang-ch'üan	66	0.23
Foochow	242	0.85	Chiang-yu	62	0.22
Ma-an-shan	241	0.85	Su-hsien	62	0.22
Fu-shun	240	0.85	Lien-yuan	61	0.22
Tsinan	230	0.81	Ch'i-hsi	61	0.22
T'ung-hua	227	0.80	Chiao-tso	58	0.20
Huai-nan	226	0.80	Hsu-chou	56	0.20
Mukden	221	0.78	Hsin-yang	51	0.18
Pen-ch'i	202	0.71	Ho-hang	51	0.18
Chu-yang-ch'i	192	0.68	Chia-mu-ssu	46	0.16
Shih-p'ing	192	0.68	Soochow	45	0.16
T'ang-shan	183	0.65	Fu-la-erh-chi	45	0.16
Kun-ming	170	0.60	Chiao-ho	43	0.15
Kuei-yang	169	0.60	Shui-ch'eng	39	0.14
Urumchi	166	0.59	Hsin-yü	38	0.13
Huang-shih	163	0.57	Tzu-hsien	38	0.13
Lo-yang	159	0.56	P'ing-chuang	38	0.13
Harbin	153	0.54	San-ming	37	0.13
Shih-chia-chuang	143	0.50	An-yang	37	0.13
Ch'eng-tu	138	0.49	Hsüan-hua	37	0.13
Ch'eng-te	135	0.48	Nan-yang	37	0.13
Han-tan	135	0.48	Ying-k'ou	36	0.13
Lin-fen	129	0.45	Feng-ch'eng	33	0.12
Pien-chüang-tzu	128	0.45	Cheng-chou	33	0.12
Ho-fei	126	0.44	An-ch'ing	32	0.11

Table B-2 (continued)

City	Annual Capacity in Value-Added (million yüan)	Percentage of Total Added	City	Annual Capacity in Value-Added (million yüan)	Percentage of Total Added
Ta-hsien	30	0.11	Chi-li-lung	20	0.07
Amoy	30	0.11	Tsun-i	20	0.07
Ho-nan	30	0.11	An-hua	20	0.07
Pi-ch'ieh	30	0.11	Wan-an	20	0.07
Lu-chou	30	0.11	Hsin-feng	19	0.07
Wu-hsi	29	0.10	Pa-pan-hsia	19	0.07
Ching-kang-shan	29	0.10	Hsia-kuan	19	0.07
Hai-la-erh	28	0.10	Chi-ch'i	19	0.07
Ch'ang-chih	26	0.09	Huan-jen	19	0.07
Hui-tse	26	0.09	Ch'ih-feng	19	0.07
Hsiao-lang-ti	26	0.09	Lao-ha-ho	19	0.07
O-ch'eng	25	0.09	Tzu-ch'uan	19	0.07
Chu-chou	25	0.09	Mu-tan-chiang	18	0.06
Tsao-chuang	25	0.09	Tzu-p'ing-pu	18	0.06
Hsin-an-chiang	24	0.08	T'an-chiang-k'ou	18	0.06
San-men-hsia	24	0.08	Yen-kuo-hsia	18	0.06
Liang-chuang	23	0.08	Tung-chiang	18	0.06
Yang-ch'un	22	0.08	Chien-ch'i	18	0.06
Hsü-ch'ang	21	0.07	Chiang-men	18	0.06
An-shun	21	0.07	Chao-p'ing	17	0.05
Ch'i-ch'i-ha-erh	21	0.07	Pang-fou	17	0.05
Liao-yüan	20	0.07	Feng-t'ai	17	0.05
Hsi-ning	20	0.07	Chin-chi	17	0.05

[a]The remaining cities account individually for 16 million yüan or less, i.e., under 0.05 per cent of total capacity.

Table B-3

FREQUENCY DISTRIBUTION OF 328 PRODUCTION LOCATIONS IN 26 PROVINCES AND
AUTONOMOUS REGIONS BY NUMBER OF INDUSTRY GROUPS

Province	Number of Industry Groups Reported at Each Location													
	1	2	3	4	5	6	7	8	9	10	11	12	13	14
Northeast China														
Liaoning	4	1	-	1	2	2	1	1	3	-	-	-	-	1
Kirin	8	2	-	2	1	-	-	-	1	-	1	-	-	-
Heilungkiang	8	-	1	2	1	-	-	2	-	1	-	-	-	-
Total	20	3	1	5	4	2	1	3	4	1	1	-	-	1
North China														
Hopeh	11	-	4	1	-	1	-	1	1	1	-	-	1	-
Shansi	7	-	2	-	-	1	1	-	-	-	-	1	-	-
Inner Mongolia	9	2	-	1	1	-	1	1	-	-	-	-	-	-
Total	27	2	6	2	1	2	2	2	1	1	-	1	1	-
East China														
Shantung	8	-	-	2	1	-	1	1	-	-	-	-	-	-
Kiangsu	3	1	2	3	-	1	1	1	-	-	-	-	-	1
Chekiang	3	4	2	-	-	-	-	-	1	-	-	-	-	-
Anhwei	5	-	4	-	3	-	-	1	-	-	-	-	-	-
Total	19	6	8	5	4	1	2	3	1	-	-	-	-	1
Central China														
Honan	10	1	1	1	3	-	2	-	-	-	-	-	-	-
Hupeh	8	-	1	-	-	-	-	-	-	-	-	1	-	-
Hunan	10	5	-	-	1	1	1	1	-	-	-	-	-	-
Kiangsi	7	2	-	1	1	1	-	1	-	-	-	-	-	-
Total	35	8	2	2	5	2	3	2	-	-	-	1	-	-
South China														
Fukien	7	2	1	2	1	-	1	1	-	-	-	-	-	-
Kwangtung	11	5	1	2	1	2	-	-	-	1	-	-	-	-
Kwangsi	5	2	2	-	-	2	-	-	-	-	-	-	-	-
Total	23	9	4	4	2	4	1	1	-	1	-	-	-	-
Northwest China														
Shensi	5	-	1	-	-	-	-	-	1	-	-	-	-	-
Kansu	3	1	1	1	-	-	-	1	-	-	-	-	-	-
Tsinghai	2	1	-	-	-	1	-	-	-	-	-	-	-	-
Ningsia	1	1	1	-	-	-	-	-	-	-	-	-	-	-
Sinkiang	2	3	-	2	-	-	-	1	-	-	-	-	-	-
Total	13	6	3	3	-	1	-	2	1	-	-	-	-	-
Southwest China														
Szechwan	12	10	1	1	-	-	1	-	-	-	1	-	-	-
Yünnan	6	3	-	-	-	-	-	1	-	-	-	-	-	-
Kweichow	6	1	-	1	-	-	-	-	1	-	-	-	-	-
Tibet	1	-	-	-	-	-	-	-	-	-	-	-	-	-
Total	25	14	1	2	-	-	1	1	1	-	1	-	-	-
Grand Total	162	48	25	23	16	12	10	14	8	3	2	2	1	2

[a]Sources: See Appendix B, Table B-1, reference a.

237

C RELATIONSHIP OF POPULATION AND INDUSTRIAL CAPACITY

Table C-1

CLASSIFICATION OF 117 CITIES ACCORDING TO TOTAL POPULATION IN 1958
AND WEIGHTED INDUSTRIAL CAPACITY BY PROVINCES AND REGIONS

Province	Cities in Indicated Group				
	Group I'	Group II'	Group V'	Group IV'	Group III'
Northeast China					
Liaoning	Fu-shun	Mukden An-tung		Lü-ta An-shan	Pen-ch'i Chin-chou Fou-hsin Liao-yang Ying-k'ou
Kirin			T'ung-hua		Ch'ang-ch'un Kirin Liao-yüan Ssu-p'ing
Heilangkiang	Harbin			Ch'i-ch'i-ha-erh Chi-hsi	Mu-tan-chiang Chia-mu-ssu Ho-kang I-ch'un Shuang-ya-shan
North China					
Hopeh	Peking Tientsin Shih-chia-chuang Han-tan		Ch'eng-te		T'ang-shan Kalgan Pao-ting Ch'in-huang-tao
Shansi	T'ai-yüan				Ta-t'ung Yang-ch'üan Ch'ang-chih Yü-t'zu
Inner Mongolia	Pao-t'ou	Huhehot			Chi-ning

Table C-1 (continued)

Province	Cities in Indicated Group				
	Group I'	Group II'	Group V'	Group IV'	Group III'
East China					
Kiangsu	Shanghai	Nanking		Hsü-chou	Soochow
					Wu-hsi
					Chang-chou
					Nan-t'ung
					Hsin-hai-lien
					T'ai-chou
					Chen-chiang
					Yang-chou
					Ch'ang-shu
Shantung	Tsingtao				Wei-fang
	Tsinan				Chefoo
	Tzu-po				
Anhwei		Ho-fei	Huai-nan		Pang-fou
					Wu-hu
					An-ch'ing
Chekiang		Hangchow			Ning-po
					Wen-chou
					Shao-hsing
					Chia-hsing
					Hu-chou
Central China					
Kiangsi		Nan-ch'ang			Ching-te-chen
Honan	Lo-yang			Chiao-tso	Cheng-chou
					K'ai-feng
					Hsin-hsiang
					Shang-ch'iu
					An-yang
Hunan			Hsiang-t'an		Ch'ang-sha
					Heng-yang
					Chu-chou
					Shao-yang
Hupeh	Wu-han				Huang-shih
South China					
Kwangsi					Nan-ning
					Liu-chou
					Kueilin
					Wu-chou
Kwangtung	Canton			Hai-k'ou	Swatow
					Chan-chiang
					Fo-shan
					Chiang-men
					Ch'ao-chou
Fukien					Foochow
					Amoy
					Ch'üan-chou
Northwest China					
Shensi	Sian				Pao-chi
Sinkiang		Urumchi			Kashgar
					I-ning
Kansu		Lan-chou			Yin-ch'uan
Tsinghai					Hsi-ning
Southwest China					
Szechwan	Chungking				Tzu-kung
	Ch'eng-tu				Nan-ch'ung
					I-pin
					Nei-chiang
					Wu-t'ung-chiao
					Lu-chou
Kweichow				Kuei-yang	
Yünnan				Kun-ming	Ko-chiu
Total	18	9	4	9	77

Table C-2

CLASSIFICATION OF 117 CITIES ACCORDING TO WEIGHTED NEW INDUSTRIAL
CAPACITY ADDED BETWEEN 1949 AND 1961 BY PROVINCES AND REGIONS

Province	Cities in Indicated Group				
	Group I	Group IV	Group V	Group II	Group III
Northeast China					
Liaoning	Mukden Fu-shun An-shan			Lü-ta Pen-ch'i An-tung Fou-hsin	Chin-chou Liao-yang Ying-k'ou
Kirin		Ch'ang-ch'un	T'ung-hua		Kirin Liao-yüan Ssu-p'ing
Heilungkiang		Ch'i-ch'i-ha-erh		Harbin	Chi-hsi Mu-tan-chiang Chia-mu-ssu Ho-kang I-ch'un Shuang-ya-shan
North China					
Hopeh	Peking Tientsin T'ang-shan			Shih-chia-chuang Han-tan	Kalgan Pao-ting Ch'in-huang-tao Ch'eng-te
Shansi	T'ai-yüan				Ta-t'ung Yang-ch'üan Ch'ang-chih Yü-t'zu
Inner Mongolia				Pao-t'ou	Huhehot Chi-ning
East China					
Kiangsu	Shanghai Nanking	Hsü-chou Soochow			Wu-hsi Ch'ang-chou Nan-t'ung Hsin-hai-lien Ch'ang-shu T'ai-chou Chen-chiang Yang-chou
Shantung	Tsingtao Tsinan Tzu-po				Wei-fang Chefoo
Anhwei				Ho-fei Huai nan	Pang-fou Wu hu An-ch'ing
Chekiang		Hangchow			Ning-po Wen-chou Shao-hsing Chia-hsing Hu-chou

240

Table C-2 (continued)

Province	Cities in Indicated Group				
	Group I	Group IV	Group V	Group II	Group III
Central China					
Kiangsi				Nan-ch'ang	Ching-te-chen
Honan		Cheng-chou		Lo-yang	K'ai-feng Chiao-tso Hsin-hsiang Shang-ch'iu An-yang
Hunan	Ch'ang-sha				Hsiang-t'an Heng-yang Chu-chou Shao-yang
Hupeh	Wu-han		Huang-shih		
South China					
Kwangsi					Nan-ning Liu-chou Kueilin Wu-chou
Kwangtung	Canton				Hai-k'ou Swatow Chan-chiang Fo-shan Chiang-men Ch'ao-chou
Fukien				Foochow	Amoy Ch'üan-chou
Northwest China					
Shensi	Sian				Pao-chi
Sinkiang				Urumchi	Kashgar I-ning
Kansu				Lan-chou	Yin-ch'uan
Tsinghai					Hsi-ning
Southwest China					
Szechwan	Chungking			Ch'eng-tu	Tzu-kung Nan-ch'ung I-pin Nei-chiang Wu-t'ung-ch'iao Lu-chou
Kweichow				Kuei-yang	
Yunnan	Kun-ming				Ko-chiu
Total	18	6	2	17	74

Table C-3

DISTRIBUTION OF 42 CITIES RECEIVING SOVIET AID FOR INDUSTRIAL PROJECTS[a]

Province	City	Iron and Steel	Coal	Electric Power	Other Heavy Industry	Total
Northeast China						
Liaoning	Mukden (A2)	–	–	2	8	10
	An-shan (A3)	9	–	–	–	9
	Fu-shun (A1)	–	1	1	4	6
	Fou-hsin (C1)	–	3	1	–	4
	Lü-ta (B6)	–	–	1	3	4
	Chin-hsi	–	–	–	1	1
	Ying-k'ou (C4)	–	–	–	1	1
	Pen-ch'i (C1)	1	–	1	–	2
	Total	10	4	6	17	37
Kirin	T'ung-hua (B2)	–	1	–	–	1
	Ch'ang-ch'un (B8)	–	–	–	2	2
	Kirin (C1)	–	–	2	3	5
	Total	–	1	2	5	8
Heilungkiang	Harbin (B3)	–	–	–	10	10
	Chia-mu-ssu (C4)	–	–	1	1	2
	Ho-kang (C4)	–	3	–	–	3
	Shuang-ya-shan (C4)	–	1	–	–	1
	Chi-hsi (C2)	–	1	–	–	1
	Fu-la-erh-chi	1	–	1	1	3
	Total	1	5	2	12	20
North China						
Hopeh	Peking (A1)	–	–	1	2	3
	Tientsin (A1)	–	–	–	2	2
	Han-tan (B3)	1	4	–	–	5
	Total	1	4	1	4	10
Shansi	Tai-yüan (A1)	–	1	2	3	6
	Yü-t'zu (C4)	–	–	–	1	1
	Total	–	1	2	4	7
Inner Mongolia	Pao-t'ou (B3)	5	–	2	–	7
East China						
Kiangsu	Shanghai (A1)	–	–	–	2	2
	Nanking (A2)	–	–	1	–	1
	Total	–	–	1	2	3
Shantung	Tsingtao (A1)	–	–	–	1	1
Anhwei	Huai-nan (B4)	–	1	–	–	1

242

Table C-3 (continued)

Province	City	Number of Industrial Projects				
		Iron and Steel	Coal	Electric Power	Other Heavy Industry	Total
Central China						
Honan	Lo-yang (B3)	–	–	1	3	4
	Hsü-ch'ang	–	1	–	–	1
	Chiao-tso (C2)	–	1	–	–	1
	Cheng-chou (B8)	–	–	1	–	1
	Total	–	2	2	3	7
Hupeh	Wu-han (A1)	7	–	1	2	10
Hunan	Chu-chou (C4)	–	–	1	–	1
Northwest China						
Shensi	Sian (A1)	–	–	3	2	5
	Hu-hsien	–	–	1	–	1
	Total	–	–	4	2	6
Kansu	Lan-chou (B5)	–	–	1	3	4
	Pai-yin	–	–	–	1	1
	Total	–	–	1	4	5
Sinkiang	Urumchi (B5)	–	–	1	1	2
Southwest China						
Szechwan	Chungking (A1)	–	–	1	–	1
	Ch'eng-tu (B3)	–	–	1	3	4
	Total	–	–	2	3	5
Yünnan	Kai-yüan	–	–	1	–	1
	Ko-chiu (C4)	–	–	–	1	1
	Total	–	–	1	1	2
Grand Total		24	18	29	61	132

[a]Sources: Yeh-hui Hsiao, "Fei-O Ching-chi Kuan-hsi chih Yen-chiu" (A Study of Sino-Russian Relations), Fei-ching Yen-chiu (Communist China Research) (Taipei), Vol. II, No. 6, February 25, 1963, pp. 63-68.

D TRANSPORTATION DATA

Table D-1

DISTRIBUTION OF OPERATING RAILWAY TRUNK LINES IN 1949 TO 1950[a]

Region	Province	Area[c] (km^2)	Approximate Length (km)	Percentage of Total	Density (km/1,000 km^2)
Northeast	Liaoning	151,000	3,820[b]		25
	Kirin	187,000 ⎫	5,943[b]		9
	Heilungkiang	463,600 ⎭			
	Total	801,600	9,763	48	12
North	Hopeh	219,800	1,791		8
	Shansi	157,100	730		5
	Inner Mongolia	1,177,500	542[b]		neg.
	Total	1,554,400	3,063	15	2
East	Shantung	153,300	950		6
	Kiangsu (including Shanghai)	108,000	831		8
	Chekiang	101,800	443		4
	Anhwei	139,900	630		5
	Total	503,000	2.854	14	6
Central	Honan	167,000	1,205		7
	Kiangsi	164,800	715		4
	Hunan	210,500	865		4
	Hupeh	187,500	329		2
	Total	729,800	3,114	16	4

Table D-1 (continued)

Region	Province	Area[c] (km^2)	Approximate Length (km)	Percentage of Total	Density (km/1,000 km^2)
South	Fukien	123,100	-		-
	Kwangtung	231,400	569		2
	Kwangsi	220,400	409		2
	Total	574,900	978	5	2
Northwest	Shensi	195.800	441		2
	Kansu and Ninghsia	432,900	-		-
	Tsinghai	721,000	-		-
	Sinkiang	1,646,800	-		-
	Total	2,996,500	441	2	neg.
Southwest	Szechwan	569,000	...		-
	Yünnan	436,200	-		-
	Kweichow	174,000	-		-
	Tibet	1,221,600	-		-
	Total	2,400,800	-		-
Grand Total		9,561,000	20,213	100	2

[a]Sources: Yuan-li Wu, "The Adequacy of Domestic Supply, Trade and Transportation of Coal in Mainland China," Interim Report 3, China's Transportation (Menlo Park, Calif.: Stanford Research Institute, June 30, 1954), Table XIII. The figure given for total railway length (20,213 km) represents the actual length of trunk lines restored up to early 1950. If the length of branch and spur lines (1740 km) were added, the total would reach 22,000 km. The length of railways in Suiyuan and Chahar has been incorporated into that of Inner Mongolia and Hopeh according to the present regional divisions. The figure of P'ing-yüan has been added to that of Honan. Yünnan's railways were probably not in operable conditon at the time. Fei-ch'ü Ti'eh-lu She-ssu Hsien-k'uang (Taipei: Communications Research Bureau, Ministry of Communications, 1961, pp. 4-13. Tu-pao shou-ts'e (A Manual for Newspaper Reading, 1950). Ch'üan-kuo Huo-ch'e Shih-k'e-piao (National Railway Time Table), No. 6, May 16, 1952. Wen Hui Pao (Hong Kong), December 6, 1953.

[b]According to the current boundaries some of the 3,800 km should probably be placed in Kirin and Hopeh and some of those in Heilungkiang should be shifted to Inner Mongolia.

[c]U.S. Dept. of Commerce, Office of Technical Service, China: Provincial Atlas of Communist Administrative Units (Washington, D.C., 1954), Plate 4.

Table D-2

DISTRIBUTION OF MAJOR NAVIGABLE INLAND WATERWAY
ROUTES UNDER THE ADMINISTRATION OF THE
CENTRAL GOVERNMENT IN 1949 TO 1950[a,b]

Waterway Route	Length of Waterway Route in Indicated Region (km)					
	Northeast	East	Central	South	Southwest	Total
Yangtze River	–	2,106	1,420	–	884	4,410
Pearl River:						
Hsi-chiang	–	–	–	2,532	–	2,532
Tung-chiang	–	–	–	1,215	–	1,215
Nan-chiang	–	–	–	328	–	328
Pei-chiang	–	–	–	1,721	–	1,721
Lin-chiang	–	–	–	850	–	850
Hsin-hsing-chiang	–	–	–	173	–	173
Ho-chiang	–	–	–	541	–	541
Hung-shui-ho	–	–	–	–	1,072	1,072
Meng-chiang	–	–	–	279	–	279
Tso-chiang	–	–	–	399	–	399
Pei-ho-chiang	–	–	–	15	–	15
Nan-ho-chiang	–	–	–	51	–	51
Pa-ch'ih-chiang	–	–	–	67	–	67
Ming-chiang	–	–	–	138	–	138
Lung-chiang	–	–	–	197	–	197
Lo-ching-ho	–	–	–	284	–	284
Wu-ming-ho	–	–	–	240	–	240
Tung-an-ho	–	–	–	168	–	168
Kuei-chiang	–	–	–	303	–	303
Kung-ch'eng-chiang	–	–	–	108	–	108
Huang-hua-ho	–	–	–	142	–	142
Chu-chiang San-chiao						
Chou (35 routes)	–	–	–	2,652	–	2,652
Hei-lung-chiang	1,555	–	–	–	–	1,555
Wu-su-li-chiang	1,794	–	–	–	–	1,794
Total	3,349	2,106	1,420	12,403	1,956	21,234
	(16%)	(10%)	(7%)	(58%)	(9%)	(100%)

[a]Sources: Shui-yün Yün-chia Hui-pien (Consolidated Tarriffs of Water Trans-
portation) (Peking: Ministry of Communications, 1956), No. 4, pp. 1-55; Chung-hua
Jen-min Kung-ho-kuo Fen-sheng Ti-t'u (Atlas of the People's Republic of China)
(Shanghai: 1953).

[b]North China and Northwest China have no major navigable inland water
routes under the administration of the central government.

DISTRIBUTION OF NAVIGABLE INLAND WATERWAY ROUTES UNDER THE
ADMINISTRATION OF PROVINCIAL AND OTHER LOCAL
GOVERNMENTS IN 1949 TO 1950[a]

Waterway Route	Length of Waterway Routes in Indicated Region (km)							
	Northeast	North	East	Central	South	Northwest	Southwest	Total
Yangtze River and Tributaries								
Chin-sha-chiang	-	-	-	-	-	-	1,000	1,000
Hung-chiang	-	-	-	-	-	-	80	80
Min-chiang	-	-	-	-	-	-	328	328
Ch'ing-shui-ho	-	-	-	-	-	-	110	110
Ta-tu-ho	-	-	-	-	-	-	100	100
Ch'ing-i-chiang	-	-	-	-	-	-	220	220
Nei-chiang	-	-	-	-	-	-	70	70
Wai-chiang	-	-	-	-	-	-	110	110
T'o-chiang	-	-	-	-	-	-	558	558
Ching-ho	-	-	-	-	-	-	160	160
Yung-ning-ho	-	-	-	-	-	-	120	120
Ch'ih-shui-ho	-	-	-	-	-	-	244	244
Ch'i-chiang	-	-	-	-	-	-	102	102
Chia-ling-chiang	-	-	-	-	-	-	1,080	1,080
Pai-shui-ho	-	-	-	-	-	-	150	150
Fu-chiang	-	-	-	-	-	-	785	785
An-ch'ang-ho	-	-	-	-	-	-	60	60
Tz'u-t'ung-ho	-	-	-	-	-	-	80	80
Ch'ü-chiang	-	-	-	-	-	-	457	457
Nan-chiang	-	-	-	-	-	-	138	138
T'ung-chiang	-	-	-	-	-	-	110	110
Chung-chiang	-	-	-	-	-	-	92	92
Hou-chiang	-	-	-	-	-	-	120	120
Wu-chiang	-	-	-	-	-	-	585	585
Ch'ing-chiang	-	-	-	-	-	-	210	210
Tung-t'ing-hu	-	-	-	505	-	-	-	505
Yüan-chiang	-	-	-	661	-	-	-	661
Chin-shui	-	-	-	--	-	-	140	140
Ch'ing-shui-chiang	-	-	-	-	-	-	490	490
Ch'ü-shui	-	-	-	-	-	-	75	75
Hung-shui	-	-	-	120	-	-	-	120
Yu-shui	-	-	-	255	-	-	-	255
Li-shui	-	-	-	342	-	-	-	342
Tzu-shui	-	-	-	350	-	-	-	350
Ch'ih-chiang	-	-	-	120	-	-	-	120
Fu-i-shui	-	-	-	120	-	-	-	120
Hsiang-chiang	-	-	-	809	-	-	-	809
Hsiao-shui	-	-	-	150	-	-	-	150

247

Table D-3 (continued)

	Length of Waterway Routes in Indicated Region (km)							
Waterway Route	Northeast	North	East	Central	South	Northwest	Southwest	Total
Yangtze River and Tributaries								
Ch'un-ling-shui	-	-	-	160	-	-	-	160
Lai-shui	-	-	-	170	-	-	-	170
Mi-shui	-	-	-	220	-	-	-	220
Lü-shui	-	-	-	90	-	-	-	90
Lien-shui	-	-	-	45	-	-	-	45
Liu-wei-shui	-	-	-	85	-	-	-	85
Mi-lo-chiang	-	-	-	75	-	-	-	75
Han-chiang	-	-	-	325	-	-	-	325
Liang-sha-yün-ho	-	-	-	110	-	-	-	110
Jen-ho	-	-	-	75	-	-	-	75
Chien-yu-ho	-	-	-	95	-	-	-	95
Tu-shui	-	-	-	257	-	-	-	257
Tan-chiang	-	-	-	450	-	-	-	450
T'ang-ho	-	-	-	170	-	-	-	170
Pai-ho	-	-	-	130	-	-	-	130
Tsuan-ho	-	-	-	60	-	-	-	60
Sun-ho	-	-	-	84	-	-	-	84
Fu-shui	-	-	-	73	-	-	-	73
Kan-chiang	-	-	-	630	-	-	-	630
Kan-yüeh-yün-ho	-	-	-	29	-	-	-	29
Po-yang-hu	-	-	-	72	-	-	-	72
Lo-an-ho	-	-	-	110	-	-	-	110
Jao-ho	-	-	-	185	-	-	-	185
Hsiu-shui	-	-	-	210	-	-	-	210
Hsi-shui	-	-	-	70	-	-	-	70
Hsin-chiang	-	-	-	375	-	-	-	375
Mien-chiang	-	-	-	220	-	-	-	220
Yüan-shui	-	-	-	225	-	-	-	225
Fu-ho	-	-	-	250	-	-	-	250
I-huang-shui	-	-	-	80	-	-	-	80
Lin-shui	-	-	-	45	-	-	-	45
Yü-chiang	-	-	-	60	-	-	-	60
Lu-shui	-	-	-	80	-	-	-	80
Ho-shui	-	-	-	250	-	-	-	250
Shang-yu-chiang	-	-	-	92	-	-	-	92
Kung-chiang	-	-	-	183	-	-	-	183
Lien-shui	-	-	-	70	-	-	-	70
T'ao-chiang	-			180			-	180
P'ing-chiang	-	-	-	60	-	-	-	60
Mei-ch'uan	-	-	-	130	-	-	-	130
Sha-ho	-	-	30	-	-	-	-	30
Ching-i-chiang	-	-	110	-	-	-	-	110
Hui-ho	-	-	35	-	-	-	-	35

248

Table D-3 (continued)

Waterway Route	Length of Waterway Routes in Indicated Region (km)							
	Northeast	North	East	Central	South	Northwest	Southwest	Total
Yangtze River and Tributaries								
Shih-hsi	–	–	105	–	–	–	–	105
Yün-tsao-ho	–	–	65	–	–	–	–	65
Tsao-hu	–	–	35	–	–	–	–	35
Fei-ho	–	–	33	–	–	–	–	33
Wu-sung-chiang	–	–	110	–	–	–	–	110
Ta-yün-ho (Canal)	–	–	360	–	–	–	–	360
Tung-feng-ta-kang to Wu-hu and to Shanghai	–	–	455	–	–	–	–	455
Major Rivers in North and Northeast								
Hsi-liao-ho	650	–	–	–	–	–	–	650
Liao-ho	761	–	–	–	–	–	–	761
Ta-ling-ho	200	–	–	–	–	–	–	200
Hsiao-ling-ho	30	–	–	–	–	–	–	30
Pei-yün-ho	–	143	–	–	–	–	–	143
Tzu-ya-ho	–	360	–	–	–	–	–	360
Fu-yang-ho	–	190	–	–	–	–	–	190
Ta-ching-ho	–	250	–	–	–	–	–	250
Ta-yün-ho	–	908	–	–	–	–	–	908
Lin-chi-yun-ho	–	120	–	–	–	–	–	120
Luan-ho	–	300	–	–	–	–	–	300
Pei-fang-ta-kang-yün-ho	–	177	–	–	–	–	–	177
Hai-ho	–	45	–	–	–	–	–	45
Chang-ho	–	80	–	–	–	–	–	80
Yellow River and Tributaries								
Yellow River	–	–	790	–	–	1,582	–	2,372
Chiao-lai-yün-ho	–	–	150	–	–	–	–	150
Huang-ho-hsiao-ch'ing-ho	–	–	205	–	–	–	–	205
Nan-lo-ho	–	–	–	170	–	–	–	170
Fen-ho	–	360	–	–	–	–	–	360
Pei-lo-ho	–	–	–	–	–	90	–	90
Wei-ho	–	–	–	–	–	350	–	350
Tao-ho	–	–	–	–	–	259	–	259
Huang-shui	–	–	–	–	–	160	–	160
Huai-ho and Tributaries								
Huai-ho	–	–	890	–	–	–	–	890
Kuan-ho	–	–	85	–	–	–	–	85
She-yang-ho	–	–	100	–	–	–	–	100
Ch'uan-ch'ang-ho	–	–	250	–	–	–	–	250
T'ung-yang-yün-ho	–	–	95	–	–	–	–	95
Hui-ho	–	–	180	–	–	–	–	180
Li-ho	–	–	100	–	–	–	–	100

249

Table D-3 (continued)

Waterway Route	Length of Waterway Routes in Indicated Region (km)							
	Northeast	North	East	Central	South	Northwest	Southwest	Total
Huai-ho and Tributaries								
Ssu-shui	-	-	60	-	-	-	-	60
Kuo-ho	-	-	190	190	-	-	-	380
Ying-ho	-	-	390	-	-	-	-	390
Pi-ho	-	-	100	-	-	-	-	100
Huang-shui	-	-	55	-	-	-	-	55
Hung-ho	-	-	90	-	-	-	-	90
Ta-yun-ho	-	-	669	-	-	-	-	669
Han-chiang	-	-	-	-	125	-	-	125
Ting-chiang	-	-	-	-	150	-	-	150
Mei-chiang	-	-	-	-	164	-	-	164
Shih-k'u-shui	-	-	-	-	168	-	-	168
Yung-chiang	-	-	105	-	-	-	-	105
Yun-ho	-	-	185	-	-	-	-	185
Tsao-o-chiang	-	-	44	-	-	-	-	44
Fu-ch'un-chiang	-	-	325	-	-	-	-	325
Hsin-an-chiang	-	-	195	-	-	-	-	195
Ling-chiang	-	-	54	-	-	-	-	54
Ou-chiang	-	-	135	-	-	-	-	135
Ta-ch'i	-	-	112	-	-	-	-	112
Fei-yün-chiang	-	-	-	180	-	-	-	180
Min-chiang and Tributaries								
Min-chiang	-	-	-	-	226	-	-	226
Chien-chi	-	-	-	-	160	-	-	160
Tung-ch'i	-	-	-	-	97	-	-	97
Tsung-ch'i	-	-	-	-	137	-	-	137
Sha-chi	-	-	-	-	160	-	-	160
Chiu-lung-ch'i	-	-	-	-	130	-	-	130
Fu-tsun-ch'i	-	-	-	-	200	-	-	200
Chin-ch'i	-	-	-	-	65	-	-	65
Yu-ch'i	-	-	-	-	40	-	-	40
Shuang-ch'i	-	-	-	-	85	-	-	85
Mu-lan-ch'i	-	-	-	-	45	-	-	45
Chin-chiang	-	-	-	-	85	-	-	85
Chiu-lung-chiang	-	-	-	-	333	-	-	333
Lung-chiang	-	-	-	-	65	-	-	65
Grand Total	1,641	2,933	6,892	10,252	2,435	2,441	7,774	34,368

[9]Sources: Hang-tao Wang (Inland Waterway Network) (Nanking: Bureau of Information, 1947), pp. 13-46; Chung-hua Jen-min Kung-ho-kuo Fen-sheng Ti-t'u (Atlas of the People's Republic of China) (Shanghai: 1953).

Table D-4

DISTRIBUTION OF ALL NAVIGABLE INLAND
WATERWAY ROUTES IN 1949 TO 1950 [a]

Region	Length of Waterway Routes Administered by the Central Government (km)	Length of Waterway Routes Administered by Provincial and Local Governments (km)	Total Length of Waterway Routes (km)
Northeast	3,349 (16%)	1,641 (5%)	4,990 (9%)
North	--	2,933 (8%)	2,933 (5%)
East	2,106 (10%)	6,892 (20%)	8,998 (16%)
Central	1,420 (7%)	10,252 (30%)	11,672 (21%)
South	12,403 (58%)	2,435 (7%)	14,838 (27%)
Northwest	--	2,441 (7%)	2,441 (4%)
Southwest	1,956 (9%)	7,774 (23%)	9,730 (18%)
Total	21,234 (100%)	34,368 (100%)	55,602 (100%)

[a]Sources: Appendix D, Tables D-2 and D-3.

E RAILWAY TRANSPORTATION DATA

Table E-1

LENGTH OF IDENTIFIED RAILWAYS IN OPERATION BY
RAILWAY LINES, REGIONS, AND PROVINCES[a]

Province	Name	Terminals		Length (km) in Operation at End of Indicated Year				
		From	To	1949	1952	1957	1960	1963
Northeast China								
Liaoning	Shen-shan	Mukden	Shan-hai-kuan	420	426	426	426	426
		Mukden (north)	Mukden (east)	...	...	11	11	11
		Mukden (north)	Huang-ku-t'sun	...	3	3	3	3
		Yü-hung	Tu-ch'eng	...	5	5	5	5
		Yü-kuo	Lan-chün-t'sun	...	13	13	13	13
		Chin-hsi	Hu-lu-tao	...	12	13	13	13
	Chin-ch'eng	Chin-chou	Yeh-pai-sh'ou	50	222	222	222	222
		Chin-ling-ssu	Pei-p'iao	...	18	18	18	18
	I-kao	I-hsien	Kao-t'ai-shan	132	192	192	192	192
	Ta-cheng	Ta-hu-shan	Cheng-chia-ts'un	366	366	370	370	370
	Ta-shen	Lü-ta	Mukden	397	397	397	397	397
		Chou-shui-tzu	Lü-shun	...	50	50	52	52
		Chou-shui-tzu	Kan-ching-tzu	...	14	14	14	14
		Chin-chou	Ch'eng-tzu-t'ung	102	102	102	102	102
		Ta-shih-ch'iao	Ying-k'ou	23	23	23	23	23
	Shen-pin	Mukden	Ch'ang-t'u	136	136	136	136	136

252

Table E-1 (continued)

Province	Name	Terminals		Length (km) in Operation at End of Indicated Year				
		From	To	1949	1952	1957	1960	1963
	Shen-an	Mukden	An-tung	261	258	277	277	277
		Su-chia-t'sun	Yü-shu-t'ai	...	13	13	13	13
		Hun-ho	Fu-shun	53	49	57	57	57
		Pen-ch'i	Liao-yang	70	71	69	69	69
		South Pen-ch'i	Shih-ch'iao-tzu	...	24	24	24	24
		South Pen-ch'i	Tien-shih-fu	...	85	86	86	86
		Feng-huang-ch'eng	Liu-chia-ho	...	35	35	35	35
		Feng-huang-ch'eng	Ch'ang-tien	...	112	143	143	143
		An-tung	East An-tung	...	13	13	13	13
	Shen-chi	Mukden	Chao-yang-chen	263	263	263	263	263
		South Fu-shun	North Fu-shun	...	4	4	4	4
	T'ieh-san[a,b]	T'ieh-ling	San Chia-tzu	–	–	–	–	33
	T'ieh-fa[a,b]	T'ieh-ling	Fa-k'u	–	–	–	53	53
	Nü-nan[a,b]	Nü-erh-ho	Nan-p'iao	–	–	–	–	29
	Total			2,273	2,906	2,979	3,034	3,096
	Total Trunk Lines							2,283
	Total Branch Lines							813
Kirin	Shen-pin	Ch'ang-tu	Hsi-chia	349	349	349	349	349
		Tao-lai-chao	Yü-shu	...	...	56	56	56
	Shen-chi	Ch'ao-yang-chen	Kirin	184	182	183	183	183
		Lung-t'an-shan	Ta-feng-man	...	23	23	23	23
		Kirin	North Kirin	...	...	12	12	12
		Kirin	Tien-kang	...	...	43	43	43
	Ssu-chi	Ssu-p'ing	Chi-an	401	400	400	400	400
		T'ung-hua	Hsin-t'ung-hua	...	...	...	4	4
		Hun-chiang	Wan-k'ou	...	18	18	48	48
		Ya-yüan	Ta-li-tzu	113	113	113	113	113
	Ch'ang-a	Kuo-ch'ien-ch'i	K'o-ken-miao	119	184	238	238	238
	Ch'ang-tu	Ch'ang-ch'un	T'u-men	528	527	529	529	529
		Hsin-chan	La-fa	...	9	8	8	8
		Lung-ching	Ho-lung	51	51	51	51	51
		Chiang-pei	Chin-chu	...	19	19	19	19
		Ch'iao-ho	Nai-tzu-shan	...	10	10	10	10
		Ch'ao-yang-ch'uan	Kai-shan-ts'un	58	58	58	58	58
	Mu-t'u	Lu-tao	T'u-men	146	146	146	146	146
		Wang-ch'ing	Hsiao-wang-ch'ing	...	9	9	9	9
	La-pin	Hsiao-ku-chia	Shui-chü-liu	97	97	97	97	97
	P'ing-ch'i	Ssu-p'ing	Pai-ch'eng-tzu	...	353	353	353	353
	Total			2,046	2,548	2,715	2,749	2,749
	Total Trunk Lines							2,295
	Total Branch Lines							454

Table E-1 (continued)

Province	Name	Terminals		Length (km) in Operation at End of Indicated Year				
		From	To	1949	1952	1957	1960	1963
Heilungkiang	Mu-t'u	Mu-tan-chiang	Lu-tao	102	102	102	102	102
	La-pin	Shui-chü-liu	Hsiang-fang	163	163	163	163	163
		Shu-lan	Mei-k'u	...	30	30	30	30
	Pin-pei	Harbin	Pei-an	326	333	333	333	333
		Harbin	San-k'o-shu	13	13	13	13	13
	Ch'i-pei	Ch'i-ch'i-ha-erh	Pei-an	...	231	231	231	231
		Fu-yü	Nen-chiang	181	182	180	180	180
	Sui-chia	Sui-hua	Lien-chiang-k'ou	382	383	369	369	369
		East Chia-mu-ssu	Shuang-ya-shan	...	...	72	72	72
	Shen-pin	Hsi-chia	Harbin	62	62	62	62	62
	P'ing-ch'i	Pai-ch'eng-tzu	Ch'i-ch'i-ha-erh	...	218	218	218	218
		Hung-ch'i-ying	Yü-shu-ts'un	...	...	3	3	3
	Chia-mu	Mu-tan-chiang	Ho-kang	392	392	392	392	392
	Lin-hu	Lin-k'ou	Hu-t'ou	172	171	171	336	336
		Hsi-chi-hsi	Hsia-ch'eng-tzu	104	104	103	103	103
		Chi-hsi	Heng-shan	12	12	12	12	12
	Sui-man	Sui-fen-ho	Nien-tzu-shan	903	903	903	903	903
		Harbin	San-k'o-shu	9	9	9	9	9
		Kou-k'ou	125 kilometers	...	...	126	126	126
		Ya-pu-li	Lou-shan	...	70	70	70	70
		Nao-t'ou	Ch'ang-ting	...	...	...	42	42
	Chia-lien	Chia-mu-ssu	Lien-chiang-k'ou	...	...	6	6	6
	Nan-lin	Nan-i	I-ch'un	105	105	104	104	104
		I-ch'un	Hsin-ch'ing	...	...	232	232	232
		I-ch'un	Tsui-luan	...	...	21	21	21
	Total			2,926	3,483	3,925	4,132	4,132
	Total Trunk Lines							3,445
	Total Branch Lines							687
Regional Total				7,245	8,937	9,619	9,915	9,977
Regional Total Trunk Lines								8,023
Regional Total Branch Lines								1,954
North China								
Hopeh	Ching-han	Peking	Tz'u-hsien	481	481	481	481	481
		Chou-k'ou-tien	Liu-li-ho	...	...	15	15	15
		Pao-ting	Pao-ting-nan	...	...	7	7	7
		Han-tan	Ho-ts'un	...	...	50	50	50
		Ma-t'ou	Feng-feng	...	...	19	19	19
		K'uang-shan	Ta-lien	...	...	35	35	35
	Ching-pao	Hsi-chih-men	Hsi-wan-p'u	256	256	256	256	256
		Kalgan	Kalgan North	...	...	10	10	10
		Hsi-chih-men	Feng-t'ai	...	...	13	13	13
		Hsi-chih-men	Tung-pien-men	...	...	12	12	12
		Tung-pien-men	T'ieh-tao-yen-chiu yüan	...	...	9	9	9
		Hsi-chih-men	Pan-chiao	...	26	56	56	56
		Hsüan-hua	P'ang-chia-pu	...	...	45	45	45

254

Province	Name	Terminals		Length (km) in Operation at End of Indicated Year				
		From	To	1949	1952	1957	1960	1963
	Feng-sha[b]	Feng-t'ai	Sha-ch'eng	–	–	104	104	104
	Ching-shan	Peking	Shan-hai-kuan	418	418	417	417	417
		Pei-tai-ho	Hai-pin	...	...	10	10	10
		Tang-ku	Hsin-kang	...	...	...	10	10
		Tang-ku	Tang-ku South	...	...	...	5	5
	Ching-ch'eng	Tung-pien-men	Ying-sh'ou-ying	90	128	128	128	128
		Shang-pan-ch'eng[b]	Ying-sh'ou-ying	–	16	120	120	120
		Huai-jou[b]	Ying-sh'ou-ying	–	–	61	61	61
		Hsü-chia-chan[b]	Miao-t'ai-tzu	–	–	11	11	11
	Chin-ch'eng(n.)	Yeh-pai-sh'ou	Ch'eng-te	...	118	215	215	215
		T'ung-hsien(w.)	T'ung-hsien(e.)	...	...	6	6	6
	Ching-p'u	Tientsin	Sang-yüan	217	217	217	217	217
		Liang-wang-chuang	Hui-tui	...	...	26	26	26
	Te-shih	Pa-li-chuang	Shih-chia-chuang	172	172	172	172	172
	Sheng-t'ai	Shih-chia-chuang	Niang-tzu-kuan	73	73	73	73	73
	Total			1,707	1,905	2,568	2,383	2,583
	Total Trunk Lines							2,244
	Total Branch Lines							339
Shansi	Ching-pao	Hsi-wan-p'u	Pao-tzu-wan	151	151	151	151	151
	Cheng-t'ai	Niang-tzu-kuan	Yü-tz'u	131	131	131	131	131
		Hsin-ching	Wei-shui	...	...	11	11	11
	T'ung-p'u	Ta-t'ung	Feng-ling-tu	164	835	860	860	860
		Chiang-ts'un	Hsi-hsien	...	...	31	31	31
		Shang-lan-ts'un	Chi-fu-fen	...	...	16	16	16
		P'ing-wang	K'ou-ch'üan	...	...	10	10	10
		Chieh-hsiu[b]	Yang-ch'uan-chu	–	–	–	–	46
		T'ai-yüan[b]	T'ao-hsing	–	–	–	–	27
		K'òu-ch'üan[b]	Wang-ts'un	–	–	–	–	60
		T'ung-kuan[b]	Feng-ling-tu	–	–	–	9	9
	Total			446	1,117	1,210	1,219	1,352
	Total Trunk Lines							1,142
	Total Branch Lines							210
Inner Mongolia	Ching-pao	Pao-tzu-wan	Pao-t'ou	211	420	420	420	420
	Chi-erh[b]	Chi-ning	Erh-lien	–	–	330	330	330
	Ch'ang-a	Ko-ken-miao	A-erh-shan	283	283	283	283	283
	Pao-lan(n.)[b]	Pao-t'ou	San-sheng-kung	–	–	–	278	278
	Pao-pai[b]	Pao-t'ou	Pai-yün-o-po	–	–	148	148	148
	Erh-shui	Erh-tao-sha-ho	Shui-mo-t'an			53	53	53
	Chin-ch'eng(n.)	Yeh-pai-ch'ou	Ch'ih-teng	–	–	147	147	147

Table E-1 (continued)

Province	Name	Terminals		Length (km) in Operation at End of Indicated Year				
		From	To	1949	1952	1957	1960	1963
	Sui-man(n.)	Nien-tzu-shan	Man-chou-li	579	579	580	580	580
	Ya-lin	Ya-k'o-shih	K'u-tu-erh	...	...	144	144	144
		K'u-tu-erh	Kan-ho	...	72	354	354	354
		I-t'u-li-ho	Ken-ho	...	...	27	27	27
	Total			1,073	1,354	2,486	2,764	2,764
	Total Trunk Lines							2,684
	Total Branch Lines							80
Regional Total				3,226	4,376	6,264	6,566	6,699
Regional Total Trunk Lines								6,070
Regional Total Branch Lines								629
East China								
Shantung	Ching-pu	Sang-yüan	Han-chuang	414	414	414	414	414
	Te-shih	Te-chou	Pa-li-chuang	9	9	8	8	8
		Hsin-t'ai	Tz'u-yao	...	66	67	67	67
		Hsüeh-ch'eng	Tsao-chuang	...	...	32	32	32
	Chiao-chi	Tsinan	Tsingtao	393	392	393	393	393
		Pa-tou	Chang-tien	...	...	49	49	49
	Lan-yen[b]	Lan-ts'un	Chefoo	–	–	183	183	183
	Total			816	881	1,146	1,146	1,146
	Total Trunk Lines							998
	Total Branch Lines							148
Kiangsu	Ching-pu	Han-chuang	P'u-k'ou	378	378	383	383	383
		Hsü-chou(e.)	Hsü-chou(n.)	...	...	6	6	6
	Te-shih	Liu-ch'üan	Chia-wang	...	...	16	16	16
	Hu-ning	Shanghai	Nanking	312	312	312	311	311
		Shanghai	Wu-sung	16	16	16	15	15
		Shanghai[b]	Wen-tsao-pin	–	–	–	14	14
		Shanghai[b]	Min-hang	–	–	–	–	42
	Hu-hang-yung	Shanghai	Feng-ching	70	70	70	70	70
		Jih-hui-kang	Hsin-lung-hua	...	4	4	4	4
	Ning-kan	Nanking	Tz'u-hu	81	81	81	81	81
	Lung-hai	Lien-yün-kang	Tang-shan	299	306	306	306	306
	Total			1,156	1,167	1,194	1,206	1,248
	Total Trunk Lines							1,151
	Total Branch Lines							97

Table E-1 (continued)

Province	Name	Terminals		Length (km) in Operation at End of Indicated Year				
		From	To	1949	1952	1957	1960	1963
Chekiang	Hu-hang-yung[b]	Feng-ching	Ch'uan-shan	126	126	294	329	329
		Nan-hsing-ch'iao	Hangchow	–	–	–	3	3
	Che-kan	Hsiao-shan	Hsin-t'ang-pien	302	302	302	302	302
		Chin-hua	Hsin-an-chiang	...	23	23	69	69
	Total			428	451	619	703	703
	Total Trunk Lines							631
	Total Branch Lines							72
Anhwei	Ning-kan	Tz'u-hu	Wu-hu	10	10	50	50	50
	Huai-nan	Pang-fou	Yü-ch'i-k'ou	131	248	248	248	248
		Pa-kung-shan	Shui-chia-hu	27	27	44	44	44
		Ta-t'ung	Tien-chia-an	...	...	6	6	6
		Wu-hu[b]	Feng-hsiang-kuo	–	–	–	–	53
		Fu-li-chi[b] (Su-hsien)	Huai-ch'i	–	–	–	–	31
	Total			168	285	348	348	432
	Total Trunk Lines							342
	Total Branch Lines							90
Regional Total				2,568	2,784	3,307	3,403	3,529
Regional Total Trunk Lines								3,122
Regional Total Branch Lines								407
Central China								
Honan	Ching-han	Tz'u-hsien	Wu-sheng-kuan	562	562	562	562	562
		T'ang-yin	Hao-pi	...	...	19	19	19
		Hsin-hsiang	Chiao-tso	64	64	62	62	62
		Wu-li-fou	Cheng-chou(w.)	–	–	6	6	6
		Meng-miao[b]	Shen-lou	–	–	61	61	61
	Lung-hai	Tang-shan	T'ung-kuan	622	622	622	622	622
		Hui-hsing[b]	San-men-hsia	–	–	14	14	14
		Lo-yang[b]	I-yang	–	–	–	–	22
		An-yang[b]	Li-chen	–	–	–	–	32
	Total			1,248	1,248	1,346	1,346	1,400
	Total Trunk Lines							1,193
	Total Branch Lines							207
Kiangsi	Che-kan	Hsin-t'ang-pien	P'ing-hsiang	366	598	598	598	598
		Ch'üan-chiang	Kao-k'eng	...	7	7	6	6
	Nan-hsün	Nan-ch'ang	Chiu-chiang	129	129	128	128	128
	Ying-hsia[b]	Ying-t'an	Tzu-ch'i	–	–	73	73	73
	Total			495	734	806	805	805
	Total Trunk Lines							799
	Total Branch Lines							6

257

Table E-1 (continued)

Province	Name	Terminals		Length (km) in Operation at End of Indicated Year				
		From	To	1949	1952	1957	1960	1963
Hupeh	Ching-han and Yüeh-han	Wu-sheng-kuan	Yang-lou-ssu	159	347	347	347	347
		Han-shui	Line	...	...	6	6	6
		Yangtze	Line	...	...	9	9	9
	Wu-sui[b]	Wu-ch'ang	Sui-hsien	–	–	–	–	216
	Wu-huang[b]	Wu-ch'ang	Huang-shih	–	–	–	98	98
	Total			159	347	362	460	676
	Total Trunk Lines							661
	Total Branch Lines							15
Hunan	Che-kan	P'ing-hsiang	Chu-chou	...	82	82	82	82
	Yüeh-han	Yang-lou-ssu	P'ing-shih	315	602	602	602	602
	Hsiang-kuei	Heng-yang	Tzu-ch'i	187	187	187	187	187
	Hsiang-ch'ien[b]	Chu-chou	Lou-ti	–	–	132	132	132
		Lou-ti	Chin-chu-shan	–	–	–	–	65
	Lou-shao[b]	Lou-ti	Shao-yang	–	–	–	–	98
	Ch'en-san	Ch'en-hsien	San-tu	...	...	47	47	47
	Wu-pai	Wu-ch'i	Pai-shih-tu	...	...	14	14	14
	Total			502	871	1,064	1,064	1,227
	Total Trunk Lines							1,101
	Total Branch Lines							126
Regional Total				2,404	3,200	3,578	3,675	4,108
Regional Total Trunk Lines								3,754
Regional Total Brnahc Lines								354
South China								
Fukien	Ying-hsia[b]	Tzu-ch'i	Lai-chou	–	–	212	212	212
		Lai-chou	Amoy	–	–	409	409	409
	Lai-fu[b]	Lai-chou	Foochow	–	–	–	194	194
		Kuo-k'eng	Lung-ch'i	–	–	–	11	11
		Chang-p'ing	Lung-yen	–	–	–	58	58
		Wai-yang	Nan-p'ing	–	–	–	24	24
	Total			–	–	621	908	908
	Total Trunk Lines							815
	Total Branch Lines							93
Kwangtung	Yüeh-han	P'ing-shih	Canton	...	334	334	334	334
	Kuang-chiu	Canton	Shen-ch'uan	146	146	146	146	146
		Chi-shan	Huang-pu	...	...	4	4	4
	Kuang-san	Canton	San-shui	...	49	49	49	49
	Lien-mao[b]	Lien-chiang (Ho-ts'un)	Mao-ming	–	–	–	61	61

258

Table E-1 (continued)

Province	Name	Terminals From	Terminals To	Length (km) in Operation at End of Indicated Year 1949	1952	1957	1960	1963
	Hai-nan	Pa-so	Shih-lu[c]	...	...	52	52	52
	Li-chan	Wen-li	Chan-chiang	...	...	106	106	106
	Total			146	529	691	752	752
	Total Trunk Lines							699
	Total Branch Lines							53
Kwangsi	Hsiang-kuei[b]	Tzu-ch'i	Mu-nan-kuan	346	838	826	826	826
	Li-chan[b]	Li-t'ang	Wen-li	–	–	209	209	209
	Ch'ien-kuei	Liu-chou	Ma-wei	262	314	314	314	314
	Total			608	1,152	1,349	1,349	1,349
	Total Trunk Lines							1,349
	Total Branch Lines							--
Regional Total				754	1,681	2,661	3,009	3,009
Regional Total Trunk Lines								2,863
Regional Total Branch Lines								146
Northwest China								
Shensi	Lung-hai	T'ung-kuan	T'o-shih	386	386	386	386	386
	Pao-ch'eng[b]	Pao-chi	Ta-t'an	–	–	–	302	302
	T'ung-hsien	T'ung-ch'uan	Hsien-yang	135	135	135	135	135
	Hsi-yü[b]	Sian	Yü-hsia	–	–	–	45	45
	Total			521	521	521	868	868
	Total Trunk Lines							688
	Total Branch Lines							180
Kansu	Lung-hai[b]	T'o-shih	Lan-chou	74	74	422	422	422
	Pao-lan[b]	Kan-t'ang	Lan-chou	–	–	–	232	232
	Lan-hsin[b]	Lan-chou	Wei-ya	–	332	942	1,185	1,185
	Ti-pai	Ti-chiu-tai	Pai-yin	...	...	23	23	23
	Lan-ch'ing[b]	Ho-k'ou	Shai-ch'e-wan	–	–	–	53	53
	Hei-lao[b]	Hei-shan-hu	Lao-chün-miao	–	–	32	32	32
	Lan-a[b]	Lan-chou	A-kan-chen	–	–	21	21	21
	Wu-kan[b]	Wu-wei	Kan-t'ang	–	–	–	–	185
	Total			74	406	1,440	1,968	2,153
	Total Trunk Lines							2,077
	Total Branch Lines							76
Ningsia	Pao-lan[b]	San-sheng-kung	Kan-t'ang	–	–	–	470	470
	Total			–	–	–	470	470
	Total Trunk Lines							470
	Total Branch Lines							–

259

Table E-1 (continued)

| Province | Name | Terminals | | Length (km) in Operation at End of Indicated Year | | | | |
		From	To	1949	1952	1957	1960	1963
Tsinghai	Lan-ch'ing[b]	Shui-ch'e-wan	Hsi-ning	-	-	-	122	122
	Hsi-hai[b]	Hsi-ning	Hai-yen	-	-	-	-	100
	Total			-	-	-	122	222
	Total Trunk Lines							222
	Total Branch Lines							-
Sinkiang	Lan-hsin	Wei-ya	Urumchi	...	...	...	142	707
	Total			...	...	...	142	707
	Total Trunk Lines							707
	Total Branch Lines							-
Regional Total				595	927	1,961	3,570	4,420
Regional Total Trunk Lines								4,164
Regional Total Branch Lines								256
Southwest China								
Szechwan	Pao-ch'eng[b]	Ta-t'an	Ch'eng-tu	-	-	-	367	367
	Ch'eng-yü[b]	Ch'eng-tu	Chungking	-	504	504	504	504
	Ch'uan-ch'ien[b]	Hsiao-nan-hai	Kan-shui	58	58	119	119	119
	San-wan	San-chiang	Wan-sheng	...	...	32	32	32
	Nei-k'un[b]	Nei-chiang	An-pien	-	-	-	142	142
	Hsin-kuan[b]	Hsin-tu	Kuan-hsien	-	-	-	-	61
	Total			58	562	655	1,164	1,225
	Total Trunk Lines							1,132
	Total Branch Lines							93
Yünnan	Nei-k'un	Kun-ming	Chan-i	174	174	180	180	180
	Tien-yüeh	Kun-ming	Ho-k'ou	...	...	469	469	469
	Pi-shih	Pi-se-chai	Shih-p'ing	...	...	143	143	143
	Ko-chi	Ko-chiu	Chi-chieh	...	...	34	34	34
	Tien-mien[b]	Kun-ming	I-p'ing-lang	-	-	-	137	137
	K'un-shih	Kun-ming	Shih-tsui	12	12	12	12	12
	Total			186	186	838	975	975
	Total Trunk Lines							929
	Total Branch Lines							46
Kweichow	Ch'ien-kuei[b]	Ma-wei	Kuei-yang	-	157	293	293	293
	Total			-	157	293	293	293
	Total Trunk Lines							293
	Total Branch Lines							-
Tibet				-	-	-	-	-
Regional Total				244	905	1,786	2,432	2,493
Regional Total Trunk Lines								2,354
Regional Total Branch Lines								139
Grand Total				17,036	22,810	29,176	32,570	34,235
Grand Total Trunk Lines								30,350
Grand Total Branch Lines								3,885

Table E-1 (continued)

[a]Source: Ling Hung-hsün, General Survey of Railways in China (1950).

[b]New railways.

[c]The railways in Hainan Island were originally listed in Ling Hung-hsün, ibid., p. 34. The latest time tables list no operating routes. According to Taiwan reports, only 52 km of railways from Pa-so to Shih-lu had been restored to normal operation by 1961.

Table E-2

RAILWAY RADIAL COUNTS OF
117 ECONOMIC CENTERS[a, b]

Rank	City	Number of Railway Radials	Rank	City	Number of Railway Radials
A	Peking	28	B	Chi-hsi	4
	Mukden	24		Chiao-tso	4
	Shanghai	17		T'ung-hua	3
	Tientsin	12		Hai-k'ou	2
	Wu-han	12		Ho-fei	2
	Nanking	12		Urumchi	2
	Ch'ang-ch'un	12		Fou-hsin	2
	T'ai-yüan	10			
	Canton	9		Chu-chou	12
	Fu-shun	8	C	Chin-chou	8
	Tsinan	8		Hsin-hai-lien	8
	Kun-ming	8		Pao-chi	8
	Hsu-chou	8		Ta-t'ung	7
	Cheng-chou	8		Pang-fou	7
	Sian	6		Yü-t'zu	6
	An-shan	5		Ssu-p'ing	6
	Tsingtao	4		Chi-ning	6
	Tzu-po	4		Wu-hu	6
	Chungking	4		An-yang	6
	T'ang-shan	4		Heng-yang	6
	Ch'ang-sha	4		Liu-chou	6
	Soochow	4		Nei-chiang	6
	Chi-chi-ha-erh	2		Mu-tan-chiang	4
				Liao-yang	5
B	Lan-chou	20		Hsin-hsiang	5
	Harbin	16		Ch'eng-te	4
	Shih-chia-chuang	16		Ying-k'ou	4
	Kirin	13		Chia-mu-ssu	4
	Pao-t'ou	12		Ho-kang	4
	Ch'eng-tu	8		Shuang-ya-shan	4
	An-tung	8		Kalgan	4
	Lu-ta	8		Pao-ting	4
	Hangchow	7		Ch'in-huang-tao	4
	Nan-ch'ang	6		Yang-ch'uan	4
	Pen-ch'i	6		Chefoo	4
	Han-tan	5		Wu-hsi	4
	Huai-nan	5		Ch'ang-chou	4
	Huang-shih	4		Chen-chiang	4
	Lo-yang	4		Ning-po	4
	Kuei-yang	4		K'ai-feng	4
	Foochow	4		Shang-ch'iu	4

Table E-2 (continued)

Rank	City	Number of Railway Radials	Rank	City	Number of Railway Radials
C	Amoy	4	C	Ching-te-chen	–
	Chan-chiang	4		Ch'üan-chou	–
	Hsi-ning	4		Fo-shan	–
	Huhehot	2		Chiang-men	–
	Hsiang-t'an	2		Wu-chou	–
	Liao-yüan	2		Kashgar	–
	Wei-fang	2		I-ning	–
	Shao-hsing	2		Wen-chou	–
	Chia-hsing	2		Lu-chou	–
	Shao-yang	2		Wu-t'ung-ch'iao	–
	Swatow	2		Nan-ch'ung	–
	Ch'ao-chou	2		An-ch'ing	–
	Nan-ning	2		Hu-chou	–
	Kue-lin	2		I-ch'un	–
	Yin-ch'uan	2		Ch'ang-chih	–
	Tzu-kung	2		Nan-t'ung	–
	I-pin	2		T'ai-chou	–
	Ko-chiu	2		Ch'ang-shu	–
				Yang-chou	–

[a]Sources: The railway radial counts are based on the following: Communist China's Railroad Passenger Time Table, Summer, 1960, JPRS, No. 8153, April 30, 1961 and No. 21963, November 21, 1963, from Ch'uan-kuo T'ieh-lu Lu-k'o Lieh-ch'e Shih-k'o-piao--1960 ho 1963 nien Hsia-chi Shih-hsing (Peking: Jen-min T'ieh-lu Chu-pan-she, 1960 and 1963); Chung-hua Jen-min Kung-ho-kuo Fen-sheng Titu (Provincial Atlas of the Chinese People's Republic (Shanghai: 1953).

[b]See Table 4-3 for the classifications of the cities. All cities having different industrial and nonindustrial rank prefixes in Table 4-3 are placed in the higher ranking group in this table.

Table E-3

NUMBER OF RAILWAY RADIALS IN 328 INDUSTRIAL LOCATIONS

Location[a]	Number of Railway Radials[b]	Location[a]	Number of Railway Radials[b]
Shanghai	17	Lan-chou	20
Tientsin	12	Lü-ta	8
Wu-han	12	Swatow	2
An-shan	5	Ha-mi	2
Chungking	4	Fou-hsin	2
Nanking	12	Shih-lu	2
Peking	28	Hsiang-t'an	2
Pao-t'ou	12	Kirin	13
Canton	9	Hangchow	7
T'ai-yüan	10	Nan-ning	2
An-tung	8	P'ing-hsiang	3
Nan-ch'ang	6	Ch'ang-ch'un	12
Tzu-po	4	Ta-t'ung	7
Tsingtao	4	T'ung-ling	-
Sian	6	Huhehot	2
Chiu-ch'üan	2	Liu-chou	6
Ch'ang-sha	4	Yang-ch'üan	4
Foochow	4	Chiang-yu	2
Ma-an-shan	2	Su-hsien	4
Fu-shun	8	Lien-yüan	2
Tsinan	8	Chi-hsi	4
T'ung-hua	3	Chiao-tso	4
Huai-nan	5	Hsu-chou	8
Mukden	24	Hsin-yang	4
Pen-ch'i	6	Ho-kang	4
Chu-yang-ch'i	-	Chia-mu-ssu	4
Shih-p'ing	-	Soochow	4
T'ang-shan	4	Fu-la-erh-chi	2
Kun-ming	8	Chiao-ho	3
Kuei-yang	4	Shui-ch'eng	-
Urumchi	2	Hsin-yü	2
Huang-shih	4	Tzu-hsien	2
Lo-yang	4	P'ing-chuang	2
Harbin	16	San-ming	2
Shih-chia-chuang	16	An-yang	6
Ch'eng-tu	8	Hsüan-hua	2
Ch'eng-te	4	Nan-yang	-
Han-tan	5	Ying-k'ou	4
Lin-fen	2	Feng-ch'eng	2
Pien-chüang-tzu	-	Cheng-chou	8
Ho-fei	2	An-ch'ing	-

264

Table E-3 (continued)

Location[a]	Number of Railway Radials[b]	Location[a]	Number of Railway Radials[b]
Ta-hsien	-	Wu-lan-hao-t'e	2
Amoy	4	Ling-ching-t'an	-
Ho-nan	-	Hu-hsien	1
Pi-ch'ieh	-	Hsüan-wei	-
Lu-chou	-	Ching-chen	-
Wu-hsi	4	Liao-yang	5
Ching-kang-shan	-	Hsin-hsiang	5
Hai-la-erh	2	Hsing-ning	-
Ch'ang-chih	-	P'ing-kuei	-
Hui-tse	-	Pao-chi	8
Hsiao-lang-ti	-	Ta-t'ung	-
O-ch'eng	2	Hsi-chung	-
Chu-chou	12	Heng-hsien	-
Tsao-chuang	2	Ku-tien	-
Hsin-an-chiang	2	Cho-hsien	4
San-men-hsia	2	Chin-chou	8
Liang-chuang	-	Nan-p'iao	2
Yang-ch'un	-	Tu-yün	2
Hsü-ch'ang	2	Shih-chiu-t'an	-
An-shun	-	Shih-tsui-shan	-
Ch'i-ch'i-ha-erh	2	Shih-ch'üan	-
Liao-yüan	2	Shang-hang	-
Hsi-ning	4	Fo-shan	-
Chi-li-lung	-	Wu-shih	4
Tsun-i	-	Heng-yang	6
An-hua	-	Hu-nan-chen	-
Wan-an	-	Wang-t'ing	4
Hsin-feng	-	Wei-fang	2
Pa-pan-hsia	-	Chan-chiang	4
Hsia-kuan	-	Hsiao-chiang-k'ou	-
Chi-ch'i	-	San-chiang	-
Huan-jen	-	Wei-yüan	-
Ch'ih-feng	4	Lu-chai	2
Lao-ha-ho	-	Shih-mo-ch'i	-
Tzu-ch'uan	2	Shui-yen	-
Mu-tan-chiang	6	Pao-ting	4
Tzu-p'ing-pu	-	Chin-hsi	2
Tan-chiang-k'ou	-	Fen-hsi	-
Yen-kuo-hsia	-	Hung-shan	-
Tung-chiang	-	Wu-hu	6
Chien-ch'i	-	K'ai-feng	4
Chiang-men	-	An-chiang	-
Chao-p'ing	-	Ch'üan-chou	-
Pang-fou	7	Nan-p'ing	6
Feng-t'ai	-	Shao-kuan	2
Chin-chi	-	Hai-k'ou	2

265

Table E-3 (continued)

Location[a]	Number of Railway Radials[b]	Location[a]	Number of Railway Radials[b]
Tsaidam	-	Nan-lin	-
Chang-chou	-	Kashgar	-
Ssu-p'ing	6	Liu-shui-ho	-
Cheng-ting	4	Hsia-ssu	-
Chefoo	4	Yang-tsung-hai	-
Hsin-cheng	-	Nan-ch'ung	-
Chai-chia-hsia	-	I-ning	-
Lo-ch'ang	4	Yung-teng	2
Ch'i-chiang	2	Ju-yüan	-
I-pin	2	Chi-an	-
Kueilin	2	I-ch'ang	-
Kuo-k'eng	2	Tzu-hsing	2
Chang-p'ing	2	Hao-pi	2
Kan-chou	-	Tang-t'u	2
Nan-t'ung	-	Yang-chou	-
I-hsien	-	Han-chuang	-
Pei-p'iao	2	Yü-t'zu	6
Mi-yün	2	Yu-chou	-
Ssu-shih-sha-ho	-	Tien-shih-fu	2
Ch'ang-chou	4	Shuang-ya-shan	4
Sha-p'o-t'ou	-	Ching-po-hu	2
Ch'ang-t'an	-	Chin-huang-tao	4
Chao-shih	-	Hsing-t'ai	4
T'ien-shui	4	Kuan-t'ing	2
Yü-men	2	Shih-hsia-li	-
Ch'ang-shou	-	Chiao-chia-wan	-
Kuang-yüan	2	Ning-wu	2
So-chia	-	Sh'ou-yang	2
K'uan-hsien	2	Chi-ning	6
Yin-ch'uan	2	Ta-hsing-an-ling	2
Hsien-yang	2	Hsin-t'ai-hsien	2
Wu-chou	-	Ch'i-shu-yen	4
P'ing-an	-	Ning-po	4
Chin-sai-hsien	-	Wen-chou	-
Chen-chiang	4	Huang-t'an-k'ou	-
Nan-ting	-	Mao-chien-shan	-
Hsin-hai-lien	8	Ma-ch'eng	-
Wu-lan-chia-pu-meng	-	Shao-yang	2
Lung-ching	-	Ch'ang-te	-
Kalgan	4	Cha-ling	-
Yü-hsien	-	Ch'ang-ning	-
Shao-hsing	2	Chiang-k'ou	-
Pai-lien-ho	-	Yung-ch'un	-
Ching-te-chen	-	Fu-an	-
Shang-yu	-	Lung-ch'i	-
Jen-hua	-	Lien-chiang	3

Table E-3 (continued)

Location[a]	Number of Railway Radials[b]	Location[a]	Number of Railway Radials[b]
T'ung-ch'uan	2	P'ing-wang	–
Tu-shan-tzu	–	Ling-shih-hsien	2
Tzu-kung	2	Hsiang-kuang-t'ung	–
Wan-hsien	–	Yen-chi	2
Lo-shan	–	T'ien-chang-tzu	2
Ko-chiu	2	Chien-kuo-chi	2
Liu-lang-tung	–	Tu-hsi	2
Lhasa	–	Chien-ch'en	2
Ho-ch'uan	–	Hun-ch'un	4
Karamai	–	Chi-ning	2
Ko-ko-to-hai	–	Tao-nan	2
Shan-tan	2	Tao-an	4
Ko-erh-mu	–	I-lan	–
Fang-ch'eng	–	Sui-fen-ho	4
Feng-huang-shan	–	Ti-tao	2
Chung-shan	–	Pei-an	2
Ch'ao-chou	2	Sun-wu	2
Ch'ü-chiang	4	Hei-ho	2
Shang-yao	2	Shuang-t'ou-shan	–
Lung-yen	–	Yü-erh-ai	–
Chin-chiang	–	T'ung-liao	2
Yüen-yang	4	Ch'ang-shu	–
Chi-ch'i	–	Ch'ang-ch'ang	–
Hsiang-fan	–	Pa-pu	–
Shang-ch'iu	4	Nan-cheng	–
Hsiang-kung-miao	–	Wu-la-po	–
Chia-hsing	2	Wu-t'ung-chiao	–
Chin-hua	4	Chien-wei	–
T'ai-chou	–	K'ang-ting	–
Wu-ho-hao-t'e	–	Shih-lung-pa	–
Cha-lai-no-erh	2	Ta-yen-men	–

[a]Table 3-1 and Appendix B, Table B-1. The cities are given in order of industrial capacity (Table B-2).

[b]The railway radial counts are devised in the same way as those in Appendix E, Table E-1.

Table E-4

NEW RAILWAYS IN COMMUNIST CHINA[a]

Railway Line	Terminals		Length (km)	Year Completed	Military Line	Connecting Line	Lines Passing Through Locations of Known Fixed Natural Resources		Lines Not Passing Through Locations of Known Fixed Natural Resources	
	From	To					Trunk Line	Other Line	Trunk Line	Other Line
Northeast China (Total Length of 3 Lines = 115 km)										
T'ieh-san[b]	T'ieh-ling	San-chia-tzu	33	1961–1963						xx
T'ieh-fa[b]	T'ieh-ling	Fa-k'u	53	1961–1963						xx
Nli-nan[b]	Nli-erh-ho	Nan-p'iao	29	1961–1963				xx		
North China (Total Length of 11 Lines = 1,194 km)										
Ching-ch'eng	Shang-pan-ch'eng	Ying-shou-ying	120	1959		xx	xx			
	Hsü-chia-chan	Miao-t'ai-tzu	11	1958						xx
	Huai-jou	Ying-shou-ying	61	1959				xx		
Feng-sha	Feng-t'ai	Sha-ch'eng	104	1955		xx	xx			
Chi-erh	Chi-ning	Erh-lien	330	1956	xx				xx	
Pao-pai	Pao-t'ou	Pai-ylin-o-po	148	1956			xx			
Pao-lan(n.)	Pao-t'ou	San-sheng-kung	278	1958			xx			
Chieh-yang	Chieh-hsiu	Yang-ch'uan-chu	46	1961–1963						xx
T'ai-t'ao	T'ai-ylian	T'ao-hsing	27	1961–1963						xx
T'ung-teng	T'ung-kuan	Feng-ling-tu	9	1958		xx	xx			
K'ou-wang	K'ou-ch'uan	Wang-ts'un	60	1961–1963						xx
East China (Total of 7 Lines = 535 km)										
Lan-yen	Lan-ts'un	Chefoo	183	1956		xx			xx	
Lan-hsin	Lan-ch'i	Hsin-an-chiang	48	1958				xx		
Ts'ao-ch'uan	Ts'ao-o-chiang	Ch'uan-shan	164	--		xx			xx	
Hu-wen	Shanghai	Wen-tsao-pin	14	1961–1963						xx
Hu-min	Shanghai	Min-hang	42	1961–1963						xx
Fu-huai	Fu-li-chi	Huai-ch'i	31	1961–1963				xx		
Wu-feng	Wu-hu	Feng-hsiang-kuo	53	1961–1963						xx

Table E-4 (continued)

| Railway Line | Terminals | | Length (km) | Year Completed | Military Line | Connecting Line | Lines Passing Through Locations of Known Fixed Natural Resources | | Lines Not Passing Through Locations of Known Fixed Natural Resources | |
	From	To					Trunk Line	Other Line	Trunk Line	Other Line
Central China (Total of 10 Lines = 811 km)										
Wu-huang	Wu-ch'ang	Huang-shih	98	1958			xx			
Meng-shen	Meng-miao	Shen-lou	61	1957						xx
Hui-san	Hui-hsing	San-men-hsia	14	1957				xx		
Ying-hsia(n.)	Ying-t'an	Tzu-ch'i	73	1957	xx		xx			xx
Lo-i	Lo-yang	I-yang	22	1961-1963						xx
An-li	An-yang	Li-chen	32	1961-1963				xx		
Lou-chin	Lou-ti	Chin-chu-shan	65	1961-1963			xx			xx
Lou-shao	Lou-ti	Shao-yang	98	1961-1963			xx			
Wu-sui	Wu-ch'ang	Sui-hsien	216	1961-1963			xx			
Hsiang-ch'ien	Chu-chou	Lou-ti	132	--					xx	
South China (Total of 8 Lines = 1,613 km)										
Ying-hsia(s.)	Tzu-ch'i	Amoy	621	1957	xx		xx			
Kuo-lung	Kuo-k'eng	Lung-ch'i	11	1958				xx		
Chang-lung	Chang-p'ing	Lung-yen	58	1958						xx
Wai-nan	Wai-yang	Nan-p'ing	24	1958						xx
Nan-fu	Nan-p'ing	Foochow	168	1958			xx			
Lai-mu	Lai-pin	Mu-nan-kuan	355	1951	xx		xx			
Li-chan	Li-t'ang	Chan-chiang	315	1955	xx				xx	
Lien-mao	Lien-chiang (Ho-ts'un)	Mao-ming	61	1959				xx		
Northwest China (Total of 11 Lines = 3,839 km)										
T'ien-lan	T'ien-shui	Lan-chou	348	1957			xx			
Lan-hsin	Lan-chou	Urumchi	1,892	1961-1963			xx			
Hei-lao	Hei-shan-hu	Lao-chün-miao	32	--	xx			xx		
Pao-lan(w.)	San-sheng-kung	Lan-chou	716	1958			xx			
Lan-ch'ing	Lan-chou	Hsi-ning	175	1959			xx			
Hsi-hai	Hsi-ning	Hai-yen	100	1961-1963						xx

Table E-4 (continued)

Railway Line	Terminals		Length (km)	Year Completed	Military Line	Connecting Line	Lines Passing Through Locations of Known Fixed Natural Resources		Lines Not Passing Through Locations of Known Fixed Natural Resources	
	From	To					Trunk Line	Other Line	Trunk Line	Other Line
Wu-kan	Wu-wei	Kan-t'ang	185	1961-1963		xx	xx			
Lan-a	Lan-chou	A-kan-chen	21	--				xx		
Pao-ch'eng(nw.)	Pao-chi	Ta-t'an	302	1958					xx	
Hsi-yü	Sian	Yü-hsia	45	1961-1963				xx	xx	
Ti-pai	Ti-chia-t'ai	Pai-yin	23	1957						xx
Southwest China (Total of 7 Lines = 1,394 km)										
Pao-ch'eng	Ta-t'an	Ch'eng-tu	367	1958					xx	
Tien-mien	An-ning	I-p'ing-lang	102	1959					xx	
Ch'eng-yü	Ch'eng-tu	Chungking	504	1952			xx			
Nei-k'un	Nei-chiang	An-pien	142	1957			xx			
Ch'ien-kuei	Tu-yün	Kuei-yang	132	1956			xx			
Ch'uan-ch'ien	Chungking	Kan-shui	86	1960			xx			
Hsin-kuan	Hsin-tu	Kuan-hsien	61	1961-1963						xx
Grand Total of 57 Lines			9,501		6	6	13	11	5	16

[a] Sources: Railroad Passenger Train Time Table (Peking: People's Railroad Publishing Bureau, 1960 and 1963); Railways in Communist China (Taipei: Bureau of Communications Research, 1961), pp. 29-33.

[b] Forest railways excluded.

Table E-5

CONSTRUCTION OF DOUBLE-TRACKS
BETWEEN 1950 AND 1962[a]

| Railway Line | Terminals | | Length (km) |
	From	To	
Man-sui	Harbin	I-mien-po	161
Shen-an	Mukden	An-tung	277
Pen-liao	Pen-ch'i	Liao-yang	69
Ha-ta	Harbin	Lü-ta	953
Shen-shan	Mukden	Shan-hai-kuan	429
Ha-sui	Harbin	Sui-hua	125
Sui-chia	Sui-hua	Chia-mu-ssu	381
Lien-ho	Lien-chiang-k'ou	Ho-kang	54
Ching-shan	Peking	Shan-hai-kuan	417
Feng-sha	Feng-tai	Sha-ch'eng	104
Lung-hai	Hsin-hai-lien	Lan-chou	1,736
Ching-han	Peking	Wu-han	1,211
Yüeh-han	Wu-han	Canton	1,115
Ching-pu	Tientsin	Pu-k'ou	1,014
Hu-ning	Nanking	Shanghai	311
Cheng-tai	Shih-chia-chuang	Yü-t'zu	204
T'ung-pu	Feng-ling-tu	Ta-t'ung	869
Total			9,430

[a]Sources: Communist China Monthly (Taipei), Vol. V, No. 7, July 1962, pp. 38-45; Geographical Knowledge (Peking), January 14, 1958, pp. 16-20; Railways in Communist China (Taipei: Bureau of Communications Research, Ministry of Communications, 1961), p. 37; China Weekly (Hong Kong), Vol. 39, No. 4, July 23, 1962; Communist China Weekly (Tokyo), No. 146, October 10, 1962, p. 17; New China News Agency (Peking), February 19, 1964.

COMPARISON OF RAILWAYS BUILT AND PROJECTED IN THE COMMUNIST PERIOD WITH NATIONALIST
PROJECTED LINES IN THE "FIRST PHASE OF POSTWAR RAILWAY RECONSTRUCTION"[a]

	Communist Railway Lines			Corresponding Nationalist Projected Lines				
Name	From	To	Length (km)	Name	From	To	Length (km)	Remarks
Northeast China								
Ya-lin[b]	Ku-tu-erh	Kan-ho	354					
	I-t'u-li-ho	Ken-ho	27					
	Ken-ho	Chin-ho	81					
Nan-lin[b]	I-ch'un	Hsin-ch'ing	232					
Yen-lung[b,c]	Yen-t'ung-shan	Lung-wang-miao	150					
	I-ch'un	Ts'ui-luan	21					
Nan-lin[b,c]	Hsin-ch'ing	Chiang-pien	239					
Nen-lin[b,d]	Nen-chiang	Ou-pu	600					
	Nen-chiang	Kan-ho	200					
	Ta-mai-kou	Han-kuei	120					
	An-t'u	Yen-pien	200					
Tieh-fa	T'ieh-ling	Fa-k'u	53					
T'ieh-san	T'ieh-ling	San-chia-tzu	33					
Nü-nan	Nü-erh-ho	Nan-p'iao	29					
North China								
Ching-ch'eng	Shang-pan-ch'eng	Ying-shou-ying	120					
	Hsü-chia-chan	Miao-t'ai-tzu	11					
	Huai-jou	Ying-shou-ying	61					
Feng-sha	Feng-t'ai	Sha-cheng	104					
Chi-erh	Chi-ning	Erh-lien	330	Chi-k'u	Chi-ning	K'u-lün	1,080	Partially identical
Pao-pai	Pao-t'ou	Pai-yün-o-po	148					
Pao-lan(n.)	Pao-t'ou	San-sheng-kung	278	Pao-ning	Pao-t'ou	Ningsia	557	Identical
Liang-ta[c]	Liang-ko-chuang	Ta-ying-chen	280					
Chang-chi[c]	Kalgan	Chi-ning	28					
Chan-lu[c]	Chan-tien	Lu-an	192					
T'ung-ku[d]	T'ung-chou	Ku-yeh	160					
T'ai-chung[d]	T'ai-yüan	Chung-wei	631					
Chieh-yang	Chieh-hsiu	Yang-ch'uan-chu	46					
T'ai-t'ao	T'ai-yüan	T'ao-hsing	27					
K'ou-wang	K'ou-ch'üan	Wang-ts'un	60					
Nen-lin	Ken-ho	Ta-mai-k'ou	63					
	Ko-i-ho	A-li-ho	75					
T'ung-feng	T'ung-kuan	Feng-ling-tu	9					

	Communist Railway Lines			Corresponding Nationalist Projected Lines				
Name	From	To	Length (km)	Name	From	To	Length (km)	Remarks
East China								
Lan-yen	Lan-ts'un	Chefoo	183					
Lan-hsin	Lan-ch'i	Hsin-an-chiang	48					
Ts'ao-ch'uan	Ts'ao-o-chiang	Ch'uan-shan	164					
Chin-wen[c]	Chin-hua	Wen-chou	253					
Chin-nan[d]	Chin-hua	Nan-p'ing	480					
Hsi-ying[d]	Hsi-hsien	Ying-t'an	332	Hsi-kuei	Hsi-hsien	Kuei-ch'i	315	Partially similar
Chi-hou[c]	Tsinan	Hou-ma	700					
Hu-wen	Shanghai	Wen-tsao-pin	14					
Hu-min	Shanghai	Min-hang	42					
Wu-feng	Wu-hu	Feng-hsiang-kuo	53					
Central China								
Wu-huang	Wu-ch'ang	Huang-shih	98					
Meng-shen	Meng-miao	Shen-lou	61					
Hui-san	Hui-hsing	San-men-hsia	14					
Lo-i[c]	Lo-yang	I-tu	660					
Ch'uan-yü[c]	Ch'eng-tu	Hsin-yang	1,000					
Pu-hsin[c]	Pu-k'ou	Hsin-yang	400					
Hsi-han[d]	Sian	Wu-han	800	Hua-hsiang	Hua-yüan	Hsiang-yang	260	Partially identical
Ying-hsia(n.)	Ying-t'an	Tzu-ch'i	73	Kuei-nan	Kuei-ch'i	Nan-p'ing	280	Partially identical
Fu-huai	Fu-li-chi (Su-hsien)	Huai-ch'i	31					
Lo-i	Lo-yang	I-yang	22					
An-li	An-yang	Li-chen	32					
Lou-chin	Lou-ti	Chin-chu-shan	65					
Lou-shao	Lou-ti	Shao-yang	98					
Wu-sui	Wu-ch'ang	Sui-hsien	216					
Hsiang-ch'ien	Chu-chou	Lou-ti	132	Hsiang-chih	Hsiang-t'an	Chih-chiang	498	Partially identical
South China								
Ying-hsia(s.)	Tzu-ch'i	Amoy	621	Kuei-nan	Kuei-ch'i	Nan-p'ing	280	Partially identical
				Nan-chang	Nan-p'ing	Chang-t'ing	220	Partially identical
	Kuo-k'eng	Lung-ch'i	11					
	Chang-p'ing	Lung-yen	58					
	Wai-yang	Nan-p'ing	24					
Nan-fu	Nan-p'ing	Foochow	168	Min-nan	Min-hou (Foochow)	Nan-p'ing	150	Identical
Lai-mu	Lai-pin	Mu-nan-kuan	355	Hsi-lai	Hsi-ying	Lai-pin	455	
Li-chan	Li-t'ang	Chan-chiang	315					
Lien-mao	Lien-chiang	Mao-ming	62					
Mei-hsing[c]	Mei-hsien	Hsing-ning	75					
Lung-mei[d]	Lung-yen	Mei-hsien	350	Chang-mei	Chang-p'ing	Mei-hsien	230	Partially identical
Ch'üan-chang[c]	Ch'üan-chou	Chang-p'ing	400					
Fu-hsia[d]	Foochow	Amoy	460					
Yü-fu[c]	Yü-shan	Foochow	568					

Table E-6 (continued)

	Communist Railway Lines			Corresponding Nationalist Projected Lines				
Name	From	To	Length (km)	Name	From	To	Length (km)	Remarks
Shih-hsing[d]	Shih-lung	Hsing-ning	220	Shih-mei	Shih-lung	Mei-hsien	330	Partially identical
Chü-shan[d]	Chü-chiang	Swatow	522					
San-mao[d]	San-shui	Mao-ming	560					
Northwest China								
T'ien-lüeh[d]	T'ien-shui	Lüeh-yang	260					
Hsi-wu[d]	Sian	Wu-wei	600					
Tien-lan	T'ien-shui	Lan-chou	348	T'ien-lan	T'ien-shui	Lan-chou	378	Identical
Lan-hsin	Lan-chou	Urumchi	1,892	Lan-ha	Lan-chou	Ha-mi	1,636	Identical
Hei-lao	Hei-shan-hu	Lao-chün-miao	32					
Pao-lan(nw.)	San-sheng-kung	Lan-chou	716	Lan-ning	Lan-chou	Ningsia	450	Identical
Lan-ch'ing	Lan-chou	Hsi-ning	175	Lan-hsi	Lan-chou	Hsi-ning	250	Identical
	Hsi-ning	Mang-ai[c]	1,125	Hsi-yü	Hsi-ning	Yü-shu	800	Partially identical
Lan-a	Lan-chou	A-kan-chen	21					
Ti-a[d]	Urumchi	A-la-shan-k'ou	771					
T'u-k'o[d]	T'u-lu-fang	Kashgar	1,500					
Wu-i[d]	Wu-su	I-ning	250					
Ch'ing-hsin[d]	Mang-ai	Jo-ch'iang	600					
Sha-ch'eng[d]	Sha-men-tzu	Ch'eng-hua	500					
Hsi-hai	Hsi-ning	Hai-yen	100					
Wu-kan	Wu-wei	Kan-t'ang	185					
Pao-ch'eng(nw.)	Pao-chi	Ta-t'an	302	T'ien-kuang	T'ien-shui	Kuang-yüan	410	Identical
Hsi-yü	Sian	Yü-hsia	45					
Pao-chung[d]	Pao-chi	Chung-wei	470					
Ti-pai	Ti-chia-t'ai	Pai-yin	23					
Southwest China								
Pao-ch'eng(sw.)	Ta-t'an	Ch'eng-tu	367	Ch'eng-kuang	Ch'eng-tu	Kuang-yüan	345	Identical
Tien-mien	An-ning	I-p'ing-lang	102	Tien-mien	An-ning	Su-ta	844	
Ch'ing-ts'ang[d]	Ko-erh-mu	Lhasa	1,330					
Hsiang-chien	Lien-yüan[b]	Tu-yün	825	Tu-chih	Tu-yün	Chih-chiang	357	
Ch'eng-yü	Ch'eng-tu	Chungking	504	Ch'eng-yü	Ch'eng-tu	Chungking	530	Identical
Nei-k'un	Nei-chiang	An-pien	142	Nei-lo	Nei-chiang	Lo-shan	180	Partially identical
Ch'ien-kuei	Tu-yün	Kuei-yang	132					
Ch'uan-ch'ien	Chungking	Kan-shui	86	Ch'uan-ch'ien	Chungking	Kuei-yang	530	Identical
Ch'eng-k'un[d]	Ch'eng-tu	I-p'ing-lang	958	Ch'eng-lo	Ch'eng-tu	Lo-shan	165	Partially identical
Hsin-kuan	Hsin-tu	Kuan-hsien	61					
Tien-ch'ien[c]	Hsüan-wei	Kuei-yang	668	Kuei-wei	Kuei-yang	Wei-ning	416	Identical
				Chan-wei	Chan-i	Wei-ning	260	

[a] Source: Railways in Communist China (Taipei: Bureau of Communications Research, 1961), pp. 29-33; Communist China Railroad Passenger Time Table (Peking: People's Railroad Publishing Bureau, 1960 and 1963); Chao Tseng-chiao, Chan-hou-Chiao-t'ung Ch'ien-she Kai-lun (Post War Communications Construction in China) (Shanghai: Commercial Press, 1947), pp. 63-65.

[b] Forest Railways.

[c] Railways under construction.

[d] Planned railways.

TRANSPORT RATE DATA

AVERAGE RAILROAD CARLOAD FREIGHT RATE IN 1955[a]

Distance of Shipment	Freight Rate (yüan/ton-km) for Indicated Commodity						
	Lowest Rate Group			Medium Rate Group		Highest Rate Group	
	Rate 9 (Pit Timber)	Rate 14 (Coal)	Rate 27 (Stone)	Rate 21 (Diesel Oil)	Rate 50 (Glass)	Rate 35 (Liquor)	Rate 36 (Furs)
50	0.0140	0.0140	0.0140	0.0340	0.0334	0.1548	0.1278
100	0.0124	0.0115	0.0106	0.0320	0.0316	0.1470	0.1214
200	0.0110	0.0103	0.0100	0.0319	0.0316	0.1469	0.1214
260	0.0108	0.0100	0.0100	0.0314	0.0314	0.1457	0.1204
300	0.0107	0.0100	0.0100	0.0311	0.0312	0.1445	0.1197
360	0.0104	0.0097	0.0098	0.0303	0.0306	0.1420	0.1173
420	0.0103	0.0096	0.0099	0.0302	0.0305	0.1416	0.1170
480	0.0103	0.0095	0.0100	0.0301	0.0304	0.1413	0.1167
540	0.0102	0.0095	0.0100	0.0296	0.0301	0.1396	0.1154
600	0.0102	0.0094	0.0100	0.0288	0.0293	0.1365	0.1128
680	0.0100	0.0093	0.0100	0.0277	0.0285	0.1324	0.1094
760	0.0099	0.0093	0.0100	0.0271	0.0279	0.1298	0.1072
840	0.0099	0.0093	0.0100	0.0265	0.0275	0.1270	0.1056
920	0.0098	0.0092	0.0101	0.0261	0.0272	0.1261	0.1042
1,000	0.0098	0.0092	0.0101	0.0257	0.0268	0.1247	0.1030
1,200	0.0094	0.0092	0.0101	0.0248	0.0248	0.1154	0.0953
1,400	0.0091	0.0092	0.0101	0.0242	0.0233	0.1084	0.0896
1,600	0.0089	0.0093	0.0101	0.0237	0.0221	0.1025	0.0846
1,800	0.0086	0.0093	0.0101	0.0232	0.0208	0.0967	0.0799
2,000	0.0086	0.0093	0.0102	0.0228	0.0198	0.0921	0.0760
2,500	0.0086	0.0093	0.0102	0.0228	0.0197	0.0918	0.0759
3,000	0.0086	0.0093	0.0102	0.0228	0.0198	0.0920	0.0760
3,500	0.0085	0.0093	0.0101	0.0227	0.0197	0.0914	0.0755
4,000	0.0085	0.0093	0.0102	0.0227	0.0197	0.0916	0.0755
4,500	0.0085	0.0093	0.0102	0.0227	0.0198	0.0918	0.0758
5,000	0.0086	0.0093	0.0102	0.0228	0.0198	0.0918	0.0759
5,500	0.0086	0.0093	0.0102	0.0228	0.0197	0.0919	0.0760
6,000	0.0086	0.0093	0.0102	0.0228	0.0198	0.0920	0.0760

[a]Source: Railway Tariff Table (Peking: 1955), pp. 2-37. In general, inland waterway rates are comparable to railway rates except for the higher rate group. However, for the average distance carried, rail rates are less. The sample rates in Table F-2 are illustrative.

Table F-2

YANGTZE RIVER TARIFF RATES IN 1955 [a-c]

Tariff Rates (yüan/ton-km)

Distance (km)	Up Stream									Down Stream								
	Upper Section			Middle Section			Lower Section			Upper Section			Middle Section			Lower Section		
	Rate 1	Rate 13	Rate 25	Rate 1	Rate 13	Rate 25	Rate 1	Rate 13	Rate 25	Rate 1	Rate 13	Rate 25	Rate 1	Rate 13	Rate 25	Rate 1	Rate 13	Rate 25
50	0.32	0.06	0.03	0.13	0.02	0.01	0.10	0.02	0.01	0.24	0.04	0.02	0.13	0.02	0.01	0.10	0.02	0.01
100	0.32	0.06	0.03	0.13	0.02	0.01	0.10	0.02	0.01	0.24	0.04	0.02	0.13	0.02	0.01	0.10	0.02	0.01
200	0.32	0.06	0.03	0.13	0.02	0.01	0.10	0.02	0.01	0.24	0.04	0.02	0.13	0.02	0.01	0.10	0.02	0.01
300	0.32	0.06	0.03	0.13	0.02	0.01	0.10	0.02	0.01	0.24	0.04	0.02	0.13	0.02	0.01	0.10	0.02	0.01
400	0.32	0.06	0.03	0.13	0.02	0.01	0.09	0.02	0.01	0.24	0.04	0.02	0.13	0.02	0.01	0.09	0.02	0.01
500	0.32	0.06	0.03	0.13	0.02	0.01	0.09	0.02	0.01	0.24	0.04	0.02	0.13	0.02	0.01	0.09	0.02	0.01
600	0.32	0.06	0.03	0.13	0.02	0.01	0.09	0.02	0.01	0.24	0.04	0.02	0.13	0.02	0.01	0.09	0.02	0.01
700	–	–	–	0.13	0.02	0.01	0.09	0.02	0.01	–	–	–	–	–	–	0.09	0.02	0.01
800	–	–	–	–	–	–	0.09	0.02	0.01	–	–	–	–	–	–	0.09	0.02	0.01
900	–	–	–	–	–	–	0.08	0.02	0.01	–	–	–	–	–	–	0.08	0.02	0.01
1,000	–	–	–	–	–	–	0.08	0.02	0.01	–	–	–	–	–	–	0.08	0.02	0.01

[a] Source: Shui-yün Yün-chia Hui-pien, op. cit., Vol. V, Section 2, pp. 1–53.

[b] Rate 1 includes various luxury food items, antiques; Rate 13 includes nonferrous metals, tires, plastics; Rate 25 includes iron ore, other ores, coal.

[c] Coastal freight rates are in general higher. (For details, see the above work, Vol. V, pp. 1–18.) Highway rates are comparable to the higher tariff groups in inland waterway traffic. See Liu and Yeh, op. cit., Rand Corporation memorandum, Vol. II, pp. 761–762.

G

ESTIMATE OF RAILWAY ENGINES, FREIGHT CARS, AND FREIGHT TRAFFIC

As mentioned in the test, one of the principal constraints to the expansion of railway freight traffic, especially during the period of the "Great Leap Forward," was the shortage of railway engines and cars. Although efficiency in using transport equipment to carry a given traffic flow does not in itself ensure efficient traffic planning, it has been a major concern of Communist China's planners. This doubtless is a reflection of the equipment shortage. The increasing economic expansion of remote regions increases the demand on rail equipment, and this "equipment constraint" can become more and more serious unless additions can be made fairly rapidly. The following computations show the possible relationship between railway freight engines and cars, on the one hand, and railway freight traffic, on the other.

On the basis of railway engines and freight cars available between 1949 and 1957, as well as railway freight traffic reported, a multiple regression equation can be fitted by the least squares method:

$$X_1 = a + b_{12.3} \, X_2 + b_{13.2} \, X_3$$

where X_1, X_2, and X_3 denote, respectively, the amount of railway freight traffic (in billion ton-km), the number of freight locomotives, and the number of freight cars.

The basic data are derived as follows:

1. <u>Railway freight engines</u>. The number of railway freight engines is estimated at 72 per cent of the total number of railway engines of all types.[1] The total number of locomotives in any year is approximated by the average of the year-end figures of the same year and of the preceding year. The year-end estimate is obtained from that of the preceding year plus reported additions during the year. The additions are the sum of domestic production and import; the number of engines restored to operating condition through repair is also included in the first few years. For details see Table G-1.

---

[1] This particular ratio was derived from a study by W. K. Chen, Ministry of Communications, Taipei (unpublished manuscript, May 1964).

2. <u>Freight cars</u>. Midyear figures are again used in the estimating equation. The year-end estimates are also obtained from an initial estimate plus annual additions. For details see Table G-2.

3. <u>Railway freight traffic</u>. See Table 8-4.

Table G-1

ESTIMATES OF RAILWAY ENGINES AVAILABLE

Year	Total Number of Railway Engines at End of Preceding Year	Number of Railway Engines Added during Year	Total Number of Railway Engines at Year-End	Estimated Number of Railway Engines at Midyear	Estimated Number of Freight Engines Only at Midyear
1949[a]	1,737	596	2,333	2,035	1,465
1950[b]	2,333	567	2,900	2,617	1,884
1951[c]	2,900	304	3,204	3,052	2,197
1952[d]	3,204	20	3,224	3,214	2,314
1953[d]	3,224	10	3,234	3,229	2,325
1954[d]	3,234	52	3,286	3,260	2,347
1955[d]	3,286	98	3,384	3,335	2,401
1956[d,e]	3,384	185	3,569	3,477	2,503
1957[d]	3,569	167	3,736	3,653	2,630
1958[d,e]	3,736	402	4,138	3,937	2,835
1959[e,f]	4,138	1,480	5,618	4,878	3,512
1960[e,g]	5,618	850	6,468	6,043	4,351

Notes and Sources:

[a] People's Railways (Peking) Vol. I, No. 2, December 1949, p. 3. The number of locomotives increased from 1,737 to 3,355 in December 1949, but the total number of locomotives in working condition was only 2,333.

[b] New China Monthly, Vol. III, No. 3, December 1950, p. 632. The 1950 year-end figure (2,900) less the 1949 year-end figure = 567 which is taken to represent the number of locomotives repaired.

[c] Yuan-li Wu, An Economic Survey of Communist China (New York: Bookman Associates, 1956), p. 364.

[d] Wei-ta ti Shih-nien (Great Ten Years) (Peking: 1959), p. 87.

[e] Torgovlia USSR, 1956 (Foreign Trade, Statistical Supplements) (Moscow: 1957), p. 124; 1959, p. 125; 1961, pp. 164-165. It was reported that locomotives used for mining were also imported from the Soviet Union: 1957, 15 units; 1958, 73 units; 1959, 96 units; 1960, 101 units. These figures are not included in the table.

[f] People's Daily, January 23, 1960; New China News Agency, March 31, 1960.

[g] People's Daily, March, 1960.

Table G-2

ESTIMATES OF RAILWAY FREIGHT CARS AVAILABLE

Year	Total Number of Railway Freight Cars at End of Preceding Year	Number of Railway Freight Cars Added during Year	Total Number of Railway Freight Cars at Year-End	Estimated Number of Railway Freight Cars at Midyear
1949[a]	29,188	10,801	39,989	34,589
1950[b]	39,989	1,500	41,489	40,739
1951[c]	41,489	7,182	48,671	45,080
1952[c,d]	48,671	5,792	54,463	51,567
1953[e]	54,463	4,500	58,963	56,713
1954[f]	58,963	5,445	64,408	61,686
1955[f]	64,408	9,258	73,666	69,037
1956[g]	73,666	8,500	82,166	77,916
1957[a]	82,166	7,300	89,466	85,816
1958[h]	89,466	11,000	100,466	94,966
1959[i]	100,466	27,500	127,966	114,216
1960[j]	127,966	32,000	159,966	143,966

Notes and Sources:

[a] People's Railways (Peking) Vol. I, No. 2, December 1, 1949, p. 3.

[b] Yuan-li Wu, An Economic Survey of Communist China (New York: Bookman Associates, 1956), p. 364.

[c] People's Daily, April 14, 1959.

[d] Hung, I., Kung-fei Chi'ao-t'ung Chien-she Chih Yen-chiu (A Study of Communication Construction in Communist China) (Taipei: 1957), p. 97.

[e] People's Daily, September 20, 1955.

[f] Kuo-chia T'ung-chi-chü 1955 Nien Kuo-min Ching-chi Chi-hua Chih-hsing Chieh-kuo Kung-pao (Report of the Implementation of the 1955 Economic Plan) (Peking: State Statistical Bureau, 1956).

[g] Idem, 1956 Report, 1957.

[h] People's Daily, April 15, 1959.

[i] Li Fu-ch'un's Report on the 1956 Economic Plan to the Second National People's Congress, First Session. The average of 27,000 and 28,000 is used for the number added during the year.

[j] People's Daily, March 31, 1960.

The regression equation thus determined has the form of

$$X'_1 = -70.6407 + 0.01647X_2 + 0.00191X_3$$

where $R^2_{1.23} = 0.99$. The estimated railway freight traffic figures for 1949 to 1962 are shown in Table G-3 with the original data.

If freight engine and car estimates for 1958 to 1960 are used in the equation, the corresponding railway freight traffic estimates would be substantially below the independent freight traffic figures in Table 8-4. Besides, these differences are much larger than those in earlier years. They may, therefore, lend support to the contention that there was a severe equipment shortage during the "Great Leap Forward."

Table G-3

RAILWAY FREIGHT TRAFFIC ESTIMATED ON THE BASIS OF THE
NUMBERS OF RAILWAY FREIGHT ENGINES AND CARS
AVAILABLE COMPARED WITH PREVIOUS ESTIMATES

Year	Freight Engines[a] X_2	Freight Cars[b] X_3	Freight Traffic[c] X_1	Estimated Freight Traffic[d] X'_1	Error[e] $X_1 - X'_1$
1949	1,465	34,589	18.40	19.55	-1.15
1950	1,884	40,739	39.41	38.20	1.21
1951	2,197	45,080	51.56	51.65	-0.90
1952	2,314	51,567	60.16	65.96	-5.80
1953	2,325	56,713	78.14	75.97	2.17
1954	2,347	61,686	93.24	85.83	7.41
1955	2,401	69,037	98.15	100.76	-2.61
1956	2,503	77,916	120.35	119.40	0.95
1957	2,630	85,816	134.59	136.58	-1.99
1958	2,835	94,966	185.52	157.44	28.08
1959	3,512	114,216	265.58	205.35	60.23
1960	4,351	143,966	326.63	276.00	50.63
1962	4,200	144,000	282.97	273.57	9.40

[a]Source: Table G-1.

[b]Source: Table G-2.

[c] Source: Table 8-5.

[d]Estimated from equation $X_1' = -70.6407 + 0.01647X_2 + 0.00191X_3$.

[e]Estimate of W. K. Chen, Ministry of Communications, Taipei (unpublished manuscript, May 1964).

H ESTIMATE OF VALUE-ADDED IN THE MODERN TRANSPORT SECTOR

The gross and net value-added in the modern transport sector are estimated in this appendix. The basic estimates are for 1956, the year for which relatively more data are available. The estimates are arrived at in several steps dealing with gross receipts, production cost excluding profit and tax, labor cost, and depreciation. Net value-added is estimated as the sum of profit, tax, and labor cost; gross value-added is obtained by aggregating depreciation and net value-added. Figure H-1 compares the estimates of gross value-added in the modern transport and industry sectors.

Gross Receipts

Gross receipts are estimated separately for railways, waterways, and highways. In all three sectors, the data are obtained by adding the appropriate values for freight and passenger traffic. The total receipts for both freight and passenger traffic are derived as the products of traffic volume and the average rate per unit of traffic. Table H-1 shows the computation of gross receipts. The average rates are derived as follows.

Railway Traffic

1. _Railway freight traffic._ Railway freight rates may be conveniently divided into three categories. According to Yu I. Fomin,[1] 55. 2 per cent of the freight consists of coal and coke (39. 8 per cent), mineral ores (5. 4 per cent), and bricks, tiles, earth, and sand (10 per cent). These commodities fall into the group of products subject to the lowest freight rates (tariff numbers[2] 9 for mine timbers or other timber materials, 12 for mineral ores, 14 and 15 for coal of all kinds, and 27 for sand and earth). The average rate amounts to 0. 01 yüan per ton-km for the average haul of railway freight traffic in Communist China. The medium rate group of freight accounts for 37. 2 per cent of the traffic, and

---

[1] Yu I. Fomin, "Success of the Railroad Transport in China," JPRS, No. 4296, December 29, 1961.

[2] Huo-wu Yün-chia-lü Piao (Freight Tariff Tables) (Peking: Ministry of Railways), pp. 2-37.

Figure H.1 Comparison of Estimates of Gross Value—Added in the Modern
Transport and Industry Sectors between 1952 and 1960

(1952 = 100)

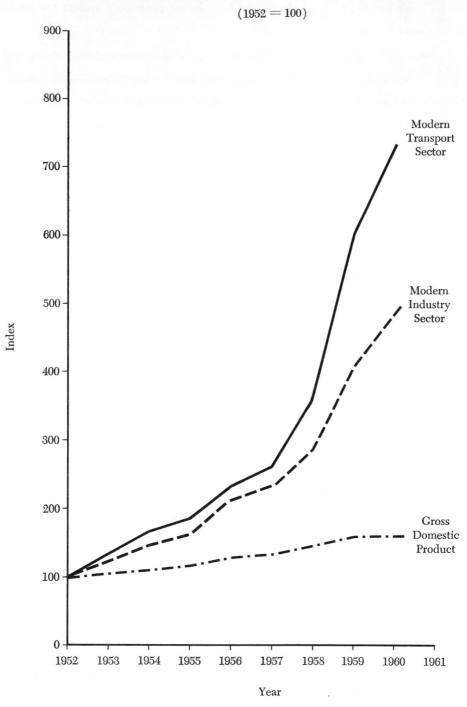

consists of agricultural products (10 per cent), lumber products (6 per cent), and iron and steel and other related products (21. 1 per cent). (The tariff numbers are 50 for agricultural products, 49 for lumber products, and 21 for petroleum and metal products.) The rate for this group is 0. 03 yüan/ton-km. The highest rate group (7. 6 per cent of total traffic), includes such items as cosmetics, furs, coffee, and liquors, and is subject to an average rate of 0. 128 yüan per ton-km. An average freight rate based on the above three rates, weighted by the percentages of traffic composition, amounts to 0. 026 yüan per ton-km. It should be noted that all these rates are for the carload. Less-than-carload rates are higher, and are assumed to be offset by special rates granted to other traffic from time to time.

2. Railway passenger traffic. Passenger rates are fixed in Communist China for hard seats, soft seats, sleepers, and special fares for children and persons traveling on military passes. For the present computation the hard seat basic ticket rate is used. The higher and lower rates for other types of accommodation are assumed to cancel out one another. The basic rate used is for an average distance of 100 to 200 kilometers, or 0. 017 yüan per passenger-km. This rate is, incidentally, very close to the rate of 0. 016 yüan employed by Liu in his national income study.[3]

Inland and Coastal Shipping

For inland freight traffic, the average rate of 0. 04 yüan per ton-km on the Yangtze is employed.[4] For coastal traffic, the average rates of the northern, southern, and Chekiang and Fukien lines are 0. 27, 0. 05, and 0. 02 yüan per ton-km (for an average haul of 600 to 700 kilometers) corresponding to tariff numbers 1, 13, and 25 respectively. These three commodity groups correspond roughly to the high, medium, and low tariff groups in railway traffic. A weighted average based on an estimated freight composition of 10, 30, and 60 per cent, respectively, comes to 0. 05 yüan per ton-km. Since coastal shipping accounts for

---

[3]"Communist China Railroad Passenger Timetable," JPRS, No. 8153, April 30, 1961, p. 18; Ta-chung Liu and Kung-chia Yeh, The Economy of the Chinese Mainland: National Income and Economic Development, 1933-1959 (Calif.: The Rand Corporation, 1963), Vol. II, pp. 761-762.

[4]Shui-yun Yun-chia Hui-pien (Consolidated Tariffs of Water Transportation) (Peking: Ministry of Communications, 1956), No. 5, Part II, pp. 6-41.

approximately 44 per cent of total freight by water, the rest being inland, the weighted average rate for both inland and coastal shipping comes to 0.044 yüan per ton-km.

For passenger traffic, the average third-class rate of 0.045 yüan per passenger-km is used in the estimate.[5]

Highway Freight Traffic

The average rate of 0.325 yüan per ton-km previously employed by Liu is adopted for our purpose for lack of more recent data.[6] For passenger traffic, an average of 0.03 yüan per passenger-km is used.[7]

Table H-1

COMPUTATION OF GROSS RECEIPTS

Transport Sector	Rate (yüan/ton-km)	Volume (billion ton-km)	Gross Receipts (billion yüan)
Railways	0.026	120.35	3.129
Shipping	0.044	28.21	1.241
Highways	0.325	3.49	1.134
	Rate (yüan/passenger-km)	Volume (billion passenger-km)	
Railways	0.017	34.38	0.584
Shipping	0.045	4.64	0.209
Highways	0.030	7.36	0.221
Railways Total Receipts (Passenger plus Freight Traffic)			3.713
Shipping Total Receipts (Passenger plus Freight Traffic)			1.450
Highways Total Receipts (Passenger plus Freight Traffic)			1.355
Total			6.518

[5] Travel Gazette (Hong-Kong: China Travel Service, March 1964), p. 27.

[6] Ta-chung Liu and Kung-chia Yeh, op. cit., p. 761.

[7] Highways in Communist China (Taipei: 1961), p. 157.

Cost of Operation

The cost of operating the railways is based on 0.0077 yüan per "cumulated ton-kilometer," defined as the sum of freight and passenger traffic. [8] Similarly, the operating cost of shipping per "cumulated ton-kilometer" is given by the same source as 0.011 yüan. The unit cost of operating the highways is estimated at 57.5 per cent of the rate charged, i.e., 0.325 yüan per ton-km. [9] This is equivalent to 0.187 yüan. At the same ration, the cost of passenger traffic would be 0.01725 yüan per passenger-km. Operating cost is computed in Table H-2.

Table H-2

COMPUTATION OF OPERATING COST

Transport Sector	Cost (yüan/ "cumulated ton-km")	Volume (billion "cumulated ton-km")	Operating Cost (billion yüan)
Railways	0.0077	154.73	1.191
Shipping	0.0110	32.85	0.361
Highways	0.1870	3.49	0.653
	Cost (yüan/ passenger-km)	Volume (billion passenger-km)	
All Sectors	0.01725	7.36	0.127
Subtotal			0.780
Total			2.332

[8] Planned Economy (Peking), No. 3, March 1958, pp. 20-23.

[9] Highway (Peking), No. 7, 1960, p. 8.

COMPUTATION OF NET VALUE-ADDED

	Railways	Waterways	Highways	Total
Gross receipts (billion yüan)	3.713	1.450	1.355	6.518
Less operating cost (billion yüan)	1.191	0.361	0.780	2.332
Profit and tax (billion yüan)	2.522	1.089	0.575	4.186
Add labor cost (billion yüan)	0.340	0.102	0.352	0.794
Net value-added (billion yüan)	2.862	1.191	0.927	4.980

Net Value-Added

Net value-added is computed in Table H-3 where the labor cost for railways is estimated at 0.0022 yüan per "cumulated ton km,"[10] for waterways at 0.0031 yüan per "cumulated ton km,"[11] and for highways at 26 per cent of total receipts.[12]

Depreciation Rates

For railways, depreciation rates are estimated at 36 per cent of costs or 11.5 per cent of gross receipts.[13] For shipping, 20 per cent of costs or 5 per cent of gross receipts are applied. For highways, depreciation is estimated at 14 per cent of receipts.[14]

---

[10] Planned Economy, loc. cit.

[11] Ibid.

[12] Automobile and Highway, Vol. I, No. 3, 1949, p. 11.

[13] Planned Economy, loc. cit., pp. 20-23.

[14] Automobile and Highway, loc. cit., p. 1.

COMPUTATION OF GROSS VALUE-ADDED

	Railways	Waterways	Highways	Total
Net value-added (billion yüan)	2. 862	1. 191	0. 927	4. 980
Add depreciation (billion yüan)	0. 427	0. 072	0. 190	0. 689
Gross value-added (billion yüan)	3. 289	1. 263	1. 117	5. 669
Net value-added to gross receipts (%)	77. 1	82. 1	68. 4	76. 4
Gross value-added to gross receipts (%)	88. 6	87. 1	82. 4	87. 0

Gross Value-Added

As a rough approximation, in Table H-4, the ratios of the gross and net values-added to gross receipts in the modern transport sectors may be applied to the gross receipts in the other years, and rough estimates obtained for the entire period of 1952 to 1960. These estimates, shown in Table H-5, may then be compared (1) with the corresponding estimates of Liu for 1952 to 1959, and (2) with the estimates of value-added in modern industry output which have been independently obtained for the same period. The first comparison shows that our estimates for 1952 to 1957 are somewhat higher than the corresponding estimates by Liu (Table H-6), thus indicating a greater degree of transport development in the modern sector than Liu has postulated. The relative importance of the modern versus the native sectors described in Chapter 6 for the beginning of the Communist regime may therefore have been substantially modified by the time of the "Great Leap Forward. " The second comparison shows a more rapid increase in the product of the transport sector than that of modern industry and of total output as a whole. This comparison lends further support to our earlier contention that use of the transport input as an intermediate product has not been particularly efficient (Table H-7).

Table H-5

GROSS AND NET VALUES-ADDED IN THE MODERN TRANSPORT SECTOR[a]

Year	Gross Value-Added (billion 1952 yüan)				Net Value-Added (billion 1952 yüan)			
	Railways	Inland and Coastal Waterways	Highways	Total	Railways	Inland and Coastal Waterways	Highways	Total
1952	1.688	0.511	0.255	2.454	1.469	0.482	0.211	2.162
1953	2.224	0.656	0.427	3.307	1.936	0.619	0.354	2.909
1954	2.592	0.859	0.612	4.063	2.255	0.810	0.508	3.573
1955	2.664	1.075	0.797	4.536	2.318	1.013	0.661	3.992
1956	3.290	1.263	1.117	5.670	2.863	1.190	0.927	4.980
1957	3.645	1.496	1.273	6.414	3.172	1.410	1.057	5.639
1958	4.890	1.880	2.138	8.908	4.255	1.772	1.775	7.802
1959	6.972	2.267	4.498	14.737	6.067	3.079	3.734	12.880
1960	8.466	4.030	5.461	17.957	7.367	3.799	4.533	15.699

[a]Sources: Tables 8-1, 8-2, and 8-5.

Table H-6

COMPARISON OF THE PRESENT ESTIMATES OF NET VALUE-ADDED
IN THE MODERN TRANSPORT SECTOR WITH LIU'S ESTIMATES

Year	New Estimates[a] (billion 1952 yuan)	Liu's Estimates[b] (billion 1952 yuan)
1952	2.16	1.92
1953	2.91	2.33
1954	3.57	2.66
1955	3.99	2.83
1956	4.98	3.20
1957	5.64	3.51
1958	7.80	3.69
1959	12.88	4.67

[a]Source: Table H-5.

[b]Source: Ta-chung Liu and Kung-chia Yeh, The Economy of the Chinese Mainland: National Income and Economic Development, 1933 to 1959, (Calif.: Rand Corporation, 1963), Vol. I, p. 243; Vol. II, pp. 764, 834, 866.

Table H-7

COMPARISON OF ESTIMATES OF GROSS VALUE-ADDED IN THE MODERN
TRANSPORT SECTOR WITH THAT OF THE MODERN INDUSTRY
SECTOR AND THE GROSS DOMESTIC PRODUCT BETWEEN
1952 AND 1960

Year	Modern Transport[a] Sector		Modern Industry[b] Sector		Gross Domestic[b] Product	
	Gross Value-Added (billion 1952 yüan)	Index	Gross Value-Added (billion 1952 yüan)	Index	Gross Value-Added (billion 1952 yüan)	Index
1952	2.45	100	9.4	100	75.6	100
1953	3.31	135	11.8	126	78.9	104
1954	4.06	166	13.8	147	82.2	109
1955	4.54	185	15.1	161	86.1	114
1956	5.67	231	19.8	211	96.6	128
1957	6.41	262	21.9	233	100.0	132
1958	8.91	364	27.1	288	110.7	146
1959	14.74	602	37.7	401	119.1	158
1960	17.96	733	45.3	482	120.7	160

[a]Source: Table H-5.

[b]Source: Yuan-li Wu et al., The Economic Potential of Communist
China (Menlo Park, Calif.: Stanford Research Institute, 1963), Vol. I, p. 241.

J KEY TO CODE NUMBERS FOR INDUSTRIAL CITIES

Region	Province	City Code Number	Name of City
Northeast	Liaoning	101	Mukden
		102	Lü-ta
		103	Fu-shun
		104	Ying-k'ou
		105	Chin-chou
		106	An-tung
		107	An-shan
		108	Chin-hsi
		109	Liao-yang
		110	Fou-hsin
		111	Pen-ch'i
		112	Pei-p'iao
		113	Nan-p'iao
		114	Tien-shih-fu
		115	T'ieh-chang-tzu
		116	Huan-yen
		760	Ch'ang-tien
		761	Ta-shih-ch'iao
		762	Lü-shun (Port Arthur)
		763	I-hsien
		764	Yeh-hai-shan
		808	T'ieh-ling
		809	San-chia-tzu
		834	Sai-ma-chi
		835	Küan-shui
		836	Feng-ch'eng
		837	Ch'eng-tzu-t'ung

Table Appendix J (continued)

Region	Province	City Code Number	Name of City
		838	Chin-hsien
		839	Hu-lu-tao
	Kirin	117	Ch'ang-ch'un
		118	Kirin
		119	T'ung-hua
		120	Ssu-p'ing
		121	Liao-yüan
		122	Yen-chi
		123	Chiao-ho
		124	Chien-kuo-chi*
		125	Tu-hsi*
		126	Lung-ching*
		127	Chien-ch'en*
		128	Hun-ch'un
		129	Chi-ning*
		130	Tao-nan
		131	Tao-an
		752	T'u-men
		753	La-fa
		754	Hu-lin
		755	Ho-lung
		756	Mei-ho-k'ou
		757	Lin-chiang
		759	Chi-an
		804	Mi-shan
		810	Hung-chiang
		829	Shu-lan
		830	Yen-chi
		831	T'u-men
		832	Ta-li-tzu
	Heilungkiang	132	Harbin
		133	Ch'i-ch'i-ha-erh
		134	Chia-mu-ssu
		135	Mu-tan-chiang
		136	Chi-hsi
		137	Ho-kang
		138	Fu-la-erh-chi
		139	Shuang-ya-shan
		140	I-lan
		141	Sui-fen-ho
		142	Ti-tao (near Chi-hsi)
		143	Pei-an
		144	Sun-wu
		145	Hei-ho
		146	Ching-po-hu

293

Region	Province	City Code Number	Name of City
		147	I-ch'un
		744	Ang-ang-ch'i
		745	Nen-chiang
		746	Fu-yü
		747	Sui-hua
		802	Tsing-hsin
		803	Nan-ch'a
		805	Ts'ui-luan
		821	K'u-erh-pin
		822	Wu-ying
		823	Chia-mu-ssu
		824	I-lan
		833	Yen-t'ung-shan
North	Hopeh	201	Peking
		202	Tientsin
		203	Shih-chia-chuang
		204	T'ang-shan
		205	Han-tan
		206	Hsüan-hua
		207	Pao-ting
		208	Ch'eng-te
		209	Chin-huang-tao
		210	Chang-chia-k'ou (Kalgan)
		211	Cho-hsien
		212	Cheng-ting
		213	Hsing-t'ai
		214	Tzu-hsien
		215	Kuan-t'ing
		216	Shuang-t'ou-shan*
		217	Mi-yün
		218	Shih-hsia-li*
		219	Hsiang-kuang-t'ung*
		220	Yu-chou*
		221	Chiao-chia-wan*
		765	Chang-chia-k'ou
		807	Ta-ku
		811	Ying-shou-ying-tzu
		812	Kuan-ch'eng
		818	Ting-hsien
		841	Luan-p'ing
		843	T'ang-ku
		844	Feng-t'ai
		845	T'ung-hsien
		846	P'ang-chia-pao
		847	Nan-ku

Table Appendix J (continued)

Region	Province	City Code Number	Name of City
		848	Men-t'ou-kou
		849	Chou-k'ou-tien
		850	Lai-yüan
		851	Yüan-p'ing
		876	Kao-i
	Shansi	222	T'ai-yüan
		223	Ta-t'ung
		224	Yang-ch'üan
		225	Ch'ang-chih
		226	Yü-t'zu
		227	P'ing-wang
		228	Lin-fen
		229	Yü-hsien
		230	Ling-shih-hsien
		231	Ning-wu
		232	Shou-yang
		233	Fen-hsi
		772	Feng-ling-tu
		773a	T'ung-kuan
		773b	Tung-kuan
		780	Hsi-hsien
		815	Wang-ts'un
		817	Kuo-hsien
		842	Ku-yeh
		852	Chiang-ts'un
		853	T'ao-hsing
		854	Yü-lin
		860	Fen-yang
		861	Hsiao-i
		862	Yang-ch'üan-chü
		863	Chieh-hsiu
		864	P'ing-yao
		865	Li-ch'eng
		867	Lu-an
	Inner Mongolia	234	Pao-t'ou
		235	Huhehot
		236	Hai-la-erh
		237	Chih-feng
		238	Chi-ning
		239	Wu-lan-hao-t'e
		240	Lao-ha-ho
		241	Ta-hsing-an-ling*
		242	P'ing-chuang
		243	Yü-erh-ai*
		244	Cha-lai-no-erh

Table Appendix J (continued)

Region	Province	City Code Number	Name of City
		245	Ssu-shih-sha-ho*
		246	T'ung-liao
		247	Wu-ho-hao-t'e
		248.	Wu-lan-cha-pu-meng
		748	Man-chan-li
		749	Wen-ch'üan (Ah-erh-shan)
		750	Lin-k'ou
		751	Ya-pu-li
		766	Kuei-sui (Huhehot)
		769	Chi-ning
		813	Erh-lien
		814	Shih-kuai-tzu
		819	Pai-yün-o-po
		820	I-t'u-li-ho
		825	Ya-k'ou-shih
		826	Po-k'o-t'u
		827	Kou-k'ou
		877	San-sheng-kung
East	Shantung	301	Tsingtao
		302	Tsinan
		303	Tzu-po
		304	Chefoo
		305	Wei-fang
		306	I-hsien
		307	Hung-shan
		308	Tsao-chuang
		309	Tzu-ch'uan
		310	Liang-chuang*
		311	Han-chuang
		312	Hsin-t'ai-hsien
		313	Nan-ting
		767	Chang-tien
		768	Po-shan
		806	Te-chou
		870	Lin-ch'eng
		871	Tzu-yang
		872	Tai-an
		873	Lan-ts'un
		874	Kao-mi
	Kiangsu	314	Shanghai
		315	Nanking
		316	Wu-hsi
		317	Soochow
		318	Ch'ang-chou

296

Table Appendix J (continued)

Region	Province	City Code Number	Name of City
		319	Nan-t'ung
		320	Hsin-hai-lien
		321	Hsü-chou
		322	Chen-chiang
		323	T'ai-chou
		324	Yang-chou
		325	Ch'i-shu-yen
		326	Ch'ang-shu
		327	Wang-t'ing
		774	Lien-yün-chiang
		776	Wu-sung
		923	Pu-k'ou
	Chekiang	328	Hangchow
		329	Chin-hua
		330	Shao-hsing
		331	Ning-po
		332	Wen-chou
		333	Chia-hsing
		334	Hsin-an-chiang
		335	Ch'i-li-lung
		336	Hu-nan-ch'en
		337	Huang-t'an-k'ou
		337a	Hu-chou
		781	Hsiao-shan
		926	Chien-te
		927	Ch'uan-shan
		928	Lan-ch'i
		929	Chin-yün
	Anhwei	338	Ho-fei
		339	Wu-hu
		340	Pang-fou
		341	Huai-nan
		342	An-ch'ing
		343	Tang-t'u
		344	T'ung-ling
		345	Ma-an-shan
		346	Feng-t'ai
		347	Ssu-hsien
		348	Chin-sai-hsien
		349	Hsiang-kung-miao*
		350	Mao-chien-shan*
		775	Pa-kung-shan
		777	Yü-ch'i-k'ou
		919	Hsiao-hsien
		920	Tsui-ch'i

297

Table Appendix J (continued)

Region	Province	City Code Number	Name of City
		921	Su-hsien
		922	Shui-chia-hu
		924	Fan-ch'ang
		925	Hsüan-ch'eng
	Honan	401	Cheng-chou
		402	Lo-yang
		403	Hsin-hsiang
		404	K'ai-feng
		405	An-yang
		406	Hsin-yang
		407	Chiao-tso
		408	Nan-yang
		409	Hao-pi
		410	Shang-ch'iu
		411	Hsü-ch'ang
		412	San-men-hsia
		413	Pa-pan-hsia*
		414	Hsin-cheng
		415	Chai-chia-hsia*
		415a	Shui-yen
		416	Sha-p'o-t'ou*
		417	Hsiao-lang-ti*
		770	Tao-k'ou
		771	Ch'in-yang
		866	Li-chen
		868	T'ang-yin
		869	Hua-hsien
		913	Wu-yang
		914	Lo-ho
		915	Meng-miao
		917	P'ing-ting-shan
	Hupeh	418	Wu-han
		419	Huang-shih
		420	I-ch'ang
		421	O-ch'eng
		422	Hsiang-fan
		423	Chi-chi*
		424	Pai-lien-ho*
		425	T'an-chiang-k'ou
		426	Ch'ang-tan*
		426a	Ma-ch'eng
		778	Han-k'ou (Hankow)
		779	Wu-ch'ang
		905	Chia-ho-kuan
		906	Kuang-hua

298

Table Appendix J (continued)

Region	Province	City Code Number	Name of City
		908	I-tu
		909	Han-yang
		910	Ying-ch'eng
		911	Hankow
		912	Sui-hsien
		939	Ta-yeh
		940	Hsiang-yang
		941	Tang-yang
	Hunan	427	Ch'ang-sha
		428	Chu-chou
		429	Heng-yang
		430	Hsiang-t'an
		431	Shao-yang
		432	Ch'ang-te
		433	Lien-yüan
		434	Cha-ling
		435	Tzu-hsing
		436	Yao-yang
		437	Chi-ch'i
		438	Tung-chiang
		439	Chao-shih
		440	Shih-mo-ch'i*
		441	Ling-ching-t'an*
		442	An-hua
		443	An-chiang
		443a	Ch'ang-ning
		443b	P'ing-an
		799	Chih-chiang
		800	Lan-t'ien
		801	Lou-ti
		942	Chao-ling
		943	Chin-chu-shan
		944	Hsin-hua
		945	Tung-an
		960	I-chang
	Kiangsi	444	Nan-ch'ang
		445	P'ing-hsiang
		446	Kan-chou
		447	Ching-te-chen
		448	Hsin-yü
		449	Chi-an
		450	Feng-ch'eng
		451	Chiu-chiang
		452	Chiang-k'ou*
		453	Shang-yu

Table Appendix J (continued)

Region	Province	City Code Number	Name of City
		454	Wan-an
		455	Shang-yao
		456	Ching-kang-shan
		782	Ying-t'an
		783	Chiang-k'ou
		930	Yü-shan
		937	Chin-hsien
		938	Sha-ho
		946	T'ai-ho
		947	Sui-ch'uan
		948	Jui-chin
South	Fukien	501	Foochow
		502	Amoy
		503	Ch'üan-chou
		504	Ch'ang-chou
		505	Nan-p'ing
		506	San-ming
		507	Kuo-k'eng*
		508	Yung-ch'un
		509	Chang-p'ing
		510	Lung-yen
		511	Chien-ch'i*
		512	Ku-tien
		512a	Fu-an
		512b	Lung-ch'i
		513	Shang-hang
		932	Cheng-ho
		933	Pa-tu
		934	Lien-chiang
		935	Chiang-lo
		936	Shun-ch'ang
		949	Ch'ang-ting
		950	Yung-ting
		952	Ch'üan-chou
		953	An-ch'i
		954	Chao-an
	Kwangtung	514	Canton
		515	Swatow
		516	Shao-kuan
		517	Chiang-men
		518	Chan-chiang
		519	Hai-k'ou
		520	Fo-shan
		521	Ch'ao-chou
		523	Yang-ch'un

300

Table Appendix J (continued)

Region	Province	City Code Number	Name of City
		524	Lo-chiang*
		525	Lien-chiang
		526	Ch'ang-ch'ang
		527	Ch'u-chiang
		528	Jen-hua
		529	Nan-lin
		530	Wu-shih
		531	Fang-ch'eng
		532	Feng-huang-shan
		533	Hsin-feng
		534	Ju-yüan*
		534a	Hsing-ning
		534b	Ho-nan
		793	Ch'ang-chiang (Shih-lu)
		794	Pa-so
		795	Yü-lin
		796	Shih-lung
		797	Chiu-lung (Kowloon), (BCC)
		798	Mei-hsien
		951	Ta-p'u
		955	Ch'ao-an
		956	Chieh-yang
		957	Hsing-ning
		958	Lung-ch'uan
		959	Nan-hsiung
		961	San-shui
		962	Hong Kong (BCC)
		963	Mao-ming
		964	Hai-an
		965	Wen-ch'ang
		966	Huang-liu
		967	Ho-p'u
		969	Tung-hsing
	Kwangsi	535	Lui-chou
		536	Nan-ning
		537	Wu-chou
		538	Kueilin
		539	Lu-chai
		540	Pa-pu
		541	Chung-shan
		542	Chao-p'ing
		543	Heng-hsien
		544	Hsi-ch'ing*
		545	P'ing-kuei

301

Table Appendix J (continued)

Region	Province	City Code Number	Name of City
		791	Lai-pin
		970	Ning-ming
		971	Fu-sui
		972	Li-t'ang
		973	Chin-ch'eng-chiang
		1004	San-chiang
Northwest	Shensi	601	Sian
		602	Pao-chi
		603	T'ung-ch'uan
		604	Hu-hsien
		605	Nan-cheng
		606	Shih-ch'üan
		607	Hsien-yang
		858	Ting-pien
		859	Yen-an
		902	Yü-hsia
		903	Lüeh-yang
		904	Tzu-yang
	Kansu	608	Lan-chou
		609	T'ien-shui
		610	Yü-men
		611	Chiu-ch'üan
		612	Yung-teng
		613	Shan-tan
		614	Yen-kuo-hsia
		878	Wu-wei
		879	Chang-yeh
		880	Lin-tse
		881	Lao-chün-miao
		897	Ho-k'ou
		898	Liu-chia-hsia
		899	Wei-yüan
		900	Lung-hsi
	Tsinghai	615	Hsi-ning
		616	Tsaidam*
		617	Ta-t'ung
		618	Ko-erh-mu
		892	Mang-ai
		893	Ta-ch'ai-tan
		895	Hai-yen
		896	Huang-yüan
	Ningsia	619	Yin-ch'uan
		620	Shih-tsui-shan

Table Appendix J (continued)

Region	Province	City Code Number	Name of City
		621	Chin-chi
		855	Chung-wei
		857	Ch'ing-t'ung-hsia
		901	T'ung-hsin
	Sinkiang	622	Urumshi
		623	Kashgar
		624	I-ning
		625	Tu-shan-tzu
		626	Karamai
		627	Ha-mi
		628	Ko-ko-to-hai
		629	Wu-la-po
		882	T'u-lu-fan
		883	Wu-erh-ho
		884	A-lo-t'ai
		885	A-la-shan-k'ou
		886	Ching-ho
		887	Sui-ting
		888	K'u-erh-lo
		890	Ho-t'ien
		891	Jo-ch'iang
Southwest	Szechwan	701	Chungking
		702	Ch'eng-tu
		703	I-pin
		704	Tzu-kung
		705	Wei-yüan
		706	Ta-hsien
		707	Ch'i-chiang
		708	Wan-hsien
		709	Lo-shan
		710	Ho-ch'uan
		711	Kuang-yüan
		712	Nan-ch'ung
		713	Wu-t'ung-chiao
		714	Lu-hsien
		715	Chien-wei*
		716	Pien-chüang-tzu*
		717	Shih-p'eng*
		718	Shih-chiu-t'an*
		719	Tzu-p'ing-pu
		720	So-chia
		721	K'uan-hsien
		722	Chiang-yu
		723	Chang-sh'ou
		724	K'ang-t'ing

303

Table Appendix J (continued)

Region	Province	City Code Number	Name of City
		725	Chu-yang-ch'i
		725a	San-chiang
		725b	Nei-chiang
		784	Ya-an
		994	Hsi-ch'ang
		996	Kung-hsien
		997	Tzu-chung
		998	Hsin-tu
		999	Kuang-han
		1000	Ch'ü-hsien
		1001	Wan-shang-ch'ang
		1002	Kan-shui-ch'ang
	Yunnan	726	Kunming
		727	Ko-chiu
		728	Hsia-kuan
		729	Hsüan-wei
		730	Hui-tse
		731	Liu-lang-tung
		732	Shih-lung-pa
		733	Liu-shui-ho*
		734	Hsiao-chiang-k'ou*
		735	Yang-tsung-hai
		786	Chan-i
		787	Pao-shan
		788	Su-ta
		789	Pi-se-chai
		790	Ho-k'ou
		978	Ch'ü-ching
		979	Lu-liang
		980	I-liang
		981	Ch'eng-chiang
		982	An-ning
		983	I-p'ing-lang (Lu-feng)
		984	Ta-li
		985	Hao-ch'ing
		986	Wan-ting
		988	Mo-chiang
		989	Shih-ping
		990	Meng-tzu
		991	K'ai-yüan
		992	Shih-tsung
		995	Yen-ching
	Kweichow	736	Kuei-yang
		737	Tsun-i
		738	Tu-yün

Table Appendix J (continued)

Region	Province	City Code Number	Name of City
		739	Shui-cheng
		740	Hsia-ssu
		741	Ching-chen
		742	Ta-yen-men*
		742a	Pi-ch'ieh
		742b	An-shun
		785	Wei-ning
		974	Ma-wei
		975	Li-po
		976	Kuei-ting
		977	Hui-shui
		993	Pi-chieh
		1003	Tu-shan
	Tibet	743	Lhasa
		894	Jih-k'o-tse (Shigatse)
	Outer Mongolia	1013	Ulan Batu
		1016	Uuldza
		1017	Choy Balsan
		1018	Dzüün
		1019	Tamsag Bulag

*Small new cities, the exact location of which cannot be located on the map.

NOTES

Chapter 1

1. Walter Isard, Location and Space-Economy (New York: John Wiley and Sons, Inc., 1956), p. 238.

2. It is not true, however, that such noneconomic costs can really be discounted completely in the long run even in a totalitarian, planned society.

3. For a comprehensive study of the economic geography of China see Norton S. Ginsburg, The Pattern of Asia (Englewood Cliffs, N. J.: Prentice-Hall, Inc., 1958), pp. 155-273.

4. See Yuan-li Wu, The Steel Industry of Communist China (New York: Praeger, 1965), Ch. 6.

5. The new Ta-ch'ing oil fields in Manchuria may have modified the expectations of the planners; however, there is no evidence that these expectations have been changed completely.

6. Jen-min Shou-t'se, 1955 (People's Handbook, 1955) (Tientsin: Ta-kung PaoShe, 1955), p. 130.

7. Chung-hua-jen-min-kung-ho-kuo Fa-chan Kuo-min-ching-chi ti Ti-i-ko Wu-nien-chi-hua (The First Five-Year Plan of the People's Republic of China) (Peking: People's Publishing House, 1955), pp. 31-33.

8. Liu Tsai-hsing and Chang Hsüeh-ch'ing, "Shih-nien-lai Chung-kuo Kung-yeh Ti-t'u ti Wei-ta Pien-ko" (Significant Changes in the Industrial Map of China during the Past Ten Years), Ti-li Chih-shih (Geographical Knowledge) (Peking), Vol. 10, No. 11, November 1959, pp. 481-484.

9. Jen-min Shou-Ts'e, 1956 (People's Handbook, 1956) (Shanghai: Ta-kung Pao-she, 1956), pp. 59-60.

10. It is rarely stated that minimization of transport input is the criterion when the markets and sources of raw materials and fuels do not coincide.

11. People's Handbook, 1956, op. cit.

12. Ibid.

13. The rate of increase of adjusted modern industrial output was 16 per cent in 1953-54 and 8 per cent in 1954-55; it rose to 26 per cent in 1955-56. The GNP rose 4 per cent in 1953-54 and 5 per cent in 1954-55; it increased 12 per cent in 1955-56. Taken from Yuan-li Wu et al., The Economic Potential of Communist China (Menlo Park, Calif.: Stanford Research Institute, 1963), Vol. I, pp. 220 and 241.

14. Jen-min Shou-ts'e, 1957 (People's Handbook, 1957) (Shanghai: Takung PaoShe, 1957), p. 192.

15. Ibid., p. 42.

16. Kao, Hsiang-kao, Ten Years of Chinese Communist Economy (Taipei: Asian People's Anti-Communist League, 1960), pp. 66-67.

17. Tseng Wen-ching, Chung-kuo ti She-hui-chu-i Kung-yeh-hua (The Socialist Industrialization of China) (Peking: People's Publishing House, 1957), pp. 257-258.

18. Lu Ta-chuang, "Ch'ung-fen Li-yung Yüan-yu Kung-yeh Chi-ti ho Chi-chi Chien-she Hsin-kung-yeh Chi-ti" (Full Utilization of Existing Industrial Bases and Active Establishment of New Industrial Bases), Ti-li Chih-shih (Geographical Knowledge) (Peking: K'o-hsüeh Ch'u-pan-she, 1959), Vol. 10, No. 12, December 1959, pp. 529-531.

19. Wu Lo-shan, "Ch'ü-yü Kuei-hua-chung ti Kung-yeh P'ei-chih Wen-t'i" (The Problem of the Industrial Location in Regional Planning), Ti-li Chih-shih (Geographical Knowledge) (Peking: K'o-hsüeh Ch'u-pan-she, 1959), Vol. 10, No. 7, July 1959, pp. 292-293.

20. Tung-pei Ti-ch'ü Ching-chi Ti-li (Northeast China Economic Geography) (Peking: 1959); Ta-kung Daily, June 27, 1962.

21. Another source places Fukien in east China, as was customary under the "Great Administrative Region." Kiangsi should also be in east China. See Liu and Chang, loc. cit.

22. Akademia der Wissenschaften des USSR, ed., Politische Ökonomie-Lehrbuch (Düsseldorf: Institut für Ökonomie, 1955), p. 242 ff. See also Holland Hunter, Soviet Transportation Policy (Cambridge, Mass.: Harvard University Press, 1957).

23. Lieh-ning Wen-hsüan Liang Ch'üan-chi (Selected Essays of Lenin) (Peking: People's Publishing House, 1954), Vol. II, p. 972.

24. Ibid.

25. Tseng, op. cit., pp. 59-66.

26. People's Handbook, 1957, op. cit., p. 48.

27. Before proceeding to the next chapter, the reader may wish to go directly to Chapter 5 for a review of the problems of coordinating locational and transportation policies.

Chapter 2

1. Morris B. Ullman, Cities of Mainland China: 1953 and 1968 (Washington, D. C.: Bureau of the Census, Foreign Manpower Research Office, U. S. Department of Commerce, 1961), Series P-95, No. 59, p. 2.

2. A municipality is defined as an urban place designated as a separate administrative unit.

3. See Walter Isard, Location and Space-Economy (New York: John Wiley and Sons, Inc., 1956), pp. 55-79.

309

4. H. W. Singer, "The 'Courbe des Populations,' A Parallel to Pareto's Law," The Economic Journal, Vol. XLVI, No. 182, June 1936, pp. 254-263.

5. G. R. Allen, "The 'Courbe des Populations,' A Further Analysis," Bulletin of the Oxford University Institute of Statistics, Vol. XVI, Nos. 5 and 6, May and June 1954, pp. 179-189.

6. Singer, loc. cit.

Chapter 3

1. Wang Hu-sheng, "Kuan-yü Chung-kung-yeh ho Ch'ing-kung-yeh Hua-fen ti Chi-ko Wen-ti" (Some Problems on the Demarcation between Heavy and Light Industries), Ching-chi Yen-chiu (Economic Research), No. 4, April 17, 1963 (Peking: Ching-chi Yen-chu Tsa-chih-she, 1963), pp. 16-26.

2. The estimates are derived from Yuan-li Wu et al., The Economic Potential of Communist China (Menlo Park, Calif.: Stanford Research Institute, 1963). The data on power and coal are taken from Yuan-li Wu, Economic Development and the Use of Energy Resources in Communist China (New York: Praeger, 1963). The ferrous metals estimates are derived from Yuan-li Wu, The Steel Industry of Communist China (New York: Praeger, 1965).

3. Ibid.

4. It should be noted in this connection that the plant data used here did not reflect the economic contraction after the "Great Leap Forward." Furthermore, because of the relatively small industrial expansion between 1963 and 1965, the spatial pattern of Communist China's industrial structure developed in this chapter can be regarded as essentially valid today (mid-1966).

5. Yuan-li Wu et al., The Economic Potential of Communist China (Menlo Park, Calif.: Stanford Research Institute, 1963), Vol. II, Appendix I. See also Yuan-li Wu, The Economy of Communist China: An Introduction (New York: Praeger, 1965).

Chapter 4

1. If we denote total industrial capacity in million yüan in the enumerated industries by X and the total population in thousands at midyear 1958 by Y, for the 117 cities employed in the text, a regression equation of the form Y = 373. 725 + 0. 8858X can be fitted, and the corresponding correlation coefficient would be equal to +0. 83. On the other hand, if X denotes the amount of new industrial capacity built or under construction since 1949 and Y denotes the increment of midyear population between 1953 and 1958, a regression equation of the form Y = 74. 146 + 0. 9966X can be fitted with a correlation coefficient of +0. 59 only. This lower but still not insignificant correlation is in line with the discussion in the text.

2. The rank prefixes are B2, B3, B4, B5, B8, C2, and C3.

3. Excluding Soochow and Kuei-yang.

4. Hsiao Yeh-hui, "Fei-O Ching-chi Kuan-hsi chih Yen-chiu" (A Study of Communist Chinese and Russian Economic Relations), Fei-ch'ing Yen-chiu (Research on Mainland China), Vol. VI, No. 2, February 25, 1963 (Taipei: Ministry of Defense, 1963), p. 51.

Chapter 5

1. If more than one set of planners are involved, which may happen given a certain degree of decentralization under the system of economic cooperation or mutual assistance regions, divergencies may appear between locational arrangements designed to maximize the rate of economic growth of an individual region with those that would maximize the national growth rate. Such discrepancies are well illustrated by examples of "regionalism" under the Sovnarkhozy in the Soviet Union. See, for example, Alec Nove, The Soviet Economy (New York: Praeger, 1961).

2. Yuan-li-Wu: The Economy of Communist China: An Introduction (New York: Praeger, 1965).

3. See Chou En-lai's report on the record of the government in Jen-min Shou-t'se, 1955 (People's Handbook, 1955) (Tientsin: Ta-kung PaoShe, 1955), pp. 129-141.

4. See Li Fu-ch'un's report on the First Five-Year Plan in Chung-hua Jen-min Kung-ho-kuo Fa-kuei Hui-pien (Compendium of Laws of the People's Republic of China, July-December 1955) (Peking: Fa-lü Ch'u-pan-she, 1956), pp. 276-358.

5. People's Handbook, 1955, op. cit., pp. 129-141.

6. Chung-hua Jen-min Kung-ho-kuo Fa-chan Kuo-min-ching-chi Ti-i-ko Wu-nien-chi-hua (The First Five Year Plan for the Development of the National Economy of the PRC) (Peking: People's Publishing House, 1955), pp. 94-95.

Chapter 6

1. Ta-chung Liu and Kung-chia Yeh, The Economy of the Chinese Mainland: National Income and Economic Development, 1933-1959 (Santa Monica, California: The Rand Corporation, April 1963), Table 48, p. 243; Table 68, p. 321; and Table H-9, p. 764. The value for the modern sector of transportation and communications has been adjusted by eliminating the portion estimated for the communications subsector (0.18 billion yüan) from the total of 2.10 billion yüan.

2. Ibid. The gross value-added in the communications subsector, estimated at about the same value as the net value-added or 0.18 billion 1952 yüan, has also been subtracted from the modern transport sector total (2.23 billion yüan). A similar adjustment, involving the subtraction of 0.24 billion yüan from the modern sector total of 3.90 billion yüan, is also made for the gross receipts.

3. Ou Pao-san, 1933 Chung-kuo Kuo-min So-te (China's National Income, 1933) (Shanghai: 1947), Vol. I, pp. 85-87, 90-91, 95-97. The estimates are adjusted to exclude the communications subsector from the modern sector

of transport and communications--90 million yüan at 1933 prices for gross receipts and 65 million yüan in net value-added, respectively.

4. Liu and Yeh, op. cit., p. 294, Table 60. The percentage figure is based on 1.46 million employed in the modern sector and 10.90 in the traditional sector.

5. Chin Chia-fung, Chung-kuo Chiao-t'ung chih Fa-chan chi Ch'i Ch'ü-hsiang (Transportation Development and Trends in China) (Shanghai: Cheng-chung shu-chü, 1937), pp. 146-147.

6. Yuan-li Wu, An Economic Survey of Communist China (New York: Bookman Associates, 1956), pp. 350 ff.

7. Wei-ta ti Shih-nien (The Great Ten Years) (Peking: Foreign Language Press, 1959), English translation, p. 129.

8. If branches and spurs (1,740 km) and the dismantled tracks (3,100 km) are subtracted from the total and if the reported operating length actually includes trunk lines only, the ratio of operating to total trackage would then be as high as 100 per cent [21,989/(24,940 - 3,100)]. This computation shows that the reported operating length probably includes branches and spurs. The estimated length of dismantled lines is derived from Railways in Communist China (Taipei: Communications Research Bureau, Ministry of Communications, 1961), pp. 25-28.

9. Yu Tsai, "Shou-chieh Ch'üan-kuo Hang-wu Kung-lu Hui-i" (The First National Navigation and Highway Conference), Hsin-hua Yüeh-pao (New China Monthly), Vol. I, No. 4, February 1950, (Peking: People's Publishing House, 1950), p. 924. The figure seems to include county roads and may also include highways and roads in Taiwan.

10. An Editorial Report on Ch'i-ch'e ho Kung-lu (Automobiles and High-ways), Vol. II, No. 4, July 1950, p. 41.

11. According to the report of Ministry of Communications, Bureau of Highway, in Kung-lu (Highway) (Peking), No. 3 March 1959, p. 12, the technical specifications of the highways in Communist China are as follows:

Specification	Grades						
	I	II	III	IV	V	VI-A	VI-B
Designed speed (km/hr)	120	100	80	60	40	25	25
Number of lanes	4	2	2	2	2	2	1
Width of road surface (meters)	14	7	7	7	7	6	3. 0-4. 5
Width of road (meters)	23	12	11	10	9	8	4. 5-6. 5
Maximum grade in plain areas (per cent)	3	4	4	4	5	5	5

Highway classification in the Nationalist period was based on the specifications given by Yü Fei-p'eng, Shih-wu-nien lai chih Chiao-t'ung Kai-k'uang) (The General Situation of Transportation during the Last Fifteen Years) (Nanking: Ministry of National Defense, 1946), pp. 31-34. These data are as follows:

Specification	National Highways		Provincial Highways	
	Grade A	Grade B	Grade A	Unclassified
Designed speed (km/hr)	100	80	60	25
Width of road surface (meters)	9-12	7. 5-9	6-7. 5	4. 5-6
Maximum grade in plain areas (per cent)	3	4	5	8
Maximum load (metric tons)	20	15	10-15	5-10

Yü Fei-p'eng also mentioned a national total (including Taiwan) of 250, 000 km attributed to the then Communist Economic and Financial Commission. If the figure for Taiwan (18, 000 km) is excluded, the net total would be 232, 000 km, which corresponds to the total given by Mao Shou-chin, in Kung-lu Ch'ang-shih (Common Sense on Highway) (Shanghai: Jen-min Chu-pan-she, 1951).

12. One-third of 232, 000 km.

13. The Great Ten Years, op cit.

14. Ching-chi Tao-pao (Economic Bulletin) (Hong Kong), No. 46, December 1953, p. 13.

15. The range is obtained from 75,000/137,000 and 81,000/137,000, respectively. If the total of 232,000 is used, the ratio of highways open to traffic would be from 32 to 35 per cent.

16. Shui-yün Yün-chia Huei-pien (Consolidated Tariff of Water Transportation) (Peking: Ministry of Communications, 1959), Part 4, pp. 1-55; Hang-tao Wang (The Inland Waterway Network) (Nanking: Executive Yuan, 1947), pp. 13-46.

17. The Great Ten Years, op. cit.

18. Ibid.

19. Hung I, Kung-fei Chiao-t'ung Chien-she chih Yen-chiu (A Study of Communication Construction in Communist China) (Taipei, 1957), p. 229.

20. Different estimates of Communist China's land area are available. The discrepancies arise from indeterminate boundaries in Southwest China and Outer Mongolia as well as from the treatment of areas outside the Chinese mainland. The figure used in the test is the sum of land areas in the mainland provinces prior to the boundary settlements with Burma and Pakistan in 1963. The figure given in The Great Ten Years, op. cit. is 9,597,000 km^2.

21. Yuan-li Wu et al., The Economic Potential of Communist China (Menlo Park, Calif.: Stanford Research Institute, 1963), Vol. I, p. 28.

22. Chin Shih-hsüan, T'ieh-tao Yün-shu-hsüeh (Railway Transportation) (Shanghai: Commercial Press, 1948), p. 221.

23. Hsin-hua Yüeh-pao (New China Monthly) (Peking: People's Publishing House), October 1950, p. 328.

Chapter 7

1. The rank prefixes are B2, B3, B4, B5, B8, C2, and C3.

2. Pao-t'ou is the autonomous region of Inner Mongolia (formerly Sui-yüan province). It is a typical example of a developing enclave in the underdeveloped portion of North China, which is relatively developed.

3. This figure is selected as an arbitrary minimum to screen out the lesser branches or spurs.

4. Yuan-li Wu, The Economy of Communist China: An Introduction (New York: Praeger, 1965), Ch. 8.

5. Only one highway (1,400 km) was listed for Inner Mongolia, and it is included with the North China figure.

6. Kung-fei ti Ti-erh-ko Wu-nien-chi-hua chih Yen-chiu (A Study on the Second Five-Year Plan of Communist China (Taipei: Bureau of Investigation, Ministry of Justice, 1961), p. 345.

7. Yu N. Kapelinskiy, Development of the Economy and Foreign Economic Contracts of the People's Republic of China, translated by J. P. R. S., No. 3234, May 23, 1960, pp. 360-361.

8. Seven when the parts are grouped by industrial capacity. I-ch'ang is a small industrial center, but is not among the economic centers with rank prefixes.

9. The relatively low position occupied by North China in part reflects the inclusion of Inner Mongolia in North China statistics.

10. People's Daily, April 9, 1960.

11. Ibid., February 8, 1963.

12. See Yuan-li Wu et al., The Economic Potential of Communist China (Menlo Park, Calif.: Stanford Research Institute, 1963), Vol. III.

13. <u>Mainland Today</u> (Taipei), No. 168, September 16, 1962, p. 10.

14. Li Po-chih, "Kao-hao Tuan-t'u Yün-shu" (Improving Short-Distance Transportation), <u>Chi-hua yü T'ung-chi</u> (Planning and Statistics) (Peking) No. 7, April 1959, p. 24; and Lei Ting and Chu Hsing-min, "Tuan-t'u Yün-shu ti T'e-tien chi Ch'i Tsai Ch'eng-hsiang Wu-tzu Chiao-liu-chung ti Tso-yung" (The Characteristics of Short-Distance Transportation and Its Function in the Commodity Flow between Rural and Urban Areas) (Peking), <u>Ching-chi Yen-chiu</u> (Economic Research), No. 6, 1963, p. 33. See also Chapter 6.

Chapter 8

1. Lü Cheng-ch'ao, "Tsen-yang Wan-ch'eng Chin-nien ti T'ieh-lu Yün-shu Jen-wu" (How to Fulfill This Year's Railway Transportation Quota), <u>Hsin-hua Pan-yüeh-k'an</u> (New China Semi-monthly) (Peking), No. 10, May 1959, pp. 32-33.

2. The business reasons, including traveling to the country for "reform through labor", may of course be entirely involuntary.

3. The dip in shipping volume in 1950 can be attributed to the coastal blockade by the Nationalists and a general lack of vessels at the time.

4. A. Bergson and S. Kuznets, <u>Economic Trends in the Soviet Union</u> (Cambridge, Mass.: Harvard University Press, 1963), p. 36.

5. H. Hunter, <u>Soviet Transportation Policy</u> (Cambridge, Mass.: Harvard University Press, 1957), pp. 331, 335, 340, 342, and 343.

6. <u>Ibid.</u>, p. 331.

7. John W. Kendrick, <u>Productivity Trends in The United States</u> (Princeton, N. J.: Princeton University Press, 1961), pp. 293-295; <u>Statistical Abstract of the United States</u> (Washington, D. C.: U. S. Department of Commerce, 1957), p. 559; <u>Ibid.</u>, 1962, p. 570.

8. Japan Power and Fuel Yearbook (Tokyo: Japan Power Association, 1961), p. 3; Japan Statistical Yearbook, 1949 (Tokyo: Prime Minister's Office, Statistics Bureau, 1949), p. 410; Asahi Yearbook, 1964 (Tokyo: 1964), p. 465; Kôlsü Yearbook, 1952 (Tokyo: 1952), p. 398.

9. A. I. Yin, "Railroad Transport in the Chinese People's Republic," J. P. R. S., No. 3484, July 6, 1960.

10. See Liu Chuang, Wo-kuo ti Yün-shu-yeh (China's Transport Industry) (Peking: 1956), pp. 49-50; Jen-min shou-t'se, 1956 (People's Handbook) (Peking: 1956), pp. 509-510.

11. Ta-kung Daily (Peking), April 13, 1963.

12. Ibid. , July 29, 1962.

13. Ibid. , August 5, 1962.

14. See the discussion on the difficulties of resource allocation in the Communist Chinese economy in Yuan-li Wu, The Economy of Communist China: An Introduction (New York: Praeger, 1965).

15. Chi-hua Ching-chi (Planned Economy), No. 4, April 9, 1958, pp. 25-26.

16. Ibid. , p. 26.

17. Ta-kung Daily (Peking), January 12, 1963.

18. Ibid. , January 23, 1963.

19. See the discussion in Mainland Today (Taipei), No. 168, September 16, 1962, pp. 10-14.

20. See Yuan-li Wu et al. , The Economic Potential of Communist China (Menlo Park, Calif. : Stanford Research Institute, 1963), Vol. II.

21. Ta-Kung Daily, February 27, 1963.

22. Fan Jo-i's article on the pricing of heavy industry products in Ching-chi Yen-chiu (Economic Research) (Peking), No. 3, June 1957, pp. 54 ff.

23. See Yuan-li Wu, The Steel Industry of Communist China (Stanford, Calif.: Hoover Institution, 1965).

24. Planned Economy, loc. cit.

25. Wei-ta ti Shih-nien (Great Ten Years) (Peking: People's Publishing House, 1959), p. 136, and Ch'i-yü, Hsin-chung-kuo ti T'ieh-tao Chien-she (New China's Railway Construction) (Peking: 1953), p. 40.

26. Ibid.

27. Ibid.; and Yu I. Formin, "Success of Railroad Transport in China," Zheleznodorzhny Transport (Railroad Transport), (Moscow), No. 6, 1960, p. 6, translated by J. P. R. S., No. 4296, December 29, 1961.

28. Chung-hua Jen-men-kung-ho-kuo Fa-kuei Hui-pien (Compendium of Laws and Regulations, January to June 1959) (Peking: 1959), pp. 208-221.

29. Ta-kung Daily (Peking), March 27, 1963.

30. See, for example, the discussion in Chi-hua yü T'ung-chi (Planning and Statistics) (Peking), No. 4, 1959, pp. 14-15.

31. Huo-wu Yün-chia Chi-suan Kuei-tze Huo-wu P'in-ming Fen-lei piao (Rules for Computing Freight Rates and Freight Classification Tables) (Peking: Communist Chinese Ministry of Railways, 1955), pp. 1-56; Huo-wu Yün-chia-lu Piao (Freight Tariff Tables) (Peking: 1955), pp. 2-37.

32. Yuan-li Wu, The Economy of Communist China: An Introduction (New York: Praeger, 1965), Ch. 3.

LIST OF PLACE NAMES*

A-erh-shan 阿爾山
Inner Mongolia
E-1

A-kan-chen 阿干鎮
Kansu
E-1, E-4, E-6

A-la-shan-k'ou 阿拉山口
Sinkiang
E-6

A-li-ho 阿里河
Inner Mongolia
E-6

A-pa 阿壩(阿坝)
Szechwan
7-16

Amoy 廈門
Fukien
155; 4-3, 4-7, 4-8, A-1,
A-2, A-4, A-5, A-6, B-
1, B-2, C-1, C-2, E-1,
E-2, E-3, E-6

An-chiang 安江
Hunan
B-1, E-3

An-ch'ing 安慶
Anhwei
4-3, 4-7, 4-8; A-1, A-2,
A-4, A-6, B-1, B-2, C-1,
C-2, E-2, E-3, J

An-hsien 安縣
Fukien
7-16

An-hua 安化
Hunan
B-1, B-2, E-3

An-ning 安寧
Yünnan
E-4, E-6

An-pien 安邊(安边)
Szechwan
E-1, E-4, E-6

An-shan 鞍山
Liaoning
1, 16, 17, 56, 60, 201; 4-
3, 4-7, 4-8, 7-8; A-1, A-
2, A-4, A-5, A-6, B-1, B-
2, C-1, C-2, C-3, E-2, E-
3, J

---

*Reference numbers are listed in the following order: text pages, tables, and appendices.

An-shun 安順
Kweichow
B-1, B-2, E-3, J

An-t'u 安圖
Kirin
E-6

An-tung 安東
Liaoning
4-3, 4-7, 4-8, 7-8; A-1, A-2, A-4, A-5, A-6, B-1, B-2, C-1, C-2, E-1, E-2, E-3, E-5, J

An-yang 安陽
Honan
4-3, 4-7, 4-8; A-1, A-2, A-4, A-5, A-6, B-1, B-2, C-1, C-2, E-1, E-2, E-3, E-4, E-6, J

Ao-t'ou 敖頭
Heilungkiang
E-1

Canton 廣州
Kwangtung
11, 16, 32, 60, 69, 165; 1-1, 1-2, 4-3, 4-7, 4-8, 7-8, 7-19, 7-20, 7-21; A-1, A-2, A-4, A-5, A-6, B-1, B-2, C-1, C-2, E-1, E-2, E-3, E-5, J

Cha-lai-no-erh 扎賚諾尔
Inner Mongolia
B-1, E-3, J

Cha-leng-k'ou 茶冷口
Tsinghai
7-16

Cha-ling 茶陵
Hunan
B-1, E-3, J

Chan-chiang 湛江
Kwangtung
155, 165; 7-20, 7-21; A-1, A-2, A-4, A-5, B-1, C-1, C-2, E-1, E-2, E-3, J

Chai-chia-hsia 翟家峽
Honan
B-1, E-3, J

Chan-i 沾益
Yünnan
E-1, E-6

Chan-tien 詹店
Shansi
E-6

Chang-chou 漳州
Fukien
B-1, E-3, J

Chang-p'ing 漳平
Fukien
B-1, E-1, E-3, E-4, E-6, J

Chang-tien 張店
Shantung
E-1

Ch'ang-ch'ang 長昌
Kwangtung
B-1, E-3, J

Ch'ang-chih 長治
    Shansi
    4-3, 4-7, 4-8; A-1, A-5,
    A-6, B-1, B-2, C-1, C-2,
    E-2, E-3

Ch'ang-chou 常州
    Kiangsu
    4-3, 4-7, 4-8; A-1, A-2,
    A-4, A-5, A-6, B-1, C-1,
    C-2, E-2, E-3, J

Ch'ang-ch'un 長春
    Kirin
    4-3, 4-7, 4-8, 7-8; A-1,
    A-2, A-4, A-5, A-6, B-1,
    B-2, C-1, C-2, C-3, E-1,
    E-2, E-3, J

Ch'ang-ning 常寧
    Hunan
    B-1, E-3, J

Ch'ang-sha 長沙
    Hunan
    11; 1-1, 1-2, 4-3, 4-7, 4-
    8, 7-8; A-1, A-2, A-4, A-
    5, A-6, B-1, B-2, C-1, C-
    2, E-2, E-3, J

Ch'ang-shou 長壽 (長寿)
    Szechwan
    B-1, E-3, J

Ch'ang-shu 常熟
    Kiangsu
    4-3, 4-7, 4-8; A-1, A-2, A-
    4, A-5, A-6, B-1, C-1, C-
    2, E-2, E-3, J

Ch'ang-t'an 長灘 (長滩)
    Hupeh
    B-1, E-3, J

Ch'ang-te 常德
    Hunan
    B-1, E-3, J

Ch'ang-tien 長甸
    Liaoning
    E-1, J

Ch'ang-ting 長汀
    Heilungkiang
    E-1

Ch'ang-tu 昌都
    Tibet
    7-16

Ch'ang-t'u 昌圖
    Liaoning
    E-1

Chao-an 詔安
    Fukien
    7-16

Chao-p'ing 昭平
    Kwangsi
    B-1, B-2, E-3, J

Chao-shih 皀市
    Hunan
    B-1, E-3, J

Ch'ao-an 潮安
    Kwangtung
    7-16

Ch'ao-chou 潮州
    Kwangtung
    4-3, 4-7, 4-8; A-1, A-2,
    A-4, A-5, B-1, C-1, C-2
    J

Ch'ao-yang-chen 朝陽鎮
Liaoning
E-1

Ch'ao-yang-ch'uan 朝陽川
Kirin
E-1

Chefoo 烟台
Shantung
165; 4-3, 4-7, 4-8, 7-19,
7-20, 7-21; A-1, A-2, A-
4, A-5, A-6, B-1, C-1, C-
2, E-1, E-2, E-3, E-4, E-
6, J

Chen-chiang 鎮江
Kiangsu
4-3, 4-7, 4-8; A-1, A-2,
A-4, A-5, A-6, B-1, C-1,
C-2, E-2, E-3, J

Ch'en hsien 郴縣
Hunan
E-1

Cheng-chia-t'sun 鄭家村
Liaoning
E-1

Cheng-chou 鄭州
Honan
16, 18; 4-3, 7-8; A-1, A-2,
A-4, A-5, A-6, B-1, B-2,
C-1, C-2, C-3, J

Cheng-ting 正定
Hopeh
B-1, E-3, J

Ch'eng-te 承德
Hopeh
4-3, 4-7, 4-8; A-1, A-5,
A-6, B-1, B-2, C-1, C-2
E-1, E-2, E-3, J

Ch'eng-tu 成都
Szechwan
1, 16, 155; 4-3, 4-7, 4-8,
7-8, 7-16; A-1, A-2, A-4,
A-5, A-6, B-1, B-2, C-1,
C-2, C-3, E-1, E-2, E-3,
E-4, E-6, J

Chi-an 吉安
Kiangsi
B-1, E-1, E-3

Chi-an 輯安
Kirin
E-1, E-2, J

Chi-ch'i 吉溪
Hunan
B-1, B-2, E-3, J

Chi-chieh 鷄街
Yünnan
E-1

Chi-hsi 鷄西
Heilungkiang
16; 4-3, 4-7, 4-8; A-1, A-
5, A-6, B-1, B-2, C-1, C-
2, C-3, E-1, E-2, E-3, J

Chi-lan-t'ai 吉蘭泰
Ningsia
7-16

Chi-mai 吉邁
    Tsinghai
    7-16

Chi-ning 集寧
    Inner Mongolia
    155; 4-3, 4-7, 4-8; A-1, A-
    5, A-6, B-1, C-1, C-2, E-
    1, E-3, J

Chi-ning 輯寧
    Kirin
    B-1, E-3, J

Chi-shan 吉山
    Kwangtung
    E-1

Ch'i-ch'i-ha-erh 齊齊哈尔
    Heilungkiang
    4-3; A-1, A-2, A-4, A-5,
    A-6, B-1, B-2, C-1, C-2,
    E-1, E-2, E-3, J

Ch'i-chiang 綦江
    Szechwan
    B-1, E-3, J

Ch'i-fu-fen 七府坟
    Shansi
    E-1

Ch'i-li-lung 七里隴
    Chekiang
    B-1, B-2, E-3

Ch'i-shu-yen 戚墅堰
    Kiangsu
    B-1, E-3, J

Chia-hsing 嘉興
    Chekiang
    4-3, 4-7, 4-8; A-1, A-5,
    A-6, B-1, C-1, C-2, E-2,
    E-3, J

Chia-mu-ssu 佳木斯
    Heilungkiang
    4-3, 4-7, 4-8, 7-19, 7-20,
    7-21; A-1, A-2, A-4, A-5,
    A-6, B-1, B-2, C-1, C-2,
    C-3, E-1, E-2, E-3, C-5, J

Chia-wang 賈旺
    Kiangsu
    E-1

Chiang-k'ou 江口
    Kiangsi
    B-1, E-3, J

Chiang-men 江門
    Kwangtung
    4-3, 4-7, 4-8; A-1, A-5,
    B-1, B-2, C-1, C-2, E-2,
    E-3, J

Chiang-pei 江北
    Kirin
    E-1

Chiang-pien 江邊
    Heilungkiang
    E-6

Chiang-shan 江山
    Chekiang
    7-16

Chiang-ts'un 蔣村
    Shansi
    E-1

Chiang-yu 江油
Szechwan
7-16; B-1, B-2, E-3, J

Chiao-chia-wan 焦家灣
Hopeh
B-1, E-3, J

Chiao-ho 蛟河
Kirin
B-1, B-2, E-1, E-3, J

Chiao-tso 焦作
Honan
4-3, 4-7, 4-8; A-1, A-5, A-6, B-1, B-2, C-2, C-3, E-1, E-2, E-3, J

Chieh-hsiu 介休
Shansi
E-1, E-4, E-6

Ch'ieh-mo 且末
Sinkiang
7-16

Chien-ch'en 建辰
Kirin
B-1, E-3, J

Chien-ch'i 建溪
Fukien
B-1, B-2, E-3, J

Chien-ho 劍河
Kweichow
7-16

Chien-kuo-chi 建國集
Kirin
B-1, E-3, J

Chien-ou 建甌
Fukien
7-16

Chien-wei 犍為
Szechwan
B-1, E-3, J

Chih-chiang 芷江
Hunan
E-4, J

Ch'ih-feng 赤峯
Inner Mongolia
B-1, B-2, E-3, J

Chin-chi 金積
Ningsia
B-1, B-2, E-3, J

Chin-chiang 錦江
Kiangsi
B-1, E-3

Chin-chou 錦州
Liaoning
4-3, 4-7, 4-8; A-1, A-2, A-4, A-5, A-6, B-1, C-1, C-2, E-1, E-2, E-3, J

Chin-chu 金珠
Kirin
E-1

Chin-chu-shan 金竹山
Hunan
E-1, E-4, E-6

Chin-ho 金河
Heilungkiang
E-6

Chin-hsi 錦西
Liaoning
B-1, C-3, E-1, E-3, J

Chin-hua 金華
Chekiang
B-1, E-1, E-3, E-6, J

Chin-ling-szu 金嶺寺
Liaoning
E-1

Chin-p'ing 錦屏
Kweichow
7-16

Chin-se-hsien 金色縣
Anhwei
B-1, E-3, J

Ch'in-huang-tao 秦皇島
Hopeh
124; 4-3, 4-7, 4-8, 7-19,
7-20, 7-21; A-1, A-4, A-5,
A-6, B-1, C-1, C-2, E-2,
E-3, J

Ching-kang-shan 井崗山
Kiangsi
7-16; B-1, B-2, E-3, J

Ching-po-hu 鏡泊湖
Heilungkiang
B-1, E-3, J

Ching-te-chen 景德鎮
Kiangsi
4-3, 4-7, 4-8; A-1, A-5,
A-6, B-1, C-1, C-2, E-2,
E-3, J

Ch'ing-chen 清鎮
Kweichow
B-1, E-3, J

Ch'ing-hua 清化
Honan
E-6

Chiu-chiang 九江
Kiangsi
1-1, 1-2; A-2, E-1

Chiu-chih 久治
Tsinghai
7-16

Chiu-ch'üan 酒泉
Kansu
B-1, E-3, J

Cho-hsien 涿縣
Hopeh
B-1, E-3, J

Chou-k'ou 周口
Honan
A-2

Chou-k'ou-tien 周口店
Hopeh
E-1

Chou-shui-tzu 周水子
Liaoning
E-1

Chu-chou 株州
Hunan
16; 4-3, 4-7, 4-8; A-1, A-
2, A-4, A-5, A-6, B-1, B-
2, C-1, C-2, C-3, E-1, E-
2, E-3, E-4, J

Chu-yang-ch'i 朱楊溪
Szechwan
B-1, B-2, E-3, J

Ch'ü-chiang 曲江
Kwangtung
E-3, E-6, J

Ch'üan-chiang 泉江
Kiangsi
E-1

Ch'üan-chou 泉州
Fukien
4-3, 4-7, 4-8; A-1, A-2,
A-4, A-5, A-6, B-1, C-1,
C-2, E-2, E-3, E-6, J

Chuang-ho 莊河
Liaoning
7-16

Ch'uan-shan 穿山
Chekiang
E-1, E-4, E-6

Chung-shan 鍾山
Kwangsi
B-1, E-3, J

Chung-wei 中衛
Ningsia
E-6

Chungking 重慶
Szechwan
11, 16, 32, 56, 69, 155, 164;
1-1, 1-2, 4-3, 4-7, 4-8, 7-
8, 7-19, 7-20, 7-21; A-1, A-
2, A-4, A-5, A-6, B-1, B-2,
C-1, C-2, C-3, E-1, E-2,
E-3, E-4, E-6, J

Erh-lien 二連
Inner Mongolia
155; E-1, E-6

Erh-tao-sha-ho 二道沙河
Inner Mongolia
E-1

Fa-k'u 法庫
Liaoning
E-1, E-4, E-6

Fang-ch'eng 房城
Kwangtung
J

Fen-hsi 汾西
Shansi
B-1, E-3

Fend-ch'eng 豐城
Kiangsi
B-1, B-2, E-3, J

Feng-ching 楓涇
Kiangsu
E-1

Feng-feng 峯峯
Hopeh
E-1

Feng-hsiang-kuo 鳳香國
Anhwei
E-1, E-4, E-6

Feng-huang-ch'eng 鳳凰城
Liaoning
E-1

Feng-huang-shan 鳳凰山
Kwangtung
B-1, E-3, J

Feng-lin 鳳林
Chekiang
7-16

Feng-ling-tu 風陵渡
Shansi
E-2, E-4, E-5, E-6

Feng-t'ai 鳳台
Anhwei
B-1, B-2, E-1, E-3, E-4,
E-5, J

Feng-t'ai 豐台 (丰台)
Hopeh
E-1, E-3, E-4, E-6

Fo-shan 佛山
Kwangtung
4-3, 4-7, 4-8; A-1, A-2,
A-4, A-5, B-1, C-1, C-2,
E-2, E-3, J

Foochow 福州
Fukien
4-3, 7-16, 7-19, 7-20, 7-
21; A-1, A-2, A-4, A-5, A-
6, B-1, B-2, C-1, C-2, E-
1, E-2, E-3, E-4, E-6, J

Fou-hsin 阜新
Liaoning
16, 124; 4-3, 4-7, 4-8; A-1,
A-2, A-4, A-5, B-1, B-2,
C-1, C-2, C-3, E-2, E-3, J

Fu-an 福安
Fukien
B-1, E-3, J

Fu-la-erh-chi 富拉尔基
Heilungkiang
B-1, C-3, E-3, J

Fu-li-chi 符離集
Anhwei
E-1, E-4, E-6

Fu-shun 撫順
Liaoning
16, 124; 4-3, 4-7, 4-8, 7-
8; A-1, A-2, A-4, A-5, A-
6, B-1, B-2, C-1, C-2, C-
3, E-1, E-2, E-3, J

Fu-ting 福鼎
Fukien
7-16

Fu-yü 富裕
Heilungkiang
E-1

Ha-mi 哈密
Sinkiang
B-1, B-2, E-3, E-6, J

Hai-k'ou 海口
Kwangtung
4-3, 7-16, 7-19, 7-20, 7-
21; A-1, A-2, A-4, A-5,
A-6, B-1, C-1, C-2, E-2,
E-3, J

Hai-la-erh 海拉尔
Inner Mongolia
7-16; B-1, B-2, E-3, J

Hai-men 海門
Chekiang
7-19

Hai-pa-chuang 海垻莊
Yünnan
7-16

Hai-pin 海濱
Hopeh
E-1

Hai-yen 海宴
Tsinghai
E-1, E-4, E-6

Han-chuang 韓莊
Shantung
B-1, E-1, E-3, J

Han-kuei 涵歸
Inner Mongolia
E-6

Han-tan 邯鄲
Hopeh
4-3, 4-7, 4-8, 7-8; A-1, A-2, A-4, A-5, A-6, B-1, B-2, C-1, C-2, C-3, E-1, E-2, E-3, J

Hangchow 杭州
Chekiang
4-3, 4-7, 4-8, 7-8; A-1, A-2, A-4, A-5, A-6, B-1, B-2, C-1, C-2, E-1, E-2, E-3, J

Hao-pi 鶴壁
Honan
B-1, E-1, J

Harbin 哈尔濱
Heilungkiang
69, 165; 4-3, 4-7, 4-8, 7-8, 7-19, 7-20, 7-21; A-1, A-2,

A-4, A-5, A-6, B-1, B-2, C-1, C-2, C-3, E-1, E-2, E-3, E-5, J

Hei-ho 黑河
Heilungkiang
B-1, E-3, J

Hei-ho 黑河
Tibet
7-16

Hei-shan-hu 黑山湖
Kansu
E-1, E-4, E-6

Heng-hsien 橫縣
Kwangsi
B-1, E-3, J

Heng-shan 恒山
Heilungkiang
E-1

Heng-yang 衡陽
Hunan
11, 16; 1-1, 1-2, 4-3, 4-7, 4-8; A-1, A-2, A-4, A-5, A-6, B-1, C-1, C-2, E-1, E-2, E-3, J

Ho-ch'uan 合川
Szechwan
B-1, E-3, J

Ho-fei 合肥
Anhwei
4-3, 4-7, 4-8, 7-8; A-1, A-2, A-4, A-5, A-6, B-1, B-2, C-1, C-2, E-2, E-3, J

Ho-kang 鶴崗
Heilungkiang
16; 4-3, 4-7, 4-8; A-1, A-
5, A-6, B-1, C-1, C-2, C-
3, E-1, E-2, E-3, E-5, J

Ho-k'ou 河口
Kansu
E-1

Ho-k'ou 河口
Yünnan
E-1

Ho-lung 和龍
Kirin
E-1

Ho-nan 和南
Kwangtung
B-2, E-3, J

Ho-shih-t'o-lo-kai 和什托洛蓋
Sinkiang
7-16

Ho-ts'un 和村
Kwangtung
E-1

Hou-ma 侯馬
Shansi
E-6

Hsi-ch'ang 西昌
Szechwan
7-16

Hsi-chi-hsi 西鷄西
Heilungkiang
E-1

Hsi-chia 西家
Heilungkiang
E-1

Hsi-chih-men 西直門
Hopeh
E-1

Hsi-ching 西津
Kwangsi
J

Hsi-chung 西鍾
Kwangsi
B-1, E-3

Hsi-hsien 忻縣
Shansi
E-1, E-6

Hsi-ning 西寧
Tsinghai
4-3, 4-7, 4-8, 7-16; A-1,
B-1, B-2, C-1, C-2, E-1,
E-2, E-3, E-4, E-6, J

Hsi-wan-p'u 西灣堡
Hopeh
E-1

Hsi-ying 西營
Kwangsi
E-6

Hsia-ch'eng-tzu 下城子
Heilungkiang
E-1

Hsia-kuan 下關 (下关)
Yünnan
B-1, B-2, E-3, J

Hsia-ssu 下司
Kweichow
B-1, E-3, J

Hsiang-fan 襄樊
Hupeh
B-1, E-3, J

Hsiang-fang 香坊
Heilungkiang
E-1

Hsiang-kuang-tung 响光洞
Hopeh
B-1, E-3, J

Hsiang-kung-miao 向公廟
Anhwei
B-1, E-3, J

Hsiang-t'an 湘潭
Hunan
4-3, 4-7, 4-8; A-1, A-2, A-
4, A-5, A-6, B-1, B-2, C-
1, C-2, E-2, E-3, E-6, J

Hsiang-yang 襄陽
Hupeh
E-6

Hsiang-yün 祥雲
Yünnan
7-16

Hsiao-chiang-k'ou 小江口
Yünnan
B-1, E-3, J

Hsiao-ku-chia 小孤家
Kirin
E-1

Hsiao-lang-ti 小浪地
Honan
B-1, B-2, E-3, J

Hsiao-nan-hai 小南海
Szechwan
E-1

Hsiao-shan 蕭山
Chekiang
E-1

Hsiao-wang-ch'ing 小汪清
Kirin
E-1

Hsien-yang 咸陽
Shensi
B-1, E-1, E-3, J

Hsin-an-chiang 新安江
Chekiang
B-1, B-2, E-1, E-3, E-4,
E-6, J

Hsin-chan 新站
Kirin
E-1

Hsin-cheng 新鄭
Honan
B-1, E-3, E-6, J

Hsin-ching 新井
Shansi
E-1

Hsin-ch'ing 新青
Heilungkiang
E-1, E-6

Hsin-feng 新豐 (新丰)
Kwangtung
B-1, B-2, E-3, J

Hsin-hai-lien 新海連
Kiangsu
4-3, 4-7, 4-8; A-1, A-2,
A-4, A-5, A-6, B-1, C-1,
C-2, E-2, E-3, J

Hsin-hsiang 新鄉
Honan
4-3, 4-7, 4-8; A-1, A-4, A-
5, A-6, B-1, C-1, C-2, E-1,
E-2, E-3, J

Hsin-i 信誼
Kwantung
7-16

Hsin-kang 新港
Hopeh
E-1

Hsin-lung-hua 新龍華
Kiangsu
E-1

Hsin-shih 新市
Szechwan
7-16

Hsin-t'ai 新泰
Shantung
E-1, J

Hsin-t'ang-pien 新塘邊
Chekiang
E-1

Hsin-tu 新都
Szechwan
E-1, E-4, E-6

Hsin-t'ung-hua 新通化
Kirin
E-1

Hsin-yang 信陽
Honan
B-1, B-2, E-3, E-6, J

Hsin-yü 新余
Kiangsi
B-1, B-2, E-3, J

Hsing-ning 興寧
Kwangtung
B-1, E-3, E-6, J

Hsing-t'ai 邢台
Hopeh
B-1, E-3, J

Hsü-ch'ang 許昌
Honan
B-1, C-3, E-3, J

Hsü-chia-chan 徐家站
Hopeh
E-1, E-4, E-6

Hsü-chou 徐州
Kiangsu
4-3; A-1, A-2, A-4, A-5,
A-6, B-1, B-2, C-1, C-2,
E-1, E-2, E-3, J

Hsüan-hua 宣化
Hopeh
B-1, B-2, E-1, E-3, J

Hsüan-wei 宣威
Yünnan
B-1, E-3, E-6, J

Hsüeh-ch'eng 薛城
Shantung
E-2

Hsün-hua 循化
Tsinghai
7-16

Hu-chou 湖州(吳興)
Chekiang
4-3, 4-7, 4-8; A-1, A-5,
A-6, C-1, C-2, E-2, J

Hu-hsien 鄠縣
Shensi
B-1, C-3, E-3, J

Hu-lu-tao 葫蘆島
Liaoning
E-1

Hu-nan-chen 湖南鎮
Chekiang
B-1, E-3, J

Hu-t'ou 虎頭
Heilungkiang
E-1

Hua-shih-hsia 花石峽
Tsinghai
7-16

Hua-yüan 花園
Hupeh
E-6

Huai-ch'i 濉溪
Anhwei
E-1, E-4, E-6

Huai-jou 懷柔(怀柔)
Hopeh
E-1, E-4, E-6

Huai-nan 淮南
Anhwei
192; 4-3, 4-7, 4-8, 7-8;
A-1, A-4, A-5, A-6, B-1,
B-2, C-1, C-2, C-3, E-2,
E-3, J

Huan-jen 桓仁
Liaoning
B-1, B-2, E-3, J

Huang-ku-ts'un 皇姑村
Liaoning
E-1

Huang-kua-liang 黄瓜梁
Tsinghai
7-16

Huang-pu 黄埔
Kwangtung
E-1

Huang-shih 黄石
Hupeh
A-1, A-2, A-4, A-5, A-6,
B-1, B-2, C-1, C-2, E-2,
E-3, E-4, J

Huang-t'an-k'ou 黄擅口
Chekiang
B-1, E-3, J

Huhehot 呼和浩特
  Inner Mongolia
  4-3, 4-7, 4-8, 7-16; A-1,
  A-2, A-3, A-4, A-5, A-6,
  B-1, B-2, C-1, C-2, E-2,
  E-3, J

Hui-hsing 會興
  Honan
  E-1, E-4, E-6

Hui-shui 惠水
  Kweichow
  7-16

Hui-tse 會澤
  Yünnan
  7-16; B-2, E-3, J

Hui-tui 灰堆
  Hopeh
  E-1

Hun-chiang 渾江
  Kirin
  E-1

Hun-ch'un 琿春
  Kirin
  B-1, E-3, J

Hun-ho 渾河
  Liaoning
  E-1

Hung-ch'i-ying 紅旗營
  Heilungkiang
  E-1

Hung-liu-yüan 紅柳園
  Kansu
  7-16

Hung-shan 洪山
  Shantung
  B-1, E-3, J

I-ch'ang 宜昌
  Hupeh
  164; 7-19, 7-21; B-1, E-3, J

I-ch'un 伊春
  Heilungkiang
  4-7, 4-8; A-1, A-5, A-6, C-
  1, C-2, E-1, E-2, E-6, J

I-hsien 義縣
  Liaoning
  E-1

I-hsien 嶧縣
  Shantung
  B-1, E-3, J

I-lan 依蘭
  Heilungkiang
  B-1, E-3, J

I-men 易門
  Yünnan
  7-16

I-mien-po 一面坡
  Heilungkiang
  E-5

I-ning 伊寧
  Sinkiang
  4-3, 4-7, 4-8; A-1, A-4,
  A-6, B-1, C-1, C-2, E-2,
  E-3, E-6, J

I-pin 宜賓
Szechwan
4-3, 4-7, 4-8; A-1, A-2,
A-4, A-5, A-6, B-1, C-1,
C-2, E-2, E-3

I-p'ing-lang 一平浪
Yünnan
E-1, E-4, E-6, J

I-tu 宜都
Hupeh
E-6

I-t'u-li-ho 伊圖里河
Inner Mongolia
E-1, E-6

I-yang 宜陽
Honan
E-1, E-4, E-6

Jen-hua 仁化
Kwangtung
B-1, E-3, J

Jih-hui-chiang 日暉港
Kiangsu
E-1

Jih-ke-tse 日喀則
Tibet
7-16

Jo-ch'iang 若羌
Sinkiang
E-6

Ju-yüan 乳源
Kwangtung
B-1, E-3, J

K'ai-feng 開封
Honan
4-3, 4-7, 4-8; A-1, A-2,
A-3, A-4, A-5, A-6, B-1,
C-1, C-2, E-2, E-3, J

K'ai-luan 開灤
Hopeh
124

Kai-p'ing 蓋平
Liaoning
7-16

K'ai-shan-ts'un 開山村
Kirin
E-1

Kalgan 張家口
Hopeh
4-3, 4-7, 4-8; A-1, A-2,
A-4, A-6, B-1, C-1, C-2,
E-1, E-2, E-3, E-6, J

Kan-chou 贛州
Kiangsi
7-16; B-1, E-3, J

Kan-ho 甘河
Inner Mongolia
E-1, E-6

Kan-shui 趕水
Szechwan
E-1, E-4, E-6

Kan-t'ang 趕堂
Kansu
E-1, E-4, E-6

K'ang-ting 康定
Szechwan
B-1, E-3, J

Kao-k'eng 高坑
Kiangsi
E-1

Kao-t'ai-shan 高台山
Liaoning
E-1

Karamai 克拉瑪依
Sinkiang
B-1, E-3

Kashgar 喀什
Sinkiang
4-3, 4-7, 4-8, 7-16; A-1,
A-5, A-6, B-1, C-1, C-2,
E-2, E-3, E-6, J

Ken-ho 根河
Inner Mongolia
E-1, E-6

Kirin 吉林
Kirin
16, 69; 4-3, 4-7, 4-8; A-1,
A-2, A-4, A-5, A-6, B-1,
B-2, C-1, C-2, C-3, E-1,
E-2, E-3, J

Ko-chiu 箇舊(箇旧)
Yünnan
4-3, 4-7, 4-8; A-1, A-2, A-
4, A-5, A-6, B-1, C-1, C-
2, C-3, E-2, E-3, J

Ko-erh-mu 噶尔穆
Tsinghai
7-16; B-1, E-3, E-6, J

Ko-i-ho 克伊河
Inner Mongolia
E-6

Ko-ken-miao 葛根廟
Inner Mongolia
E-1

Ko-ko-to-hai 克克托海
Sinkiang
B-1, E-3, J

Ko-ta-ke 葛大克
Tibet
7-16

Kou-k'ou 溝口
Heilungkiang
E-1

K'ou-ch'üan 口泉
Shansi
E-1, E-4, E-6

Ku-t'ien 古田
Fukien
B-1, E-3

K'u-lün 庫倫
Center Mongolia
E-6

K'u-tu-erh 庫都爾
Inner Mongolia
E-1, E-6

K'u-yeh 古冶
Hopeh
E-6

Kuan-hsien 灌縣
Szechwan
E-1, E-4, J

Kuan-t'ing 官廳
Hopeh
B-1, E-3, J

Kuan-yin-t'ang 觀音堂
Hopeh
192

Kuang-yüan 廣元
Szechwan
B-1, E-3, E-6, J

K'uang-shan 礦山
Hopeh
E-1

Kuei-ch'i 貴溪
Kiangsi
E-6

Kuei-tung 桂東
Hunan
7-16

Kuei-yang 貴陽
Kweichow
1-1, 1-2, 4-3; A-1, A-2,
A-4, A-5, A-6, B-1, B-2,
C-1, C-2, E-2, C-3, E-4,
E-6, J

K'ung-ke-shan-k'ou 空喀山口
Sinkiang
7-16

Kunming 昆明
Yünnan
1-1, 1-2, 4-3; A-1, A-2,
A-4, A-5, A-6, B-1, B-2,
C-1, C-2, C-3, J

Kuo-ch'ien-ch'i 郭前旗
Kirin
E-1

Kuo-k'eng 郭坑
Fukien
B-1, E-1, E-3, E-4, E-6, J

Kuo-lo 果洛
Tsinghai
7-16

Kweilin 桂林
Kwangsi
4-7; A-1, A-2, A-4, A-5,
A-6, B-1, C-1, C-2, E-2,
E-3, J

La-fa 拉法
Kirin
E-1

Lai-chou 賚州
Fukien
E-1, E-4

Lai-pin 來賓
Kwangsi
155; E-6

Lan-ch'i 蘭谿
Chekiang
E-4, E-6

Lan-chou 蘭州 (兰州)
Kansu
16, 18; 1-1, 1-2, 4-3, 4-7,
4-8, 7-8, 7-16; A-1, A-2,
A-4, A-5, A-6, B-1, B-2,
C-1, C-2, C-3, E-1, E-2,
E-3, E-4, E-5, E-6, J

Lan-chün-ts'un 攬軍村
Liaoning
E-1

Lan-ts'ang 瀾滄
Yünnan
7-16

Lan-ts'un 蘭村 (兰村)
Shantung
E-1, E-4, E-6

Lang-mu-ssu 郎木寺
Kansu
7-16

Lao-chün-miao 老君廟 (老君庙)
Kansu
E-1, E-6

Lao-ha-ho 老哈河
Inner Mongolia
B-1, B-2, E-3, J

Lei-shan 雷山
Kweichow
7-16

Leng-hu 冷湖
Tsinghai
7-16

Lhasa 拉薩
Tibet
7-16; B-1, E-3, J

Li-chen 利鎮
Honan
E-1, E-4, E-6

Li-t'ang 黎塘
Kwangsi
E-1, E-4, E-6

Liang-chuang 梁莊
Shantung
B-1, E-3, J

Liang-ko-chuang 梁各莊
Hopeh
E-6

Liang-wang-chuang 良王莊
Hopeh
E-1

Liao-yang 遼陽
Liaoning
4-3, 4-7, 4-8; A-1, A-2, A-
4, A-5, A-6, B-1, C-1, C-2,
E-1, E-2, E-3, E-5, J

Liao-yüan 遼源
Kirin
4-3, 4-7, 4-8; A-1, A-2,
A-4, A-5, A-6, B-1, B-2,
C-1, C-2, E-2, E-3, J

Lien-chiang 濂江
Kwangtung
B-1, E-1, E-3, E-4, J

Lien-chiang-k'ou 蓮江口
Heilungkiang
E-1, E-5

Ling-ching-t'an 凌津攤
Hunan
B-1, E-3, J

Lien-yüan (Lan T'ien) 連源(藍田)
Hunan
B-1, B-2, E-3, J

Lien-yün 連雲
Kiangsu
7-19, 7-20, 7-21

Lien-yün-chiang 連雲港
Kiangsu
E-1

Lin-fen 臨汾
Shansi
B-1, B-2, E-3, J

Lin-hai 臨海
Chekiang
7-16

Lin-k'ou 林口
Heilungkiang
E-2

Ling-ching-t'an 凌津灘
Hunan
J

Ling-shih-hsien 靈石縣
Shansi
B-1, E-3, J

Liu-chia-ho 劉家河
Liaoning
E-1

Liu-chou 柳州
Kwangsi
4-3, 4-7, 4-8; A-1, A-2, A-4, A-5, A-6, B-1, B-2, C-1, C-2, E-1, E-2, E-3, J

Liu-ch'üan 柳泉
Kiangsu
E-1

Liu-lang-tung 六郎洞
Yünnan
B-1, E-3, J

Liu-li-ho 琉璃河
Hopeh
E-1

Liu-shui-ho 流水河
Yünnan
B-1, E-3, J

Lo-ch'ang 樂昌
Kwangtung
E-3

Lo-chiang 羅江
Kwangtung
B-1, J

Lo-shan 樂山
Szechwan
B-1, E-3, E-6, J

Lo-tien 羅甸
Kweichow
7-16

340

Lo-ting 羅定
Kwangtung
7-16

Lo-yang 洛陽
Honan
1, 16, 18; 4-3, 4-7, 4-8, 7-
8; A-1, A-2, A-4, A-5, A-6,
B-1, B-2, C-1, C-2, C-3,
E-1, E-2, E-3, E-4, E-6, J

Lou-shan 樓山
Heilungkiang
E-1

Lou-ti 婁底
Hunan
E-1, E-4, E-6

Lu-an 潞安
Shansi
E-6

Lu-chai 鹿寨
Kwangsi
B-1, E-3, J

Lu-chou 瀘州 (泸州)
Szechwan
4-3, 4-7, 4-8; A-1, A-2,
A-4, A-5, A-6, B-1, B-2,
C-1, C-2, E-2, E-3, J

Lü-ta (Port Arthur and Dairen) 旅大
Liaoning
81, 124; 4-3, 4-7, 4-8, 7-8,
7-19, 7-20, 7-21; A-1, A-2,
A-4, A-5, A-6, B-1, B-2,
C-1, C-2, C-3, E-1, E-2,
E-3, J

Lu-tao 鹿道
Heilungkiang
E-1

Lüeh-yang 略陽
Shensi
E-6

Lung-ch'i 龍溪 (龙溪)
Fukien
B-1, E-1, E-3, E-4, E-6

Lung-ch'ing 龍清
Kirin
B-1, E-1, E-3

Lung-jih 龍日
Szechwan
7-16

Lung-k'ou 龍口
Shantung
165; 7-19

Lung-t'an-shan 龍潭山
Kirin
E-1

Lung-wang-miao 龍王廟

E-6

Lung-yen 龍岩
Fukien
B-1, E-1, E-3, E-4, E-6, J

Ma-an-shan 馬鞍山
Anhwei
B-1, B-2, E-3, J

Ma-ch'eng 麻城
Hupeh
B-1, E-3, J

Men-t'ou-kou 門頭溝
Hopeh
192

Ma-ni-kang-kuo 馬尼崗果
Szechwan
7-16

Meng-hai 勐海
Yünnan
7-16

Ma-t'ou 馬頭
Hopeh
E-1

Meng-miao 孟廟 (孟庙)
Honan
E-1, E-4, E-6

Ma-wei 麻尾
Kweichow
E-1

Meng-ting 孟定
Yünnan
7-16

Man-chou-li 滿州里
Inner Mongolia
E-1

Mi-chih-na 密支那
Yünnan
7-16

Mang-ai 茫崖
Tsinghai
7-16; E-6

Mi-yün 密雲
Hopeh
B-1, E-3, J

Mao-chien-shan 毛尖山
Anhwei
B-1, E-3, J

Miao-t'ai-tzu 廟台子
Hopeh
E-1, E-4, E-6

Mao-ming 茂名
Kwangtung
E-1, E-4, E-6, J

Min-hang 閔行
Kiangsu
E-1, E-4, E-6

Mei-hsien 梅縣
Kwangtung
E-6

Min-hou 閩候
Fukien
285; E-6

Mei-k'u 煤窰
Heilungkiang
E-1

Mo-ho 莫河
Tsinghai
7-16

342

Mu-nan-kuan 睦南關
    Kwangsi
    155; E-1, E-4, E-6

Mu-tan-chiang 牡丹江
    Heilungkiang
    4-3, 4-7, 4-8; A-1, A-2,
    A-4, A-5, A-6, B-1, B-2,
    C-1, C-2, E-1, E-2, J

Mukden 瀋陽
    Liaoning
    16, 69; 4-3, 4-7, 4-8, 7-8;
    A-1, A-2, A-4, A-5, A-6,
    B-1, B-2, C-1, C-2, C-3,
    E-1, E-2, E-3, E-5, J

Na-ta 那大
    Kwangtung
    7-16

Nai-tzu-shan 奶子山
    Kirin
    E-1

Nan-ch'ang 南昌
    Kiangsi
    1-1, 1-2, 4-3, 4-7, 4-8; A-
    1, A-2, A-4, A-5, A-6, B-
    1, B-2, C-1, C-2, E-1, E-
    2, E-3, J

Nan-cheng 南鄭
    Shensi
    7-16; B-1, E-3, J

Nan-chien 南澗
    Yünnan
    7-16

Nan-ch'ung 南充
    Szechwan
    16; 4-3, 4-7, 4-8, A-1, A-
    2, A-4, A-5, A-6, B-1, C-
    1, C-2, E-2, E-3, J

Nan-hsing-ch'iao 南星橋
    Chekiang
    E-1

Nan-i 南義
    Heilungkiang
    E-1

Nan-lin 南林
    Kwangtung
    B-1, E-3, J

Nan-ning 南寧 (南宁)
    Kwangsi
    4-3, 4-7, 4-8; A-1, A-2,
    A-4, A-5, A-6, B-1, B-2,
    C-1, C-2, E-2, E-3, J

Nan-p'iao 南票
    Liaoning
    B-1, E-1, E-3, E-4, E-6, J

Nan-p'ing 南平
    Fukien
    7-16; B-1, E-1, E-3, E-4,
    E-6, J

Nan-pu 南部
    Szechwan
    7-16

Nan-ta 南大
    Yünnan
    7-16

Nan-ting 南定
Shantung
B-1, E-3, J

Nan-t'ung 南通
Kiangsu
4-3, 4-7, 4-8; A-1, A-2, A-4, A-5, A-6, B-1, C-1, C-2, E-2, E-3, J

Nan-yang 南陽
Honan
B-1, B-2, E-3, J

Nanking 南京
Kiangsu
11, 16, 32; 1-1, 1-2, 4-3, 4-7, 4-8, 7-8, 7-19, 7-20, 7-21; A-1, A-2, A-4, A-5, A-6, B-1, B-2, C-2, C-3, E-1, E-2, E-3, E-5, J

Nei-chiang 内江
Szechwan
16; 4-3, 4-7, 4-8; A-1, A-2, A-4, A-5, A-6, C-1, C-2, E-1, E-2, E-4, E-6, J

Nen-chiang 嫩江
Heilungkiang
E-1, E-6

Niang-tzu-kuan 娘子關
Shansi
E-1

Nieh-la-mu 聶拉木
Tibet
7-16

Nien-tzu-shan 碾子山
Heilungkiang
E-1

Ning-po 寧波
Chekiang
4-3, 4-7, 4-8, 7-19, 7-20, 7-21; A-1, A-2, A-4, A-5, A-6, B-1, C-1, C-2, E-2, E-3, J

Ning-wu 寧武
Shansi
B-1, E-3, J

Nü-erh-ho 女兒河
Liaoning
E-1, E-4, E-6

O-ch'eng 鄂城
Hupeh
B-1, B-2, E-3, J

O-p'u-liang 鄂溥梁
Tsinghai
7-16

Ou-p'u 鷗浦
Inner Mongolia
E-6

Pa-kung-shan 八公山
Anhwei
E-1

Pa-li-chuang 八里莊
Hopei
E-1

Pa-pan-hsia 八盤峽
Honan
B-1, B-2, E-3, J

Pa-pu 八步
Kwangsi
B-1, E-3, J

344

Pa-so 八所
Kwangtung
7-16, 7-19; E-1

Pa-tou 八陡
Shantung
E-1

Pa-yü-kuan 巴裕關
Szechwan
7-16

Pai-ch'eng-tzu 白城子
Kirin
E-1

Pai-lien-ho 白蓮河
Hupeh
B-1, E-3, J

Pai-shih-tu 白石渡
Hunan
E-1

Pai-Yin 白銀
Kansu
C-3, E-1, E-4, E-6

Pai-yüh-o-po 白雲鄂博
Inner Mongolia
E-4, E-6

Pan-ch'iao 板橋
Hopeh
E-1

Pang-fou 蚌埠
Anhwei
164; 4-3, 4-7; A-1, A-2,
A-3, A-4, A-5, A-6, B-1,
B-2, C-1, C-2, E-1, E-2,
E-3, J

Pang-ta 邦達
Tibet
7-16

P'ang-chia-pu 龐家堡
Hopeh
E-1

Pao-chi 寶鷄（宝鸡）
Shensi
4-3, 4-7, 4-8; A-1, A-2,
A-4, A-5, A-6, B-1, C-1,
C-2, E-1, E-2, E-3, E-4,
E-6, J

Pao-ting 保定
Hopeh
4-3, 4-7, 4-8; A-1, A-2,
A-4, A-5, A-6, B-1, C-1,
C-2, E-1, E-2, E-3, J

Pao-ting-nan 保定南
Hopeh
E-1

Pao-t'ou 包頭
Inner Mongolia
16, 18, 60; 4-3, 4-7, 4-8,
7-8; A-1, A-2, A-4, A-5,
A-6, B-1, B-2, C-1, C-2,
C-3, E-1, E-2, E-3, E-4,
E-6, J

Pao-tzu-wan 豹子灣
Inner Mongolia
E-1

Pei-an 北安
Heilungkiang
B-1, E-1, E-3, J

Pei-piao 北票
Liaoning
124; B-1, E-1, E-3, J

Pei-tai-ho 北戴河
Hopeh
E-1

Peking 北京
Hopeh
11, 25, 50, 69, 192; 1-1,
1-2, 4-3, 4-7, 4-8, 7-8,
A-1, A-2, A-4, A-5, A-6,
B-1, B-1, C-1, C-2, C-3,
E-1, E-2, E-3, E-5, J

Pen-ch'i 本溪
Liaoning
16; 4-3, 4-7, 4-8; A-1, A-2,
A-4, A-5, A-6, B-1, B-2,
C-1, C-2, C-3, J

Peng-shih 蓬市
Fukien
7-16

P'eng-k'ou 朋口
Fukien
7-16

Pi-chiang 碧江
Yünnan
7-16

Pi-chieh 畢節
Kweichow
B-1, E-3, J

Pi-se-chai 碧色寨
Yünnan
E-1

Pien-ch'uang-tzu 偏窗子
Szechwan
B-1, B-2, E-3, J

P'ing-an 平安
Hunan
B-1, E-3, J

P'ing-chuang 平莊
Inner Mongolia
B-1, B-2, E-3, J

P'ing-ho 平和
Fukien
7-16, J

P'ing-hsiang 萍鄉
Kiangsi
B-1, B-2, E-1, E-3, J

P'ing-kuei 平桂
Kwangsi
B-1, E-3

P'ing-shih 坪石
Kwangtung
E-1

P'ing-wang 平旺
Shansi
B-1, E-1, E-3, J

Pu-ch'eng 蒲城
Fukien
7-16

Pu-erh 晉洱
Yünnan
7-16

P'u-lan-tsung 普蘭宗
    <u>Tibet</u>
    7-16

P'u-k'ou 浦口
    <u>Kiangsu</u>
    E-1, E-5, E-6

Sai-ch'i 賽岐
    <u>Fukien</u>
    7-16

San-chia-tzu 三家子
    <u>Liaoning</u>
    E-1, E-4, E-6

San-chiang 三江
    <u>Szechwan</u>
    7-16; B-1, E-1, E-3, J

San-k'o-shu 三棵樹
    <u>Heilungkiang</u>
    E-1

San-men-hsia 三門峽
    <u>Honan</u>
    B-1, B-2, E-1, E-3, E-4,
    E-6, J

San-ming 三明
    <u>Fukien</u>
    B-1, B-2, E-3, J

San-sheng-kung 三盛公
    <u>Inner Mongolia</u>
    E-1

San-shui 三水
    <u>Kwangtung</u>
    E-1, E-6

San-tu 三都
    <u>Hunan</u>
    E-1

Sang-yüan 桑園
    <u>Hopeh</u>
    E-1

Sha-ch'eng 沙城
    <u>Hopeh</u>
    E-1, E-4, E-5, E-6

Sha-men-tzu 沙門子
    <u>Sinkiang</u>
    E-6

Sha-p'o-t'ou 沙坡頭
    <u>Honan</u>
    B-1, E-3, J

Shan-hai-kuan 山海關
    <u>Hopeh</u>
    E-1, E-5

Shan-tan 山丹
    <u>Kansu</u>
    B-1, E-3, J

Shang-ch'iu 商邱
    <u>Honan</u>
    4-3, 4-7, 4-8, A-1, A-2,
    A-4, A-5, A-6, B-1, C-1,
    C-2, E-2, E-3, J

Shang-hang 上杭
    <u>Fukien</u>
    B-1, E-3, J

Shang-lan-ts'un 上蘭村
    <u>Shansi</u>
    E-1

Shang-pan-ch'eng 上板城
Hopeh
E-1, E-4, E-6

Shang-yao 上饒
Kiangsi
7-16; B-1, E-3, J

Shang-yu 上猶
Kiangsi
B-1, E-3, J

Shanghai 上海
Kiangsu
1, 11, 16, 17, 25, 56, 60,
62, 69, 124, 164, 165, 201;
1-1, 1-2, 4-3, 4-7, 4-8, 7-
8, 7-19, 7-20, 7-21; A-1,
A-2, A-4, A-5, A-6, B-1,
B-2, C-1, C-2, C-3, E-1,
E-2, E-3, E-4, E-5, E-6, J

Shao-hsing 紹興
Chekiang
4-3, 4-7, 4-8; A-1, A-2,
A-4, A-5, A-6, B-1, C-1,
C-2, E-2, E-3, J

Shao-kuan 韶關
Kwangtung
B-1, E-3, J

Shao-liang-tzu 少梁子
Tsinghai
7-16

Shao-yang 邵陽
Hunan
4-3, 4-7, 4-8; A-1, A-2,
A-4, A-5, A-6, B-1, C-1,
C-2, E-1, E-2, E-3, E-4,
E-6, J

Shen-ch'uan 深圳
Kwangtung
E-1

Shen-lou 申樓
Honan
E-1, E-4, E-6

Shih-chia-chuang 石家莊
Hopeh
16; 4-3, 4-7, 4-8, 7-8; A-
1, A-2, A-4, A-5, A-6,
B-1, B-2, C-1, C-2, E-1,
E-2, E-3, E-5, J

Shih-ch'iao-tzu 石橋子
Liaoning
E-1

Shih-chiu-t'an 獅九灘
Szechwan
B-1, E-3, J

Shih-ch'üan 石泉
Shensi
B-1, E-3, J

Shih-hsia-li 石匣里
Hopeh
B-1, E-3

Shih-lu 石碌
Kwangtung
B-1, B-2, E-1, E-3, J

Shih-lung 石龍 (石尤)
Kwangtung
E-6

Shih-lung-pa 石龍壩(石龙坝)
　　Yünnan
　　B-1, E-3, J

Shih-mo-ch'i 石摸溪
　　Hunan
　　B-1, E-3, J

Shih-p'eng 石棚
　　Szechwan
　　B-1, J

Shih-p'ing 石屏
　　Yünnan
　　B-2, E-1, E-3

Shih-tsui 石嘴
　　Yünnan
　　E-1

Shih-tsui-shan 石嘴山
　　Ningsia
　　B-1, E-3, J

Shih-tsui-tzu 石嘴子
　　Ningsia
　　7-16

Shou-ning 壽寧(寿宁)
　　Fukien
　　7-16

Shou-yang 壽陽
　　Shansi
　　B-1, E-3, J

Shu-lan 舒蘭(舒兰)
　　Heilungkiang
　　E-1

Shuang-t'ou-shan 雙頭山(双头山)
　　Hopeh
　　B-1, E-3, J

Shuang-ya-shan 雙鴨山
　　Heilungkiang
　　16; 4-3, 4-7, 4-8; A-1, A-
　　5, A-6, B-1, C-1, C-2, C-
　　3, E-1, E-2, E-3, J

Shui-ch'e-wan 水車灣
　　Kansu
　　E-1

Shui-ch'eng 水城
　　Kweichow
　　7-16; B-1, B-2, E-3, J

Shui-chia-hu 水家湖
　　Anhwei
　　E-2

Shui-chü-liu 水曲柳
　　Kirin
　　E-1

Shui-mo-t'an 水磨潭
　　Inner Mongolia
　　E-1

Shui-yen 水堰
　　Honan
　　B-1, E-3, J

Sian 西安
　　Shensi
　　16, 18; 1-1, 1-2, 4-3, 4-7,
　　4-8, 7-8; A-1, A-2, A-4,
　　A-5, A-6, B-1, B-1, C-1,
　　C-2, C-3, E-1, E-2, E-3,
　　E-4, E-6, J

So-chia 所家
Szechwan
B-1, E-3, J

So-erh-k'u-li 素爾庫里
Tsinghai
7-16

Soochow 蘇州
Kiangsu
4-3; A-1, A-2, A-4, A-5,
A-6, B-1, B-2, C-1, C-2,
E-2, E-3, J

Ssu-nan 思南
Kweichow
7-16

Ssu-p'ing 四平
Kirin
4-3, 4-7, 4-8; A-1, A-2, A-
4, A-5, A-6, B-1, C-1, C-
2, E-1, E-2, E-3, J

Ssu-shih-sha-ho 四什沙河
Inner Mongolia
B-1, E-3, J

Su-chia-t'sun 蘇家村
Liaoning
E-1

Su-hsien 宿縣
Anhwei
B-1, B-2, E-3, E-6, J

Su-ta 蘇達
Yünnan
E-6

Sui-fen-ho 綏芬河
Heilungkiang
B-1, E-1, E-3, J

Sui-hsien 隨縣
Hupeh
E-1, E-4, E-6

Sui-hua 綏化
Heilungkiang
E-1, E-5

Sui-te 綏德
Shensi
7-16

Sun-wu 孫武
Heilungkiang
B-1, E-3, J

Swatow 汕頭
Kwangtung
1-1, 1-2, 4-3, 4-7, 7-19,
7-20, 7-21; A-1, A-2, A-4,
B-1, B-1, C-1, C-2, E-2,
E-3, E-6, J

Ta-ch'eng 大城
Liaoning
E-1

Ta-ch'ing (oil fields) 大慶(大庄)
Manchuria

Ta-feng-man 大豐滿
Kirin
E-1

Ta-hsien 達縣
Szechwan
B-1, B-2, E-3, J

Ta-hsing-an-ling 大興安嶺
Inner Mongolia
B-1, E-3, J

Ta-hu-shan 大虎山
Liaoning
E-1

Ta-li-tzu 大力子
Kirin
E-1

Ta-li-yüan 大栗園
Yünnan
7-16

Ta-lien 褡褳
Hopeh
E-1

Ta-mai-kou 達麥溝
Inner Mongolia
E-6

Ta-o-po-t'u 大鄂博圖
Tsinghai
7-16

Ta-pu 大埔
Kwangtung
7-16

Ta-shih-ch'iao 大石橋
Liaoning
E-1

Ta-t'an 大灘
Shensi
E-1, E-4, E-6

Ta-t'ung 大通
Anhwei
E-1

Ta-t'ung 大同
Shansi
4-3, 4-7, 4-8; A-1, A-2,
A-4, A-5, A-6, B-1, B-
2, C-1, C-2, E-1, E-2,
E-3, E-5, J

Ta-t'ung 大通
Tsinghai
B-1, J

Ta-yen-men 大言門
Kwiechow
B-1, E-3, J

Ta-ying-chen 大營鎮
Hopeh
E-6

Ta-yung 大庸
Hunan
7-16

T'ai-shun 泰順
Chekiang
7-16

T'ai-chiang 台江
Kweichow
7-16

T'ai-chou 泰州
Kiangsu
4-3, 4-7, 4-8; A-1, A-2,
A-4, A-5, A-6, B-1, C-1,
C-2, E-2, E-3, J

T'ai-ho 泰和
　　Kiangsi
　　7-16

T'ai-yüan 太原
　　Shansi
　　8, 16, 62; 4-7, 4-8, 7-8; A-
　　1, A-2, A-4, A-5, A-6, B-1,
　　B-2, C-1, C-2, C-3, E-1,
　　E-2, E-4, E-6, J

Tan-chiang-k'ou 丹江口
　　Hupeh
　　B-1, B-2, E-3, J

Tang-chin-shan-k'ou 當金山口
　　Tsinghai
　　7-16

Tang-t'u 當塗
　　Anhwei
　　B-1, E-3, J

Tang-shan 碭山
　　Kiangsu
　　E-1

T'ang-k'o 唐克
　　Szechwan
　　7-16

T'ang-ku 塘沽
　　Hopeh
　　E-1

T'ang-shan 唐山
　　Hopeh
　　4-3, 4-7, 4-8; A-1, A-2,
　　A-4, A-5, A-6, B-1, B-2,
　　C-1, C-2, E-2, E-3, J

T'ang-yin 湯陰
　　Honan
　　E-1

T'ao-an 洮安
　　Kirin
　　B-1, E-3, J

T'ao-lai-chao 陶賴昭
　　Kirin
　　E-1, J

T'ao-nan 洮南
　　Kirin
　　B-1, E-3

Tao-t'ang-ho 倒淌河
　　Tsinghai
　　7-16

T'ao-hsing 陶興
　　Shansi
　　E-1, E-4, E-6

Te-chou 德州
　　Shantung
　　E-1

Ti-chia-t'ai 狄家台
　　Kansu
　　E-1, E-4, E-6

Ti-tao 滴道
　　Heilungkiang
　　B-1, E-3, J

T'ieh-ch'ang-tzu 鐵廠子
　　Liaoning
　　J

T'ieh-ling 鐵嶺
Liaoning
E-1, E-4, E-6

Tientsin 天津
Hopeh
11, 16, 56, 60, 69, 165,
201; 1-1, 1-2, 4-3, 4-7, 4-
8, 7-8, 7-19, 7-20, 7-21;
A-1, A-2, A-4, A-5, A-6,
B-1, B-2, C-1, C-2, C-3,
E-1, E-2, E-3, E-5, J

T'ien-chang-tzu 天章子
Liaoning
B-1, E-3

T'ien-chia-an 田家庵
Anhwei
E-1

T'ien-kang 天崗
Kirin
E-1

T'ien-shih-fu 田師付
Liaoning
B-1, E-1, E-3, J

T'ien-shui 天水
Kansu
B-1, E-3, E-4, E-6, J

Ting-hai 定海
Chekiang
7-19

Ting-pien 定邊
Shensi
7-16

T'o-shih 拓石
Shensi
E-1

Tsaidam 柴達木
Tsinghai
194; B-1, E-3, J

Tsao-chuang 棗莊
Shantung
B-1, B-2, E-1, E-3, J

Ts'ao-o-chiang 曹娥江
Chekiang
E-4, E-6

Tse-tang 澤當
Tibet
7-16

Ts'e-heng 冊亨
Kweichow
7-16

Tsinan(Chinan) 濟南
Shantung
4-3, 4-7, 4-8, 7-8; A-1,
A-2, A-3, A-4, A-5, A-6,
B-1, B-2, C-1, C-2, E-1,
E-2, E-3, E-6, J

Tsingtao 青島
Shantung
11, 16, 165; 1-1, 1-2, 4-3,
4-7, 4-8, 7-8, 7-19, 7-20,
7-21; A-1, A-2, A-3, A-4,
A-5, A-6, B-1, B-2, C-1,
C-2, C-3, E-1, E-2, E-3
J

Ts'ui-luan 翠灤
Heilungksiang
E-1, E-6

Tsun-i 遵義
Kweichow
B-1, B-2, E-3, J

Tu-hsi 拓西
Kirin
B-1, E-3, J

Tu-shan-tzu 獨山子
Sinkiang
7-16; B-1, E-3, J

Tu-yün 都勻
Kweichow
B-1, E-3, E-4, E-6, J

T'u-erh-to-te 吐爾朵特
Sinkiang
7-16

T'u-lu-fan 吐魯番
Sinkiang
E-6

T'u-men 圖門
Kirin
E-1

Tun-huang 敦煌
Kansu
7-16

Tung-chiang 東江
Hunan
B-1, B-2, E-3, J

Tung-o-lo 東俄洛
Tibet
7-16

Tung-pien-men 東便門
Hopeh
E-1

T'ung-chou 通州
Hopeh
E-1, E-6

T'ung-ch'uan 銅川
Shensi
B-1, J

T'ung-kuan 潼關
Shensi
E-1, E-4, E-6

T'ung-hua 通化
Kirin
4-3, 4-7, 4-8, 7-8; A-2,
A-4, A-5, A-6, B-1, B-2,
C-1, C-2, C-3, E-1, E-2,
E-3, J

T'ung-jen 同仁
Tsinghai
7-16

T'ung-liao 通遼
Inner Mongolia
B-1, E-3, J

T'ung-ling 銅陵
Anhwei
B-1, B-2, E-3, J

T'ung-te 同德
  Tsinghai
  7-16

T'ung-yüan-pao 通遠堡
  Liaoning
  7-16

Tzu-ch'i 紫溪
  Hunan
  E-1, E-4, E-6

Tzu-ch'i 資溪
  Kiangsi
  E-1

Tzu-ch'uan 淄川
  Shantung
  B-1, B-2, E-3, J

Tzu-hsing 資興
  Hunan
  7-16, B-1, E-3, J

Tzu-kung 自貢
  Szechwan
  16; 4-3, 4-7, 4-8; A-1, A-2,
  A-4, A-5, A-6, C-1, C-2,
  E-2, E-3, J

Tzu-p'ing-p'u 紫坪舖
  Szechwan
  B-1, B-2, E-3, J

Tzu-po 淄博
  Shantung
  4-3, 4-7, 4-8; A-1, A-4,
  A-5, A-6, B-1, B-2, C-1,
  C-2, E-2, E-3, J

Tz'u-hsien 磁縣
  Hopeh
  B-1, B-2, E-3, J

Tz'u-hu 慈湖
  Anhwei
  E-1

Tz'u-li 慈利
  Hunan
  7-16

Tz'u-yao 磁窰
  Shantung
  E-1

Urumchi (Ti-hua) 烏魯木齊
  Sinkiang
  4-3, 4-7, 4-8, 7-8, 7-16;
  A-1, A-2, A-4, A-5, A-6,
  B-1, B-2, C-1, C-2, C-3,
  E-2, E-3, E-4, E-6, J

Wai-yang 外洋
  Fukien
  E-1, E-4, E-6

Wan-an 萬安
  Kiangsi
  B-1, B-2, E-3, J

Wan-hsien 萬縣
  Szechwan
  B-1, E-3, J

Wan-k'ou 萬口
  Kirin
  E-1

Wan-sheng 萬盛
Szechwan
E-1

Wang-ch'ing 汪清
Kirin
E-1

Wang-t'ing 望亭
Kiangsu
B-1, E-3, J

Wang-ts'un 王村
Shansi
E-1, E-4, E-6

Wei-fang 濰坊
Shantung
7-16; 4-3, 4-7, 4-8; A-1,
A-2, A-4, A-5, A-6, B-1,
C-1, C-2, E-2, E-3, J

Wei-hai-wei 威海衛
Shantung
7-19; A-2

Wei-ning 威寧
Kweichow
7-16; E-6

Wei-shui 微水
Shansi
E-1

Wei-ya 維亞
Kansu
E-1

Wei-yüan 威遠
Szechwan
B-1, E-3, J

Wen-chou 溫州
Chekiang
4-3, 4-7, 4-8, 7-16, 7-19,
7-20, 7-21; A-1, A-2, A-
4, A-5, A-6, B-1, C-1, C-
2, E-2, E-3, E-6, J

Wen-li 文里
Kwangsi
E-1

Wen-tsao-pin 文糟賓
Kiangsu
E-1, E-4, E-6

Wu-ch'ang 武昌
Hupeh
E-1, E-4, E-6

Wu-ch'i 語溪
Hunan
E-1

Wu-chou 梧州
Kwangsi
4-3, 4-7, 4-8; A-1, A-2,
A-4, A-5, A-6, B-1, C-1,
C-2, E-2, E-3, J

Wu-han 武漢
Hupeh
1, 11, 16, 18, 32, 56, 60,
69, 102, 192, 201; 1-1, 1-
2, 4-3, 4-7, 4-8, 7-8, 7-19,
7-20; A-1, A-2, A-4, A-5,
A-6, B-1, B-2, C-1, C-2,
C-3, E-2, E-3, E-5, J

Wu-ho-hao-t'e 烏和浩特
Inner Mongolia
B-1, E-3, J

Wu-hsi 無錫
Kiangsi
4-3, 4-7, 4-8; A-1, A-2, A-4, A-5, B-1, C-1, C-2, E-2, E-3, J

Wu-hu 蕪湖
Anhwei
4-3, 4-7, 4-8; A-1, A-2, A-4, A-5, A-6, B-1, C-1, C-2, E-1, E-2, E-3, E-4, E-6, J

Wu-la-po 烏拉泊
Sinkiang
B-1, E-3, J

Wu-lan-cha-pu-meng 烏蘭扎布盟
Inner Mongolia
B-1, E-3, J

Wu-lan-hao-t'e 烏蘭浩特
Inner Mongolia
B-1, E-2, J

Wu-li-fou 五里堡
Honan
E-1

Wu-sheng-kuan 武勝關
Hupeh
E-1

Wu-shih 烏石
Kwangtung
B-1, E-3, J

Wu-su 烏蘇
Sinkiang
E-6

Wu-sung 吳淞
Kiangsu
E-1

Wu-tu 武都
Kansu
7-16

Wu-t'ung-ch'iao 五通橋
Szechwan
4-3, 4-7, 4-8 A-1, A-4, A-5, A-6, B-1, C-1, C-2, E-2, E-3, J

Wu-wei 武威
Kansu
E-1, E-4, E-6

Ya-an 雅安
Szechwan
7-16

Ya-k'o-shih 牙克石
Inner Mongolia
E-1

Ya-pu-li 亞布力
Heilungkiang
E-1

Ya-tung 亞東
Tibet
7-16

Ya-yüan 鴨園
Kirin
E-1

Yang-chieh 羊街
Yünnan
7-16

Yang-chou 楊州
Kiangsu
4-3, 4-7, 4-8; A-1, A-2,
A-4, A-5, A-6, B-1, C-1,
C-2, E-2, E-3, J

Yang-ch'üan 陽泉
Shansi
165; 4-3, 4-7, 4-8; A-1, A-
4, A-5, A-6, B-1, B-2, C-
1, C-2, E-3, J

Yang-ch'üan-chü 陽泉曲
Shansi
E-1, E-4, E-6, J

Yang-ch'un 陽春
Kwangtung
B-1, E-3, J

Yang-lin 楊林
Yünnan
7-16

Yang-lou-ssu 羊樓司
Hunan
E-1

Yang-tsung-hai 楊宗海
Yünnan
B-1, E-3

Yao-p'ing 饒平
Kwangtung
7-16

Yeh-ch'eng 葉城
Sinkiang
7-16

Yeh-pai-shou 葉柏壽
Liaoning
E-1

Yen-chi 延吉
Kirin
B-1, E-3, J

Yen-kuo-hsia 塩鍋峽
Kansu
B-1, B-2, E-3, J

Yen-pien 延邊
Heilungkiang
E-6

Yen-t'ung-shan 烟筒山
Heilungkiang
E-6

Yin-ch'uan 銀川
Ningsia
7-16; A-1, A-6, B-1, C-1
C-2, E-2, E-3, J

Ying-k'ou 營口
Liaoning
124; 4-3, 4-7, 4-8; A-1, A-
2, A-4, A-5, A-6, B-1, B-
2, C-1, C-2, C-3, E-2, E-
3, J

Ying-shou-ying 鷹手營
Hopeh
E-1, E-4, E-6

Ying-t'an 鷹潭
Kiangsi
155; E-1, E-4, E-6

Yü-ch'i-k'ou 裕溪口
Anhwei
165; 7-19; E-1

Yü-erh-ai 玉兒崖
Inner Mongolia
B-1, E-3, J

Yu-chou 幽州
Hopeh
B-1, E-3, J

Yü-hsia 玉狹
Shensi
E-1, E-4, E-6

Yü-hsien 盂縣
Shansi
B-1, E-3, J

Yü-hung 于洪
Liaoning
E-1

Yü-kuo 裕國
Liaoning
E-1

Yü-lin 玉林
Kwangsi
7-16, 7-19

Yü-men 玉門
Kansu
A-5, B-1, E-3, J

Yü-shan 玉山
Kiangsi
E-6

Yü-shu 榆樹
Kirin
E-1, E-6

Yü-shu 玉樹
Tsinghai
7-16

Yü-shu-t'ai 榆樹台
Liaoning
E-1

Yü-shu-ts'un 榆樹村
Heilungchiang
E-1

Yü-tz'u 榆次
Shansi
4-7, 4-8; A-1, A-5, A-6,
B-1, C-1, C-2, C-3, E-1,
E-2, E-3, E-5, J

Yüeh-yang 岳陽
Hunan
B-1, E-3

Yün-ch'eng 鄆城
Shantung
7-16

Yün-ho 雲和
Chekiang
7-16

Yün-hsiao 雲宵
Kwangtung
7-16

Yung-chiang 榕江
    Kweichow
    7-16

Yung-ch'un 永春
    Fukien
    B-1, E-3, J

Yung-k'ang 永康
    Chekiang
    7-16

Yung-teng 永登
    Kansu
    B-1, E-3, J

Yung-ting 永定
    Fukien
    7-16

INDEX

Agriculture: pre-Communist period, 7, 12. See also Grain.

Aviation: First Five-Year Plan, 102; length of routes, 110. See also Transportation facilities, Transportation industry.

Chou En-lai: on industry, 16, 18-9, 23; on transportation policy, 101

Cities: changes in population, 1953, 1958; 26-30, 32-50, 228-31, 235-6; changes in population, 1948-53; 30-1, 32-50, 201, 228-31; provincial distribution by size, 32-8; regional distribution by size, 32-8; growth rates, 1953-8; 41-52; industrial capacity, 56-60, 70-85, 201-2, 247-8; population as index of industrial capacity, 70-1, 80, 84; regional distribution by industrial rank, 74, 76, 79-80; industrial changes under Communist regime, 80-4; Soviet aid to industrial development, 85-9, 202-3, 254-5; and industrial economy, 200; economic ranking, 202; ranked by population, 1953; 231-2; ranked by population, 1958; 233-4; classified by 1958 population and industrial capacity, 250-1; classified by new industrial capacity, 1949-61; 252-3; key to code numbers, 3-4-11. See also Economic centers, Industry, Market areas, Population, Urbanization.

Coal: 7; mining, 67; dominated freight traffic, 124; shipping errors, 192; passim, 211. See also Natural resources.

Coastal areas: population changes, 1953-8; 38, 41; industrial development, 74, 79-80; Soviet industrial aid to, 85, 88-9; highway transportation, 101; industrial development, 199, 202. See also Industrial location policy, Transportation industry, Transportation policy.

Colonization: 4, 6

Commerce: pre-Communist period, 7. See also Transportation industry.

Commune movement, 1956: 26

Cooperative farms: 175

Defense: and Communist industrial planning, 22-4; and transportation policy, 101

Domestic product, 303

Economic centers: distribution by motive power, employment, and factories, pre-Communist period, 8-9; ranking in pre-Communist period, 8, 10-11; new, defined, 145; old, defined, 145; located on railway lines, 147; location policy of new, 153; and railway construction, 204; railway radials in, 274-5, 276-9. See also Cities, Industry, Market areas, Population, Urbanization.

Economic Cooperative Regions: development of, 18, 19, 20-1, 22; comparative industrial capacity, 61; passim, 38

Economic development: constraints during pre-Communist period, 6-15; indicated by population growth, 25-6; Soviet aid to, 85-9; and railway construction, 144. See also Transportation industry.

Economic region: defined by Russian Regional Planning Commission, 22

Economy. See Economic development, Industrial economy, Spatial economy, Transportation industry.

Employment: at end of World War II, 8-9, 11; and population growth, 26, 42

Factories: distribution, end of World War II, 8-9, 11. See also Industry.

Ferrous metals: production, 67; passim, 211. See also Natural resources.

Five-Year Plan, First: industrial location policy, 16-8, 20, 45, 206-7; development of heavy industry, 18, 19; and population changes, 27; industrial decentralization policy, 66; transportation policy, 100-2, 200; and railway construction, 155, 206; and urban development, 200; passim, 23, 89, 188, 191, 195

Five-Year Plan, Second: and industrial construction, 18-9; and population changes, 27; economic development at end of, 90; and Fig. 4-2, passim, 23

Five-Year Plan, Third: economic development at start of, 90; passim, 24, 85, 169

Freight rate. See Freight traffic, Highways, Railways, Waterways.

Freight traffic: volume and haul, 1949; 120-4; growth of, 1949-60; 175, 180, 181-2, 204-5; total, 1952-63; 180, 185; growth of transport input coefficient, 1952-63; 180, 185; 186; 187; 188-94; average haul, 1953-8; 182, 188; excessive cost, 195; rates, 196-7, 287. See also Highways, Railway, Transportation industry, Waterways.

Geological surveys: pre-Communist period, 7

Government control: effect on transportation facilities; 99-100; effect on industrial location policy, 99-100

Grain: production, 1931-7; 12, 14; Third Five-Year Plan, 90-7

Great depression, 1960-2; 207

"Great Leap Forward": failure of, 24; industrial decentralization policy, 62, 66; and railways, 130; and waterway construction, 164; increase in transport input, 187; development of remote areas, 188; transport expenses excessive, 194; agricultural crisis, 197; freight traffic congestion, 206; railway car shortage, 289; passim, 38, 89, 172, 193, 211, 301

Harbors: construction of, 1949-61; 165-6; economic influence of railways on, 165-9; data on, 166. See also Waterways.

Heavy industry: Tseng Wen-ching on, 22, 23; classification of, 53-55; regional distribution of, 66-9; and transportation policy, 101. See also Industrial plants, Industry

Highways: First Five-Year Plan, 101, 102; ambiguity of statistics, 107; length in 1949; 107, 108, 110, 111, 113; grades, 107; regional distribution, 117, 118, 158-60; construction of, 1949-60; 158-64; increase compared with railroads, 1949-60; 160; construction in less developed regions, 1950-60; 160; preparatory to railroad construction, 160; regional distribution of new, 1960; 160-2; distribution of new by length, 160, 163, 164; route density, 1960; 169-70; and local transport, 172; growth of passenger traffic, 1949-60; 175, 176 80; growth of freight traffic, 180, 181-2, 205; average haul, 1953-58; 182, 188; development, 1952; 199-200; development, 204; technical specifications, 215;

Waterways (cont'd): regional distribution, 1949-50; 114, 116, 117, 118, 120, 258-63; navigable by steamers, 163, 164; length increase, 1949-60; 163; 164; dredging of, 1949-59; 164; constructions compared with railway, 165; "native" carriers, 1958; 172; passenger traffic, 1949-60; 175, 176-80; freight traffic increase, 180, 181-2, 205, 218; average haul, 1953-8; 182, 188; development, 1952; 199; Yangtze tariff rates, 1955; 288; gross receipt, 1956; 295, 298; freight rates, derivation, 297-8; passenger rates, 298; cost of shipping operations, 299; shipping, net value-added, 300, 301-2; shipping depreciation rates, 300; shipping, gross value-added, 301-2. <u>See also</u> Freight traffic, Harbors, Transportation facilities, Transportation industry, Transportation policy.